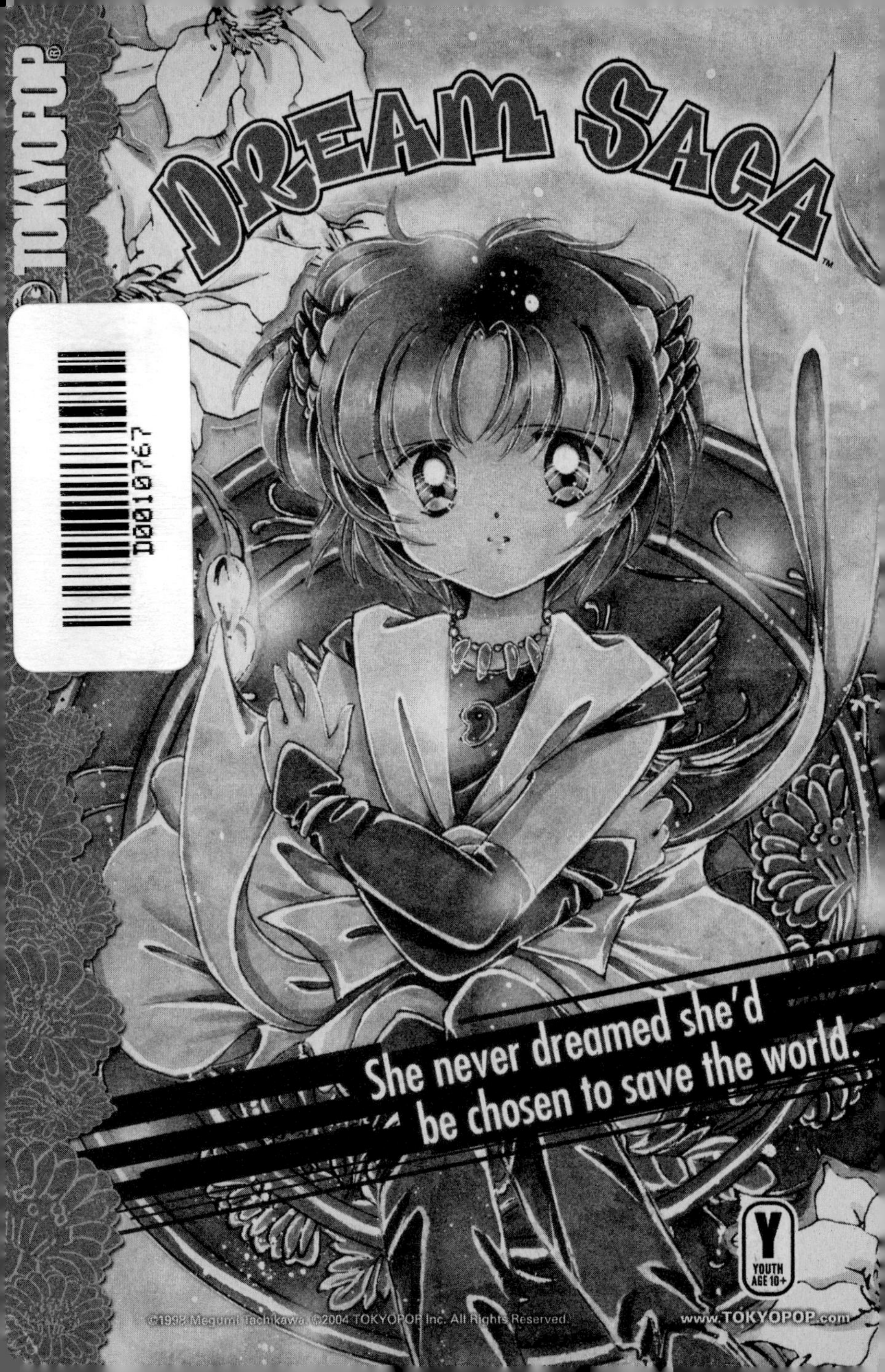
TOKYOPOP®
DREAM SAGA™
She never dreamed she'd
be chosen to save the world.
Y
YOUTH
AGE 10+
www.TOKYOPOP.com

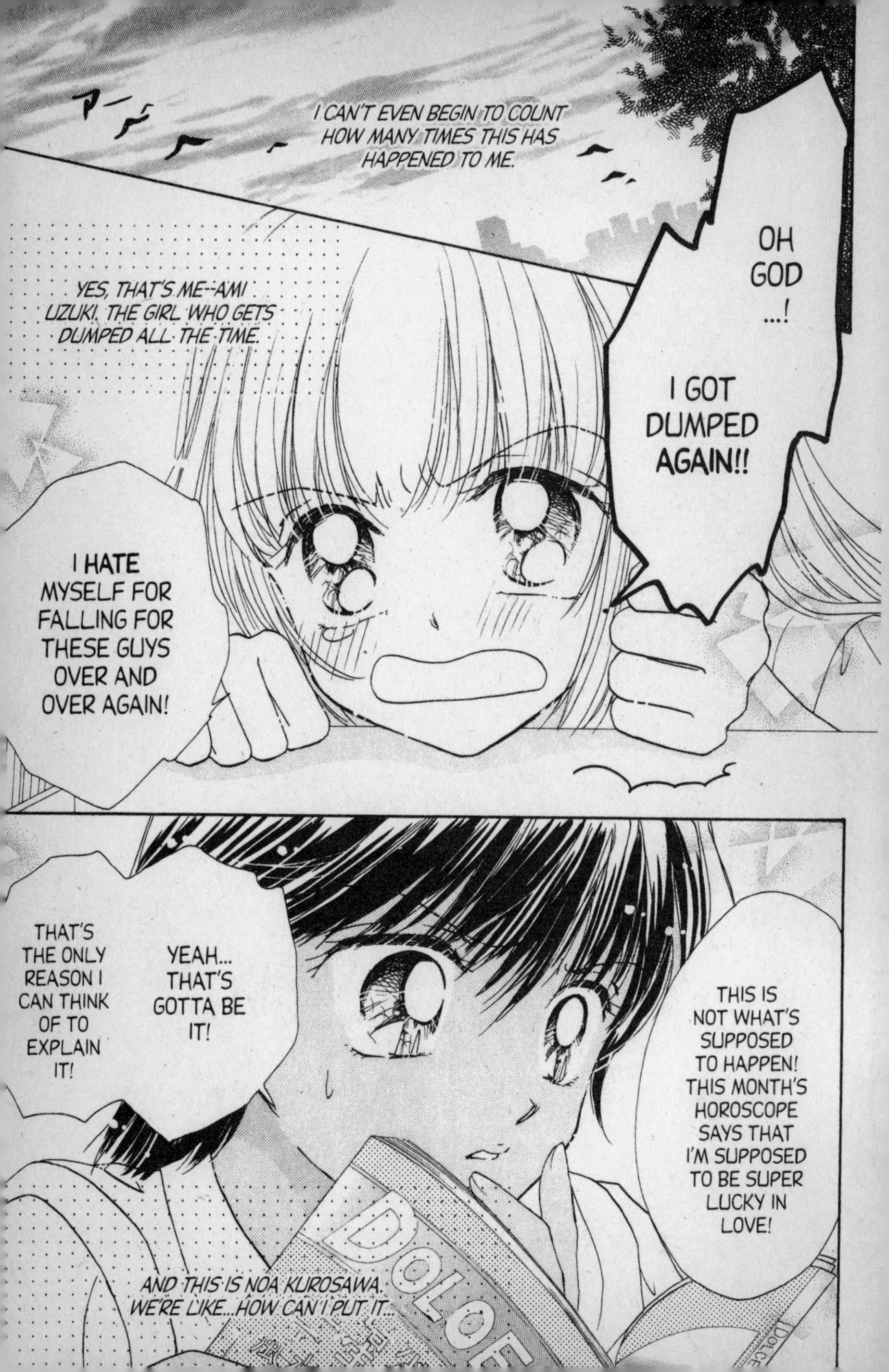
I CAN'T EVEN BEGIN TO COUNT HOW MANY TIMES THIS HAS HAPPENED TO ME.
OH GOD ...!
I GOT DUMPED AGAIN!!
YES, THAT'S ME--AMI UZUKI. THE GIRL WHO GETS DUMPED ALL THE TIME.
I HATE MYSELF FOR FALLING FOR THESE GUYS OVER AND OVER AGAIN!
THIS IS NOT WHAT'S SUPPOSED TO HAPPEN! THIS MONTH'S HOROSCOPE SAYS THAT I'M SUPPOSED TO BE SUPER LUCKY IN LOVE!
YEAH... THAT'S GOTTA BE IT!
THAT'S THE ONLY REASON I CAN THINK OF TO EXPLAIN IT!
AND THIS IS NOA KUROSAWA. WE'RE LIKE...HOW CAN I PUT IT...

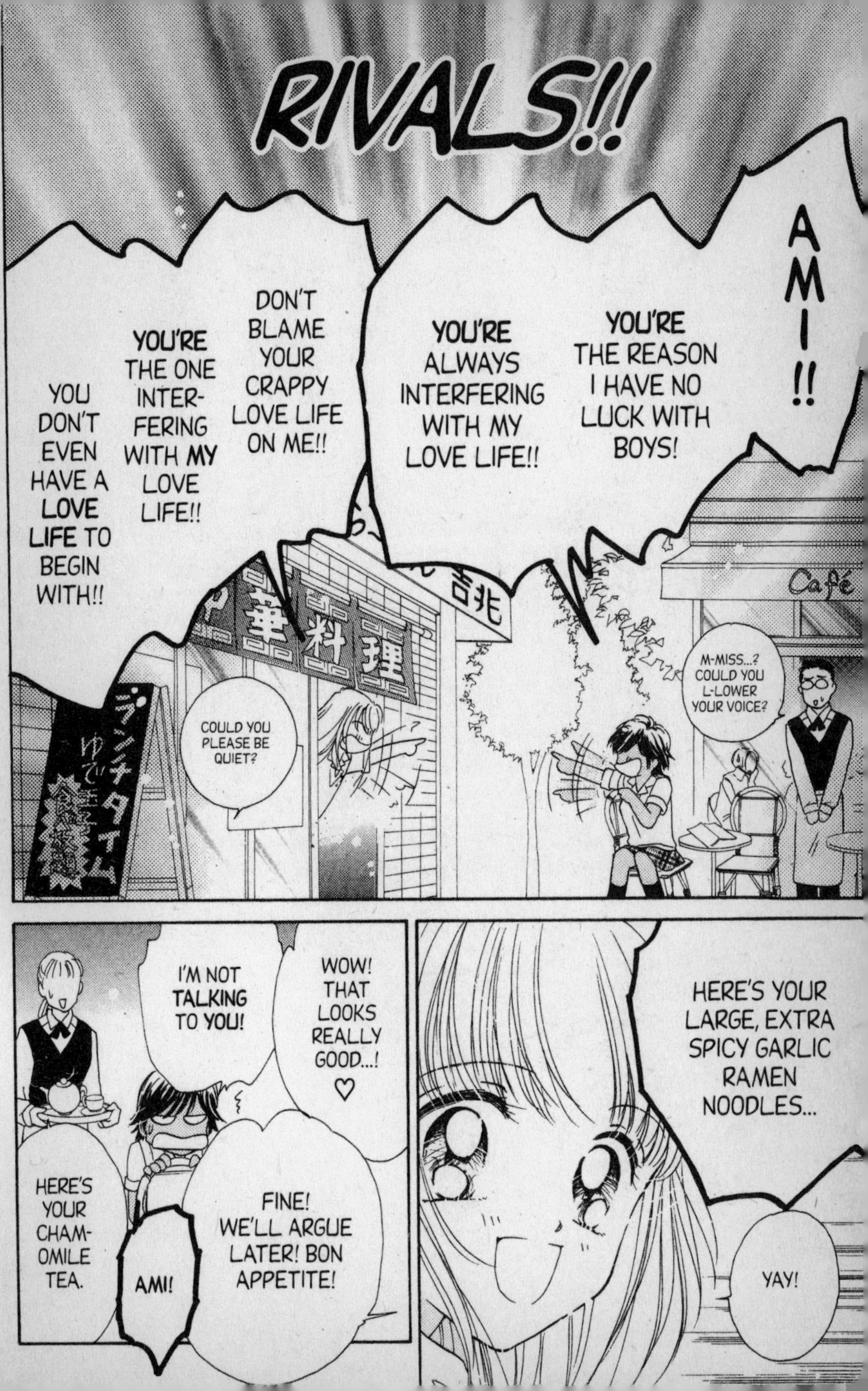
RIVALS!!
AMI!!
YOU'RE THE REASON I HAVE NO LUCK WITH BOYS!
YOU'RE ALWAYS INTERFERING WITH MY LOVE LIFE!!
DON'T BLAME YOUR CRAPPY LOVE LIFE ON ME!!
YOU'RE THE ONE INTERFERING WITH MY LOVE LIFE!!
YOU DON'T EVEN HAVE A LOVE LIFE TO BEGIN WITH!!
Café
M-MISS...? COULD YOU L-LOWER YOUR VOICE?
COULD YOU PLEASE BE QUIET?
HERE'S YOUR LARGE, EXTRA SPICY GARLIC RAMEN NOODLES...
YAY!
WOW! THAT LOOKS REALLY GOOD...! ♡
I'M NOT TALKING TO YOU!
FINE! WE'LL ARGUE LATER! BON APPETITE!
AMI!
HERE'S YOUR CHAMOMILE TEA.

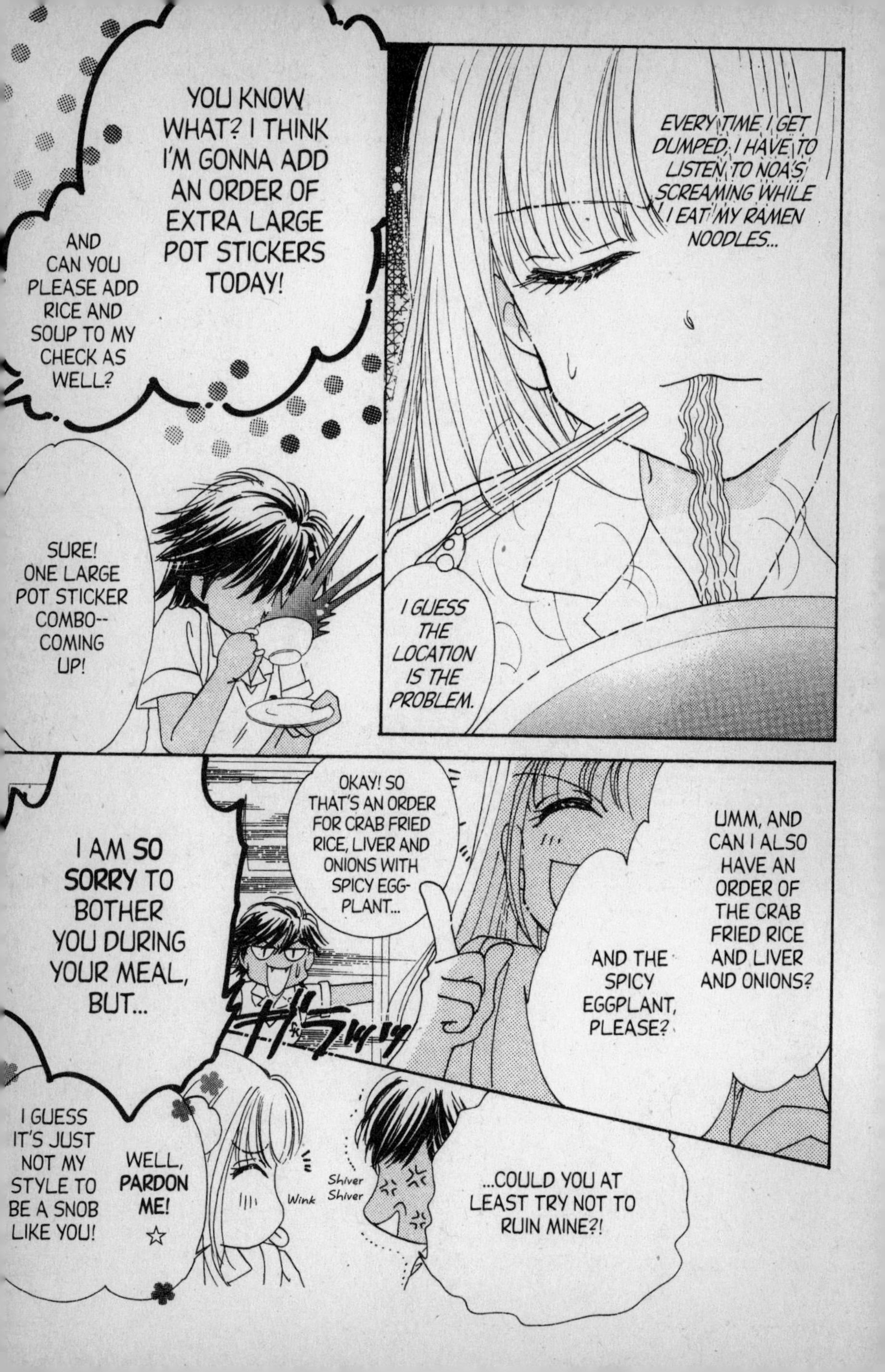
EVERY TIME I GET DUMPED, I HAVE TO LISTEN TO NOA'S SCREAMING WHILE I EAT MY RAMEN NOODLES...
I GUESS THE LOCATION IS THE PROBLEM.
YOU KNOW WHAT? I THINK I'M GONNA ADD AN ORDER OF EXTRA LARGE POT STICKERS TODAY!
AND CAN YOU PLEASE ADD RICE AND SOUP TO MY CHECK AS WELL?
SURE! ONE LARGE POT STICKER COMBO-- COMING UP!
UMM, AND CAN I ALSO HAVE AN ORDER OF THE CRAB FRIED RICE AND LIVER AND ONIONS?
AND THE SPICY EGGPLANT, PLEASE?
OKAY! SO THAT'S AN ORDER FOR CRAB FRIED RICE, LIVER AND ONIONS WITH SPICY EGG-PLANT...
I AM **SO SORRY** TO BOTHER YOU DURING YOUR MEAL, BUT...
...COULD YOU AT LEAST TRY NOT TO RUIN MINE?!
Shiver Shiver
Wink
WELL, **PARDON ME!** ☆
I GUESS IT'S JUST NOT MY STYLE TO BE A SNOB LIKE YOU!

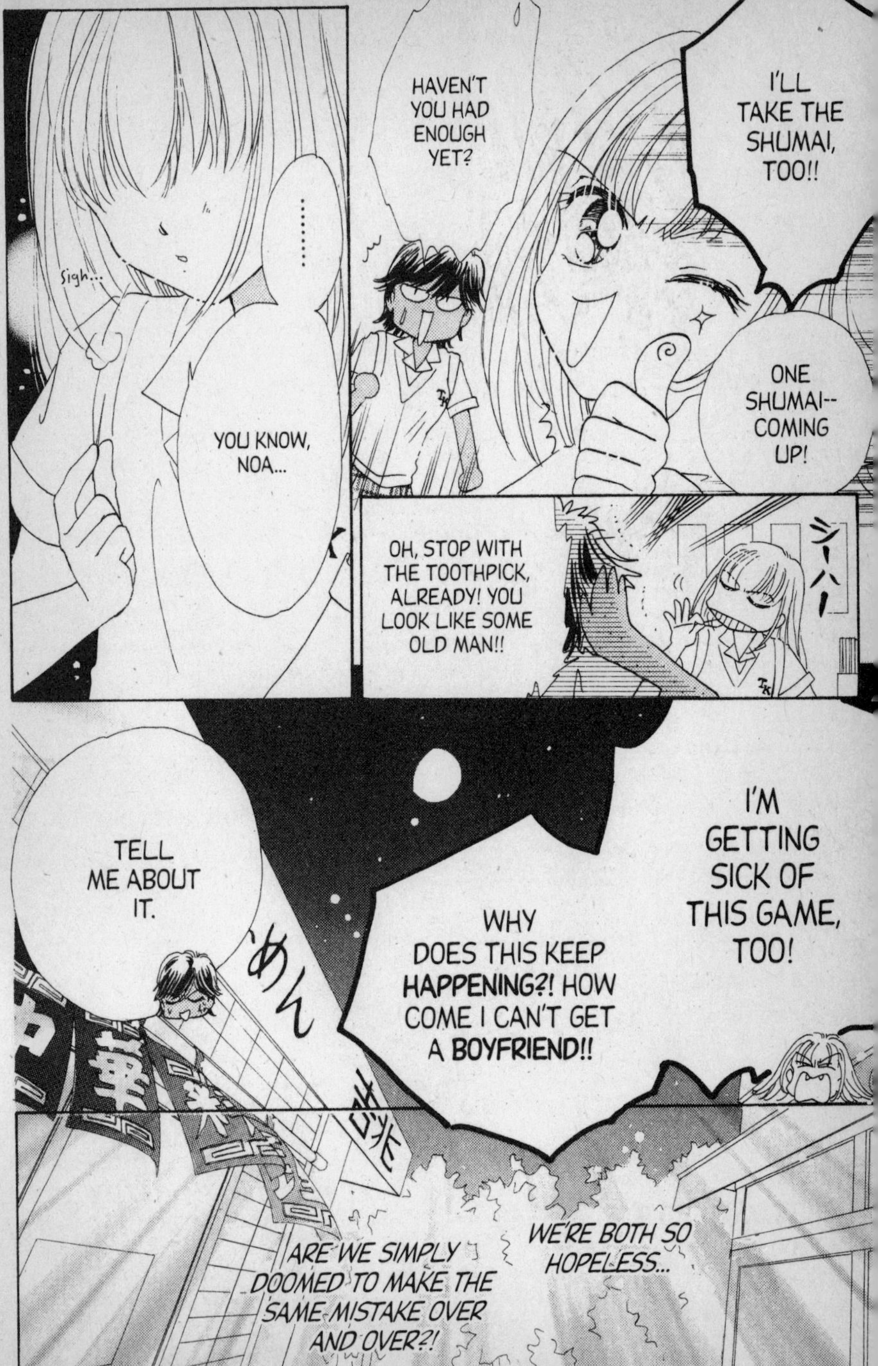
I'LL TAKE THE SHUMAI, TOO!!
ONE SHUMAI--COMING UP!
HAVEN'T YOU HAD ENOUGH YET?
シーハー
OH, STOP WITH THE TOOTHPICK, ALREADY! YOU LOOK LIKE SOME OLD MAN!!
......
YOU KNOW, NOA...
Sigh...
I'M GETTING SICK OF THIS GAME, TOO!
WHY DOES THIS KEEP HAPPENING?! HOW COME I CAN'T GET A BOYFRIEND!!
TELL ME ABOUT IT.
めん
WE'RE BOTH SO HOPELESS...
ARE WE SIMPLY DOOMED TO MAKE THE SAME MISTAKE OVER AND OVER?!

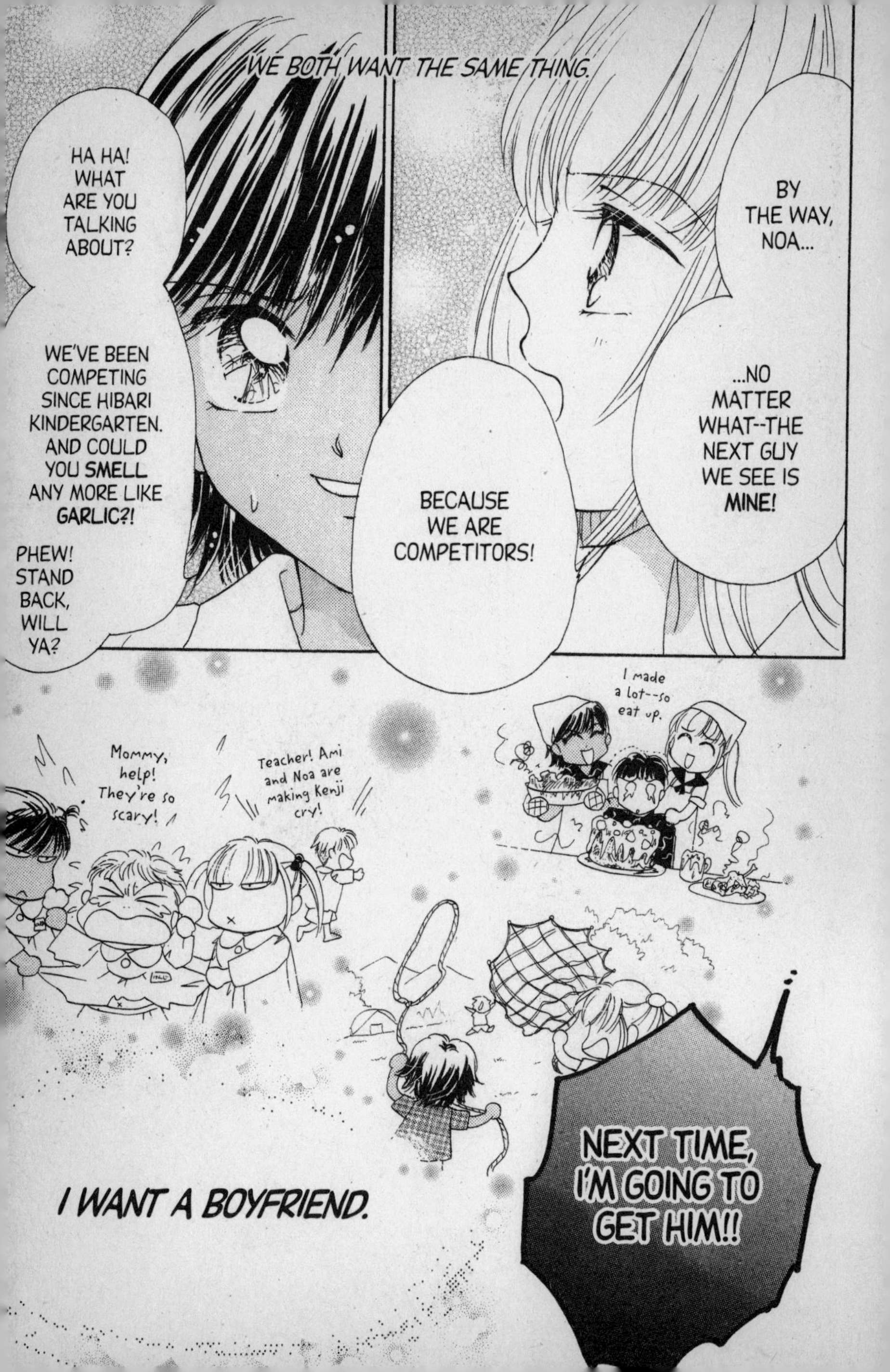
WE BOTH WANT THE SAME THING.
BY THE WAY, NOA...
...NO MATTER WHAT--THE NEXT GUY WE SEE IS MINE!
BECAUSE WE ARE COMPETITORS!
HA HA! WHAT ARE YOU TALKING ABOUT?
WE'VE BEEN COMPETING SINCE HIBARI KINDERGARTEN. AND COULD YOU SMELL ANY MORE LIKE GARLIC?!
PHEW! STAND BACK, WILL YA?
I made a lot--so eat up.
Teacher! Ami and Noa are making Kenji cry!
Mommy, help! They're so scary!
NEXT TIME, I'M GOING TO GET HIM!!
I WANT A BOYFRIEND.

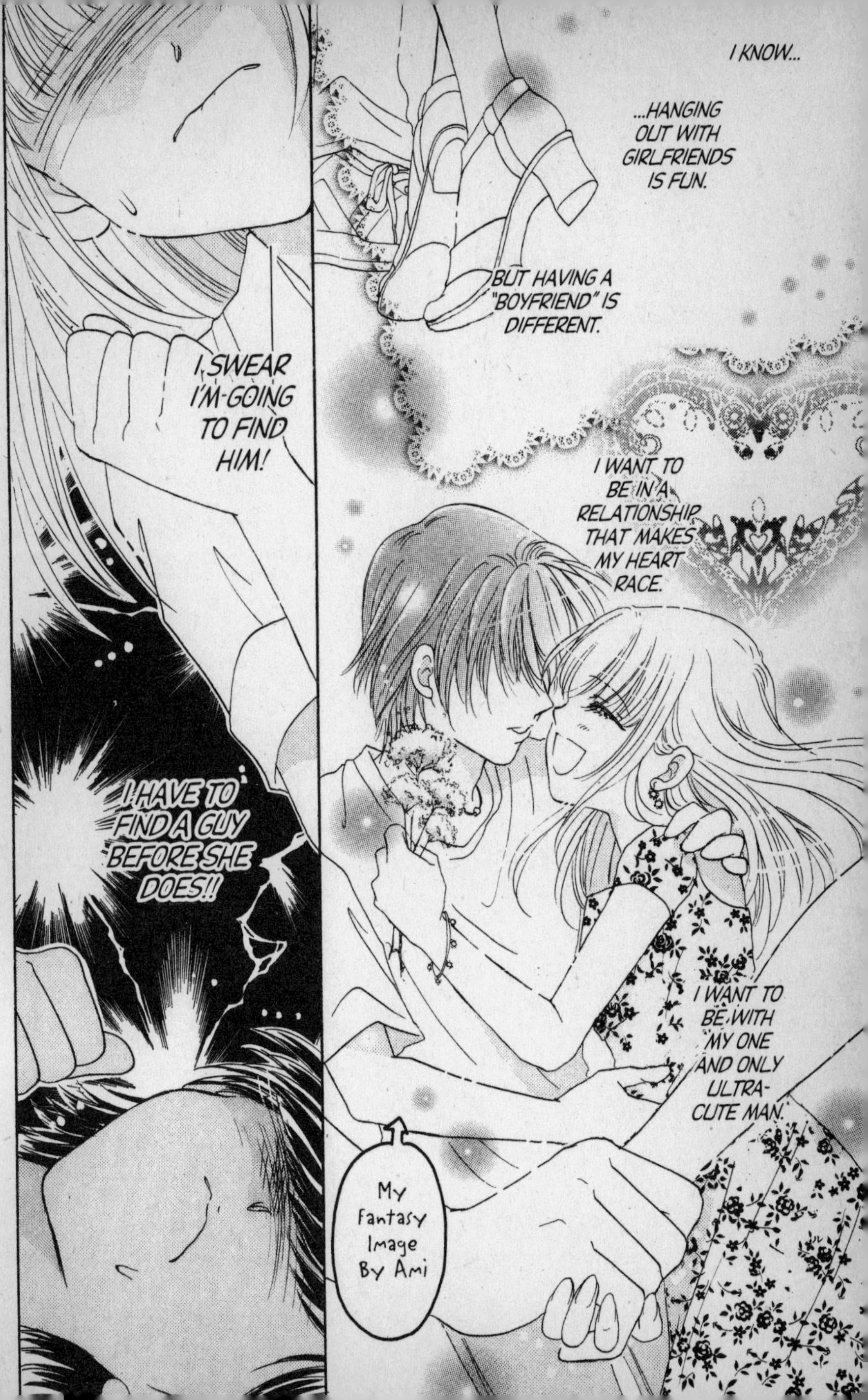
I KNOW...
...HANGING OUT WITH GIRLFRIENDS IS FUN.
BUT HAVING A "BOYFRIEND" IS DIFFERENT.
I WANT TO BE IN A RELATIONSHIP THAT MAKES MY HEART RACE.
I WANT TO BE WITH MY ONE AND ONLY ULTRA-CUTE MAN.
My Fantasy Image By Ami
I SWEAR I'M GOING TO FIND HIM!
I HAVE TO FIND A GUY BEFORE SHE DOES!!

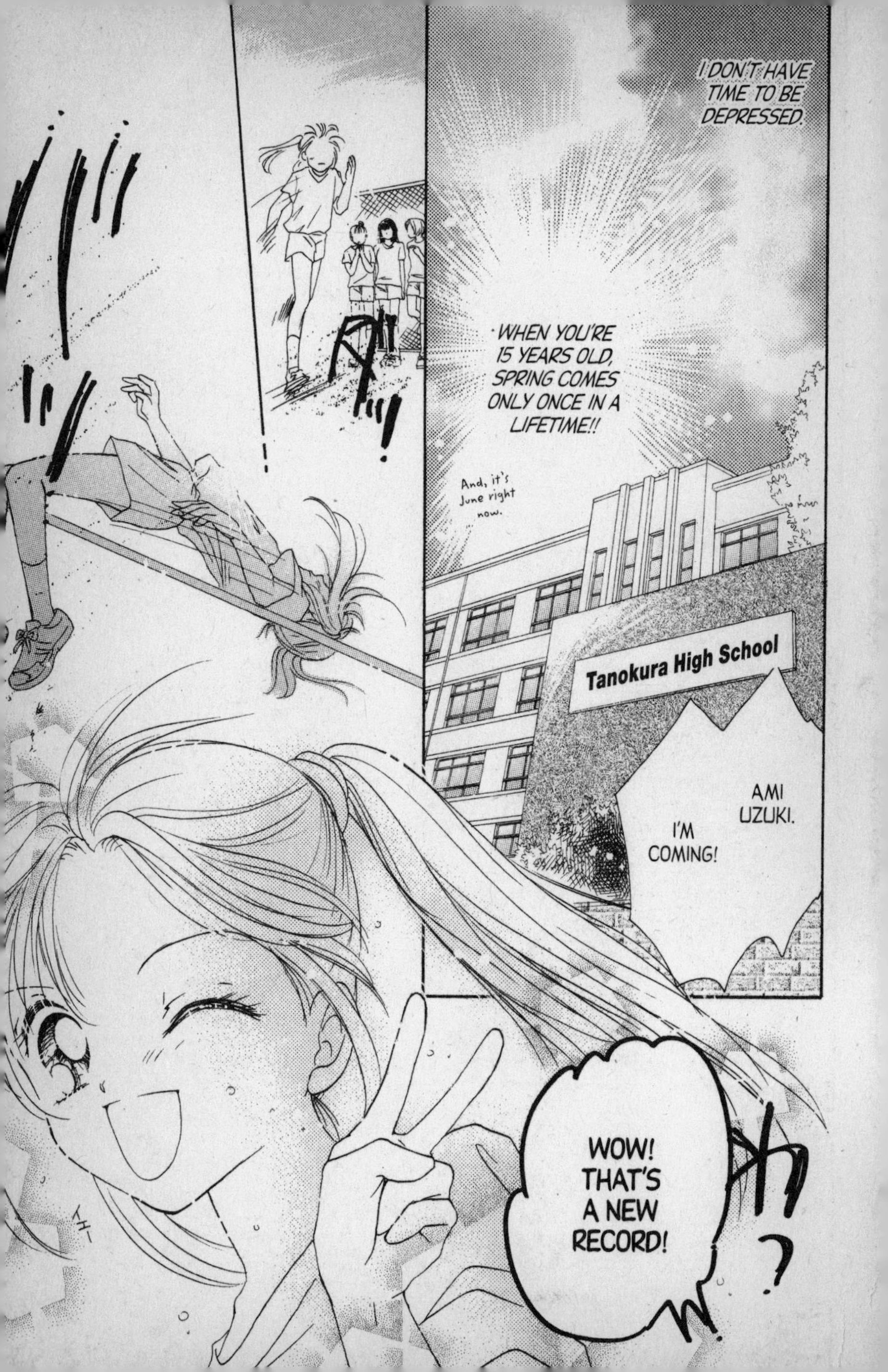
I DON'T HAVE TIME TO BE DEPRESSED.
WHEN YOU'RE 15 YEARS OLD, SPRING COMES ONLY ONCE IN A LIFETIME!!
And, it's June right now...
Tanokura High School
AMI UZUKI.
I'M COMING!
WOW! THAT'S A NEW RECORD!

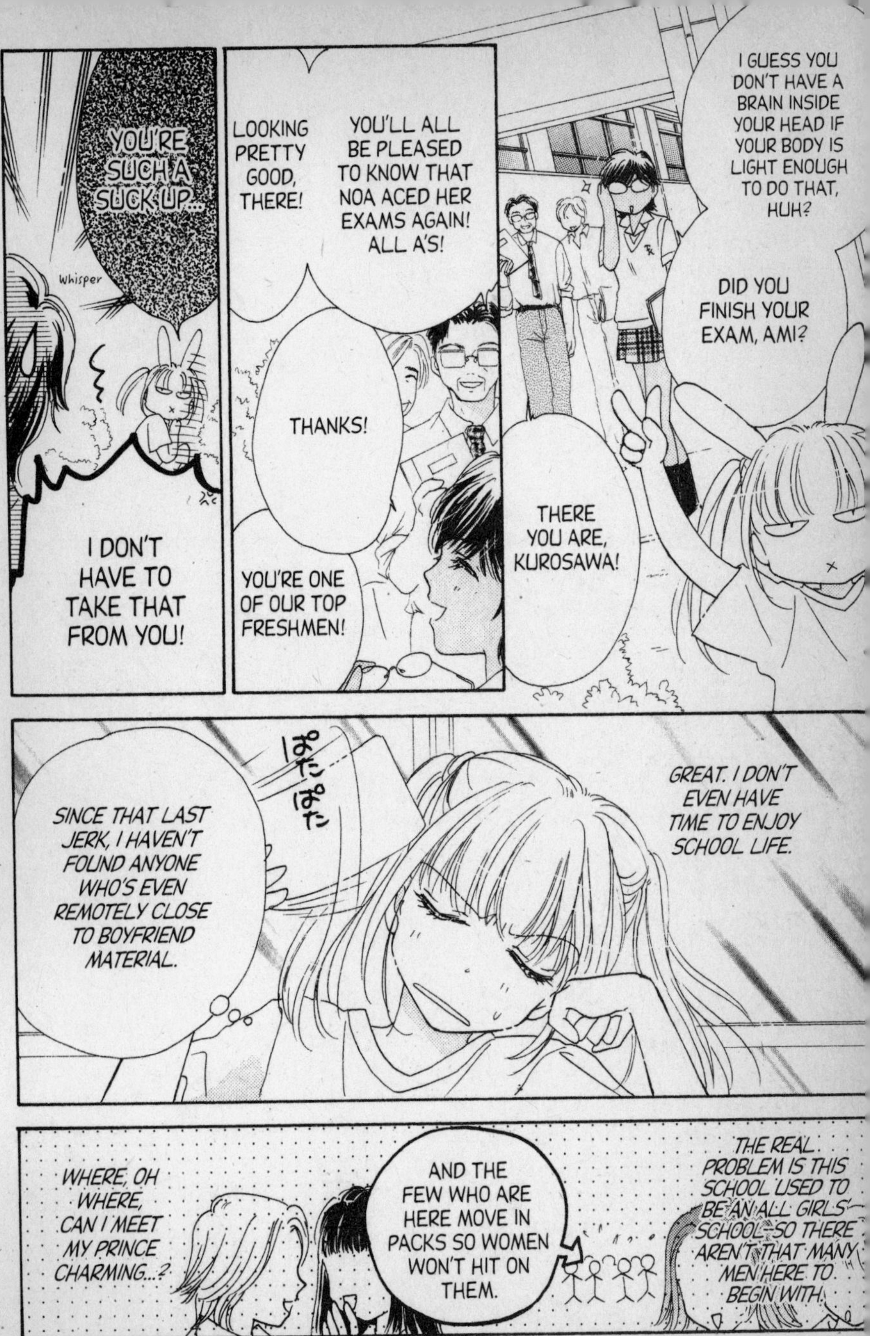

I GUESS YOU DON'T HAVE A BRAIN INSIDE YOUR HEAD IF YOUR BODY IS LIGHT ENOUGH TO DO THAT, HUH?
DID YOU FINISH YOUR EXAM, AMI?
THERE YOU ARE, KUROSAWA!
YOU'LL ALL BE PLEASED TO KNOW THAT NOA ACED HER EXAMS AGAIN! ALL A'S!
LOOKING PRETTY GOOD, THERE!
THANKS!
YOU'RE ONE OF OUR TOP FRESHMEN!
YOU'RE SUCH A SUCK UP...
Whisper
I DON'T HAVE TO TAKE THAT FROM YOU!
GREAT. I DON'T EVEN HAVE TIME TO ENJOY SCHOOL LIFE.
ぱたぱた
SINCE THAT LAST JERK, I HAVEN'T FOUND ANYONE WHO'S EVEN REMOTELY CLOSE TO BOYFRIEND MATERIAL.
THE REAL PROBLEM IS THIS SCHOOL USED TO BE AN ALL GIRLS SCHOOL--SO THERE AREN'T THAT MANY MEN HERE TO BEGIN WITH.
AND THE FEW WHO ARE HERE MOVE IN PACKS SO WOMEN WON'T HIT ON THEM.
WHERE, OH WHERE, CAN I MEET MY PRINCE CHARMING...?

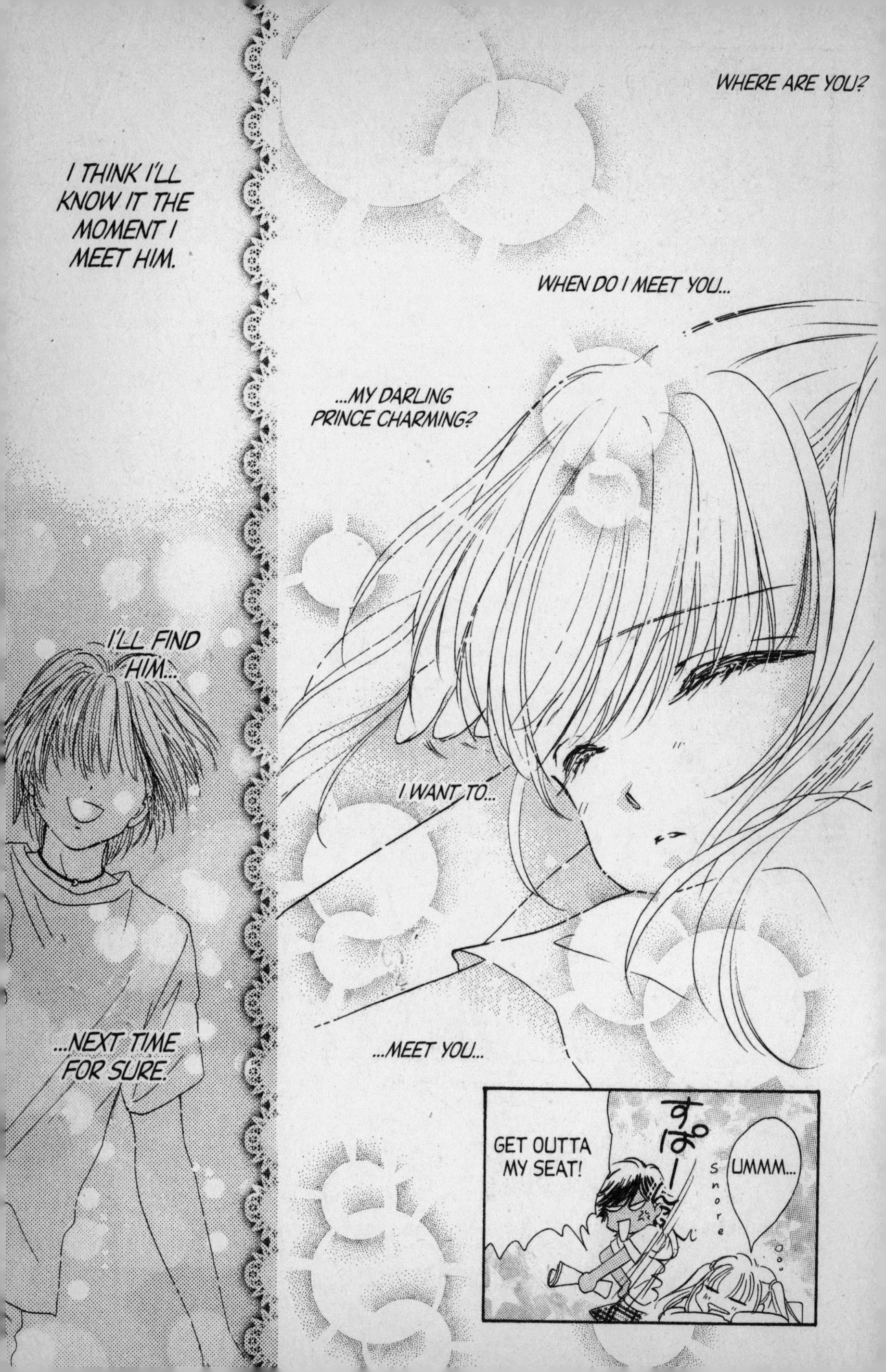
WHERE ARE YOU?
WHEN DO I MEET YOU...
...MY DARLING PRINCE CHARMING?
I WANT TO...
...MEET YOU...
UMMM...
すぱー
Snore
GET OUTTA MY SEAT!
I THINK I'LL KNOW IT THE MOMENT I MEET HIM.
I'LL FIND HIM...
...NEXT TIME FOR SURE.

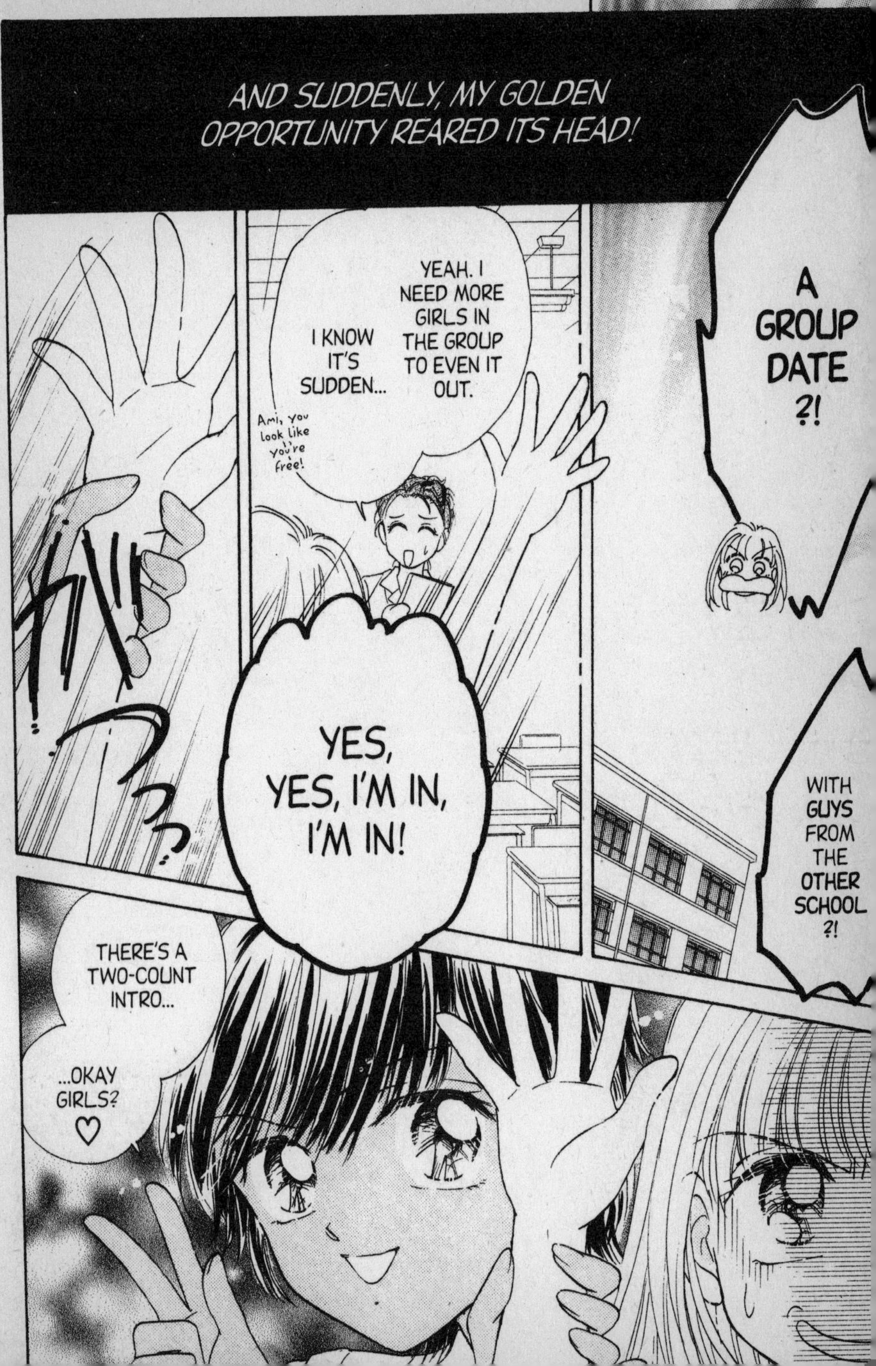
AND SUDDENLY, MY GOLDEN OPPORTUNITY REARED ITS HEAD!
A GROUP DATE ?!
YEAH. I NEED MORE GIRLS IN THE GROUP TO EVEN IT OUT.
I KNOW IT'S SUDDEN...
Ami, you look like you're free!
YES, YES, I'M IN, I'M IN!
WITH GUYS FROM THE OTHER SCHOOL ?!
THERE'S A TWO-COUNT INTRO...
...OKAY GIRLS? ♡

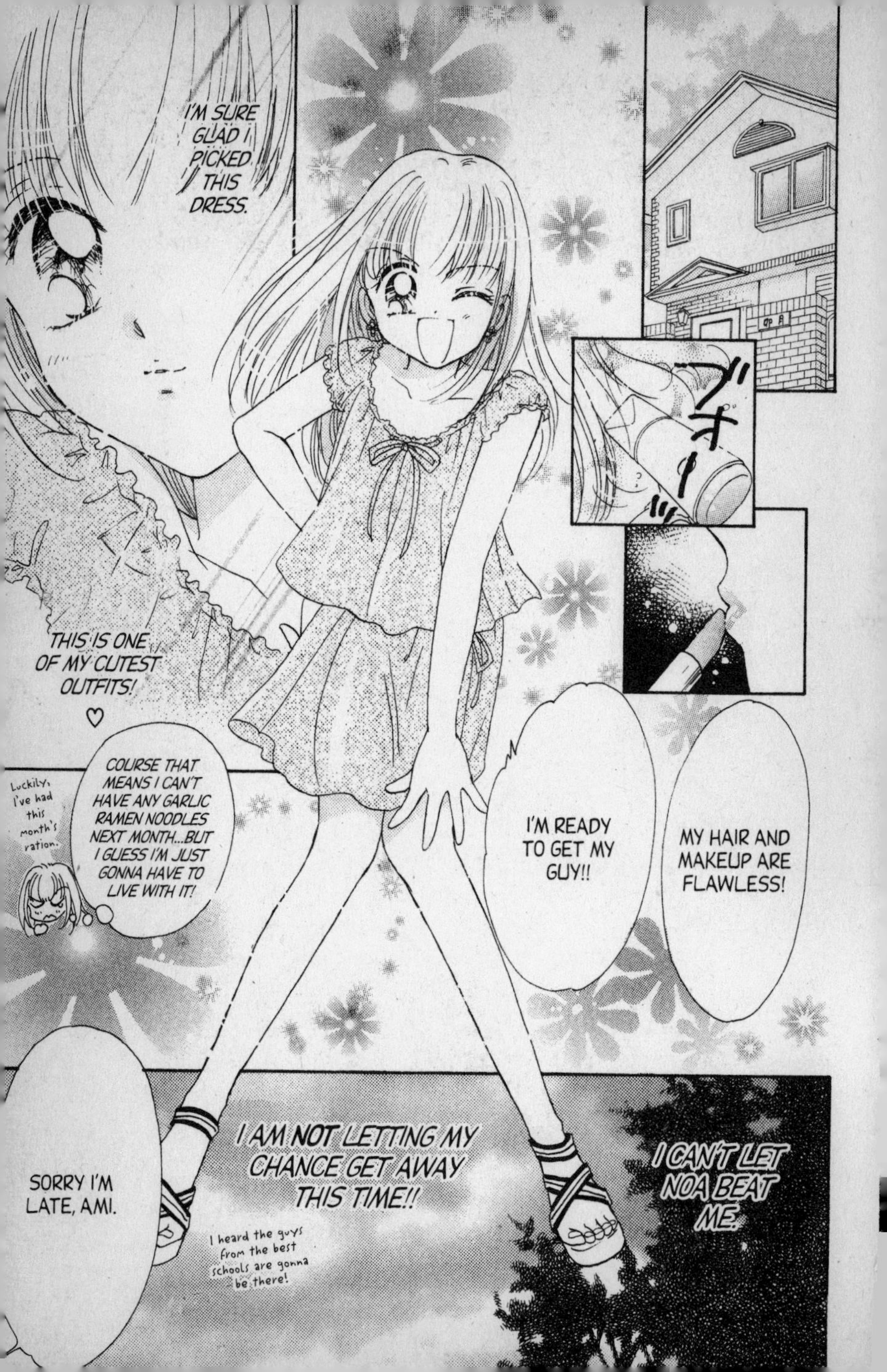

ブオーッ
MY HAIR AND MAKEUP ARE FLAWLESS!
I'M READY TO GET MY GUY!!
I'M SURE GLAD I PICKED THIS DRESS.
THIS IS ONE OF MY CUTEST OUTFITS! ♡
COURSE THAT MEANS I CAN'T HAVE ANY GARLIC RAMEN NOODLES NEXT MONTH...BUT I GUESS I'M JUST GONNA HAVE TO LIVE WITH IT!
Luckily, I've had this month's ration.
I CAN'T LET NOA BEAT ME.
I AM NOT LETTING MY CHANCE GET AWAY THIS TIME!!
I heard the guys from the best schools are gonna be there!
SORRY I'M LATE, AMI.

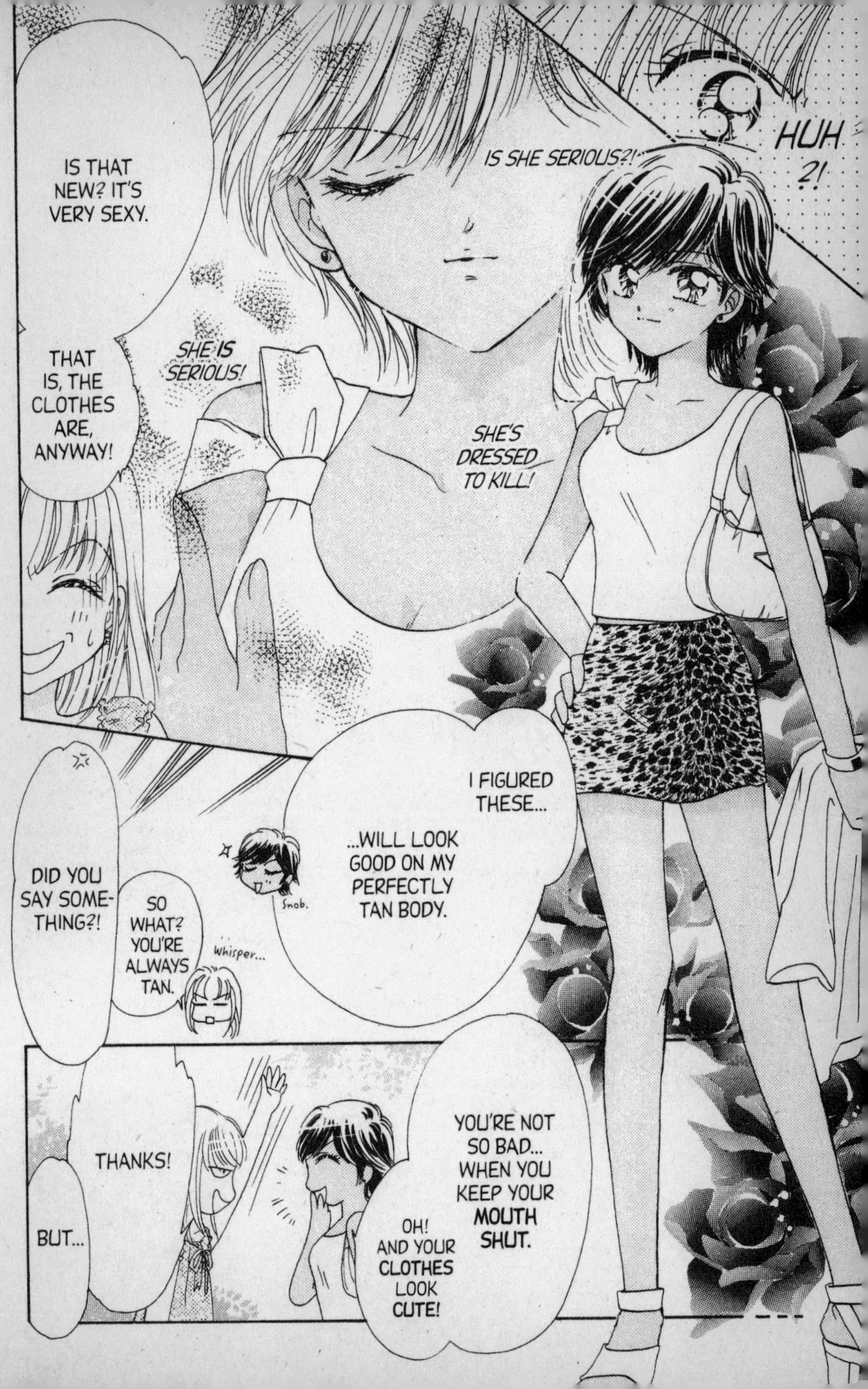
HUH ?!
IS SHE SERIOUS?!
SHE'S DRESSED TO KILL!
SHE IS SERIOUS!
IS THAT NEW? IT'S VERY SEXY.
THAT IS, THE CLOTHES ARE, ANYWAY!
I FIGURED THESE...
...WILL LOOK GOOD ON MY PERFECTLY TAN BODY.
Snob.
SO WHAT? YOU'RE ALWAYS TAN.
Whisper...
DID YOU SAY SOME-THING?!
YOU'RE NOT SO BAD... WHEN YOU KEEP YOUR MOUTH SHUT.
OH! AND YOUR CLOTHES LOOK CUTE!
THANKS!
BUT...

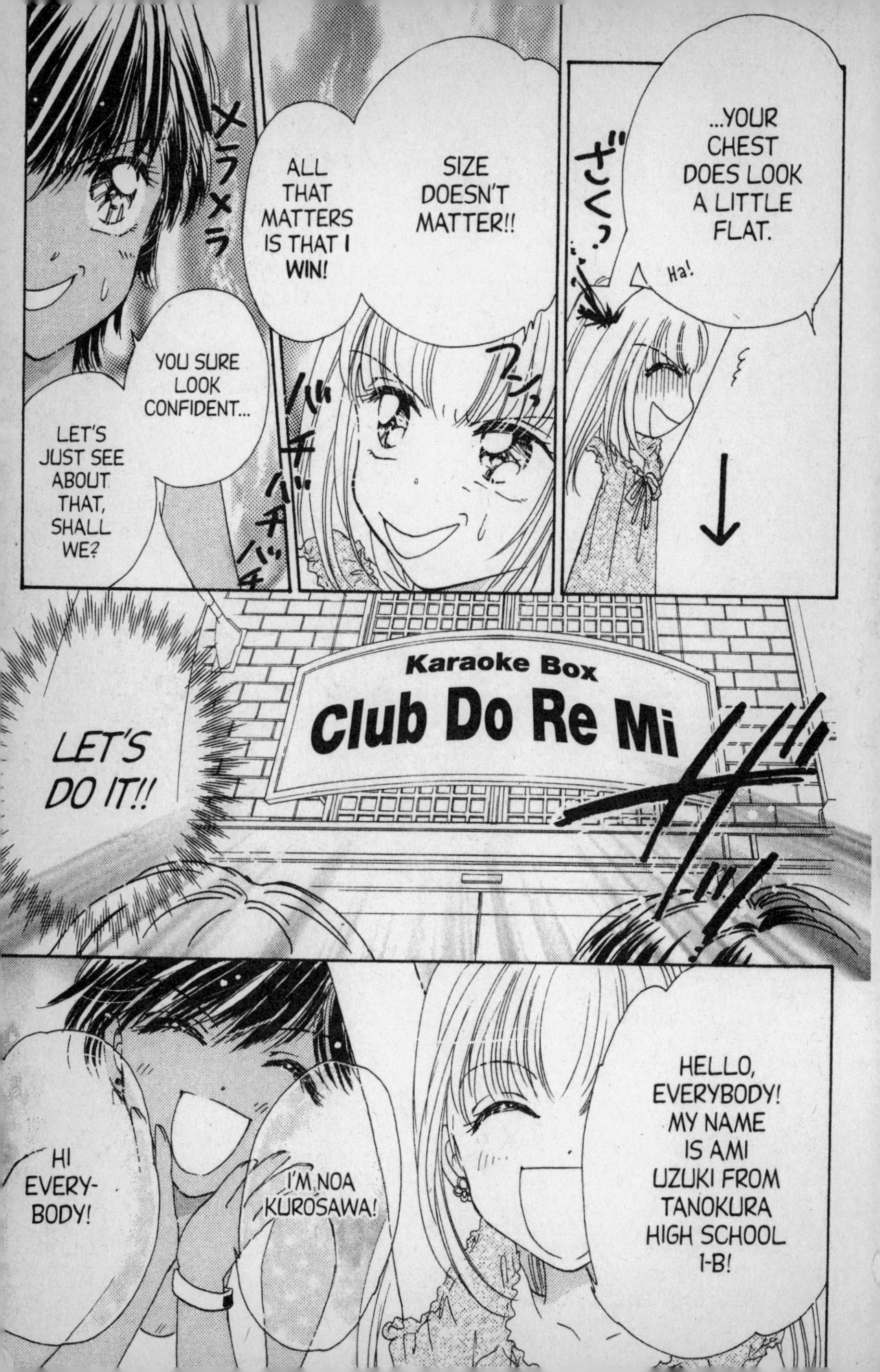
...YOUR CHEST DOES LOOK A LITTLE FLAT.
Ha!
ざくっ
SIZE DOESN'T MATTER!!
ALL THAT MATTERS IS THAT I WIN!
フン
バチバチバチ
メラメラ
YOU SURE LOOK CONFIDENT...
LET'S JUST SEE ABOUT THAT, SHALL WE?
Karaoke Box
Club Do Re Mi
LET'S DO IT!!
HELLO, EVERYBODY! MY NAME IS AMI UZUKI FROM TANOKURA HIGH SCHOOL 1-B!
I'M NOA KUROSAWA!
HI EVERY-BODY!

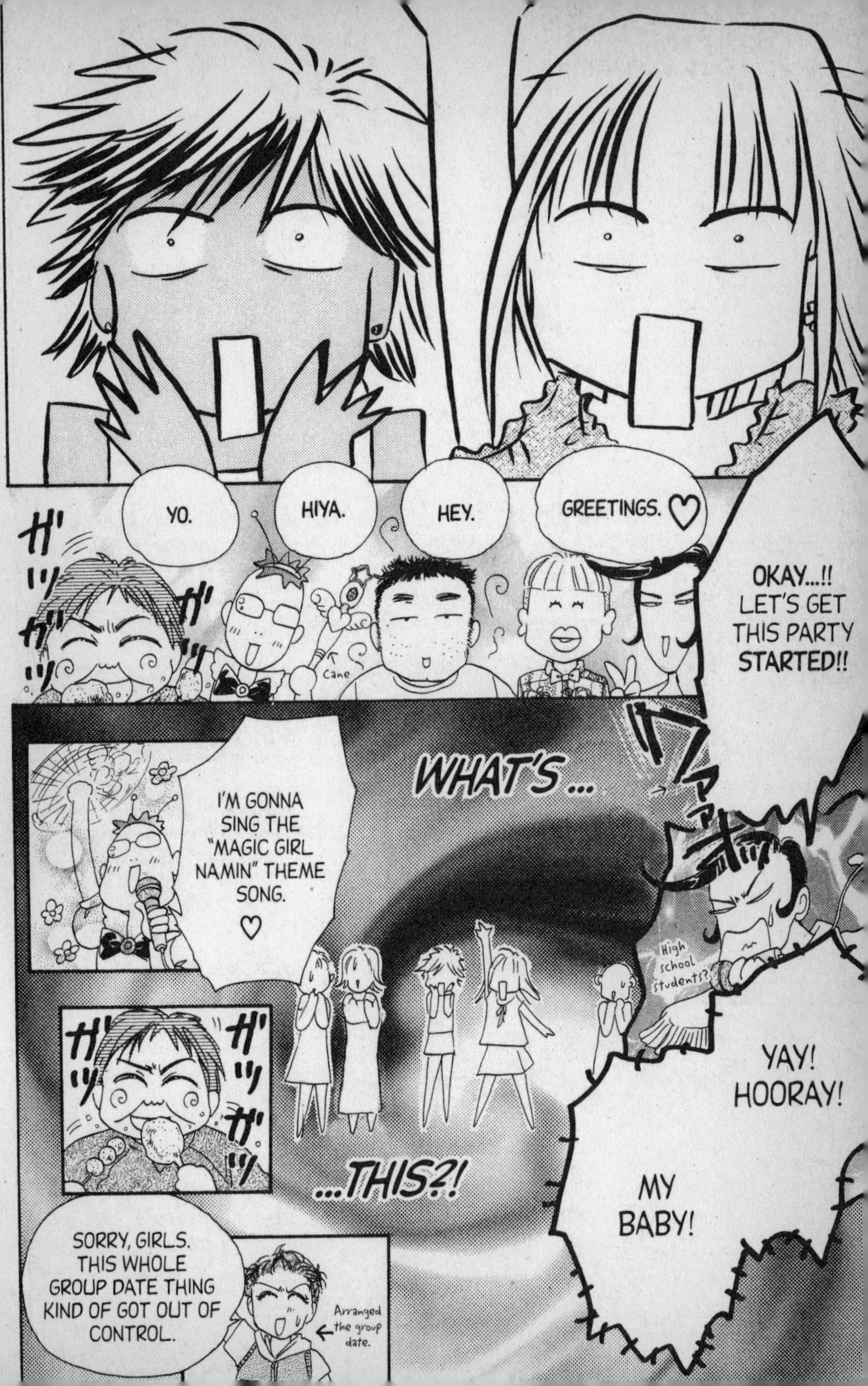

GREETINGS. ♡
HEY.
HIYA.
YO.
Cane
ガツガツガツ
OKAY...!! LET'S GET THIS PARTY STARTED!!
WHAT'S...
High school students?
YAY! HOORAY!
MY BABY!
...THIS?!
I'M GONNA SING THE "MAGIC GIRL NAMIN" THEME SONG. ♡
ガツガツガツ
SORRY, GIRLS. THIS WHOLE GROUP DATE THING KIND OF GOT OUT OF CONTROL.
Arranged the group date.

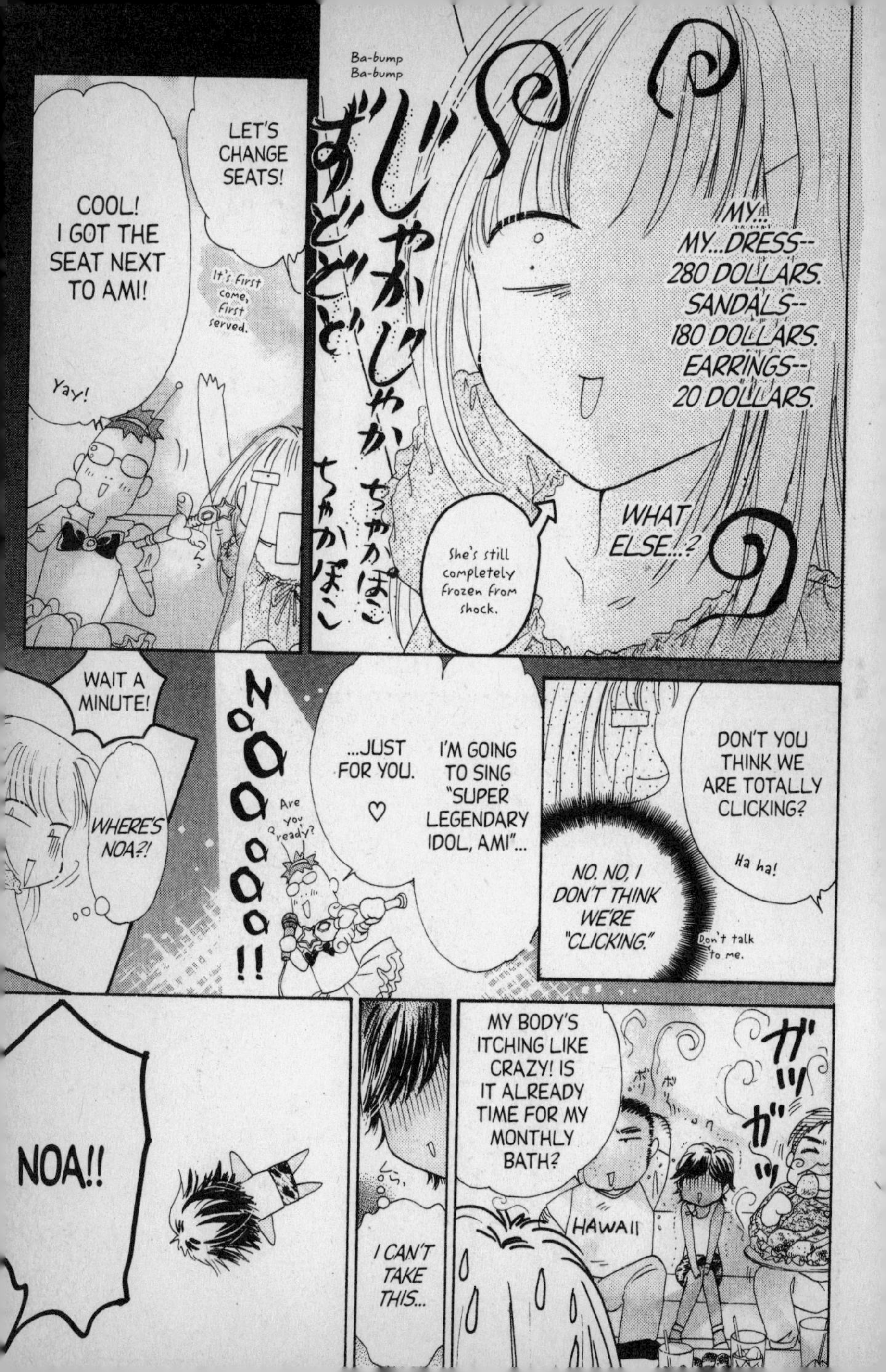
Ba-bump
Ba-bump
ずどどど
じゃかじゃかじゃか
ちゃかぽこちゃかぽこ
MY... MY...DRESS-- 280 DOLLARS. SANDALS-- 180 DOLLARS. EARRINGS-- 20 DOLLARS.
WHAT ELSE...?
She's still completely frozen from shock.
LET'S CHANGE SEATS!
COOL! I GOT THE SEAT NEXT TO AMI!
It's first come, first served.
Yay!
DON'T YOU THINK WE ARE TOTALLY CLICKING?
Ha ha!
NO. NO, I DON'T THINK WE'RE "CLICKING."
Don't talk to me.
I'M GOING TO SING "SUPER LEGENDARY IDOL, AMI"...
...JUST FOR YOU. ♡
Are you ready?
NOOOOOOO!!
WAIT A MINUTE!
WHERE'S NOA?!
ガッガッ
MY BODY'S ITCHING LIKE CRAZY! IS IT ALREADY TIME FOR MY MONTHLY BATH?
HAWAII
I CAN'T TAKE THIS...
NOA!!

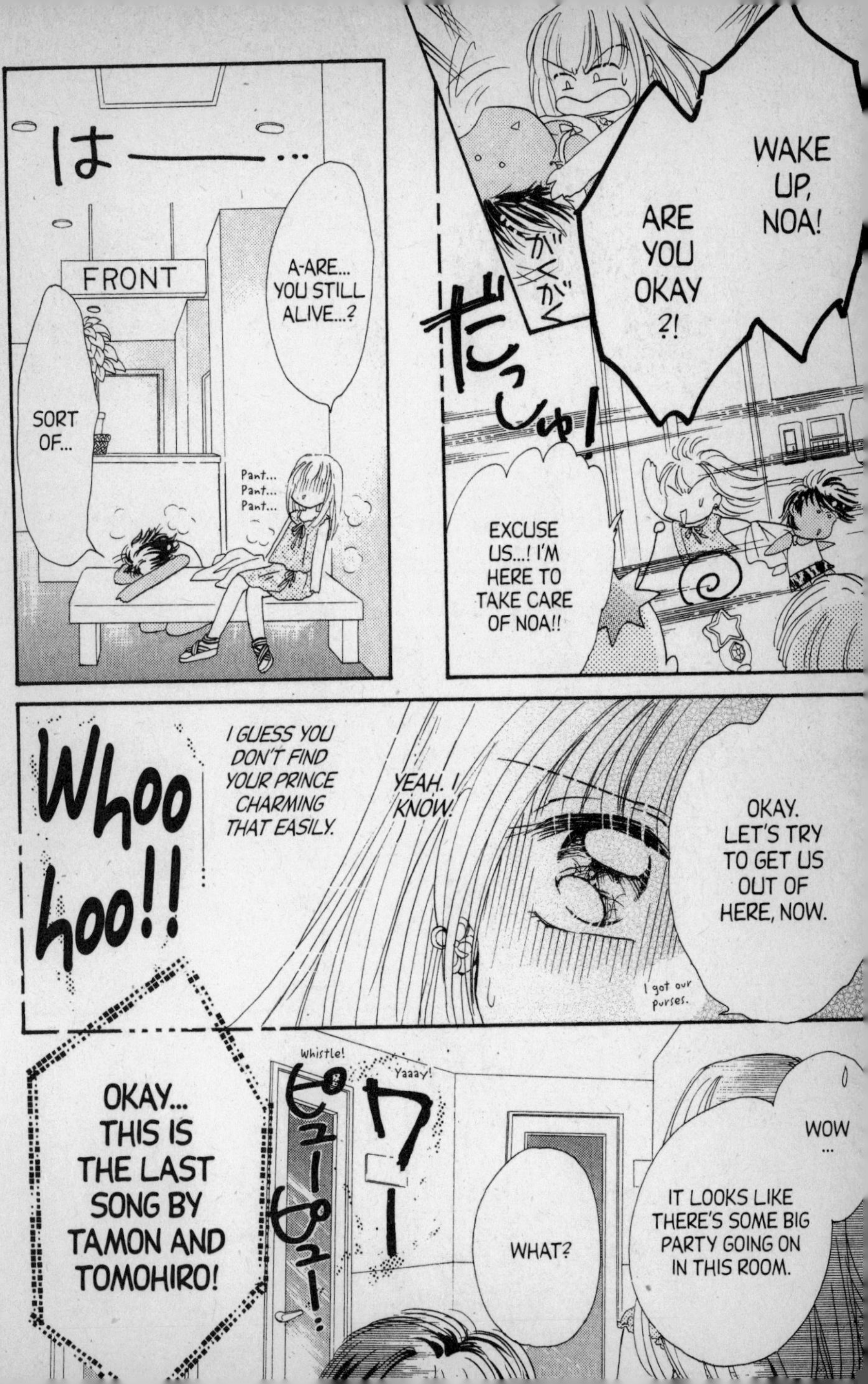
WAKE UP, NOA!
ARE YOU OKAY ?!
がくがく
だっしゅ!
EXCUSE US...! I'M HERE TO TAKE CARE OF NOA!!
は——…
FRONT
A-ARE... YOU STILL ALIVE...?
SORT OF...
Pant... Pant... Pant...
OKAY. LET'S TRY TO GET US OUT OF HERE, NOW.
I got our purses.
YEAH. I KNOW.
I GUESS YOU DON'T FIND YOUR PRINCE CHARMING THAT EASILY.
Whoo hoo!!
WOW ...
IT LOOKS LIKE THERE'S SOME BIG PARTY GOING ON IN THIS ROOM.
WHAT?
ワー
Yaaay!
ピューピュー
Whistle!
OKAY... THIS IS THE LAST SONG BY TAMON AND TOMOHIRO!

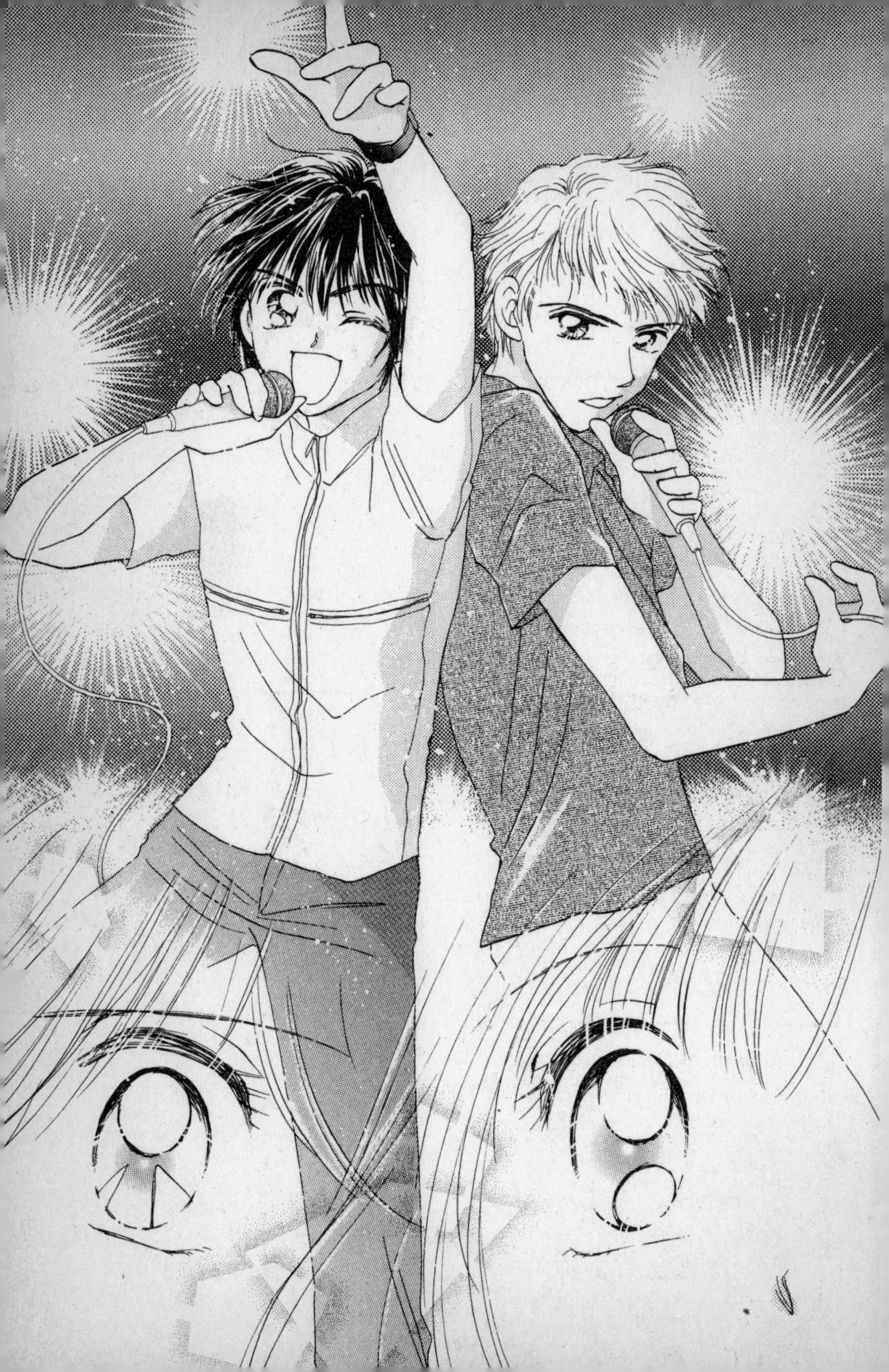

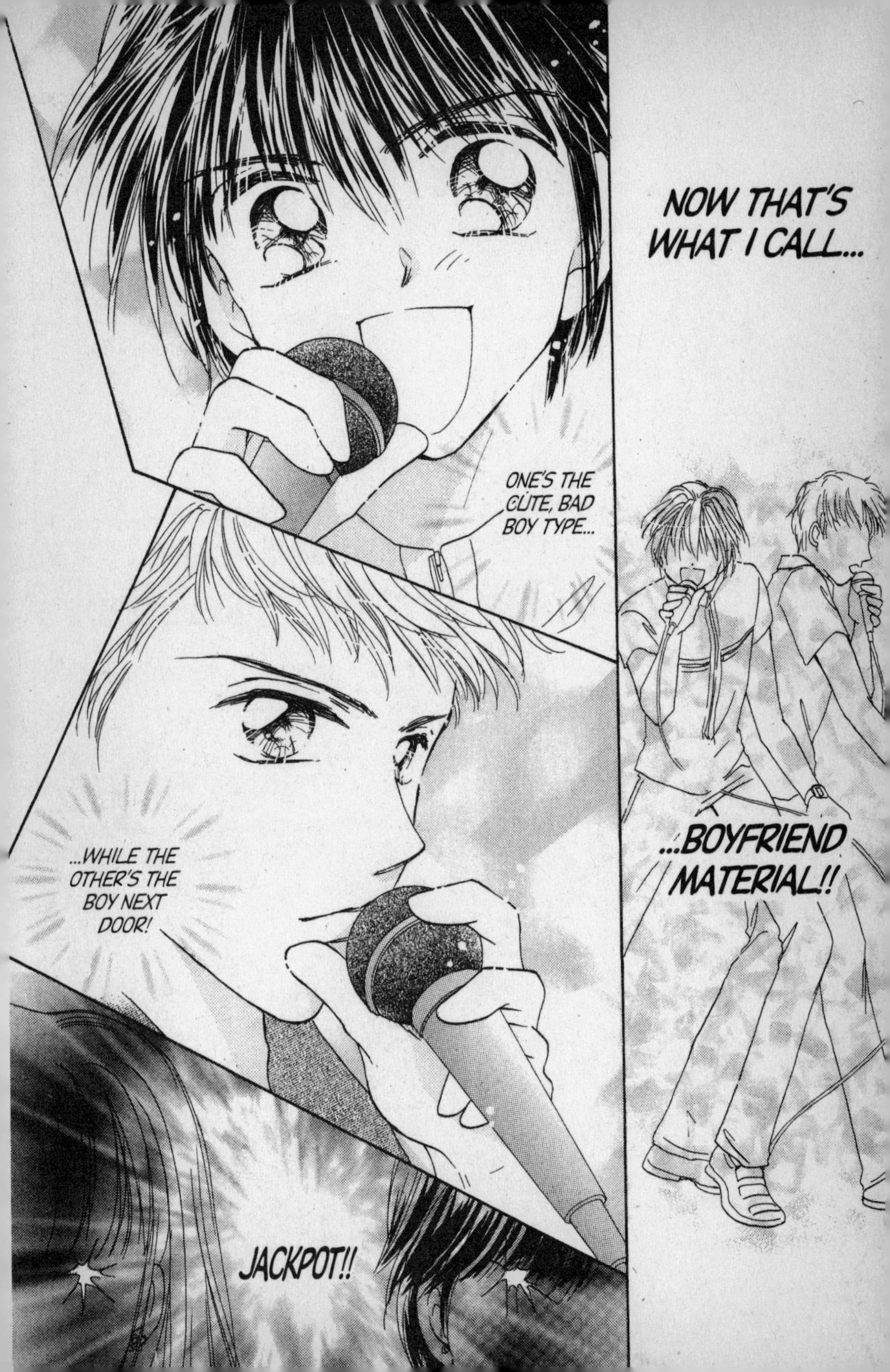
NOW THAT'S WHAT I CALL...
...BOYFRIEND MATERIAL!!
ONE'S THE CUTE, BAD BOY TYPE...
...WHILE THE OTHER'S THE BOY NEXT DOOR!
JACKPOT!!

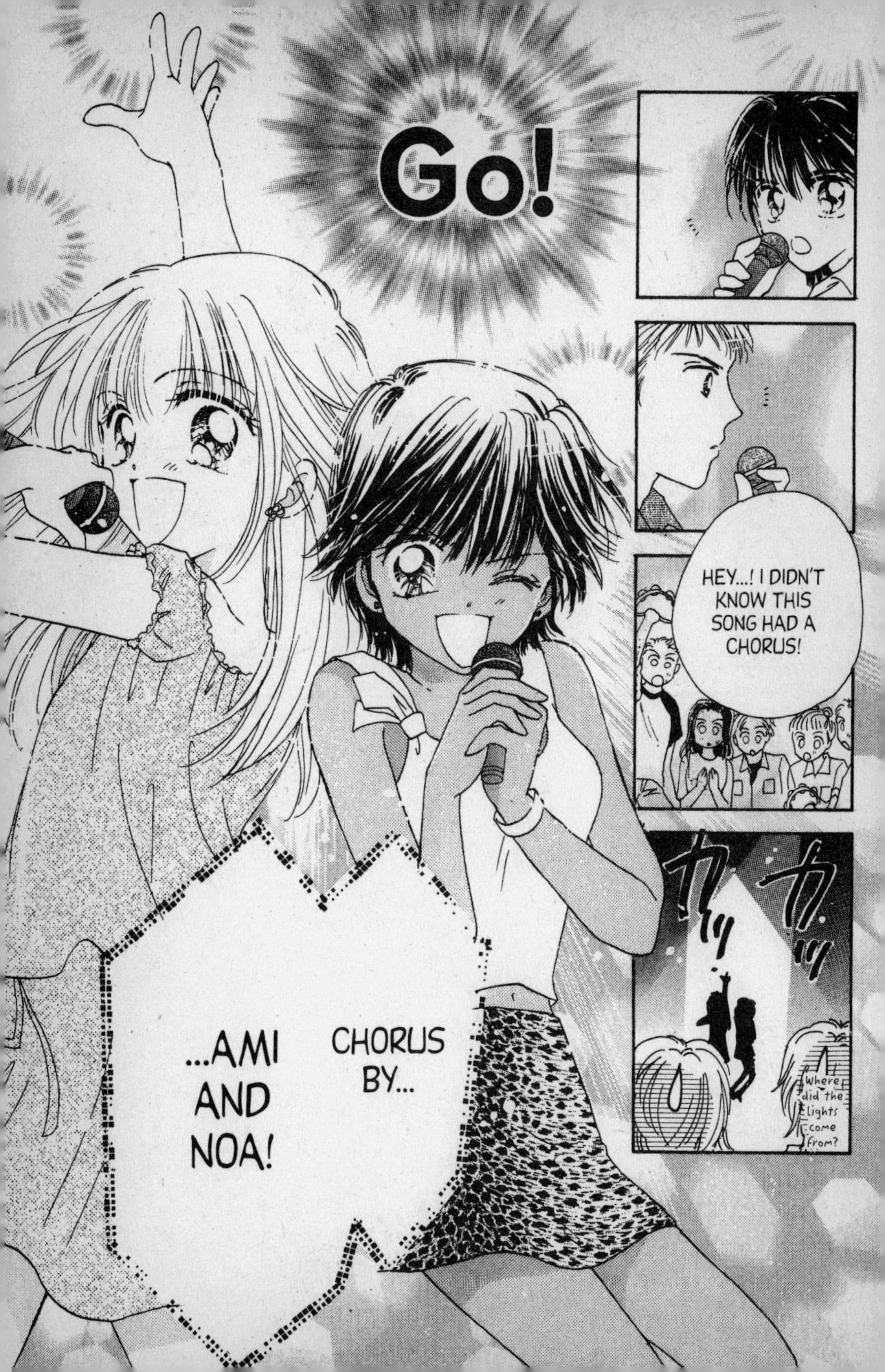
HEY...! I DIDN'T KNOW THIS SONG HAD A CHORUS!
カッ
カッ
Where did the lights come from?
Go!
CHORUS BY...
...AMI AND NOA!

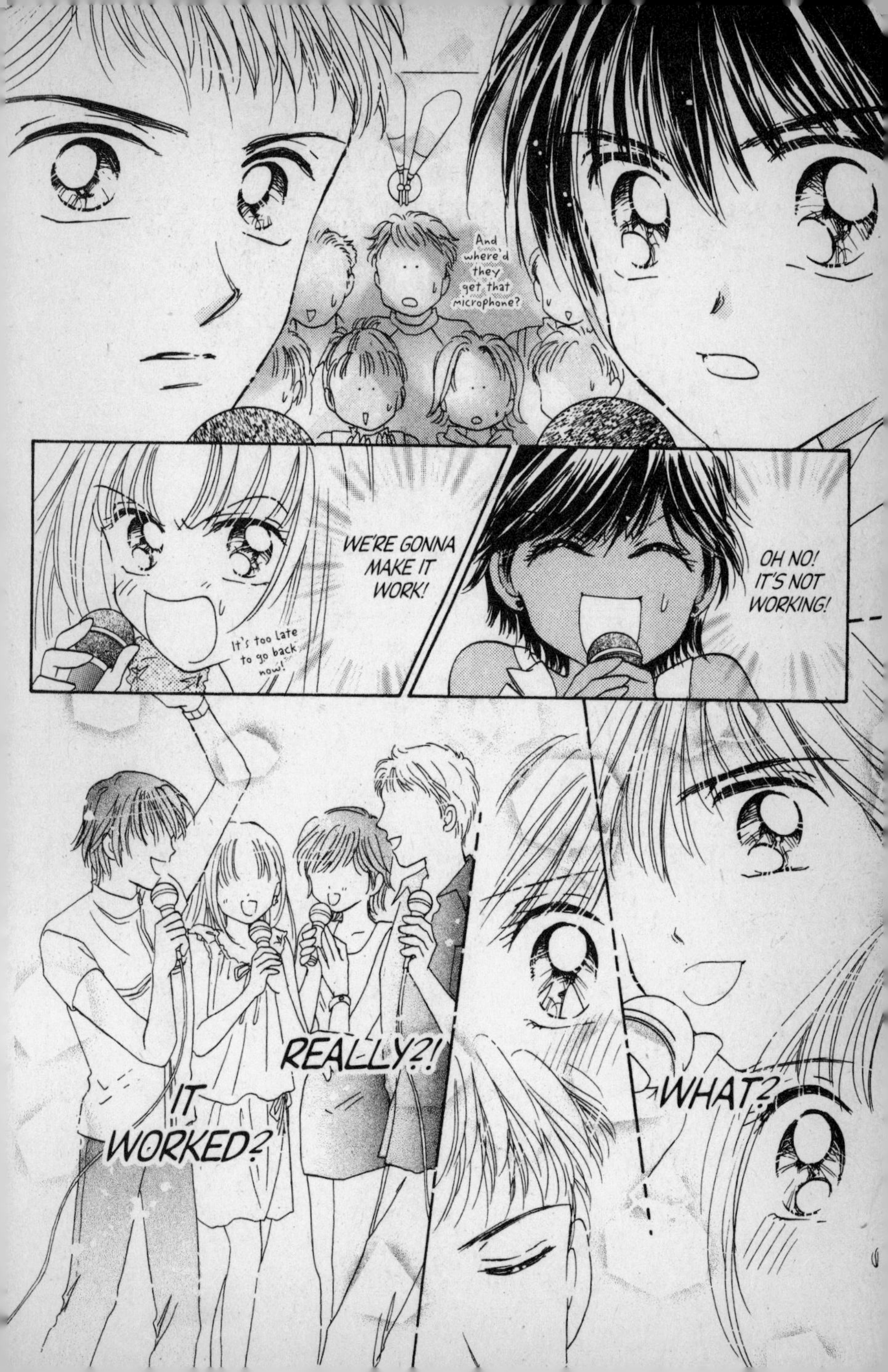
And where'd they get that microphone?
OH NO! IT'S NOT WORKING!
WE'RE GONNA MAKE IT WORK!
It's too late to go back now!
WHAT?
REALLY?!
IT WORKED?

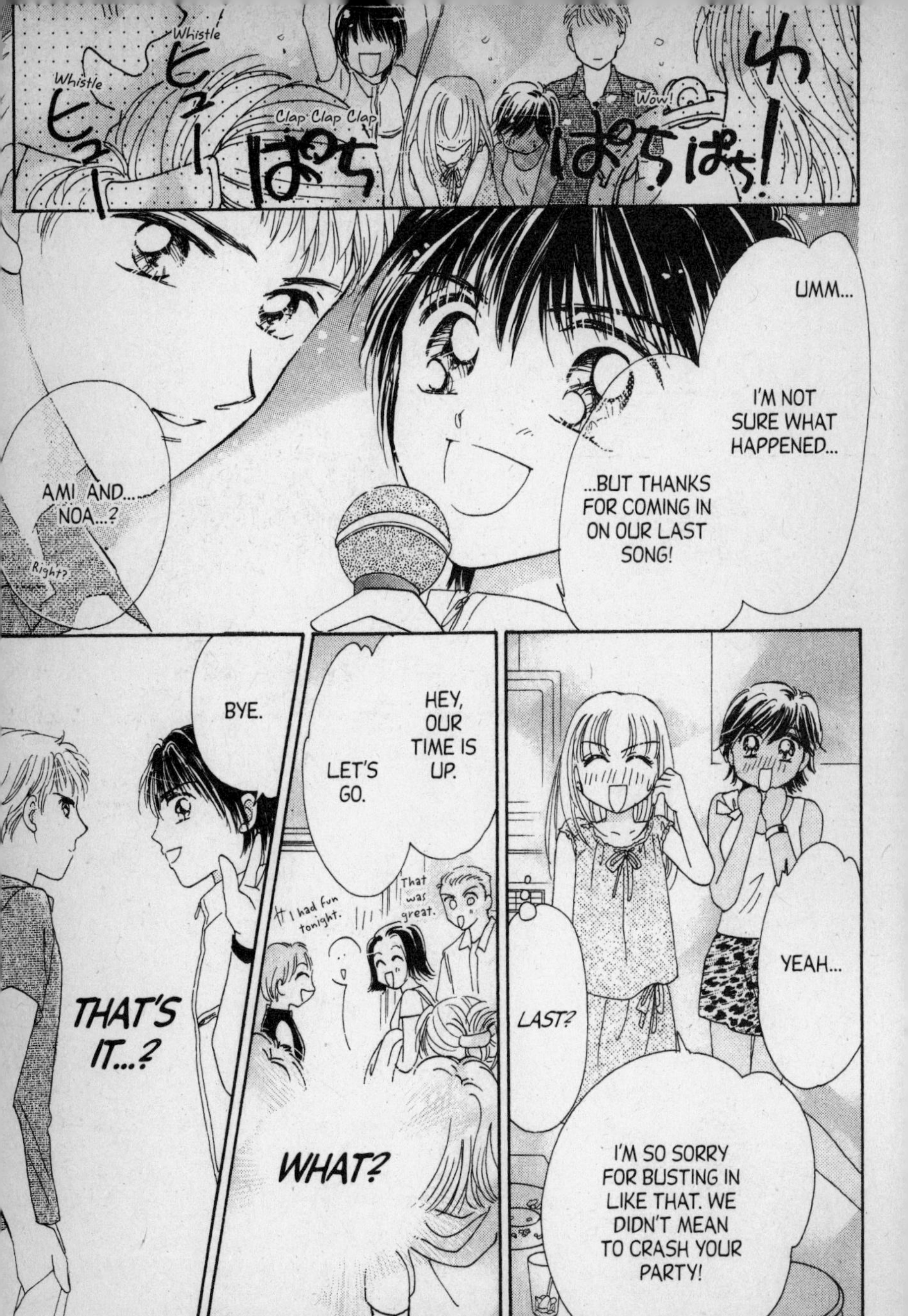
わ
Wow!
ぱちぱち!
ぱち
Clap Clap Clap
ヒュー
Whistle
ヒュー
Whistle
UMM...
I'M NOT SURE WHAT HAPPENED...
...BUT THANKS FOR COMING IN ON OUR LAST SONG!
AMI AND... NOA...?
Right?
YEAH...
LAST?
I'M SO SORRY FOR BUSTING IN LIKE THAT. WE DIDN'T MEAN TO CRASH YOUR PARTY!
HEY, OUR TIME IS UP.
LET'S GO.
That was great.
I had fun tonight.
WHAT?
BYE.
THAT'S IT...?

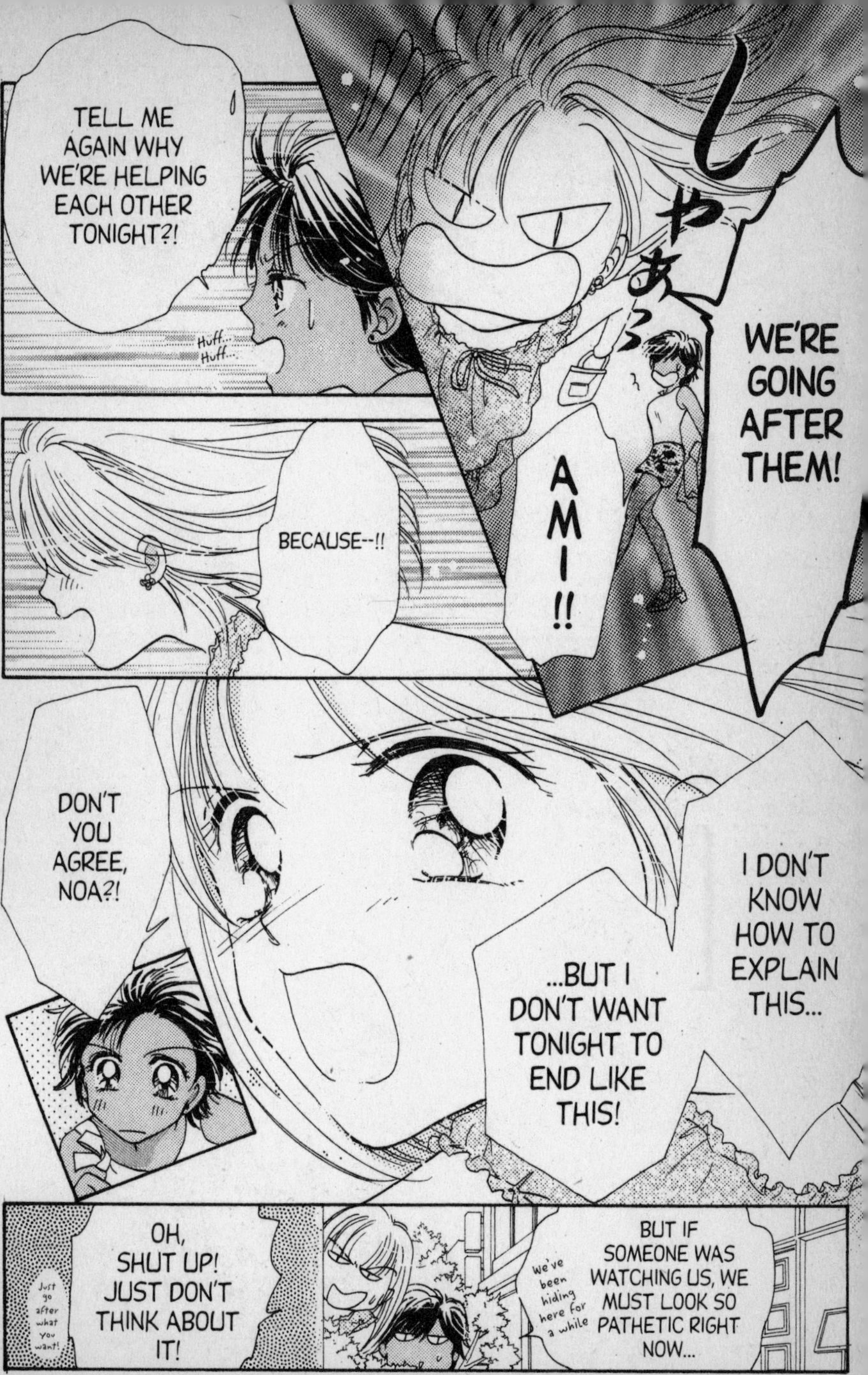
しゃあっ
WE'RE GOING AFTER THEM!
AMI!!
TELL ME AGAIN WHY WE'RE HELPING EACH OTHER TONIGHT?!
Huff... Huff...
BECAUSE--!!
I DON'T KNOW HOW TO EXPLAIN THIS...
...BUT I DON'T WANT TONIGHT TO END LIKE THIS!
DON'T YOU AGREE, NOA?!
BUT IF SOMEONE WAS WATCHING US, WE MUST LOOK SO PATHETIC RIGHT NOW...
We've been hiding here for a while
OH, SHUT UP! JUST DON'T THINK ABOUT IT!
Just go after what you want!

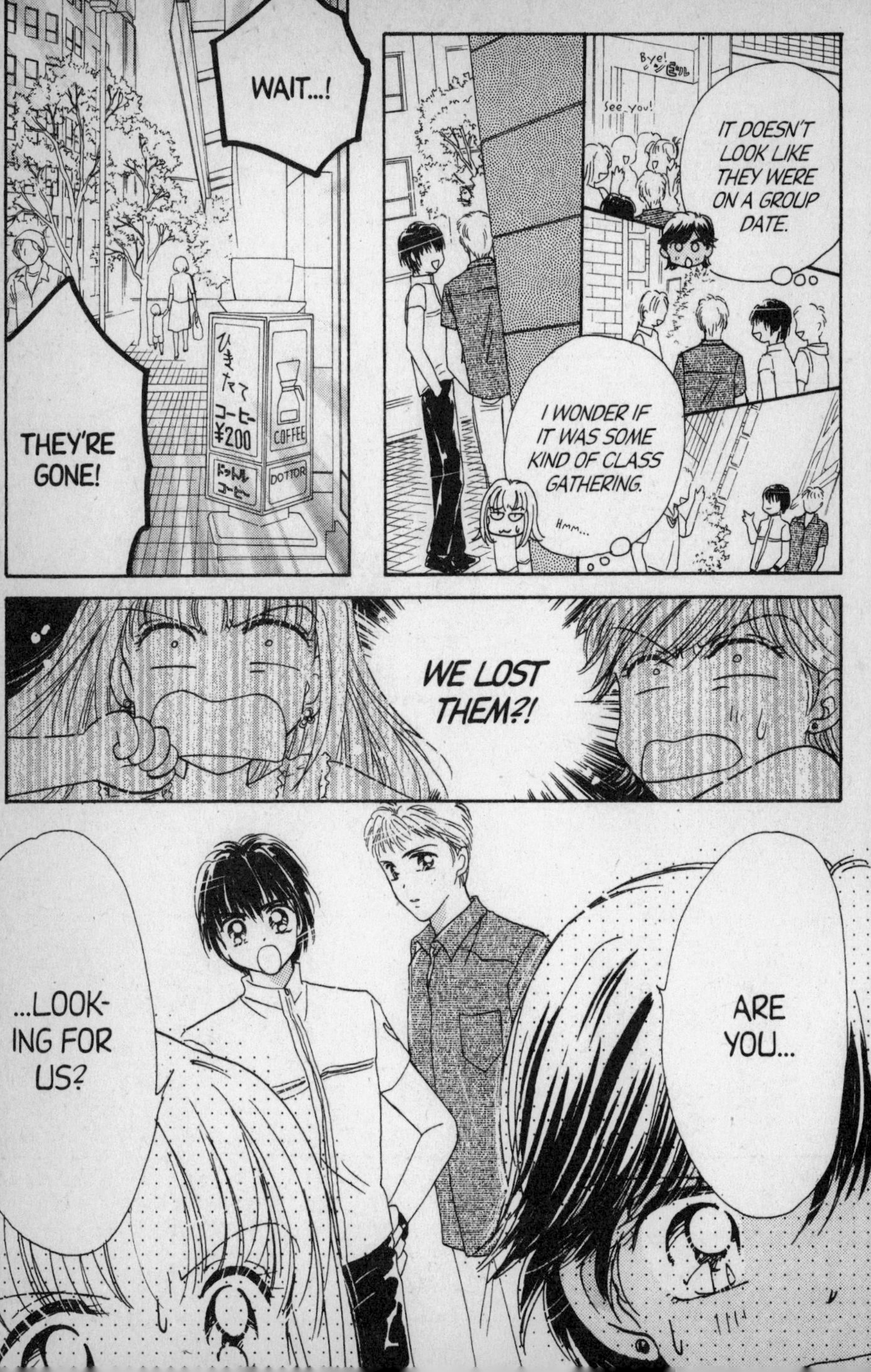
IT DOESN'T LOOK LIKE THEY WERE ON A GROUP DATE.
Bye!
See you!
I WONDER IF IT WAS SOME KIND OF CLASS GATHERING.
Hmm...
WAIT...!
THEY'RE GONE!
ひきたて コーヒー ¥200
COFFEE
ドトール コーヒー
DOTTOR
WE LOST THEM?!
ARE YOU...
...LOOKING FOR US?

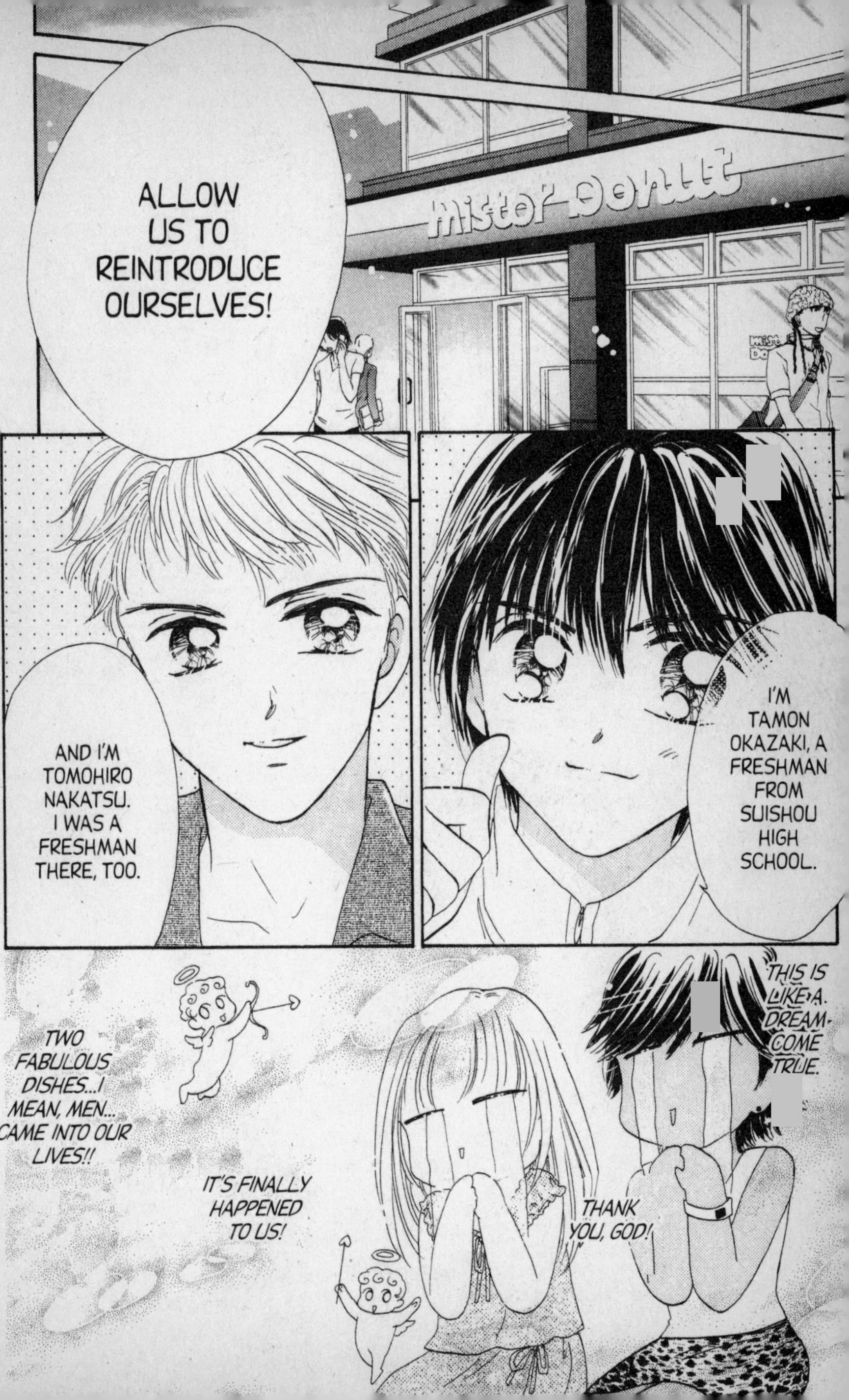
mister Donut
ALLOW US TO REINTRODUCE OURSELVES!
I'M TAMON OKAZAKI, A FRESHMAN FROM SUISHOU HIGH SCHOOL.
AND I'M TOMOHIRO NAKATSU. I WAS A FRESHMAN THERE, TOO.
THIS IS LIKE A DREAM COME TRUE.
THANK YOU, GOD!
IT'S FINALLY HAPPENED TO US!
TWO FABULOUS DISHES...I MEAN, MEN... CAME INTO OUR LIVES!!

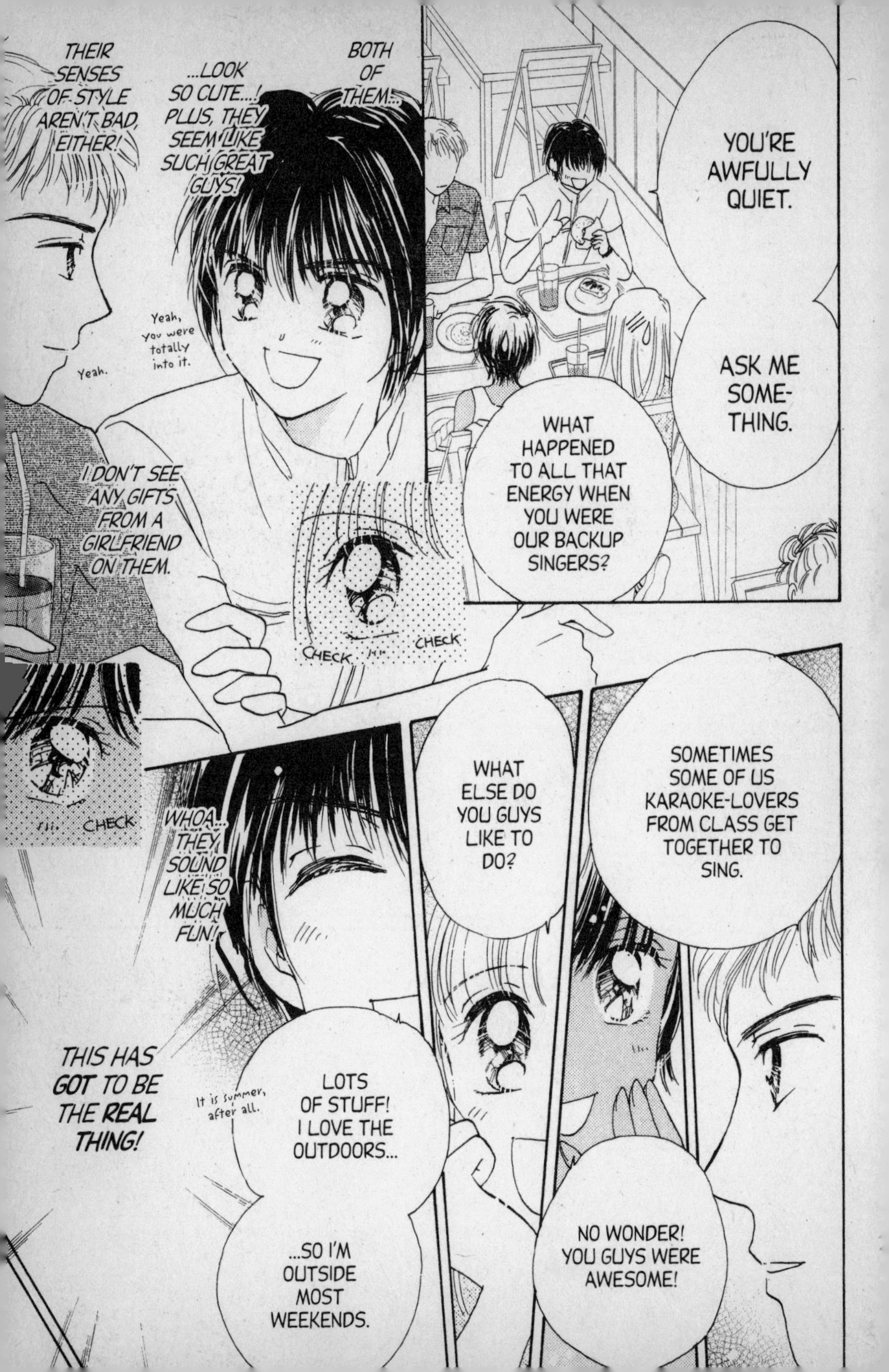
YOU'RE AWFULLY QUIET.
ASK ME SOMETHING.
WHAT HAPPENED TO ALL THAT ENERGY WHEN YOU WERE OUR BACKUP SINGERS?
BOTH OF THEM...
...LOOK SO CUTE...! PLUS, THEY SEEM LIKE SUCH GREAT GUYS!
THEIR SENSES OF STYLE AREN'T BAD, EITHER!
Yeah, you were totally into it.
Yeah.
I DON'T SEE ANY GIFTS FROM A GIRLFRIEND ON THEM.
CHECK
CHECK
CHECK
SOMETIMES SOME OF US KARAOKE-LOVERS FROM CLASS GET TOGETHER TO SING.
NO WONDER! YOU GUYS WERE AWESOME!
WHAT ELSE DO YOU GUYS LIKE TO DO?
WHOA... THEY SOUND LIKE SO MUCH FUN!
LOTS OF STUFF! I LOVE THE OUTDOORS...
...SO I'M OUTSIDE MOST WEEKENDS.
It is summer, after all.
THIS HAS GOT TO BE THE REAL THING!

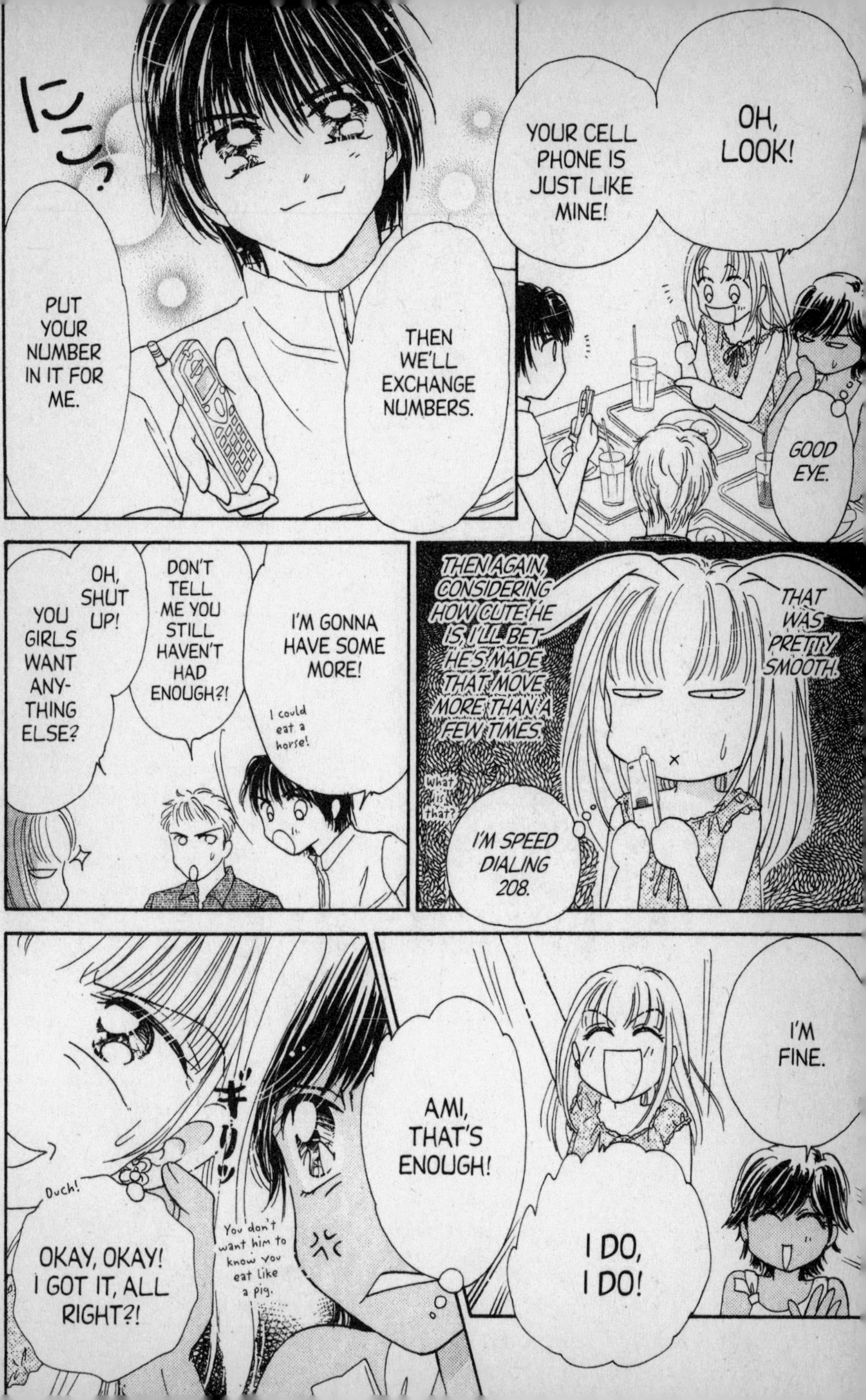

OH, LOOK!
YOUR CELL PHONE IS JUST LIKE MINE!
GOOD EYE.
にこっ
THEN WE'LL EXCHANGE NUMBERS.
PUT YOUR NUMBER IN IT FOR ME.
THAT WAS PRETTY SMOOTH.
THEN AGAIN, CONSIDERING HOW CUTE HE IS, I'LL BET HE'S MADE THAT MOVE MORE THAN A FEW TIMES.
what is that?
I'M SPEED DIALING 208.
I'M GONNA HAVE SOME MORE!
I could eat a horse!
DON'T TELL ME YOU STILL HAVEN'T HAD ENOUGH?!
OH, SHUT UP!
YOU GIRLS WANT ANY-THING ELSE?
I'M FINE.
I DO, I DO!
AMI, THAT'S ENOUGH!
ギリッ
You don't want him to know you eat like a pig.
Ouch!
OKAY, OKAY! I GOT IT, ALL RIGHT?!

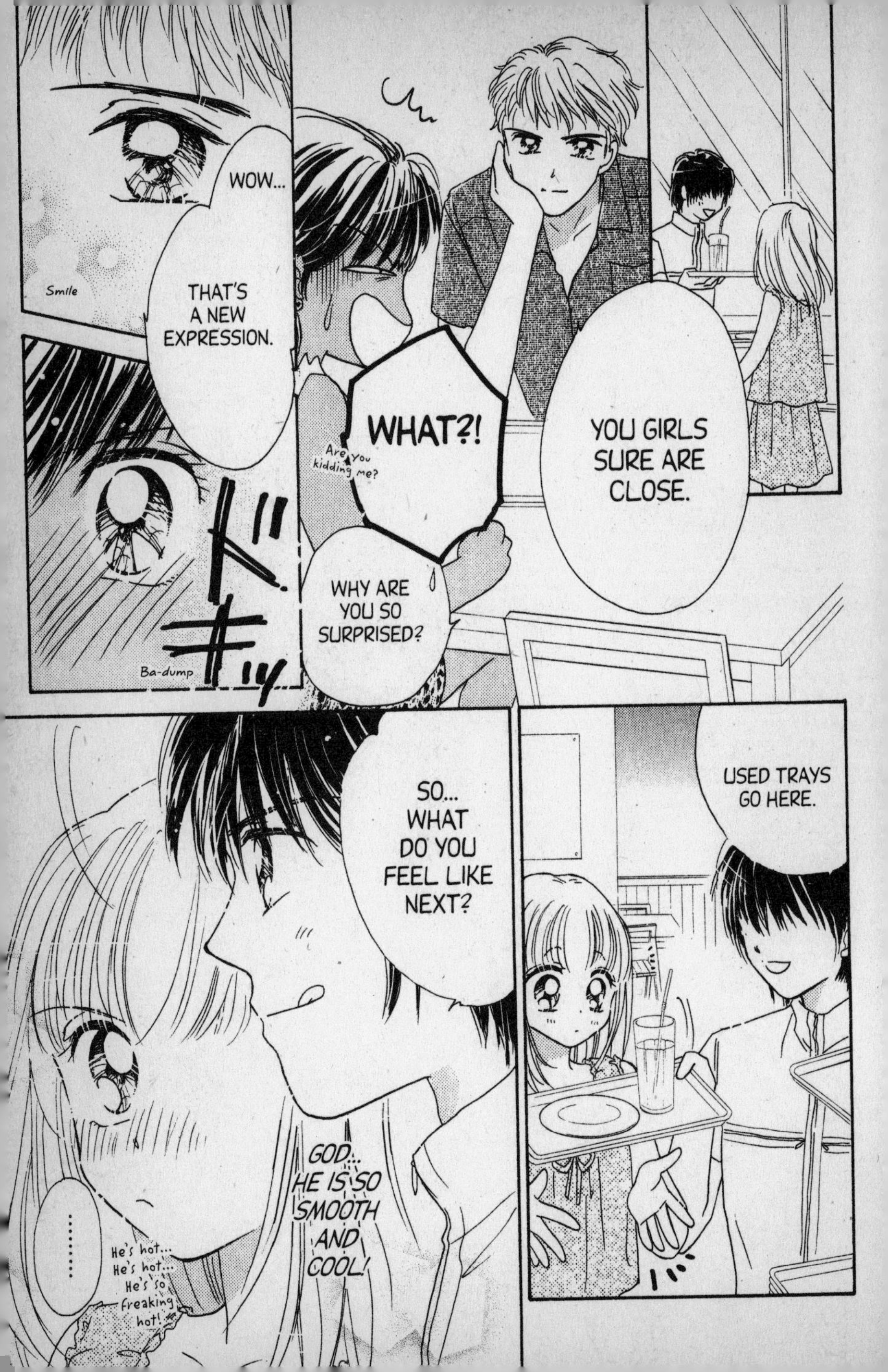

YOU GIRLS SURE ARE CLOSE.
WHAT?!
Are you kidding me?
WHY ARE YOU SO SURPRISED?
WOW...
THAT'S A NEW EXPRESSION.
Smile
ドキッ
Ba-dump
USED TRAYS GO HERE.
SO... WHAT DO YOU FEEL LIKE NEXT?
GOD... HE IS SO SMOOTH AND COOL!
......
He's hot... He's hot... He's so freaking hot!

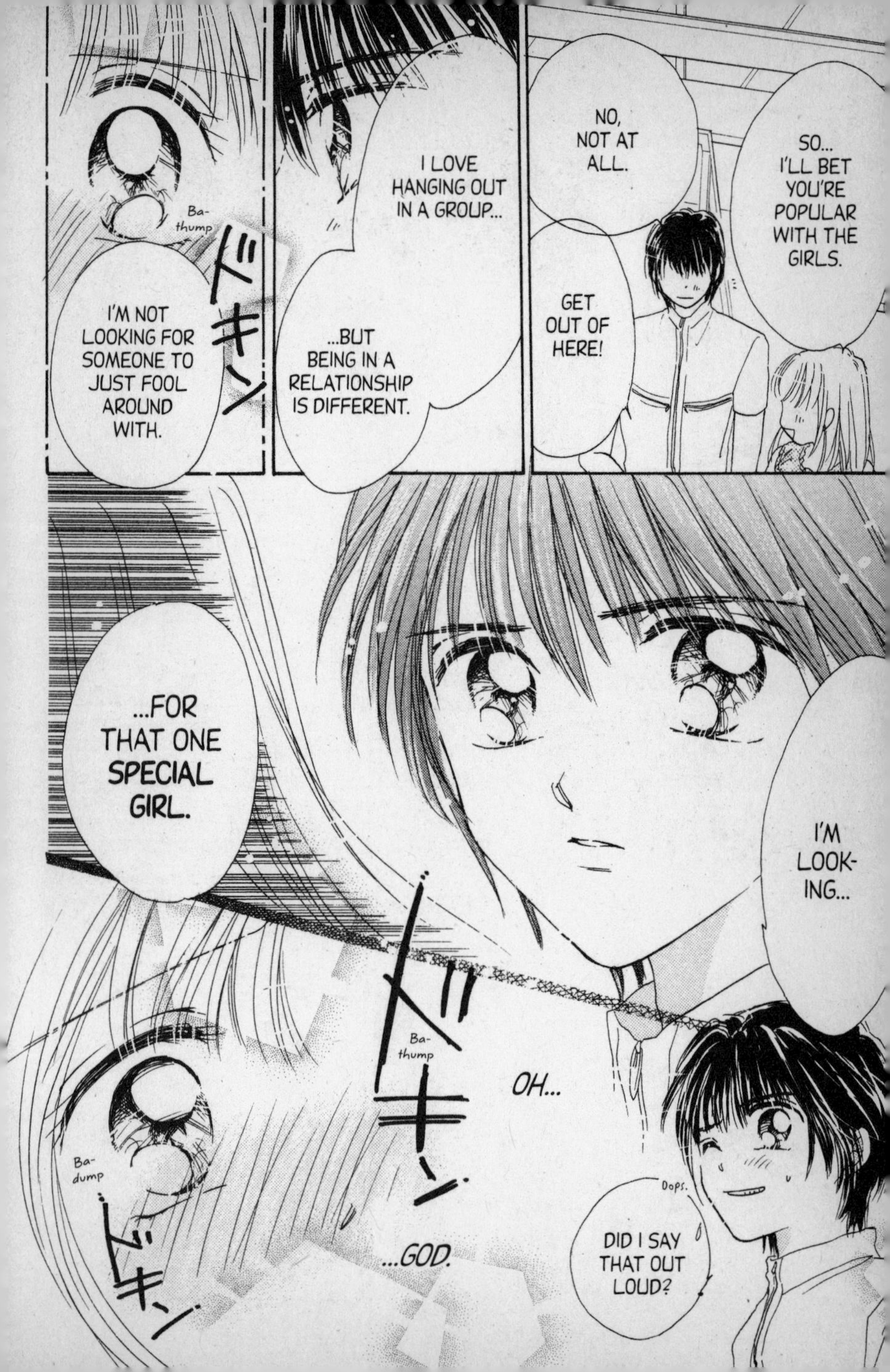
SO... I'LL BET YOU'RE POPULAR WITH THE GIRLS.
NO, NOT AT ALL.
GET OUT OF HERE!
I LOVE HANGING OUT IN A GROUP...
...BUT BEING IN A RELATIONSHIP IS DIFFERENT.
ドキン
Ba-thump
I'M NOT LOOKING FOR SOMEONE TO JUST FOOL AROUND WITH.
I'M LOOKING...
...FOR THAT ONE SPECIAL GIRL.
ドキン
Ba-thump
OH...
Oops.
DID I SAY THAT OUT LOUD?
...GOD.
ドキン
Ba-dump

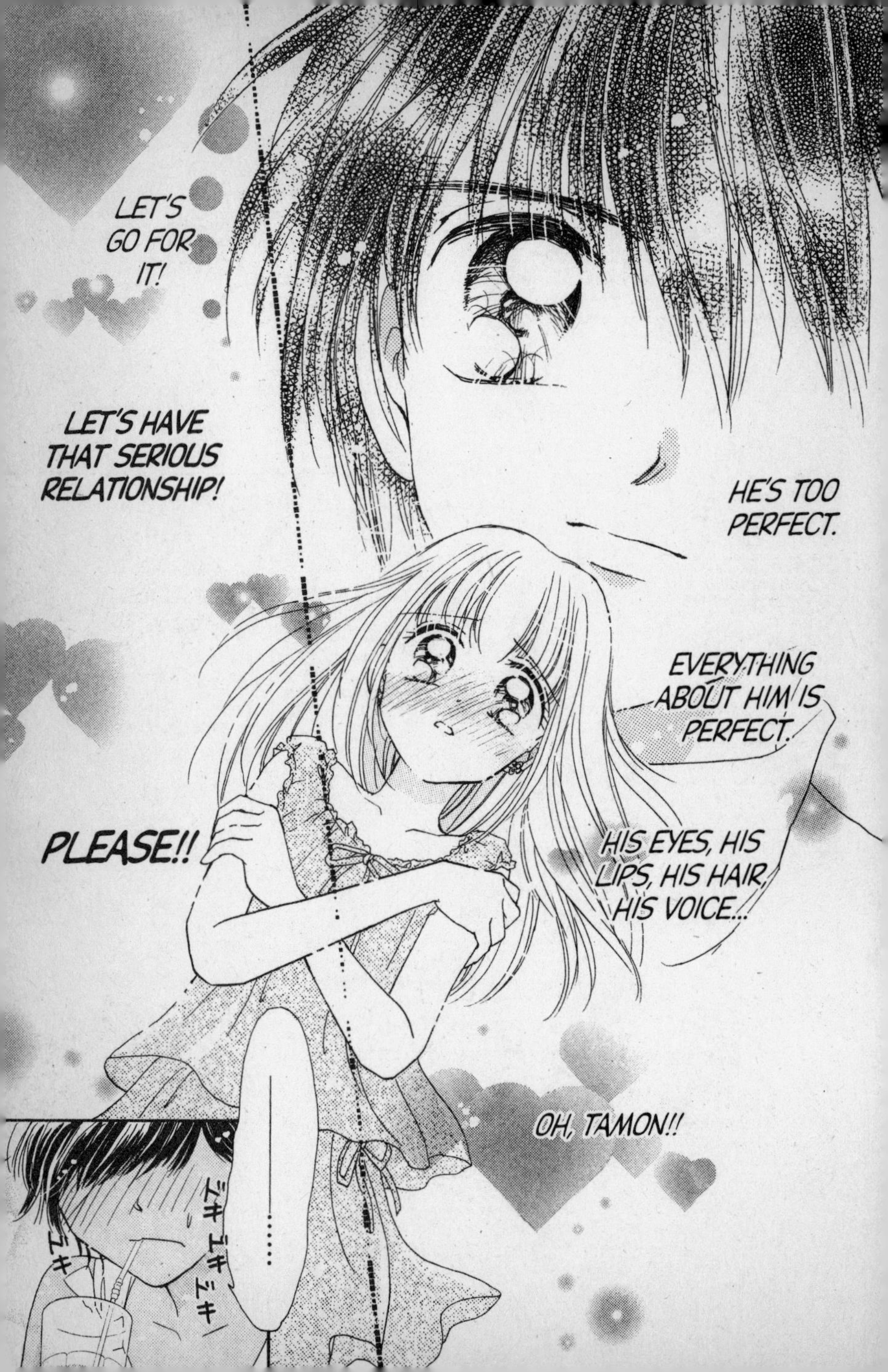
HE'S TOO PERFECT.
EVERYTHING ABOUT HIM IS PERFECT.
HIS EYES, HIS LIPS, HIS HAIR, HIS VOICE...
OH, TAMON!!
LET'S GO FOR IT!
LET'S HAVE THAT SERIOUS RELATIONSHIP!
PLEASE!!

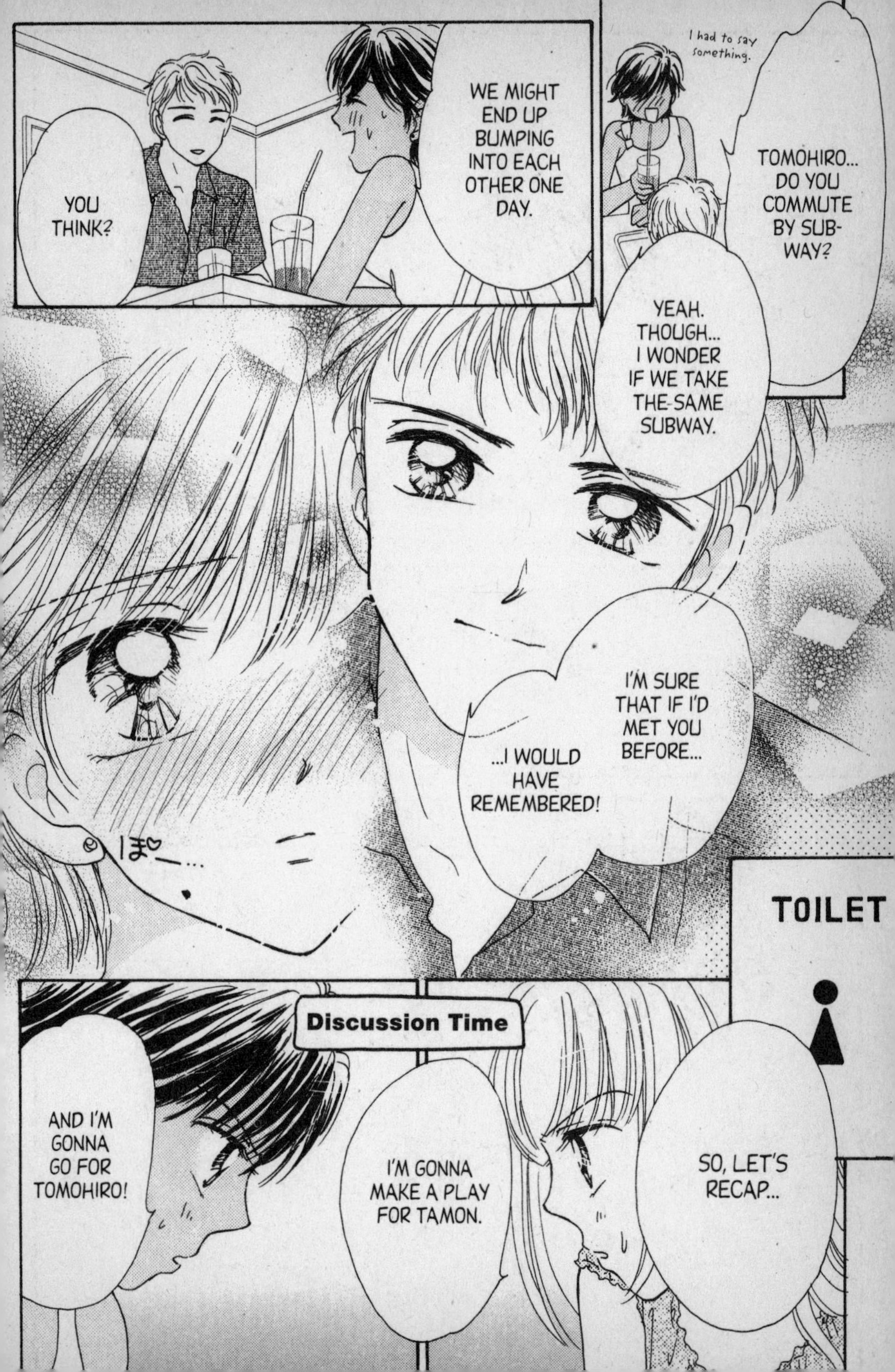

I had to say something.
TOMOHIRO... DO YOU COMMUTE BY SUBWAY?
YEAH. THOUGH... I WONDER IF WE TAKE THE SAME SUBWAY.
WE MIGHT END UP BUMPING INTO EACH OTHER ONE DAY.
YOU THINK?
I'M SURE THAT IF I'D MET YOU BEFORE...
...I WOULD HAVE REMEMBERED!
ぽ~...
TOILET
Discussion Time
SO, LET'S RECAP...
I'M GONNA MAKE A PLAY FOR TAMON.
AND I'M GONNA GO FOR TOMOHIRO!

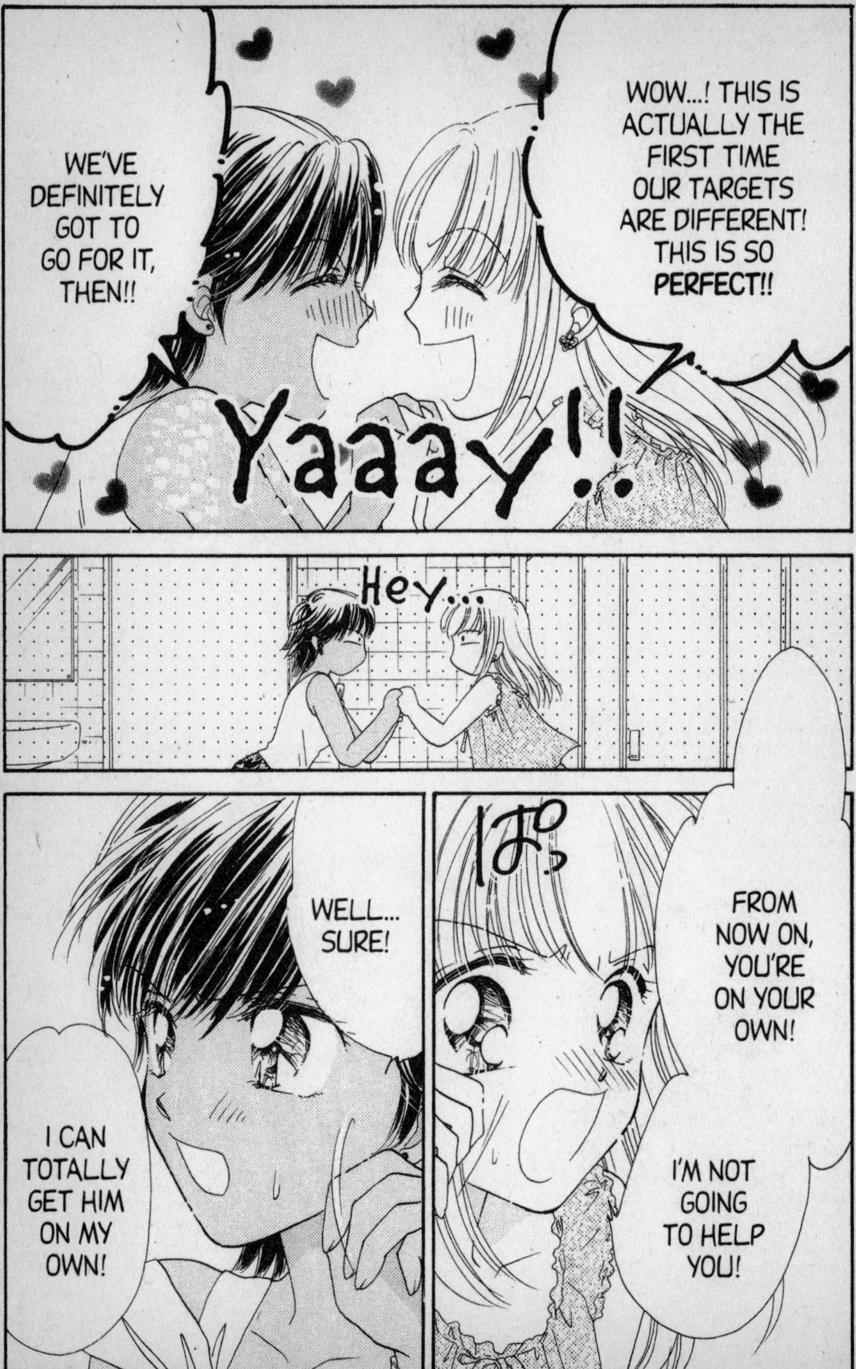
WOW...! THIS IS ACTUALLY THE FIRST TIME OUR TARGETS ARE DIFFERENT! THIS IS SO PERFECT!!
WE'VE DEFINITELY GOT TO GO FOR IT, THEN!!
Yaaay!!
Hey...
ぱっ
FROM NOW ON, YOU'RE ON YOUR OWN!
I'M NOT GOING TO HELP YOU!
WELL... SURE!
I CAN TOTALLY GET HIM ON MY OWN!

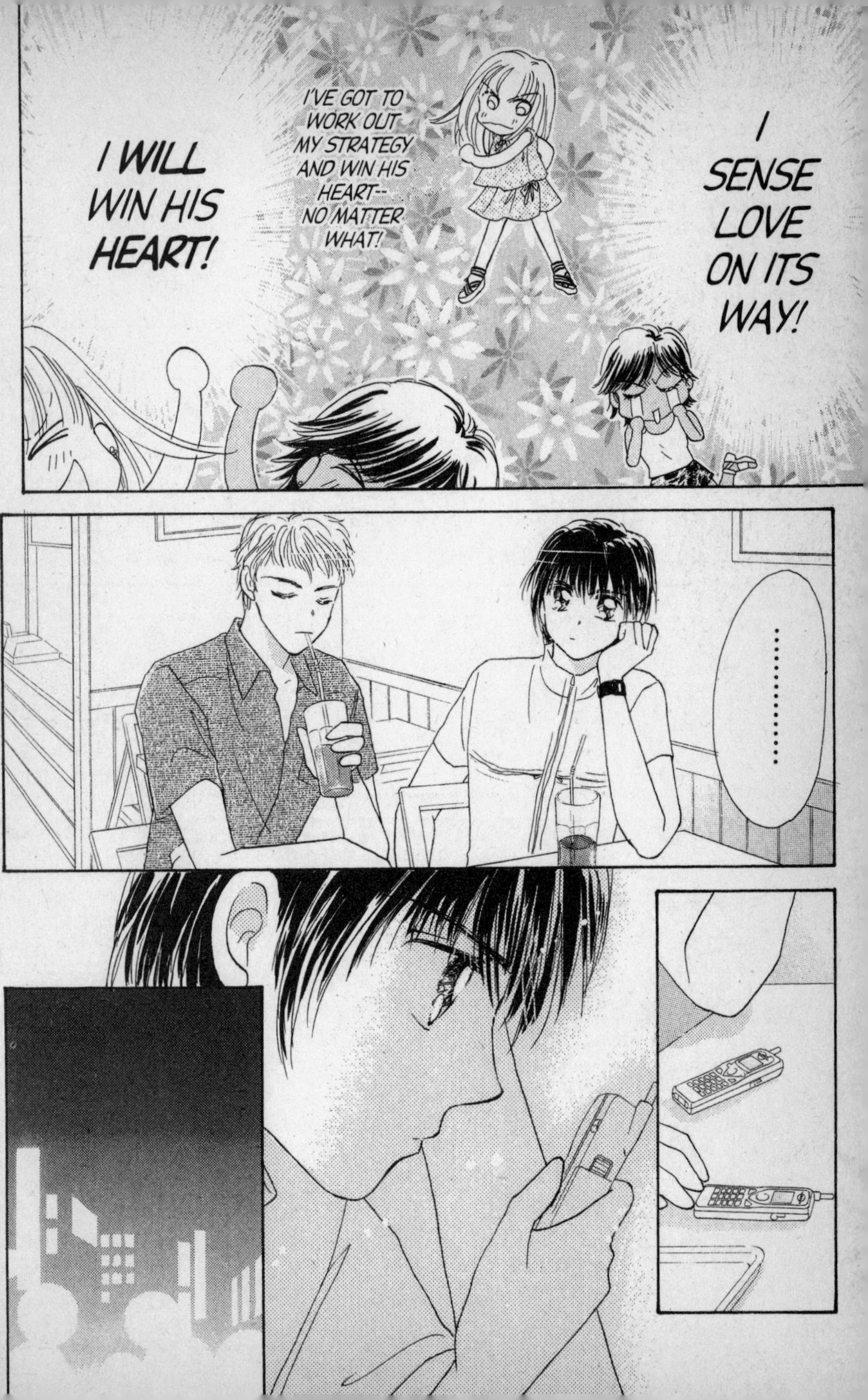
I SENSE LOVE ON ITS WAY!
I'VE GOT TO WORK OUT MY STRATEGY AND WIN HIS HEART--NO MATTER WHAT!
I WILL WIN HIS HEART!
......

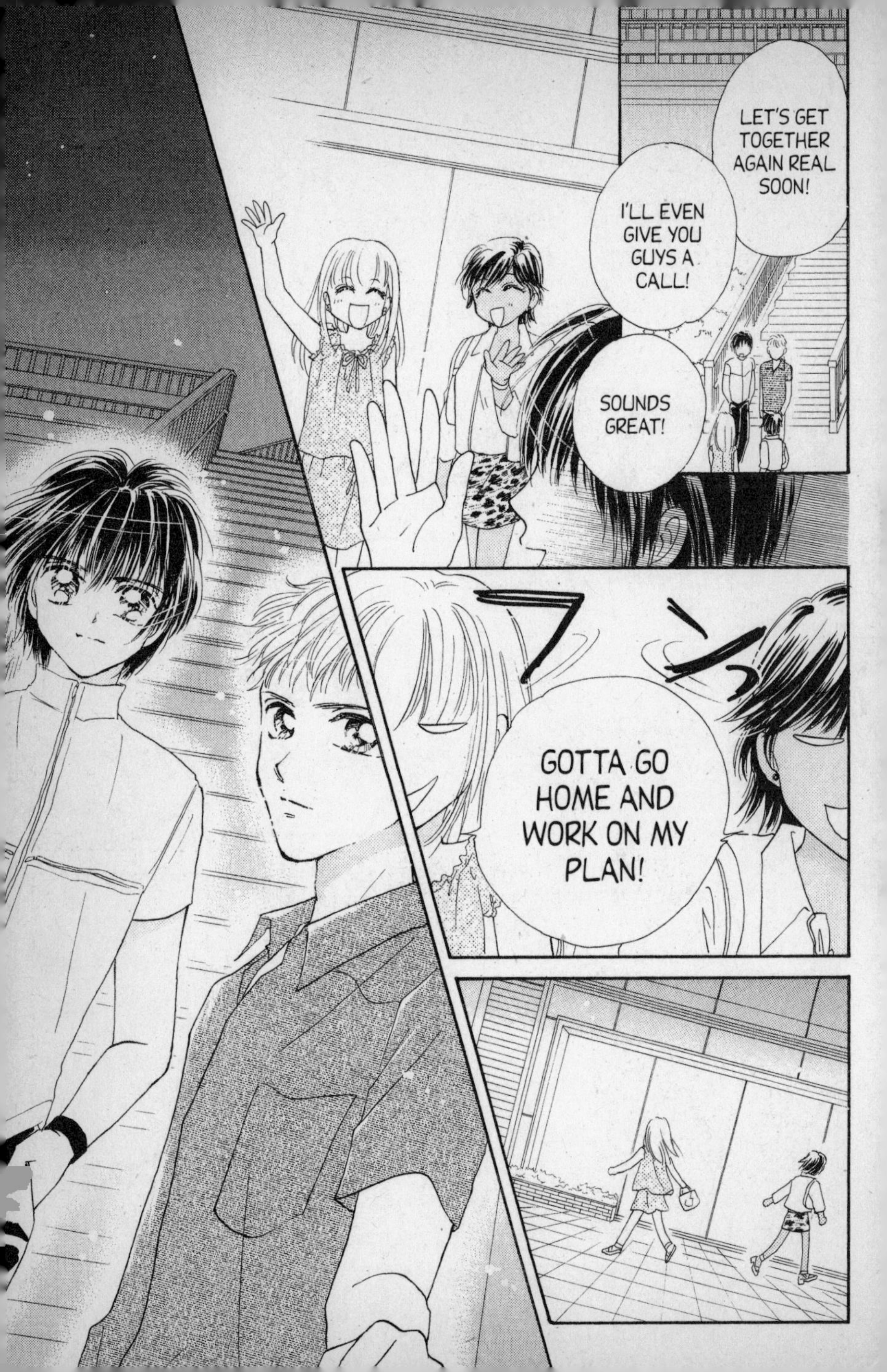
LET'S GET TOGETHER AGAIN REAL SOON!
I'LL EVEN GIVE YOU GUYS A CALL!
SOUNDS GREAT!
GOTTA GO HOME AND WORK ON MY PLAN!

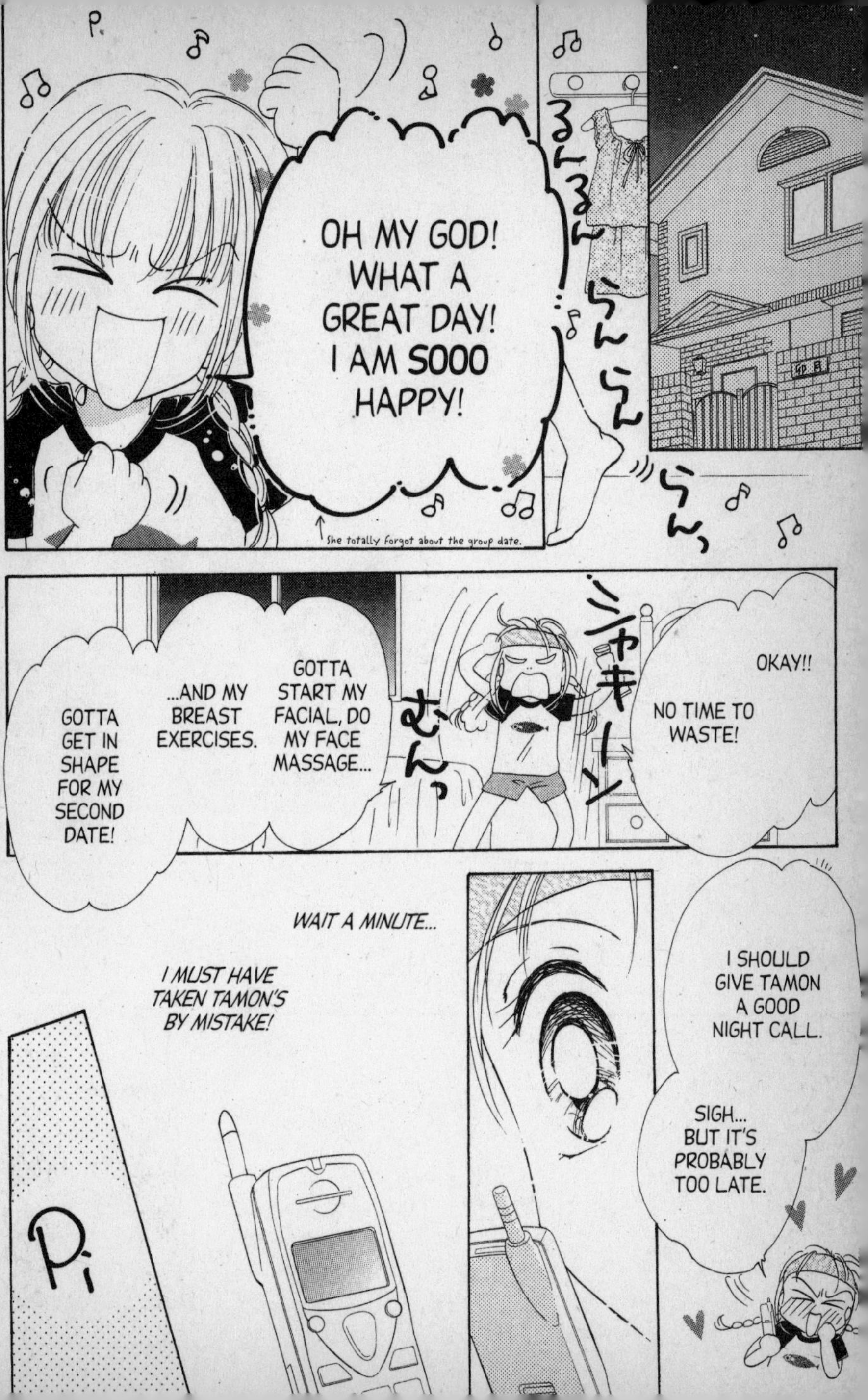
P.
るんるん
らんらん
らんっ
OH MY GOD! WHAT A GREAT DAY! I AM SOOO HAPPY!
She totally forgot about the group date.
OKAY!!
NO TIME TO WASTE!
シャキーン
むんっ
GOTTA START MY FACIAL, DO MY FACE MASSAGE...
...AND MY BREAST EXERCISES.
GOTTA GET IN SHAPE FOR MY SECOND DATE!
I SHOULD GIVE TAMON A GOOD NIGHT CALL.
SIGH... BUT IT'S PROBABLY TOO LATE.
WAIT A MINUTE...
I MUST HAVE TAKEN TAMON'S BY MISTAKE!
Pi

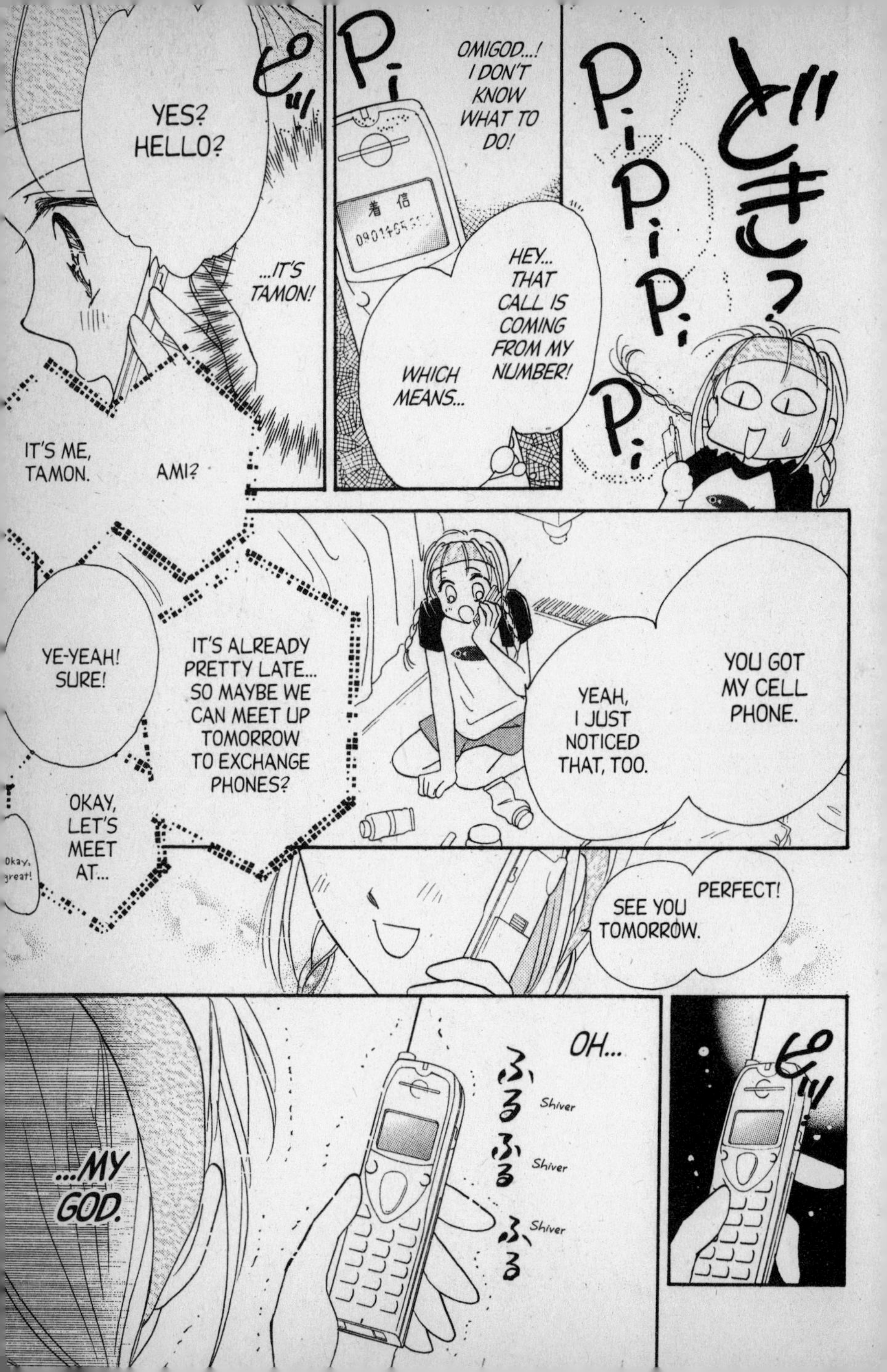
どきっ
Pi Pi Pi Pi
OMIGOD...! I DON'T KNOW WHAT TO DO!
着信
HEY... THAT CALL IS COMING FROM MY NUMBER!
WHICH MEANS...
Pi
ピッ
YES? HELLO?
...IT'S TAMON!
AMI?
IT'S ME, TAMON.
YOU GOT MY CELL PHONE.
YEAH, I JUST NOTICED THAT, TOO.
IT'S ALREADY PRETTY LATE... SO MAYBE WE CAN MEET UP TOMORROW TO EXCHANGE PHONES?
YE-YEAH! SURE!
OKAY, LET'S MEET AT...
Okay, great!
PERFECT! SEE YOU TOMORROW.
ピッ
OH...
ふる
Shiver
ふる
Shiver
ふる
Shiver
...MY GOD.

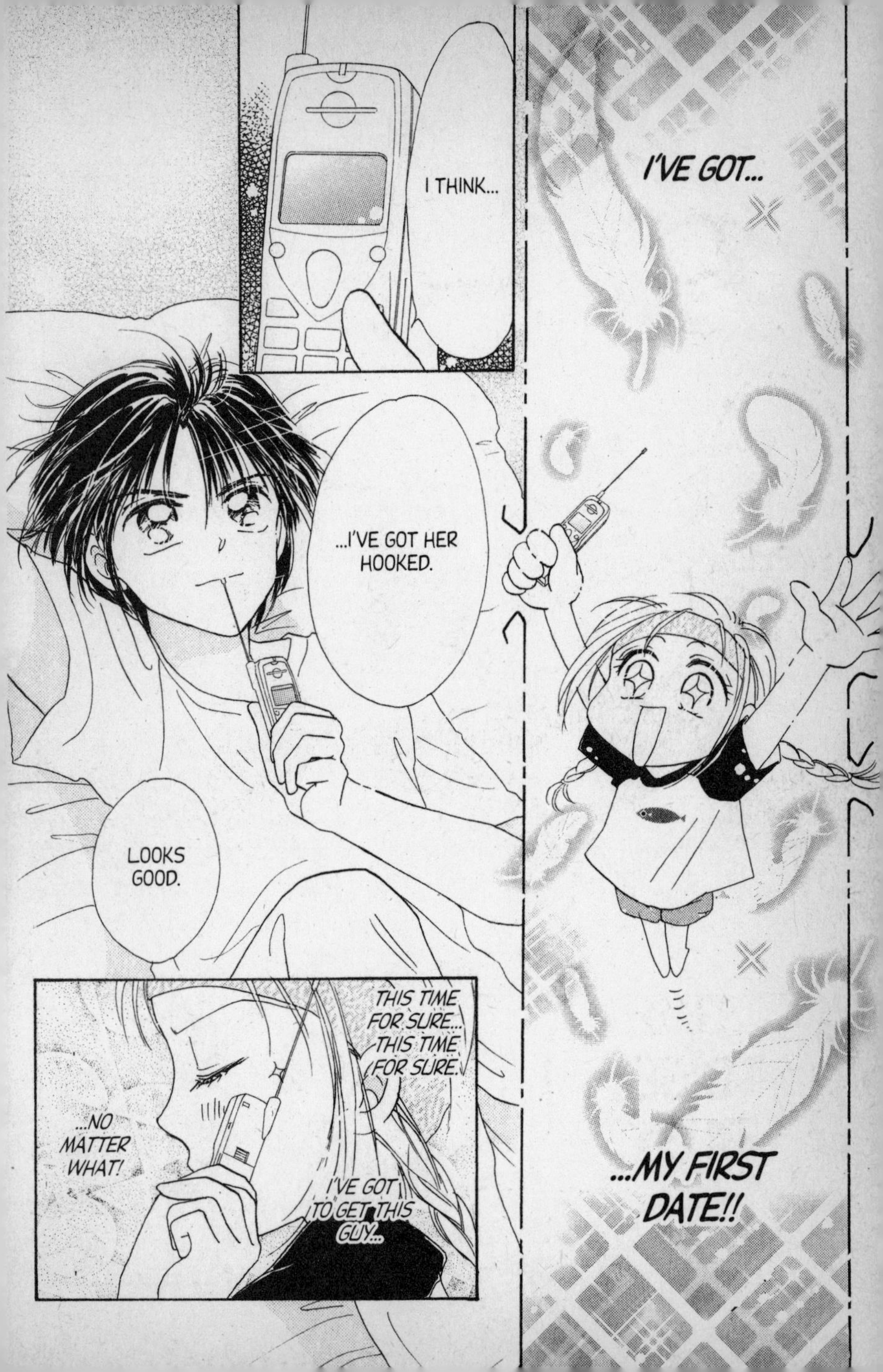
I'VE GOT...
...MY FIRST DATE!!
I THINK...
...I'VE GOT HER HOOKED.
LOOKS GOOD.
THIS TIME FOR SURE... THIS TIME FOR SURE.
I'VE GOT TO GET THIS GUY...
...NO MATTER WHAT!

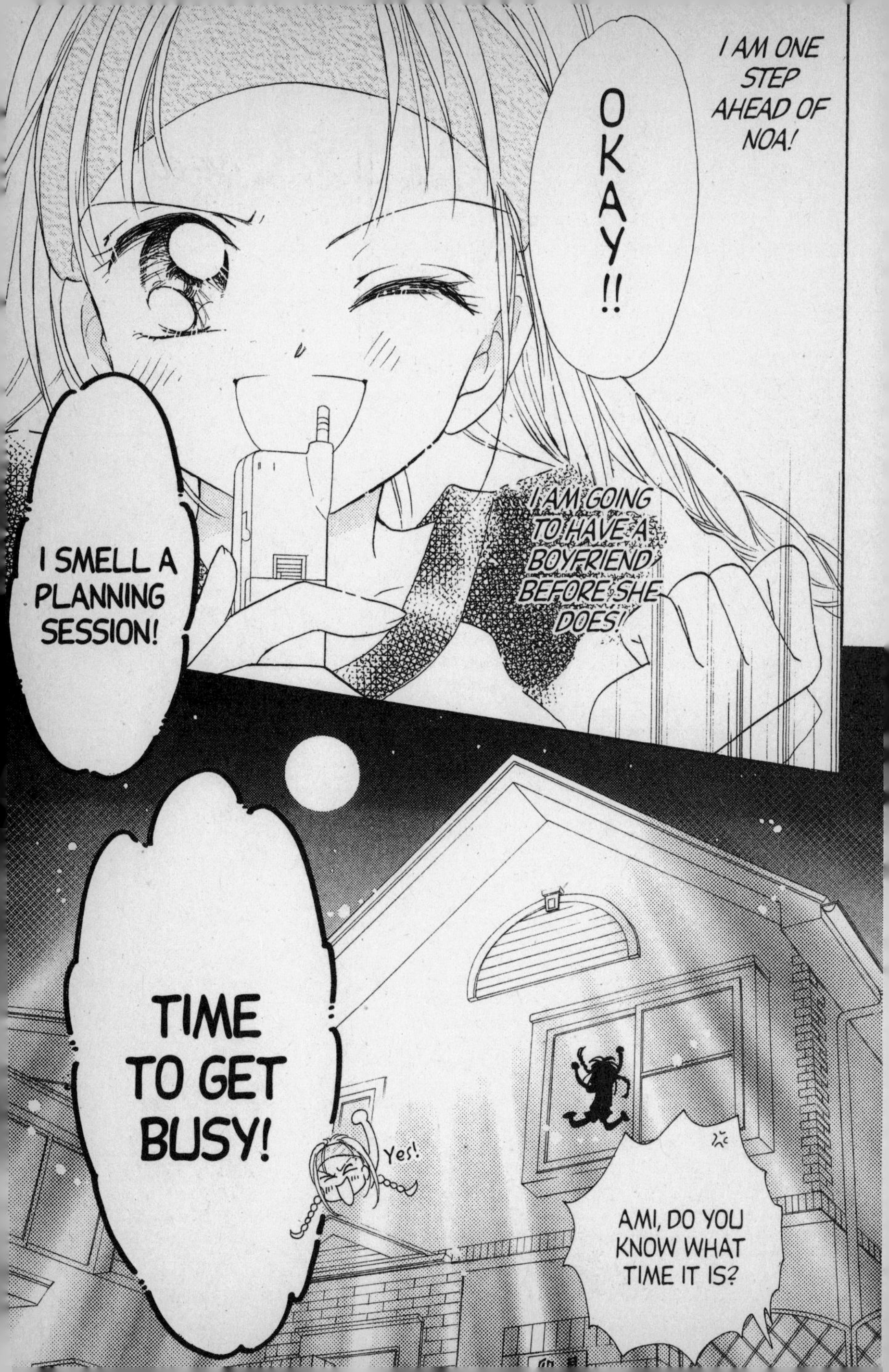

I AM ONE STEP AHEAD OF NOA!
OKAY!!
I AM GOING TO HAVE A BOYFRIEND BEFORE SHE DOES!
I SMELL A PLANNING SESSION!
AMI, DO YOU KNOW WHAT TIME IT IS?
Yes!
TIME TO GET BUSY!

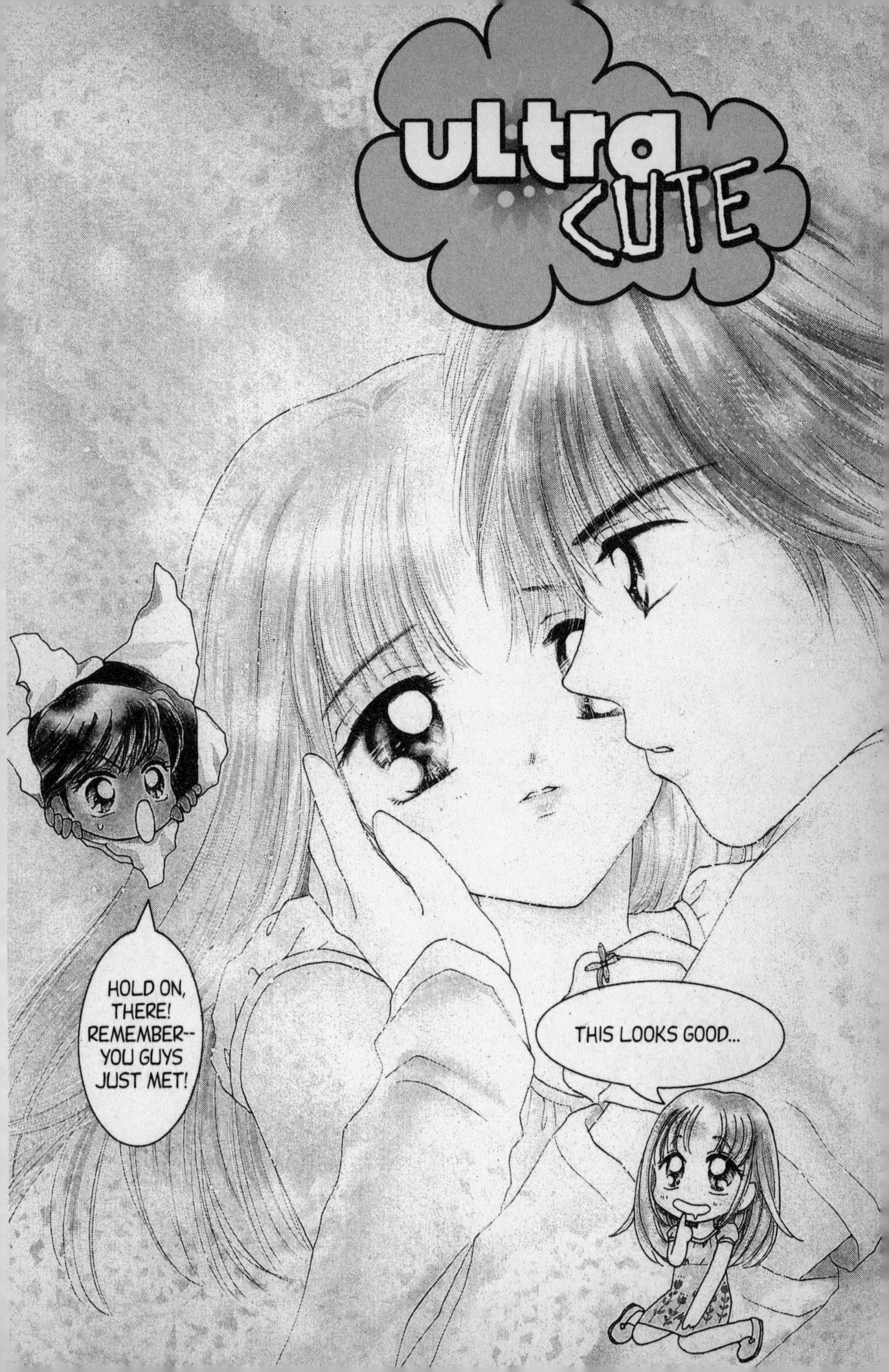
ultra CUTE
THIS LOOKS GOOD...
HOLD ON, THERE! REMEMBER-- YOU GUYS JUST MET!

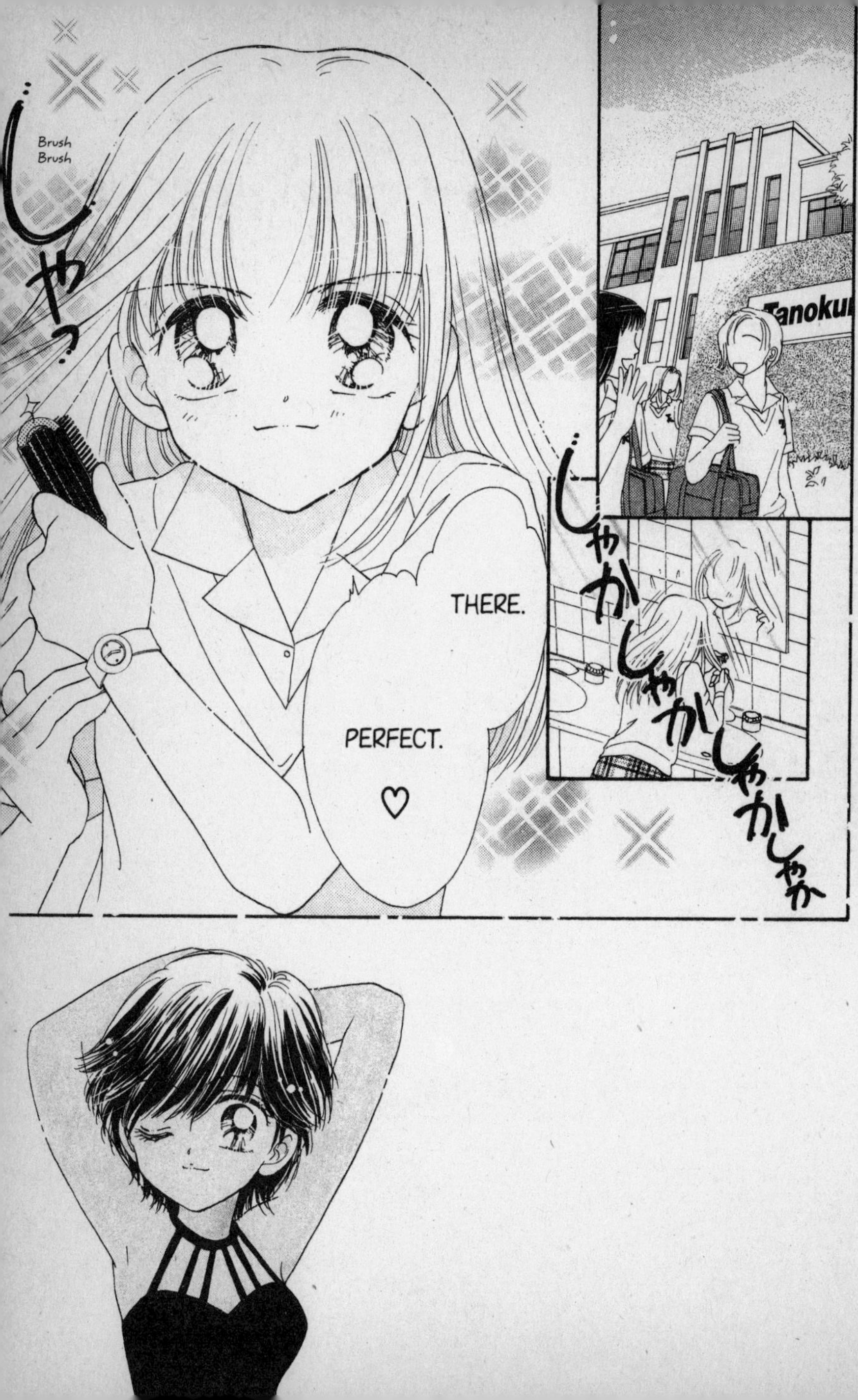

Tanoku
しゃかしゃかしゃかしゃかしゃか
しゃっ
Brush Brush
THERE.
PERFECT.
♡

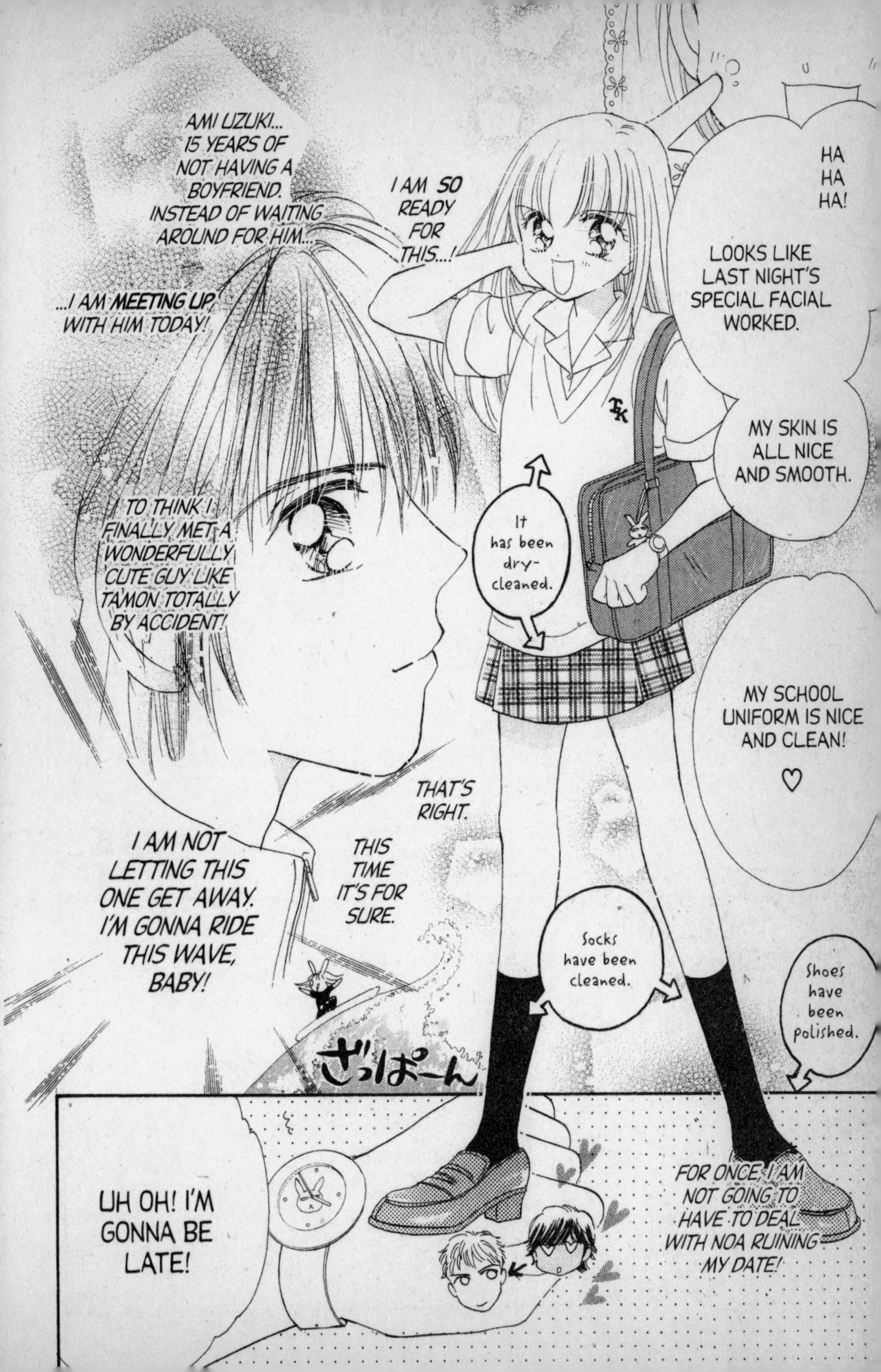
HA HA HA!
LOOKS LIKE LAST NIGHT'S SPECIAL FACIAL WORKED.
MY SKIN IS ALL NICE AND SMOOTH.
It has been dry-cleaned.
MY SCHOOL UNIFORM IS NICE AND CLEAN! ♡
Socks have been cleaned.
Shoes have been polished.
I AM SO READY FOR THIS...!
AMI UZUKI... 15 YEARS OF NOT HAVING A BOYFRIEND. INSTEAD OF WAITING AROUND FOR HIM...
...I AM MEETING UP WITH HIM TODAY!
TO THINK I FINALLY MET A WONDERFULLY CUTE GUY LIKE TAMON TOTALLY BY ACCIDENT!
THAT'S RIGHT.
THIS TIME IT'S FOR SURE.
I AM NOT LETTING THIS ONE GET AWAY. I'M GONNA RIDE THIS WAVE, BABY!
ざっぱーん
FOR ONCE, I AM NOT GOING TO HAVE TO DEAL WITH NOA RUINING MY DATE!
UH OH! I'M GONNA BE LATE!

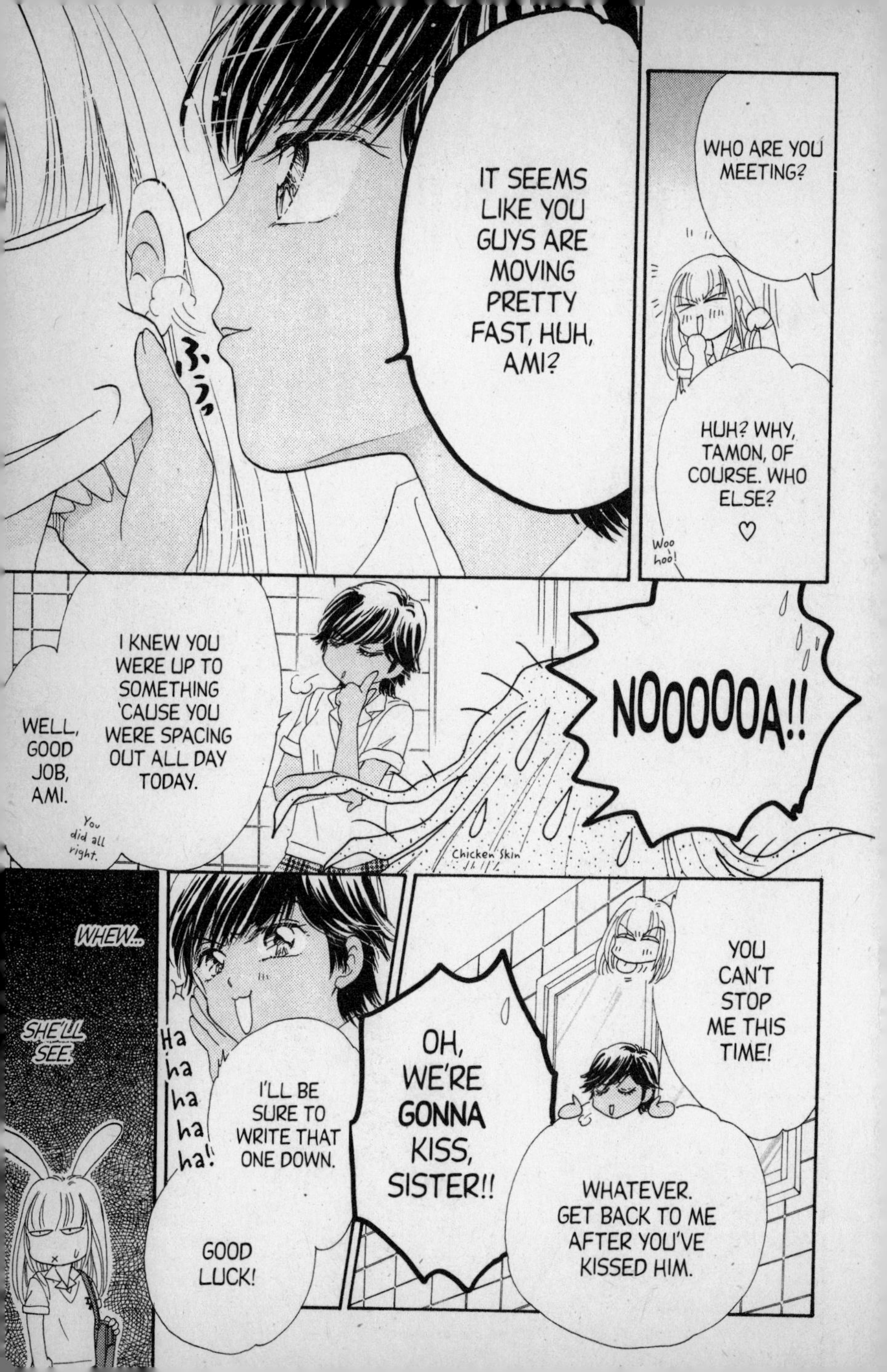
WHO ARE YOU MEETING?
HUH? WHY, TAMON, OF COURSE. WHO ELSE? ♡
Woo hoo!
IT SEEMS LIKE YOU GUYS ARE MOVING PRETTY FAST, HUH, AMI?
ふぅ
NOOOOOA!!
I KNEW YOU WERE UP TO SOMETHING 'CAUSE YOU WERE SPACING OUT ALL DAY TODAY.
WELL, GOOD JOB, AMI.
You did all right.
Chicken Skin
YOU CAN'T STOP ME THIS TIME!
OH, WE'RE GONNA KISS, SISTER!!
WHATEVER. GET BACK TO ME AFTER YOU'VE KISSED HIM.
Ha ha ha ha ha!
I'LL BE SURE TO WRITE THAT ONE DOWN.
GOOD LUCK!
WHEW...
SHE'LL SEE.

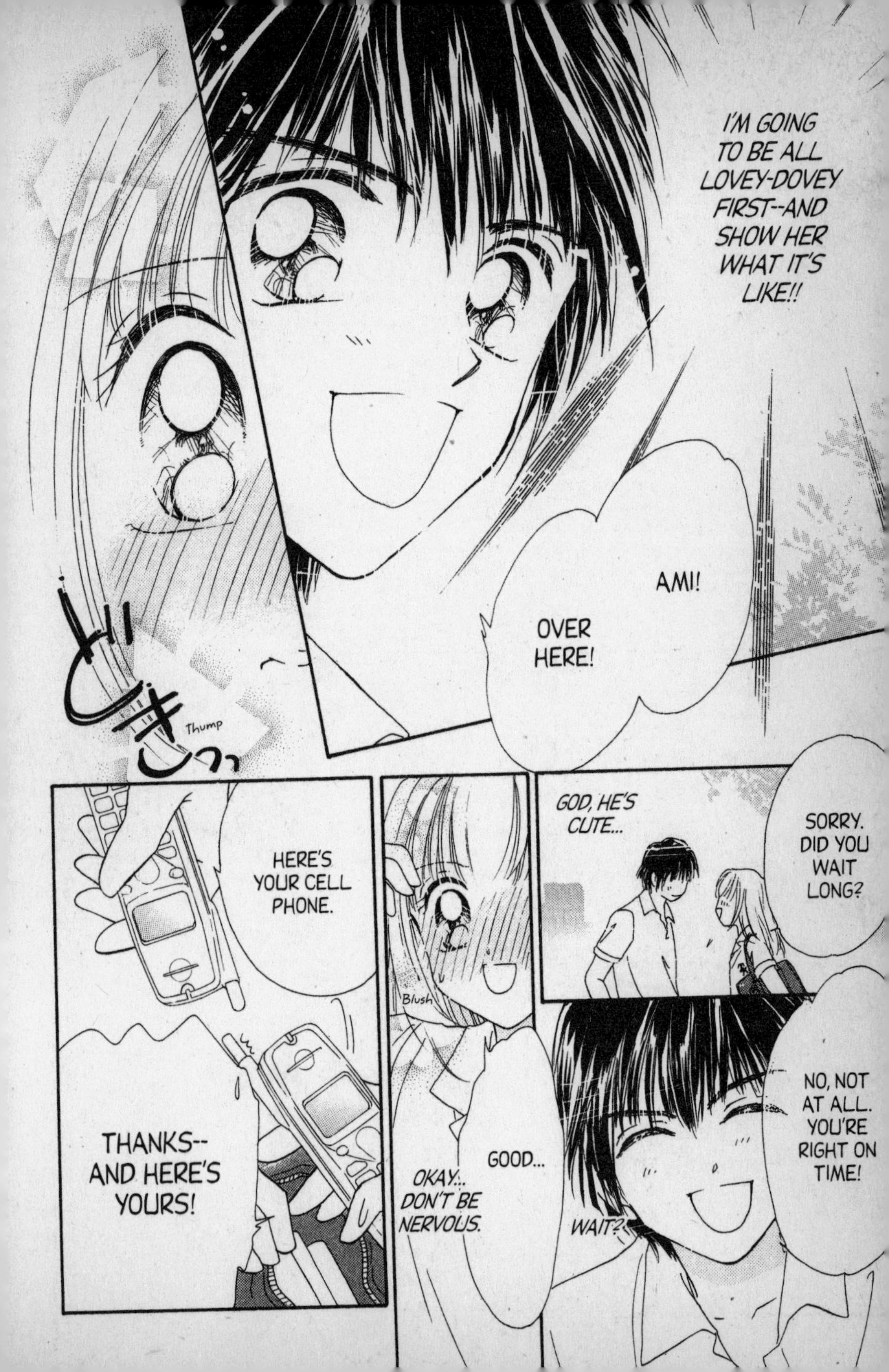
I'M GOING TO BE ALL LOVEY-DOVEY FIRST--AND SHOW HER WHAT IT'S LIKE!!
AMI!
OVER HERE!
Thump
SORRY. DID YOU WAIT LONG?
GOD, HE'S CUTE...
NO, NOT AT ALL. YOU'RE RIGHT ON TIME!
WAIT?
GOOD...
OKAY... DON'T BE NERVOUS.
Blush
HERE'S YOUR CELL PHONE.
THANKS-- AND HERE'S YOURS!

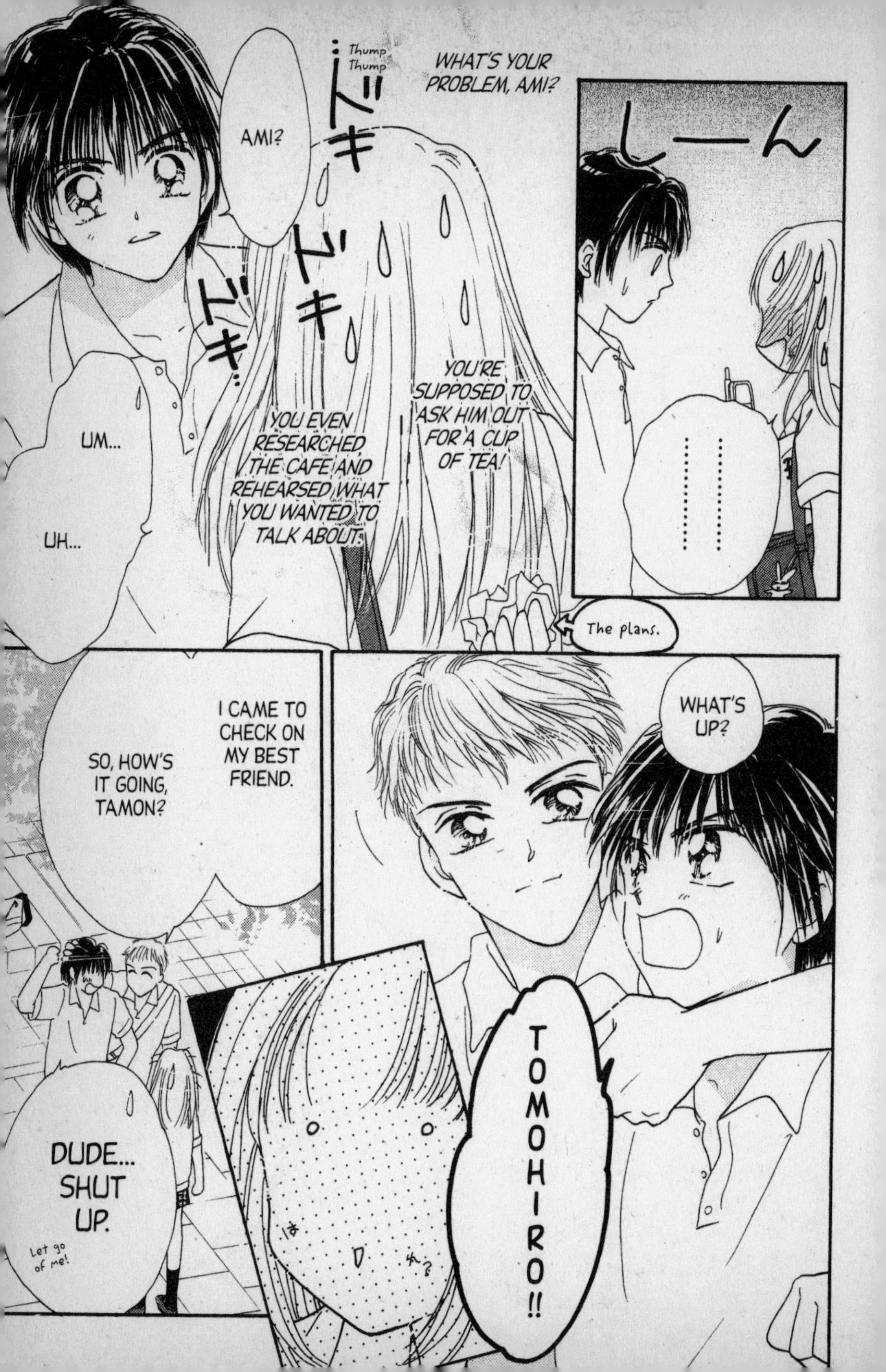
しーん
......
WHAT'S YOUR PROBLEM, AMI?
YOU'RE SUPPOSED TO ASK HIM OUT FOR A CUP OF TEA!
YOU EVEN RESEARCHED THE CAFE AND REHEARSED WHAT YOU WANTED TO TALK ABOUT.
Thump Thump
ドキドキドキ
AMI?
UM...
UH...
The plans.
WHAT'S UP?
TOMOHIRO!!
I CAME TO CHECK ON MY BEST FRIEND.
SO, HOW'S IT GOING, TAMON?
DUDE... SHUT UP.
Let go of me!

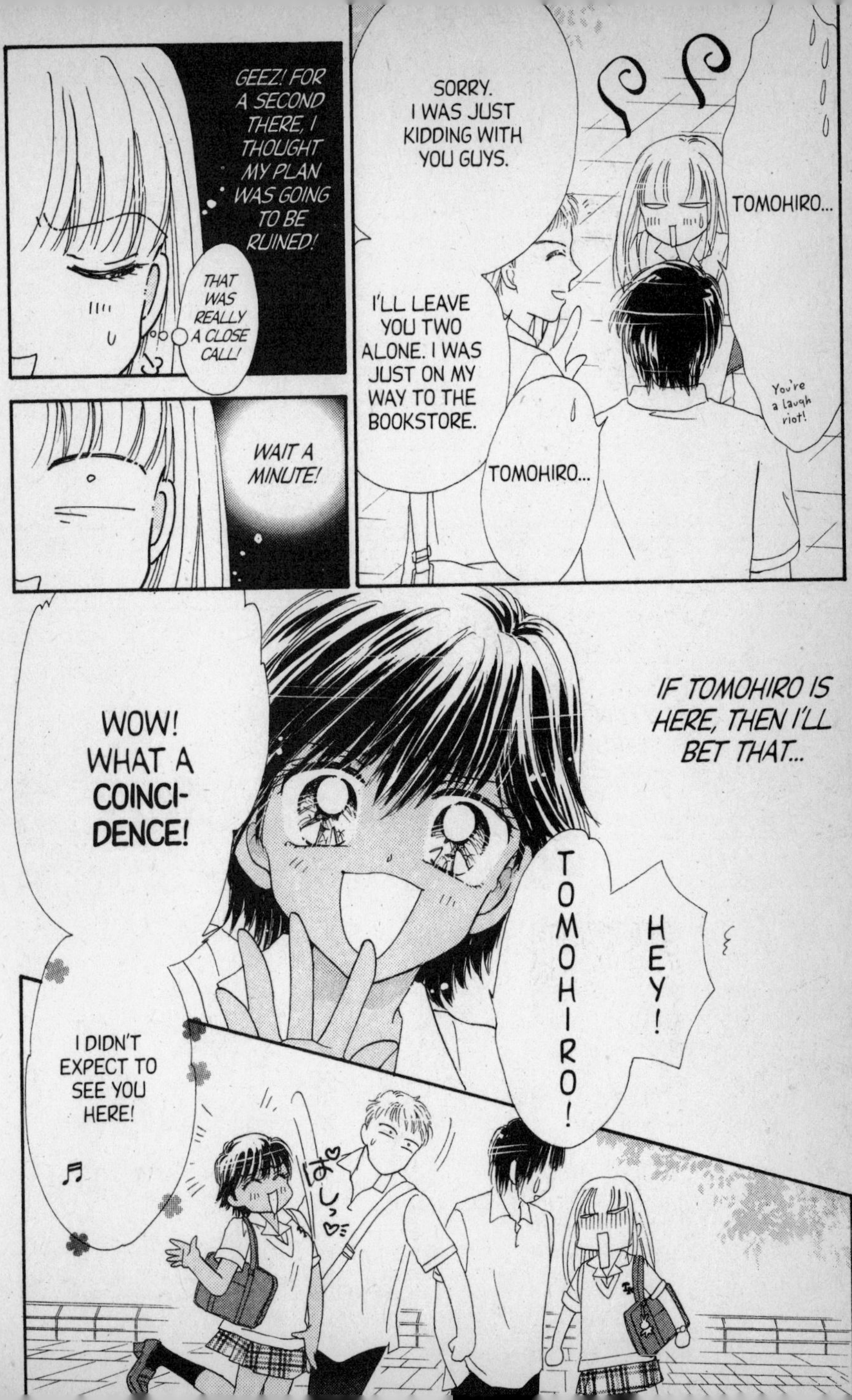

SORRY. I WAS JUST KIDDING WITH YOU GUYS.
TOMOHIRO...
I'LL LEAVE YOU TWO ALONE. I WAS JUST ON MY WAY TO THE BOOKSTORE.
You're a laugh riot!
TOMOHIRO...
GEEZ! FOR A SECOND THERE, I THOUGHT MY PLAN WAS GOING TO BE RUINED!
THAT WAS REALLY A CLOSE CALL!
WAIT A MINUTE!
IF TOMOHIRO IS HERE, THEN I'LL BET THAT...
HEY!
TOMOHIRO!
WOW! WHAT A COINCIDENCE!
I DIDN'T EXPECT TO SEE YOU HERE!

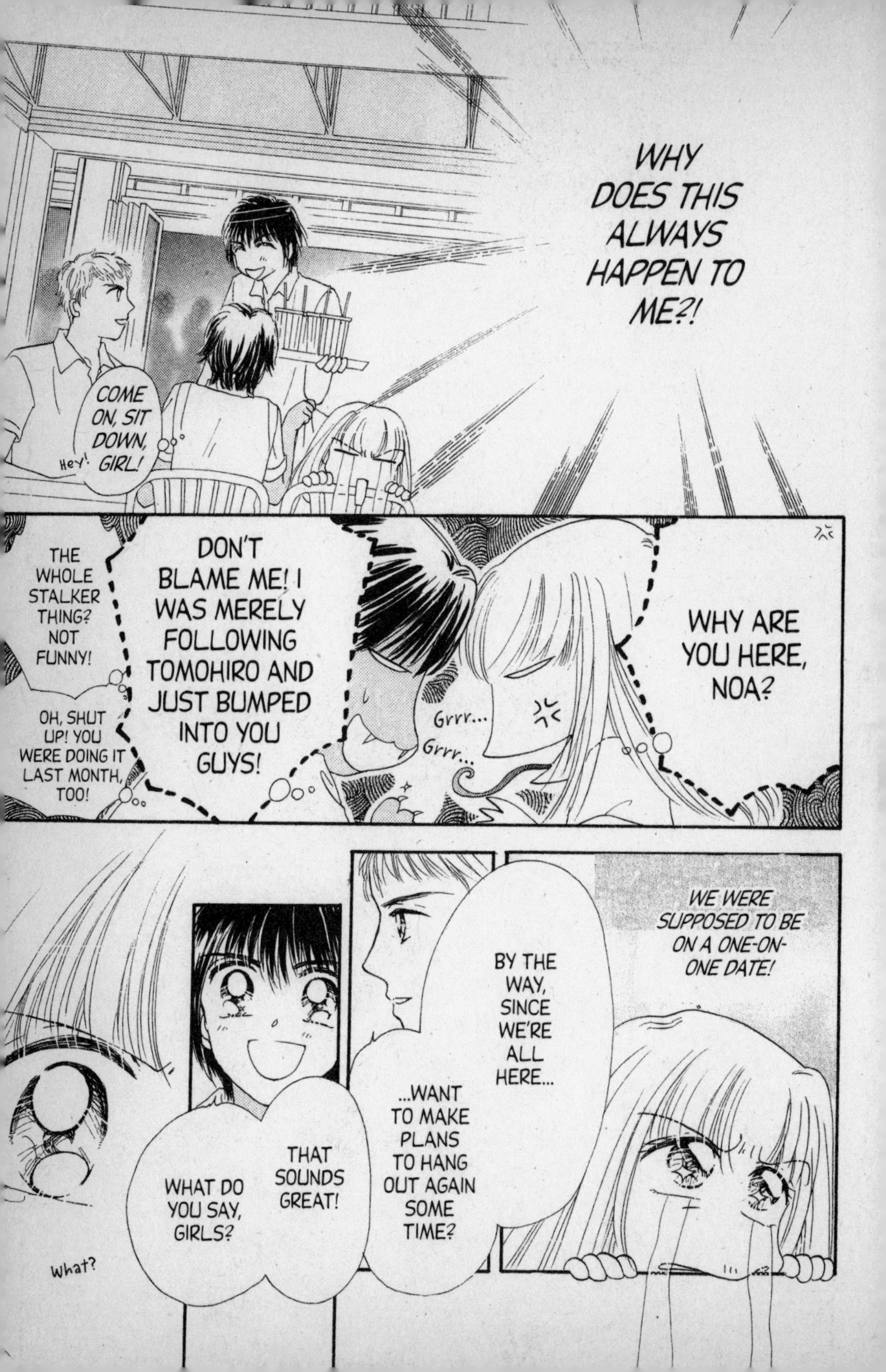
WHY DOES THIS ALWAYS HAPPEN TO ME?!
COME ON, SIT DOWN, GIRL!
Hey!
WHY ARE YOU HERE, NOA?
DON'T BLAME ME! I WAS MERELY FOLLOWING TOMOHIRO AND JUST BUMPED INTO YOU GUYS!
Grrr...
Grrr...
THE WHOLE STALKER THING? NOT FUNNY!
OH, SHUT UP! YOU WERE DOING IT LAST MONTH, TOO!
WE WERE SUPPOSED TO BE ON A ONE-ON-ONE DATE!
BY THE WAY, SINCE WE'RE ALL HERE...
...WANT TO MAKE PLANS TO HANG OUT AGAIN SOME TIME?
WHAT DO YOU SAY, GIRLS?
THAT SOUNDS GREAT!
What?

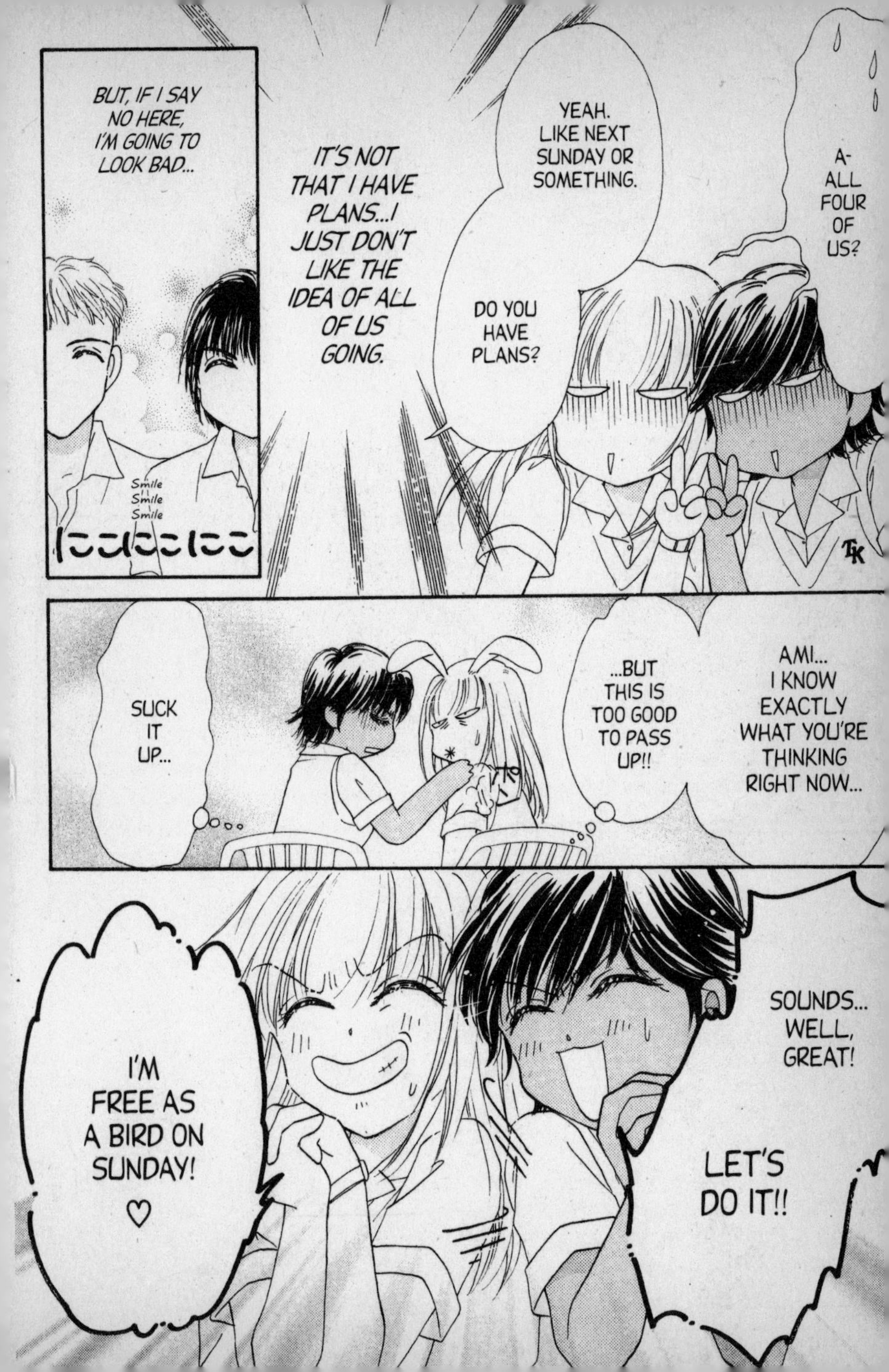
A- ALL FOUR OF US?
YEAH. LIKE NEXT SUNDAY OR SOMETHING.
DO YOU HAVE PLANS?
IT'S NOT THAT I HAVE PLANS...I JUST DON'T LIKE THE IDEA OF ALL OF US GOING.
BUT, IF I SAY NO HERE, I'M GOING TO LOOK BAD...
Smile Smile Smile
にこにこにこ
AMI... I KNOW EXACTLY WHAT YOU'RE THINKING RIGHT NOW...
...BUT THIS IS TOO GOOD TO PASS UP!!
SUCK IT UP...
SOUNDS... WELL, GREAT!
LET'S DO IT!!
I'M FREE AS A BIRD ON SUNDAY! ♡

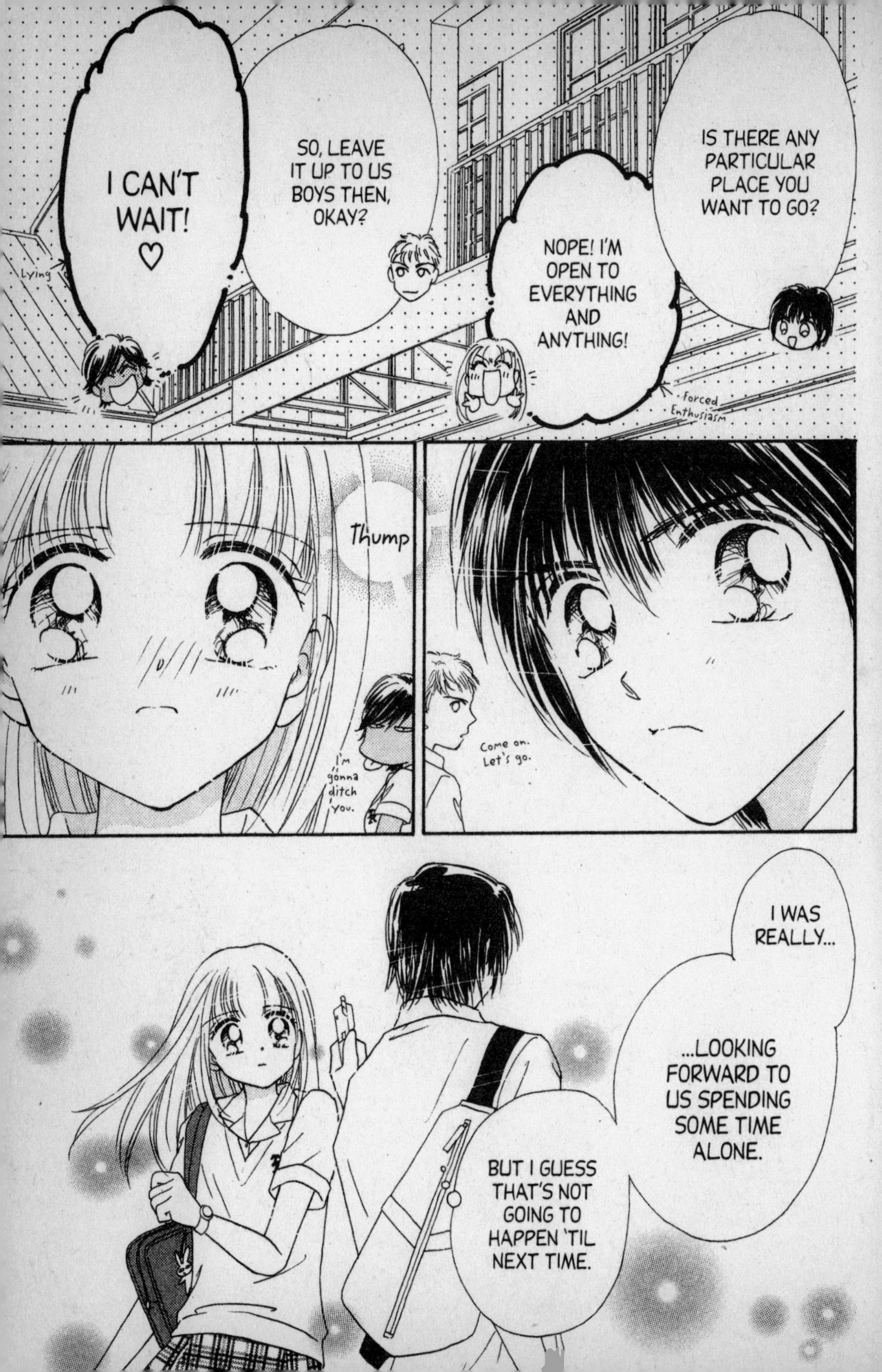
IS THERE ANY PARTICULAR PLACE YOU WANT TO GO?
NOPE! I'M OPEN TO EVERYTHING AND ANYTHING!
Forced Enthusiasm
SO, LEAVE IT UP TO US BOYS THEN, OKAY?
I CAN'T WAIT! ♡
Lying
Come on. Let's go.
Thump
I'm gonna ditch you.
I WAS REALLY...
...LOOKING FORWARD TO US SPENDING SOME TIME ALONE.
BUT I GUESS THAT'S NOT GOING TO HAPPEN 'TIL NEXT TIME.

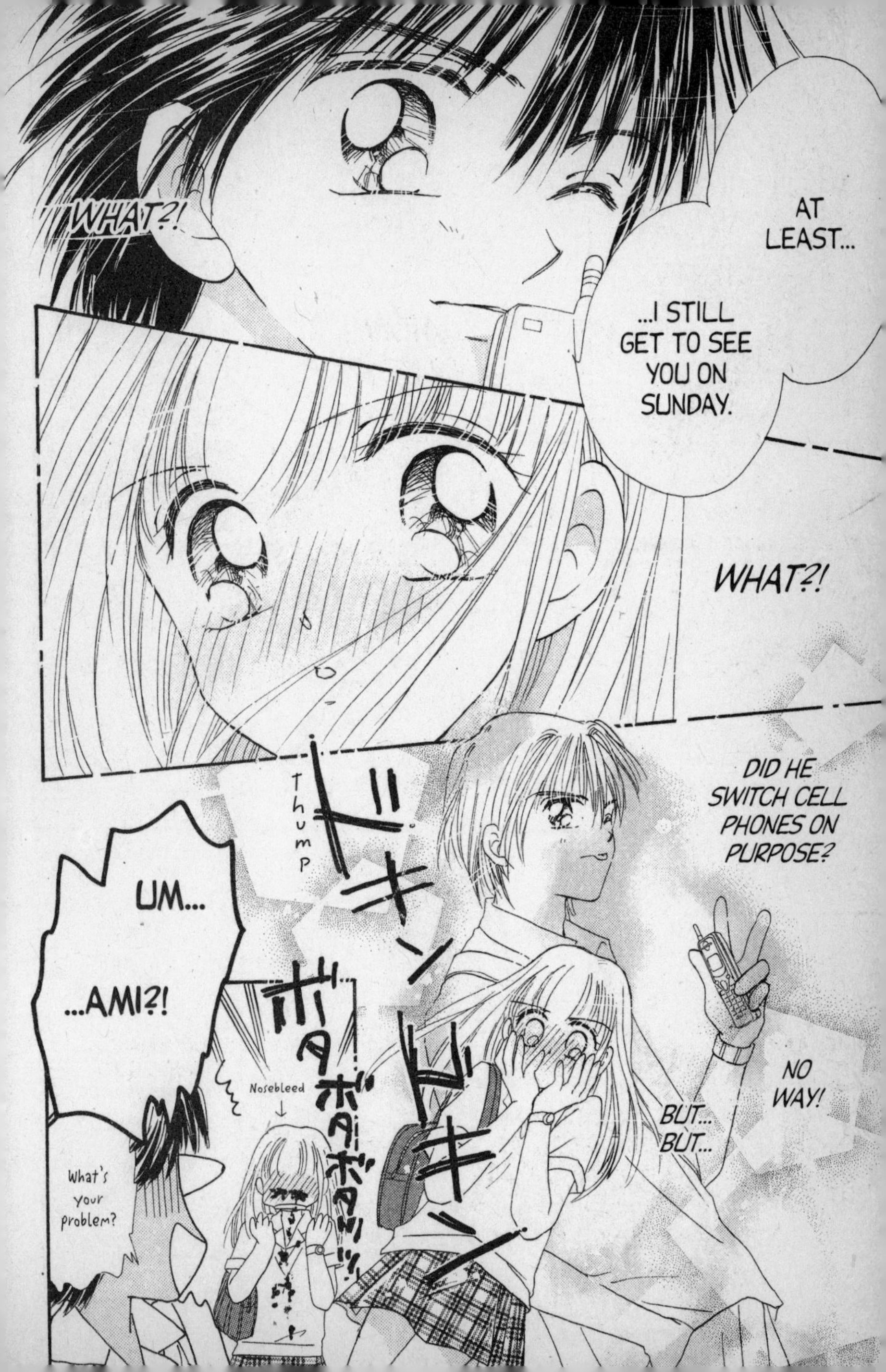
AT LEAST...
...I STILL GET TO SEE YOU ON SUNDAY.
WHAT?!
WHAT?!
DID HE SWITCH CELL PHONES ON PURPOSE?
NO WAY!
BUT... BUT...
Thump
UM...
...AMI?!
Nosebleed
What's your problem?

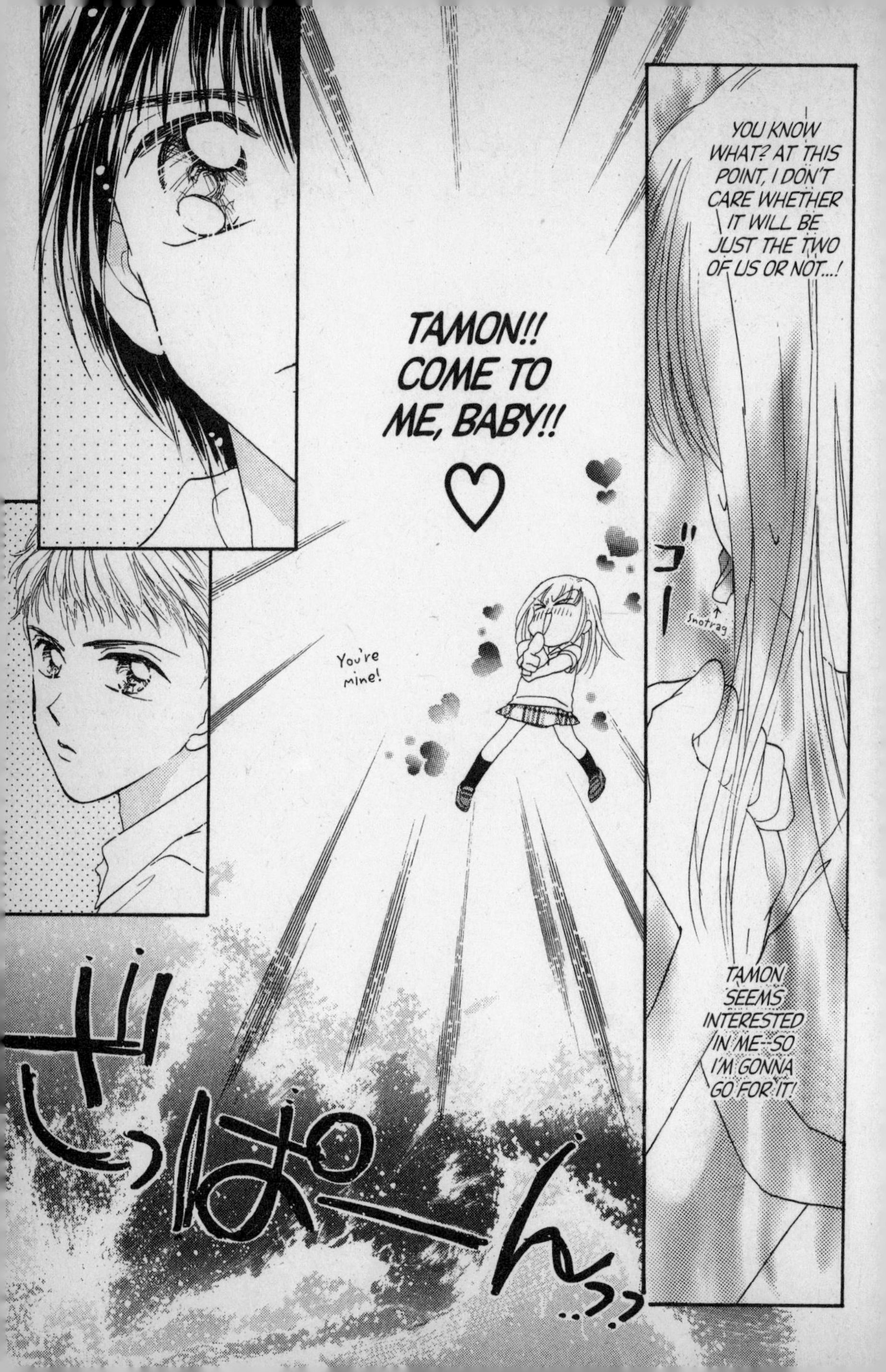
YOU KNOW WHAT? AT THIS POINT, I DON'T CARE WHETHER IT WILL BE JUST THE TWO OF US OR NOT...!
TAMON SEEMS INTERESTED IN ME--SO I'M GONNA GO FOR IT!
ゴー
Snotrag
TAMON!! COME TO ME, BABY!! ♡
You're mine!
ざっぱーん

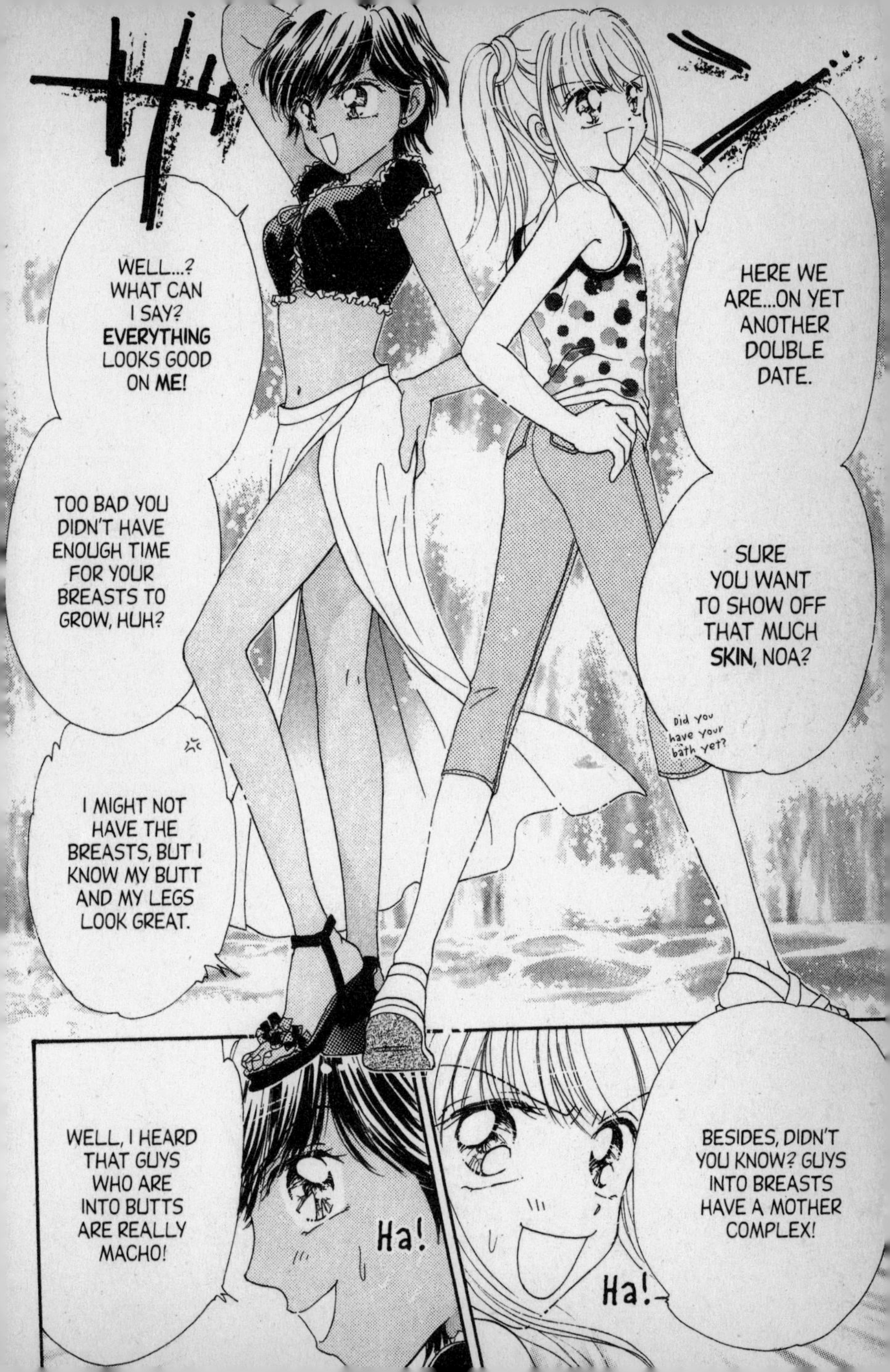

HERE WE ARE...ON YET ANOTHER DOUBLE DATE.
WELL...? WHAT CAN I SAY? EVERYTHING LOOKS GOOD ON ME!
SURE YOU WANT TO SHOW OFF THAT MUCH SKIN, NOA?
Did you have your bath yet?
TOO BAD YOU DIDN'T HAVE ENOUGH TIME FOR YOUR BREASTS TO GROW, HUH?
I MIGHT NOT HAVE THE BREASTS, BUT I KNOW MY BUTT AND MY LEGS LOOK GREAT.
BESIDES, DIDN'T YOU KNOW? GUYS INTO BREASTS HAVE A MOTHER COMPLEX!
Ha!
Ha!
WELL, I HEARD THAT GUYS WHO ARE INTO BUTTS ARE REALLY MACHO!

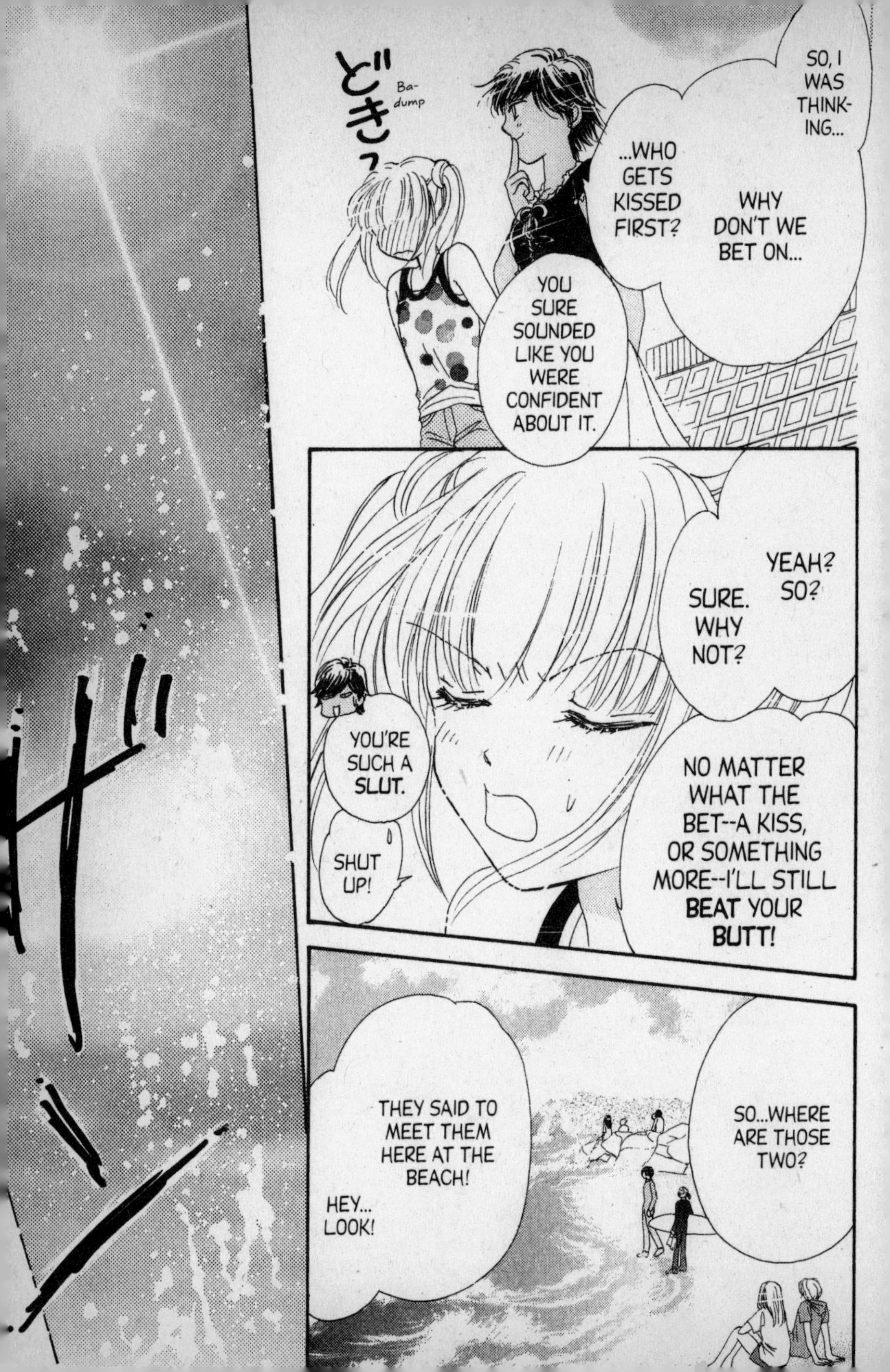
SO, I WAS THINKING...
WHY DON'T WE BET ON...
...WHO GETS KISSED FIRST?
どきっ
Ba-dump
YOU SURE SOUNDED LIKE YOU WERE CONFIDENT ABOUT IT.
YEAH? SO?
SURE. WHY NOT?
NO MATTER WHAT THE BET--A KISS, OR SOMETHING MORE--I'LL STILL BEAT YOUR BUTT!
YOU'RE SUCH A SLUT.
SHUT UP!
SO...WHERE ARE THOSE TWO?
THEY SAID TO MEET THEM HERE AT THE BEACH!
HEY... LOOK!
ザ

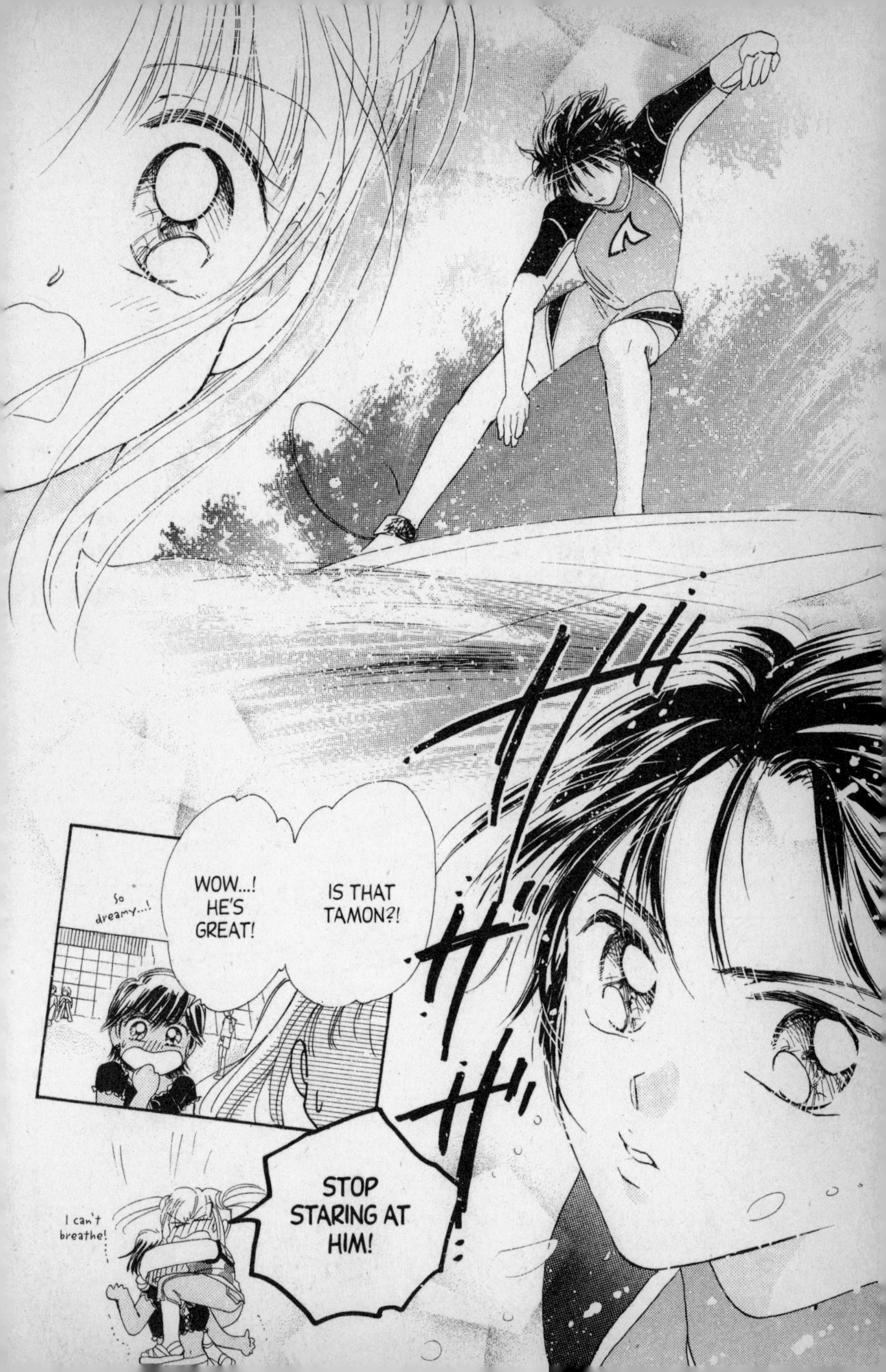
IS THAT TAMON?!
WOW...! HE'S GREAT!
So dreamy...!
STOP STARING AT HIM!
I can't breathe!

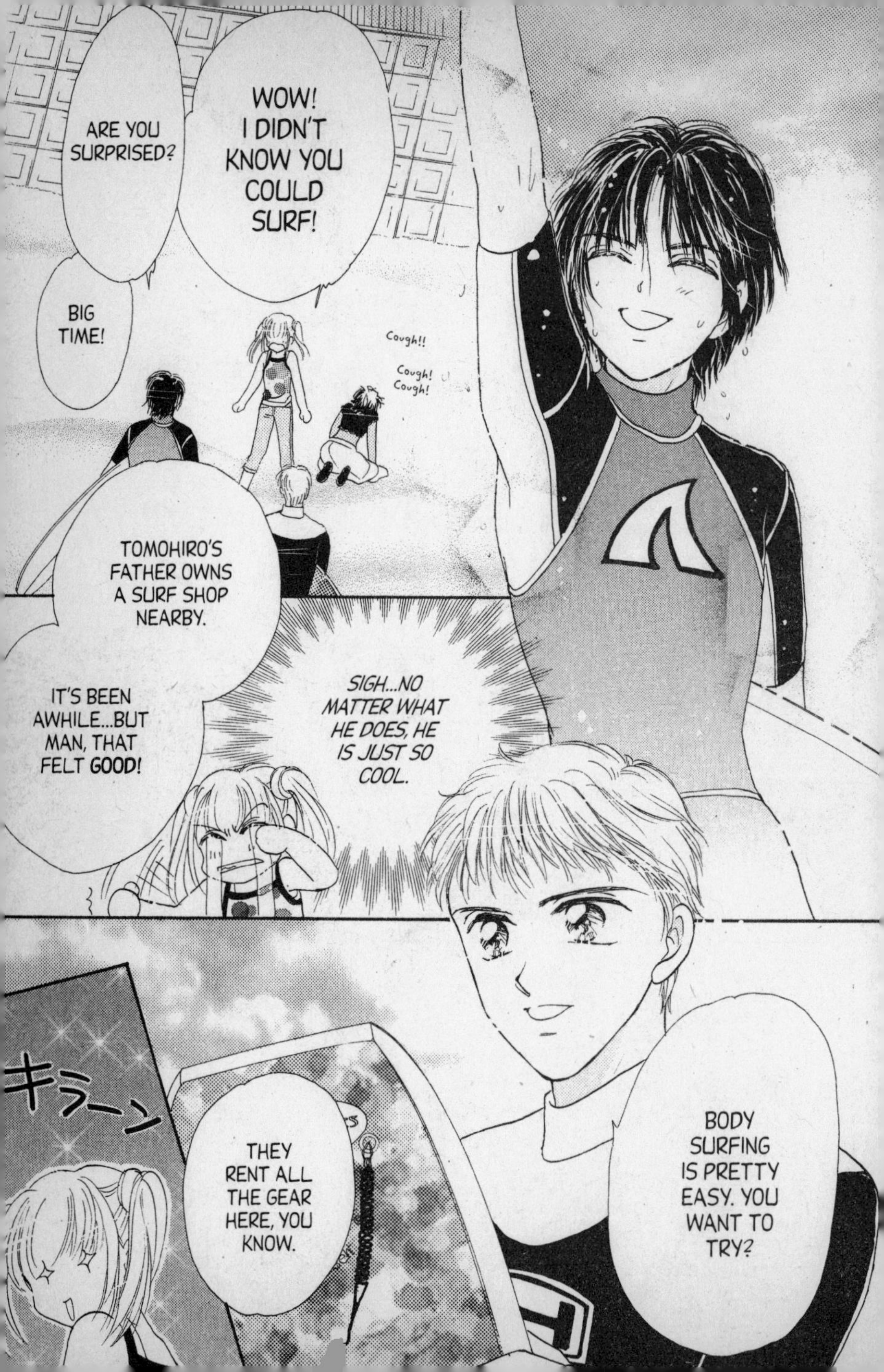
WOW! I DIDN'T KNOW YOU COULD SURF!
ARE YOU SURPRISED?
BIG TIME!
Cough!!
Cough! Cough!
TOMOHIRO'S FATHER OWNS A SURF SHOP NEARBY.
IT'S BEEN AWHILE...BUT MAN, THAT FELT **GOOD**!
SIGH...NO MATTER WHAT HE DOES, HE IS JUST SO COOL.
BODY SURFING IS PRETTY EASY. YOU WANT TO TRY?
THEY RENT ALL THE GEAR HERE, YOU KNOW.
キラーン

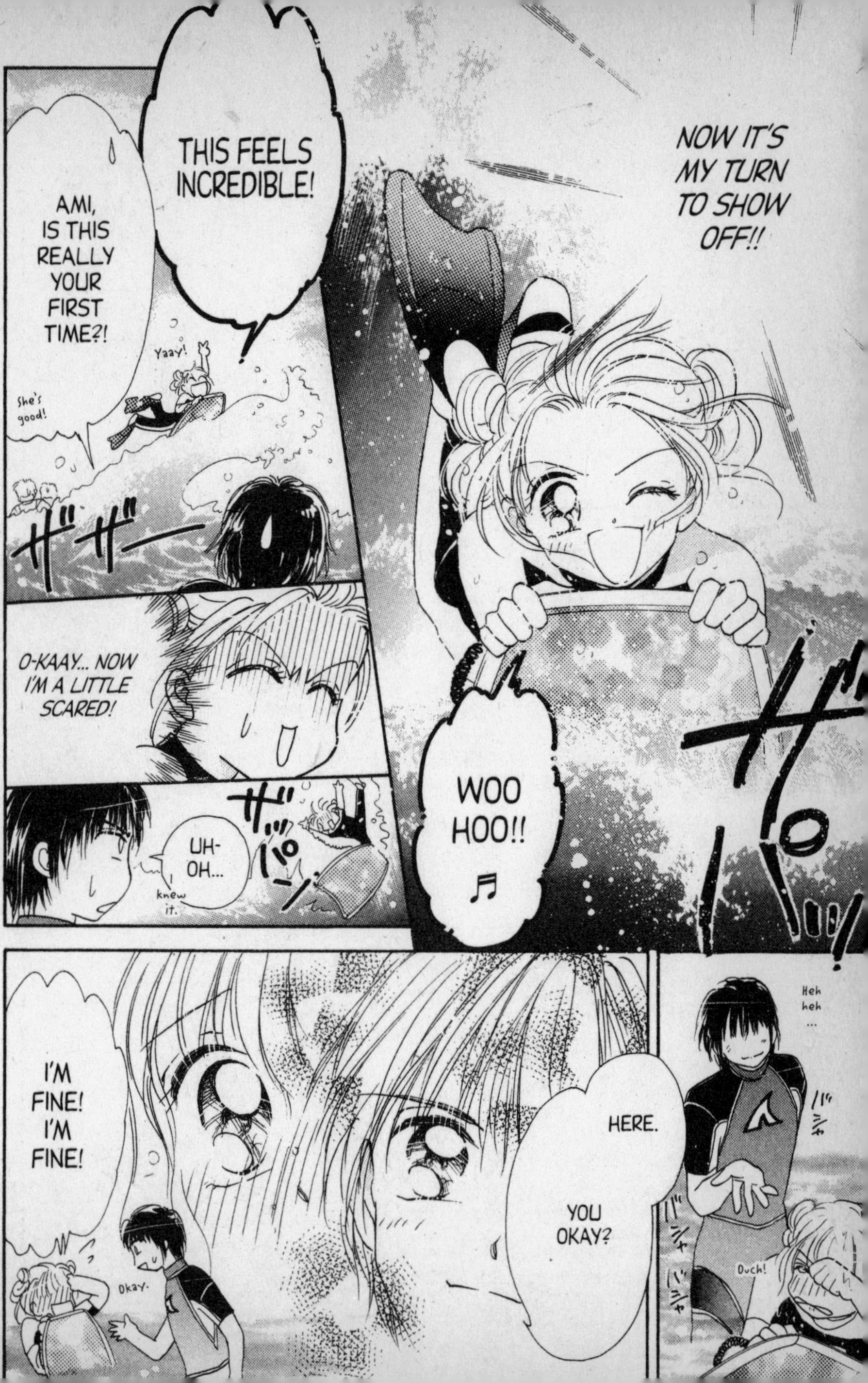
NOW IT'S MY TURN TO SHOW OFF!!
WOO HOO!! ♬
THIS FEELS INCREDIBLE!
AMI, IS THIS REALLY YOUR FIRST TIME?!
Yaay!
She's good!
ザザー
O-KAAY... NOW I'M A LITTLE SCARED!
UH-OH...
I knew it.
Heh heh ...
Ouch!
HERE.
YOU OKAY?
I'M FINE! I'M FINE!
Okay.

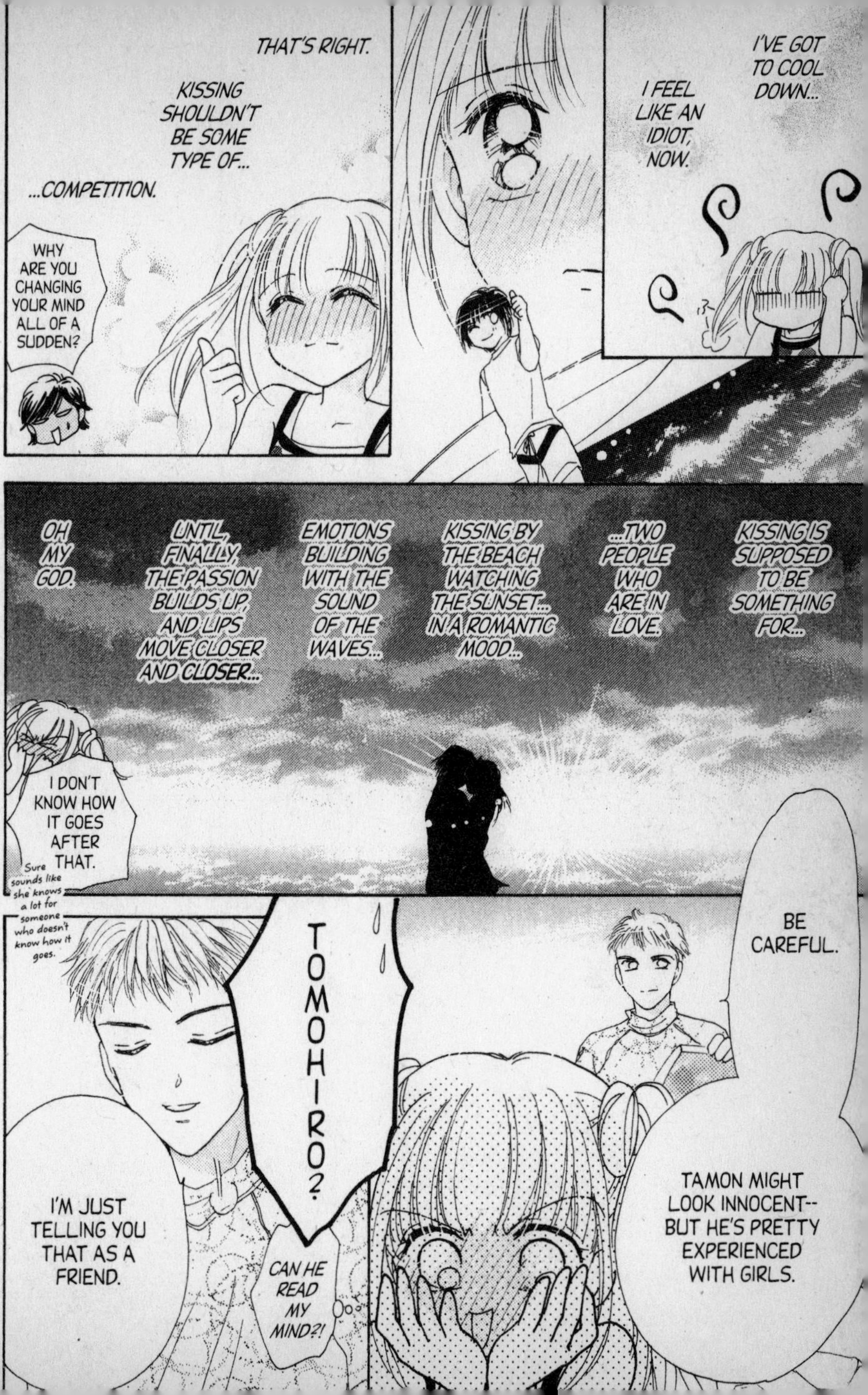
I'VE GOT TO COOL DOWN...
I FEEL LIKE AN IDIOT, NOW.
THAT'S RIGHT.
KISSING SHOULDN'T BE SOME TYPE OF...
...COMPETITION.
WHY ARE YOU CHANGING YOUR MIND ALL OF A SUDDEN?
KISSING IS SUPPOSED TO BE SOMETHING FOR...
...TWO PEOPLE WHO ARE IN LOVE.
KISSING BY THE BEACH WATCHING THE SUNSET... IN A ROMANTIC MOOD...
EMOTIONS BUILDING WITH THE SOUND OF THE WAVES...
UNTIL, FINALLY, THE PASSION BUILDS UP, AND LIPS MOVE CLOSER AND CLOSER...
OH MY GOD.
I DON'T KNOW HOW IT GOES AFTER THAT.
Sure sounds like she knows a lot for someone who doesn't know how it goes.
BE CAREFUL.
TAMON MIGHT LOOK INNOCENT-- BUT HE'S PRETTY EXPERIENCED WITH GIRLS.
TOMOHIRO?
CAN HE READ MY MIND?!
I'M JUST TELLING YOU THAT AS A FRIEND.

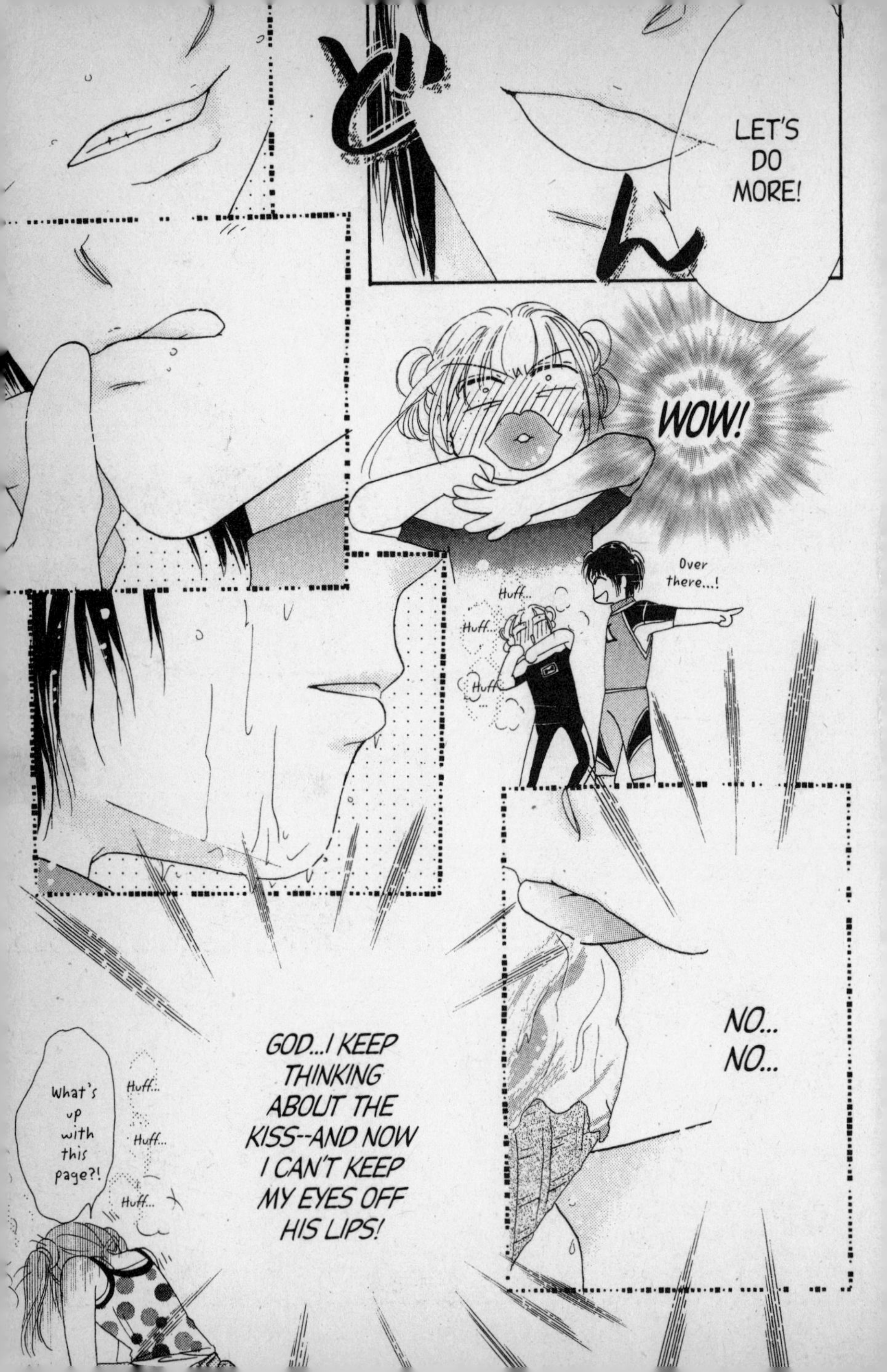
LET'S DO MORE!
WOW!
Over there...!
Huff... Huff... Huff...
NO... NO...
GOD...I KEEP THINKING ABOUT THE KISS--AND NOW I CAN'T KEEP MY EYES OFF HIS LIPS!
What's up with this page?!
Huff... Huff... Huff...

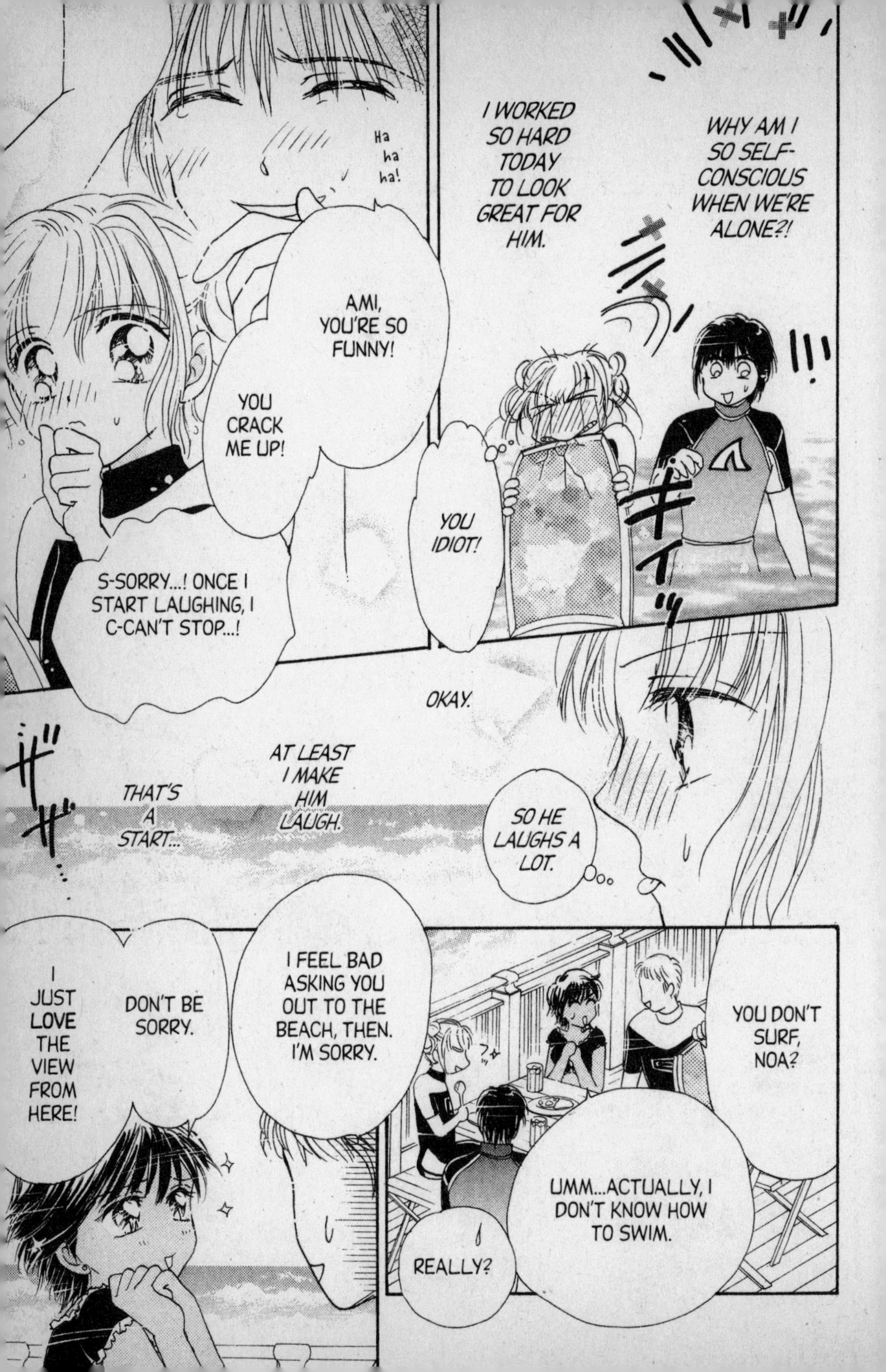
WHY AM I SO SELF-CONSCIOUS WHEN WE'RE ALONE?!
I WORKED SO HARD TODAY TO LOOK GREAT FOR HIM.
YOU IDIOT!
Ha ha ha!
AMI, YOU'RE SO FUNNY!
YOU CRACK ME UP!
S-SORRY...! ONCE I START LAUGHING, I C-CAN'T STOP...!
SO HE LAUGHS A LOT.
OKAY.
AT LEAST I MAKE HIM LAUGH.
THAT'S A START...
YOU DON'T SURF, NOA?
UMM...ACTUALLY, I DON'T KNOW HOW TO SWIM.
REALLY?
I FEEL BAD ASKING YOU OUT TO THE BEACH, THEN. I'M SORRY.
DON'T BE SORRY.
I JUST LOVE THE VIEW FROM HERE!

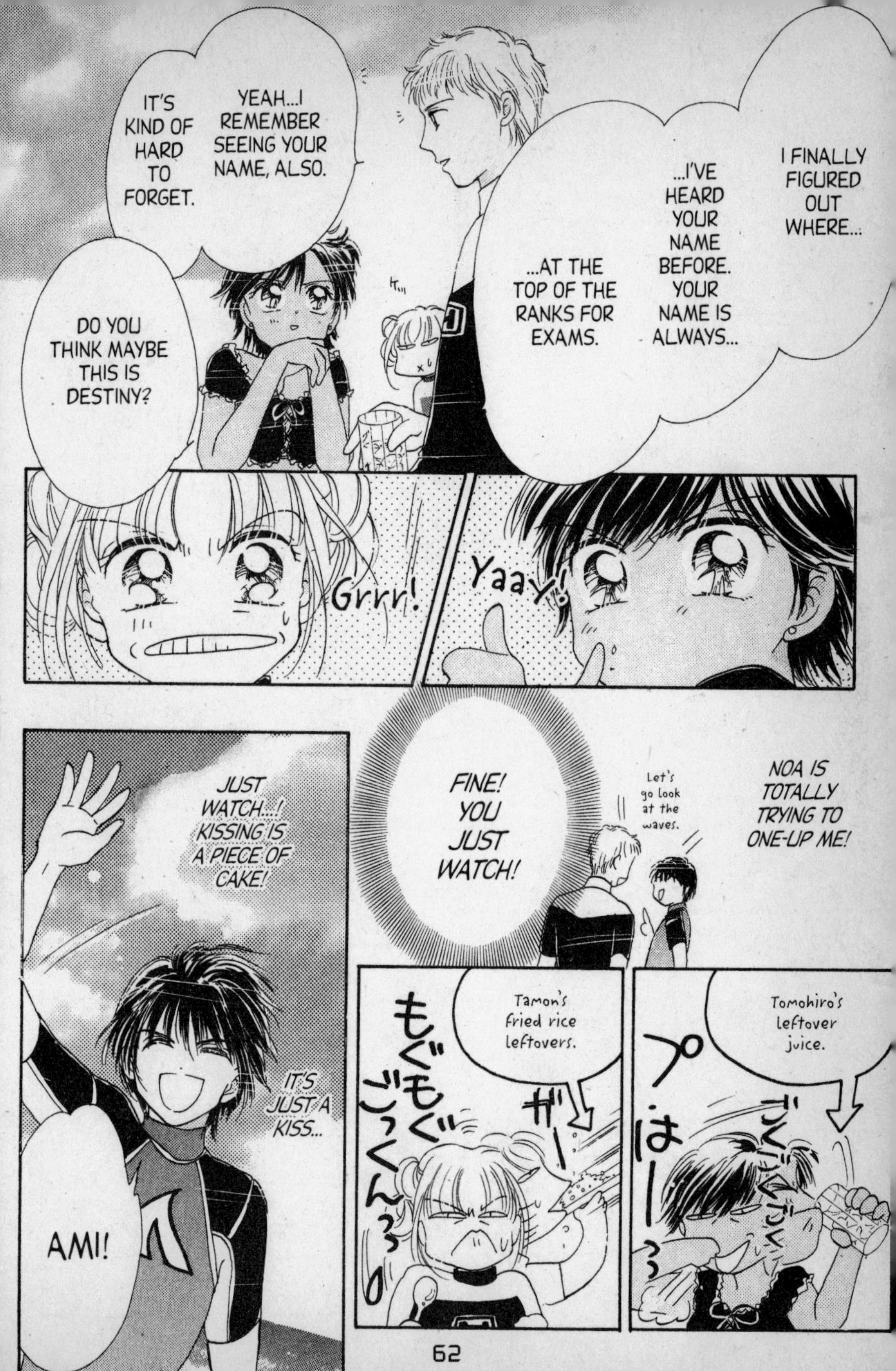
I FINALLY FIGURED OUT WHERE...
...I'VE HEARD YOUR NAME BEFORE. YOUR NAME IS ALWAYS...
...AT THE TOP OF THE RANKS FOR EXAMS.
YEAH...I REMEMBER SEEING YOUR NAME, ALSO.
IT'S KIND OF HARD TO FORGET.
DO YOU THINK MAYBE THIS IS DESTINY?
Yaay!
Grrr!
NOA IS TOTALLY TRYING TO ONE-UP ME!
Let's go look at the waves.
FINE! YOU JUST WATCH!
Tomohiro's leftover juice.
ごくごく
プはーっ
Tamon's fried rice leftovers.
もぐもぐ
ごっくんっっ
ガーー
JUST WATCH...! KISSING IS A PIECE OF CAKE!
IT'S JUST A KISS...
AMI!

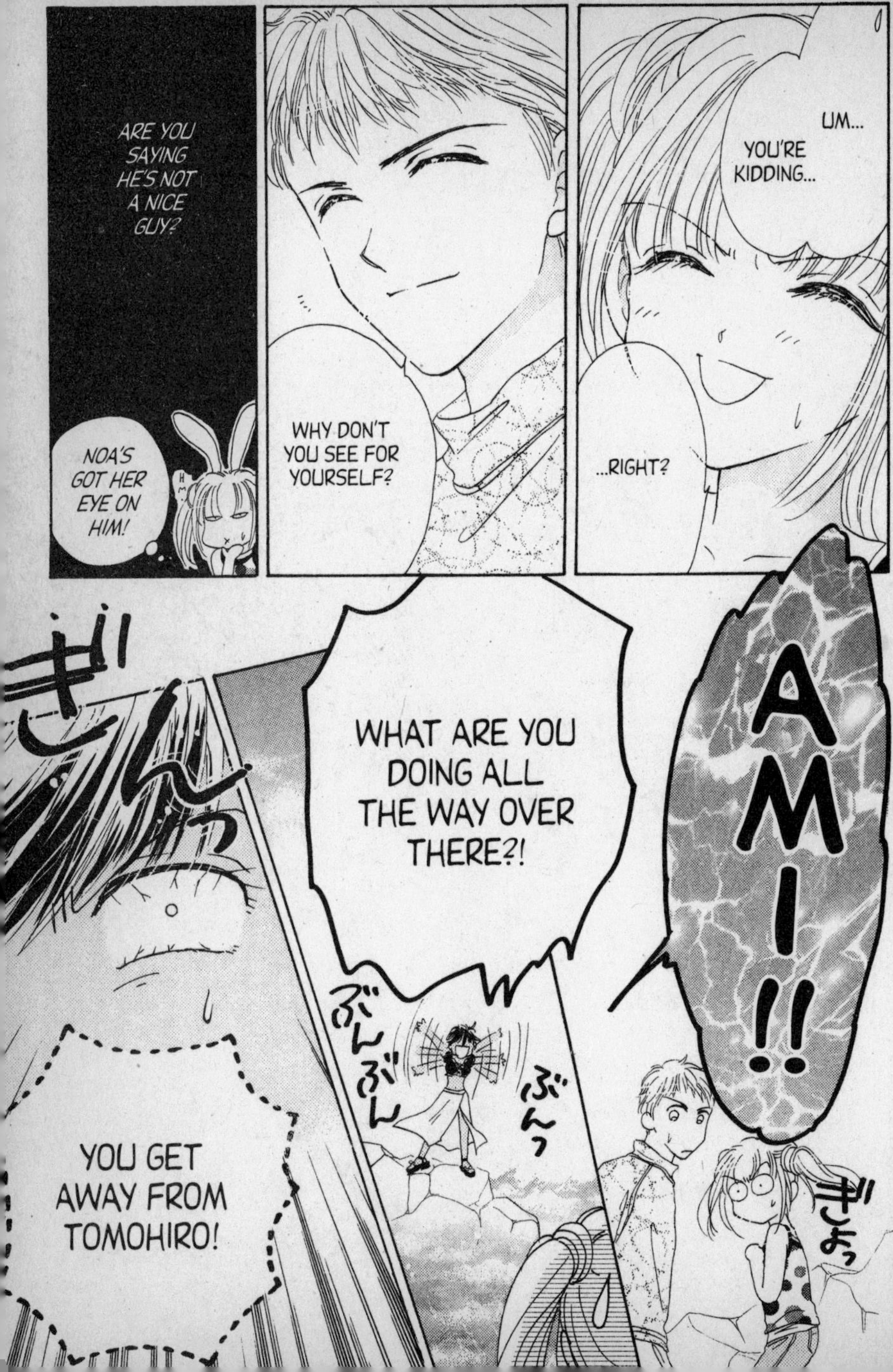
UM... YOU'RE KIDDING...
...RIGHT?
WHY DON'T YOU SEE FOR YOURSELF?
ARE YOU SAYING HE'S NOT A NICE GUY?
NOA'S GOT HER EYE ON HIM!
ぎょっ
AMI-!!
ぶんっ
ぶんぶん
WHAT ARE YOU DOING ALL THE WAY OVER THERE?!
ぎんっ
YOU GET AWAY FROM TOMOHIRO!

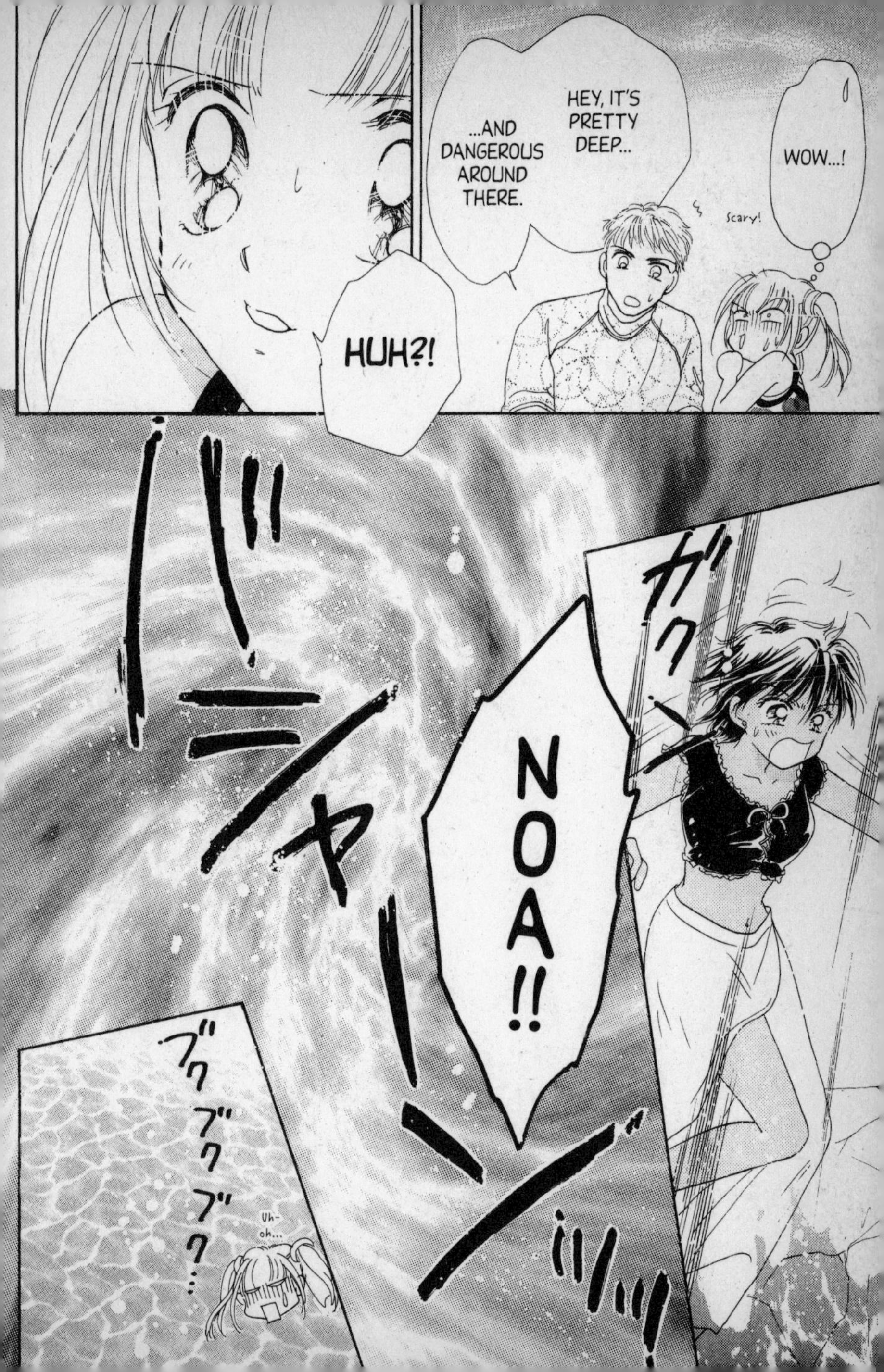
WOW...!
Scary!
HEY, IT'S PRETTY DEEP...
...AND DANGEROUS AROUND THERE.
HUH?!
ガクッ
NOA!!
バシャーン
ブクブクブク...
Uh-oh...

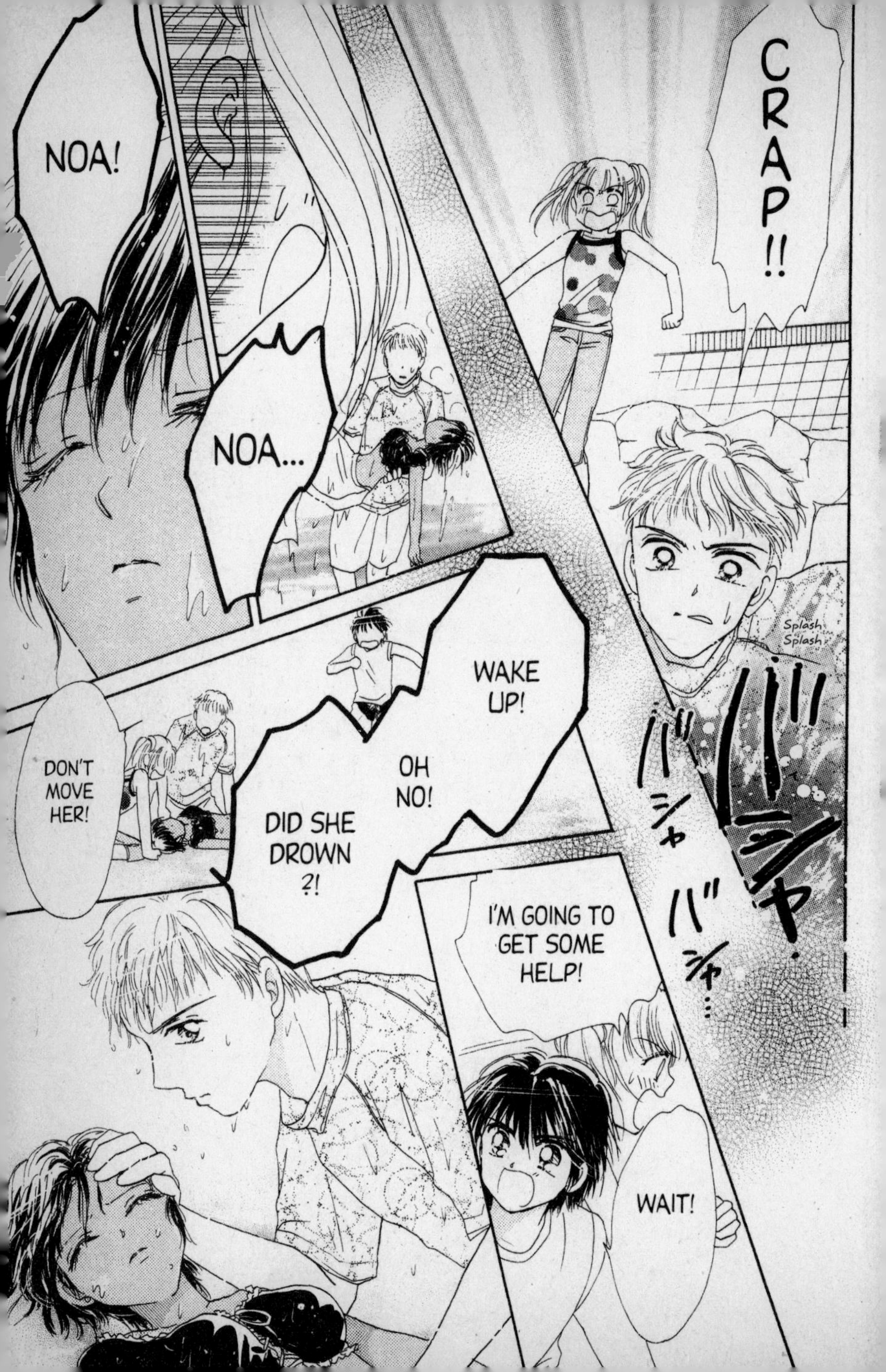
CRAP!!
Splash Splash
NOA...
NOA!
WAKE UP!
OH NO!
DID SHE DROWN ?!
DON'T MOVE HER!
I'M GOING TO GET SOME HELP!
WAIT!

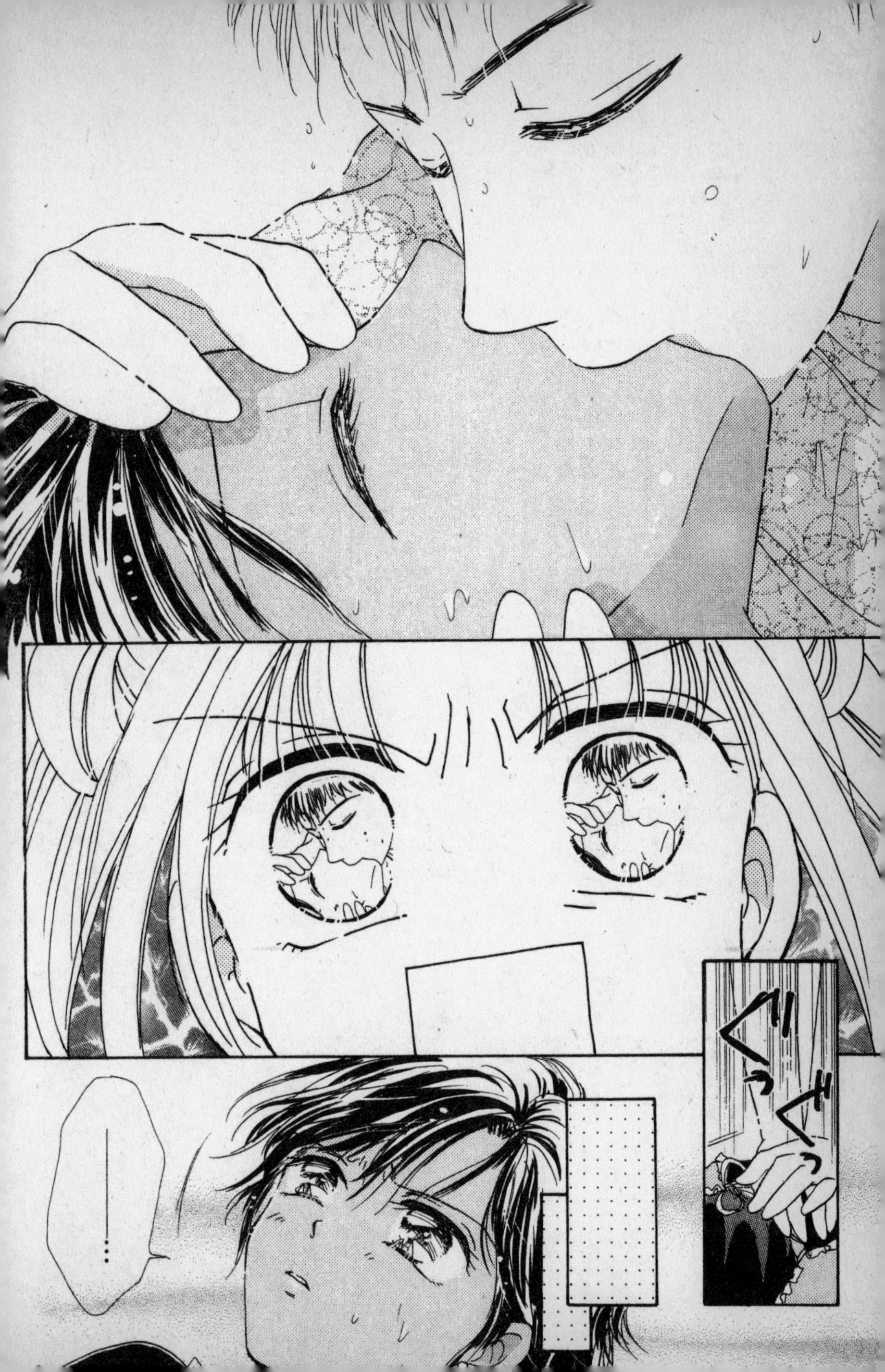
……

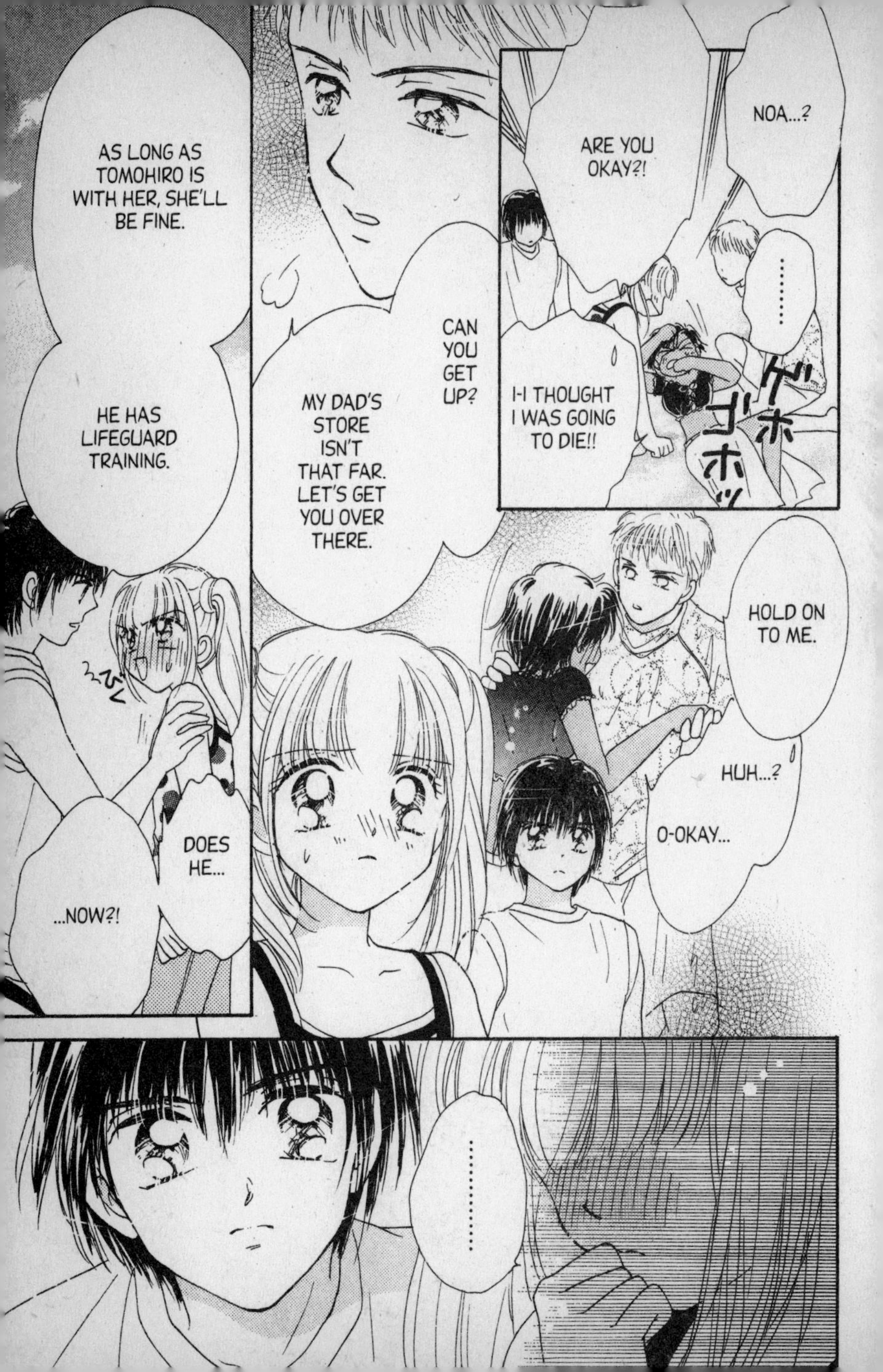
NOA...?
ARE YOU OKAY?!
......
I-I THOUGHT I WAS GOING TO DIE!!
ゲホゴホッ
CAN YOU GET UP?
MY DAD'S STORE ISN'T THAT FAR. LET'S GET YOU OVER THERE.
HOLD ON TO ME.
HUH...?
O-OKAY...
AS LONG AS TOMOHIRO IS WITH HER, SHE'LL BE FINE.
HE HAS LIFEGUARD TRAINING.
DOES HE...
...NOW?!
......

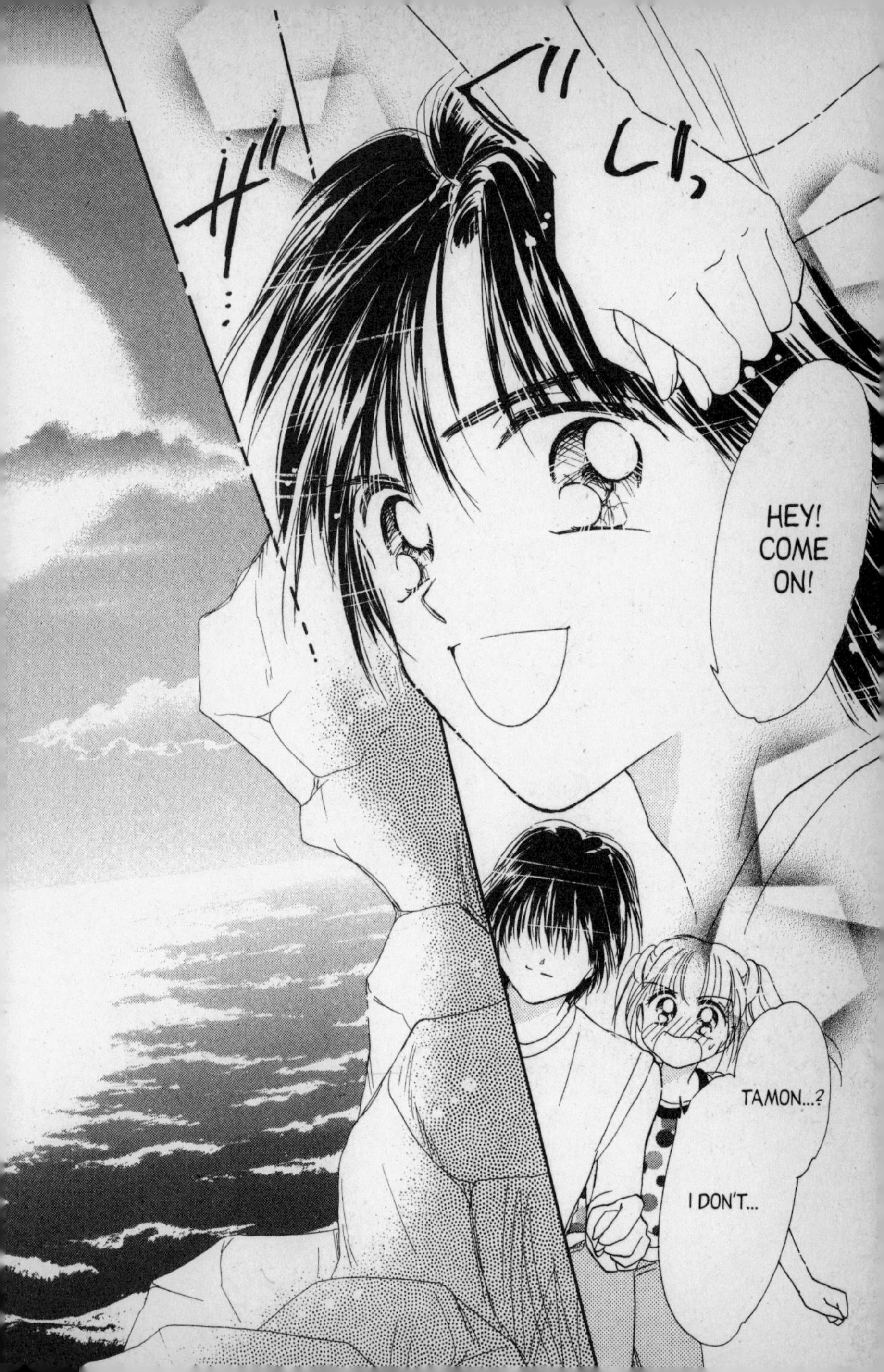
ぐい
HEY! COME ON!
ザ
TAMON...?
I DON'T...

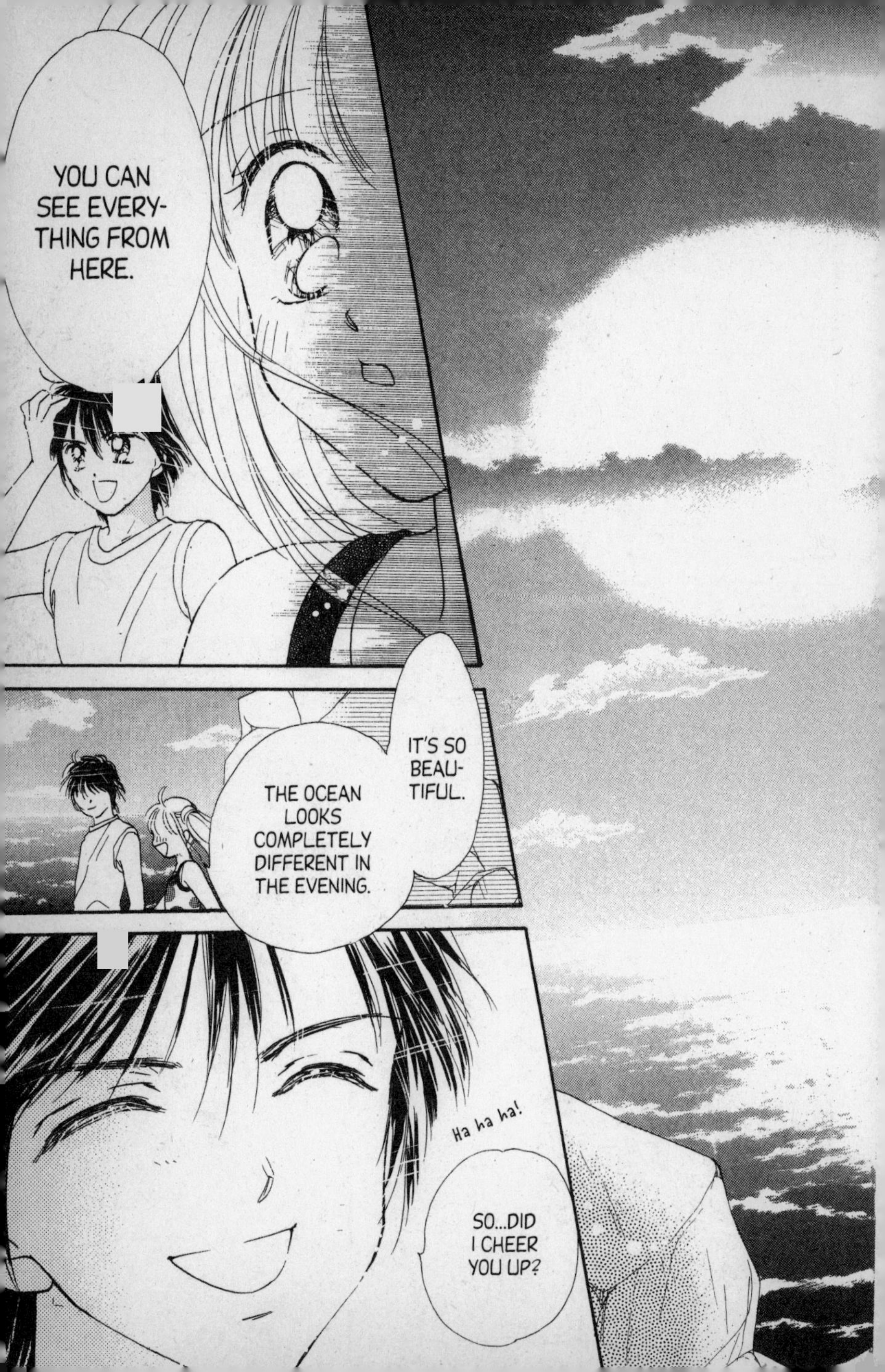
YOU CAN SEE EVERY-THING FROM HERE.
IT'S SO BEAU-TIFUL.
THE OCEAN LOOKS COMPLETELY DIFFERENT IN THE EVENING.
Ha ha ha!
SO...DID I CHEER YOU UP?

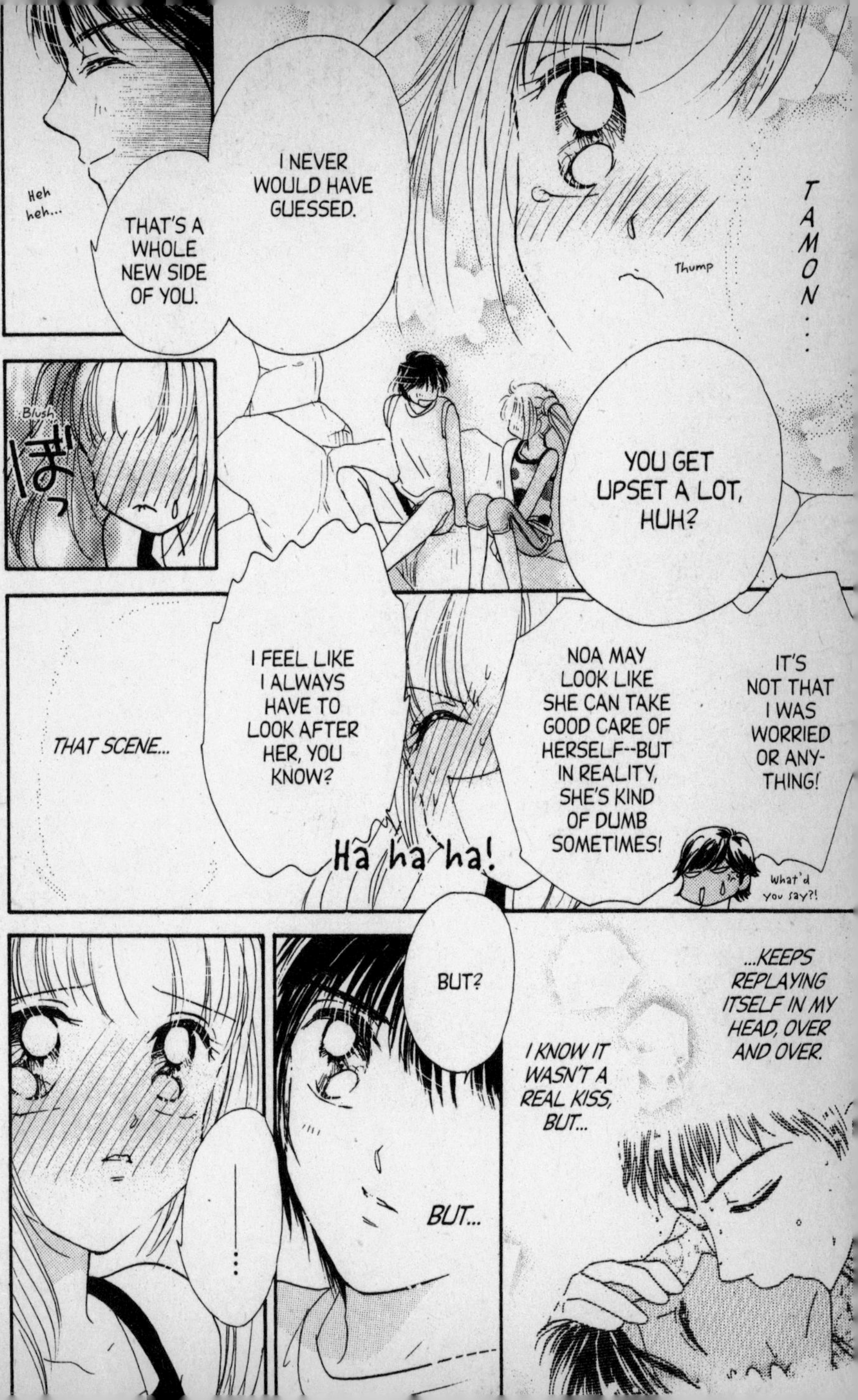

TAMON...
Thump
Heh heh...
I NEVER WOULD HAVE GUESSED.
THAT'S A WHOLE NEW SIDE OF YOU.
YOU GET UPSET A LOT, HUH?
Blush
ぼっ
IT'S NOT THAT I WAS WORRIED OR ANYTHING!
What'd you say?!
NOA MAY LOOK LIKE SHE CAN TAKE GOOD CARE OF HERSELF--BUT IN REALITY, SHE'S KIND OF DUMB SOMETIMES!
I FEEL LIKE I ALWAYS HAVE TO LOOK AFTER HER, YOU KNOW?
Ha ha ha!
THAT SCENE...
...KEEPS REPLAYING ITSELF IN MY HEAD, OVER AND OVER.
I KNOW IT WASN'T A REAL KISS, BUT...
BUT?
BUT...
......

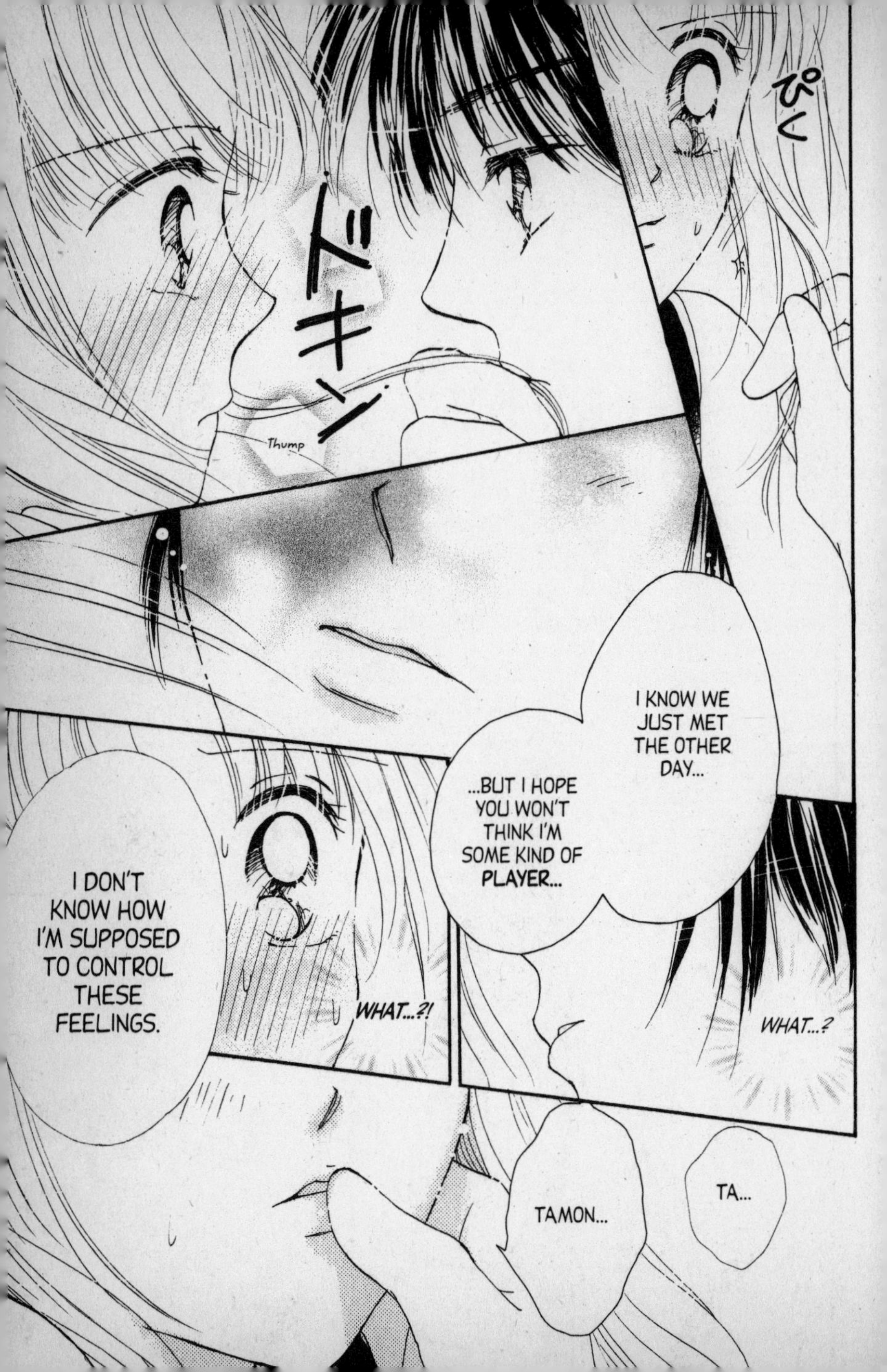
ぴく
ドキン
Thump
I KNOW WE JUST MET THE OTHER DAY...
...BUT I HOPE YOU WON'T THINK I'M SOME KIND OF PLAYER...
WHAT...?
WHAT...?!
I DON'T KNOW HOW I'M SUPPOSED TO CONTROL THESE FEELINGS.
TA...
TAMON...

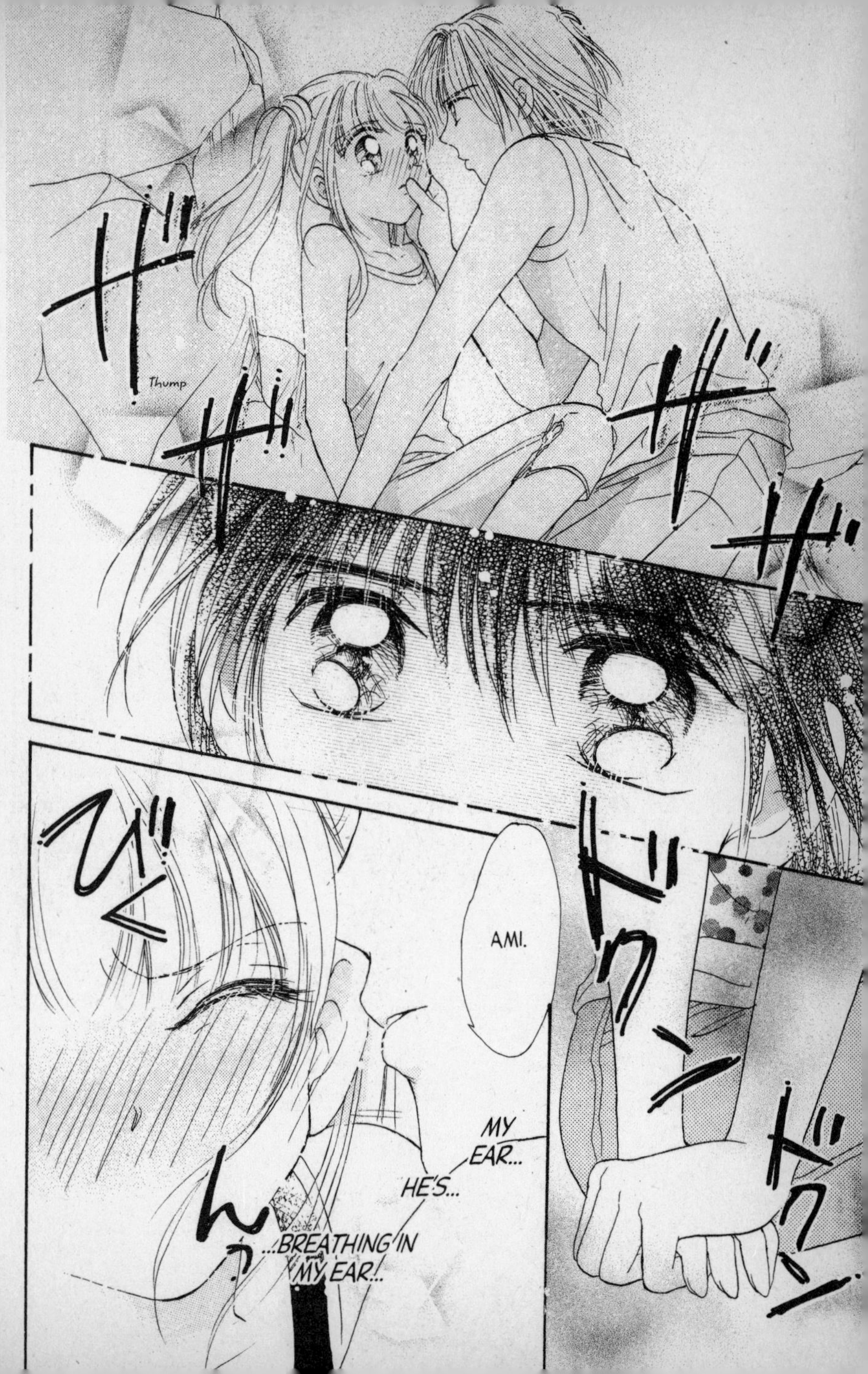
Thump
AMI.
MY EAR...
HE'S...
...BREATHING IN MY EAR!..

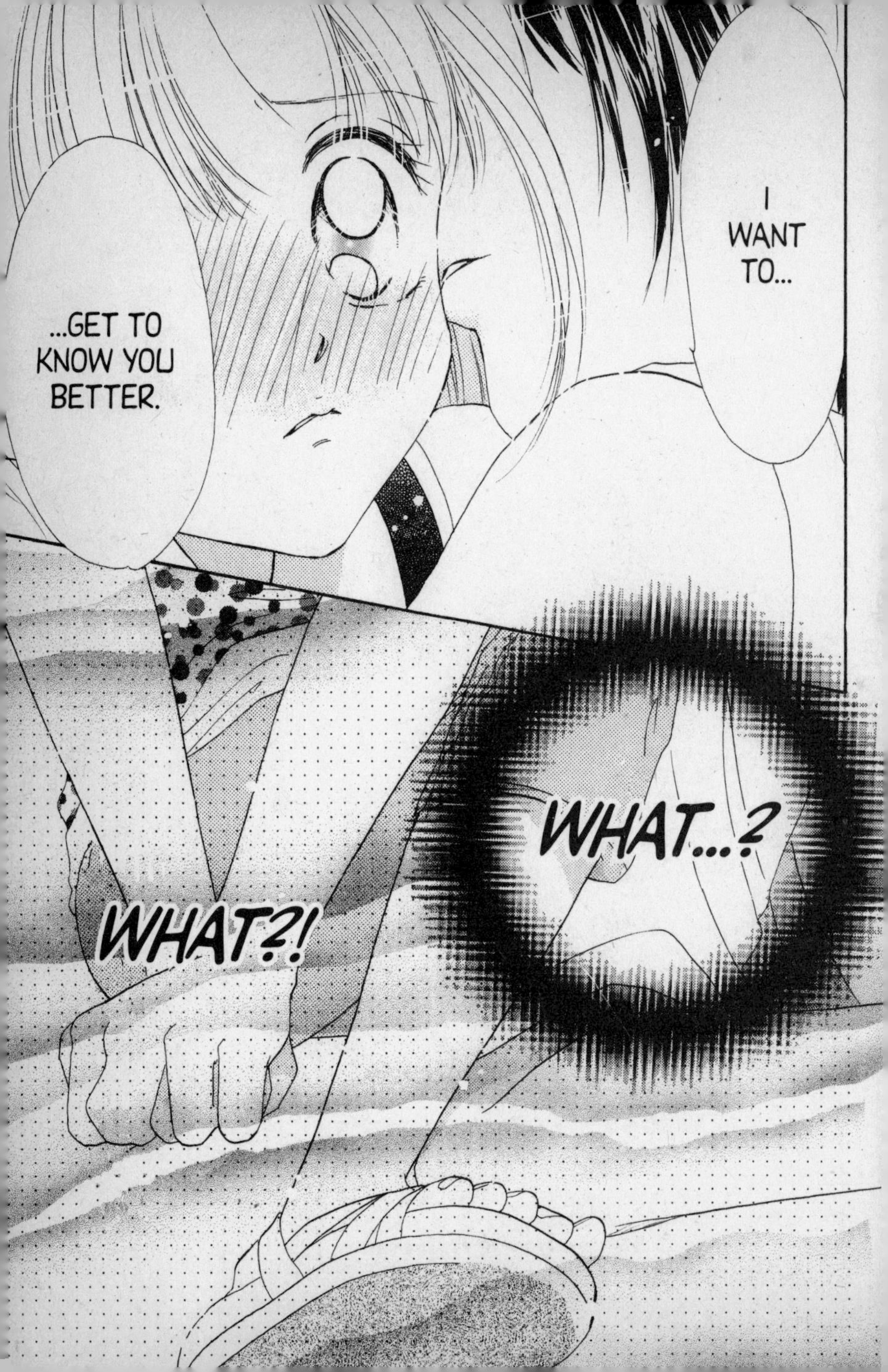
I WANT TO...
...GET TO KNOW YOU BETTER.
WHAT...?
WHAT?!

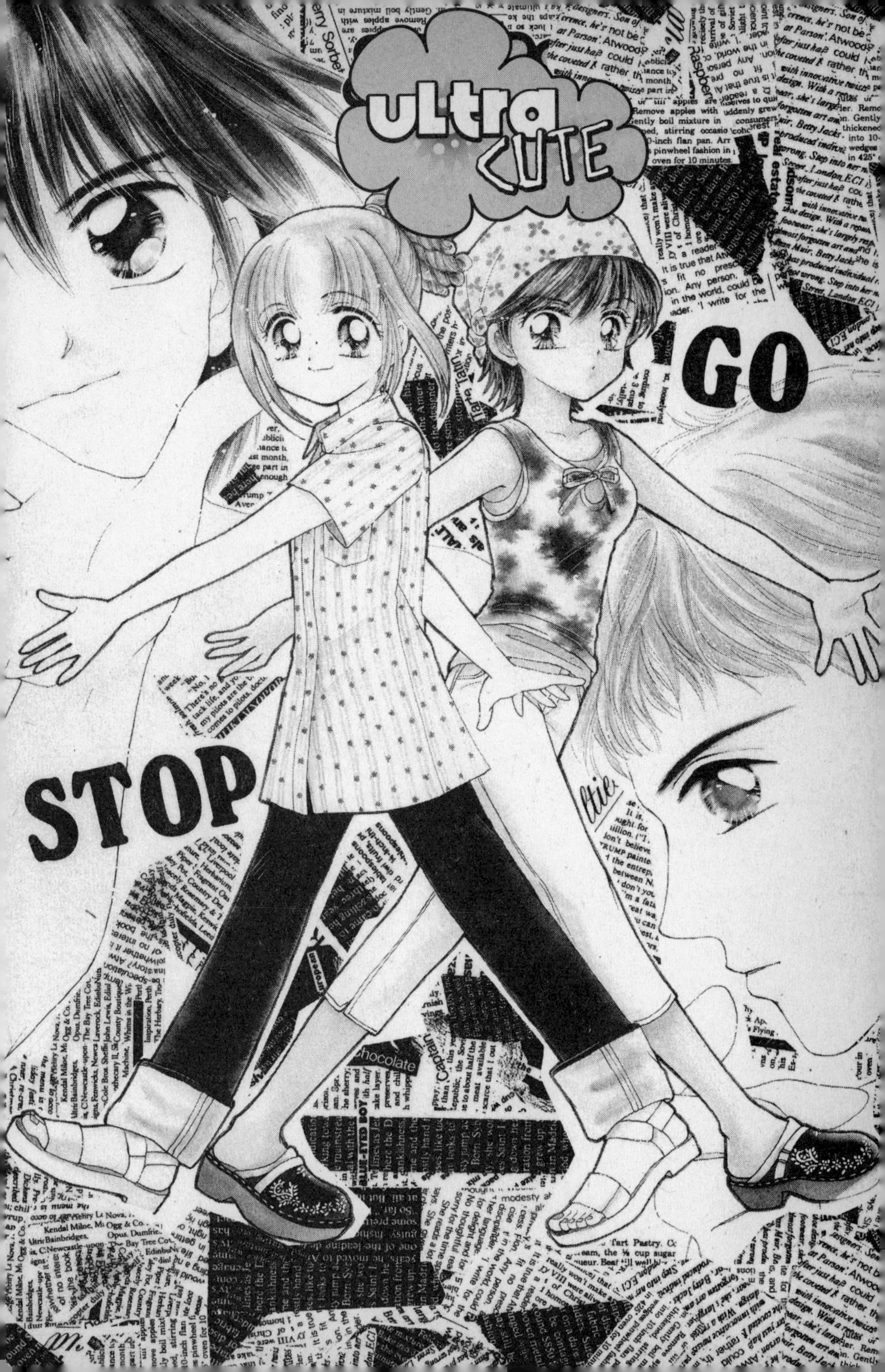
ultra
CUTE
GO
STOP

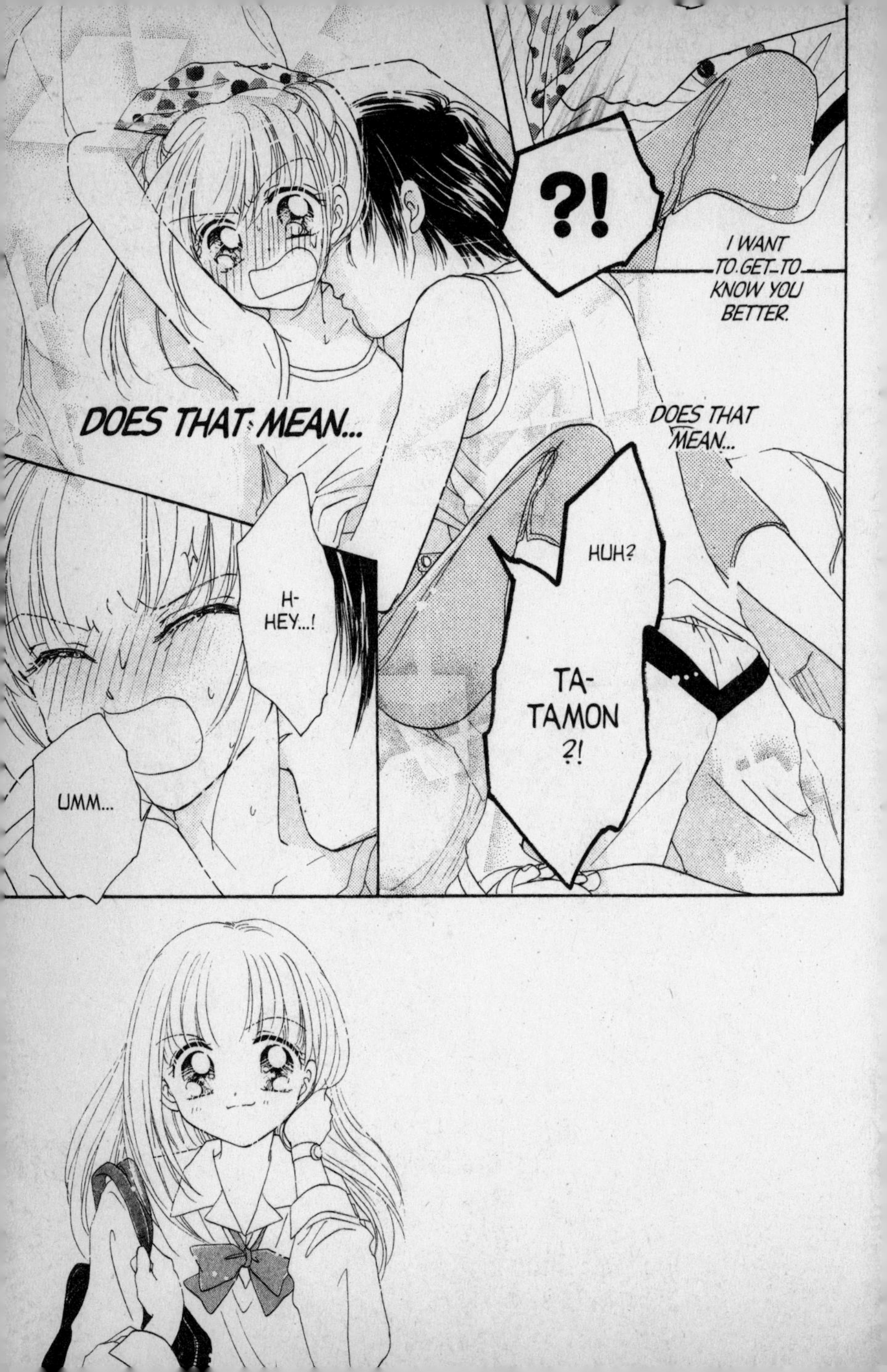
?!
I WANT TO GET TO KNOW YOU BETTER.
DOES THAT MEAN...
DOES THAT MEAN...
HUH?
TA-TAMON?!
H-HEY...!
UMM...

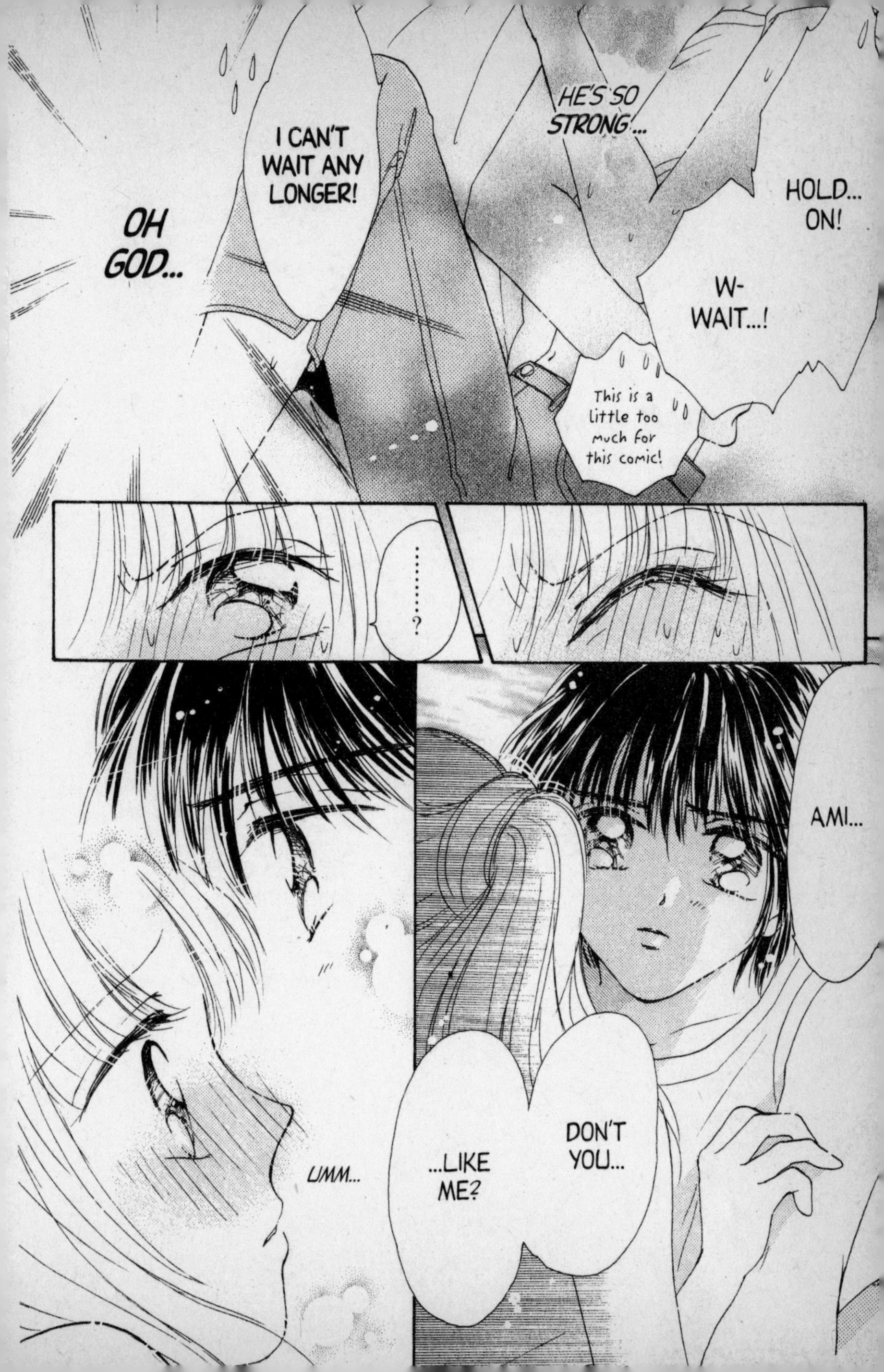
HOLD... ON!
W- WAIT...!
HE'S SO STRONG...
This is a little too much for this comic!
I CAN'T WAIT ANY LONGER!
OH GOD...
......?
AMI...
DON'T YOU...
...LIKE ME?
UMM...

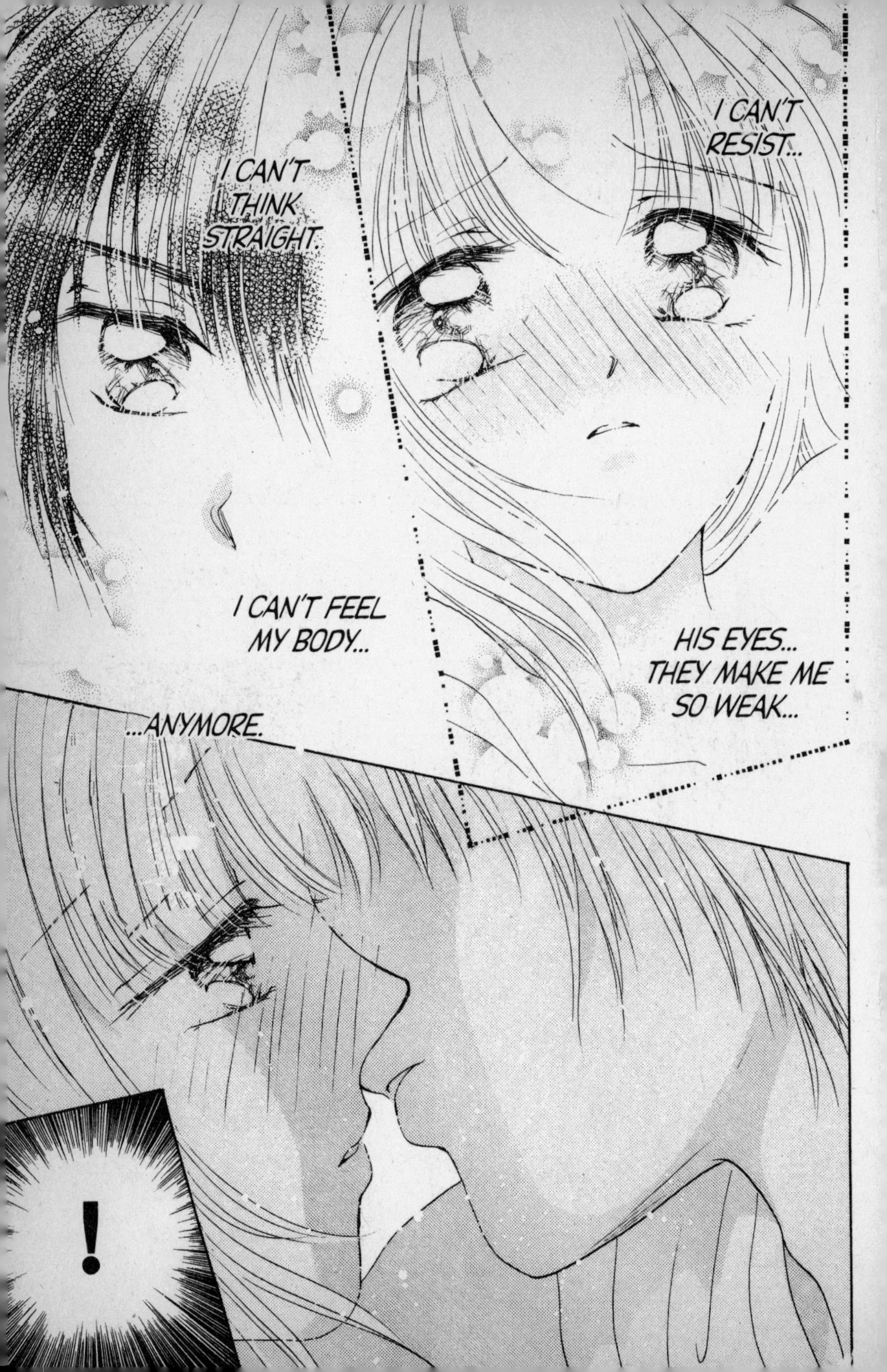
I CAN'T RESIST...
HIS EYES... THEY MAKE ME SO WEAK...
I CAN'T THINK STRAIGHT.
I CAN'T FEEL MY BODY...
...ANYMORE.
!

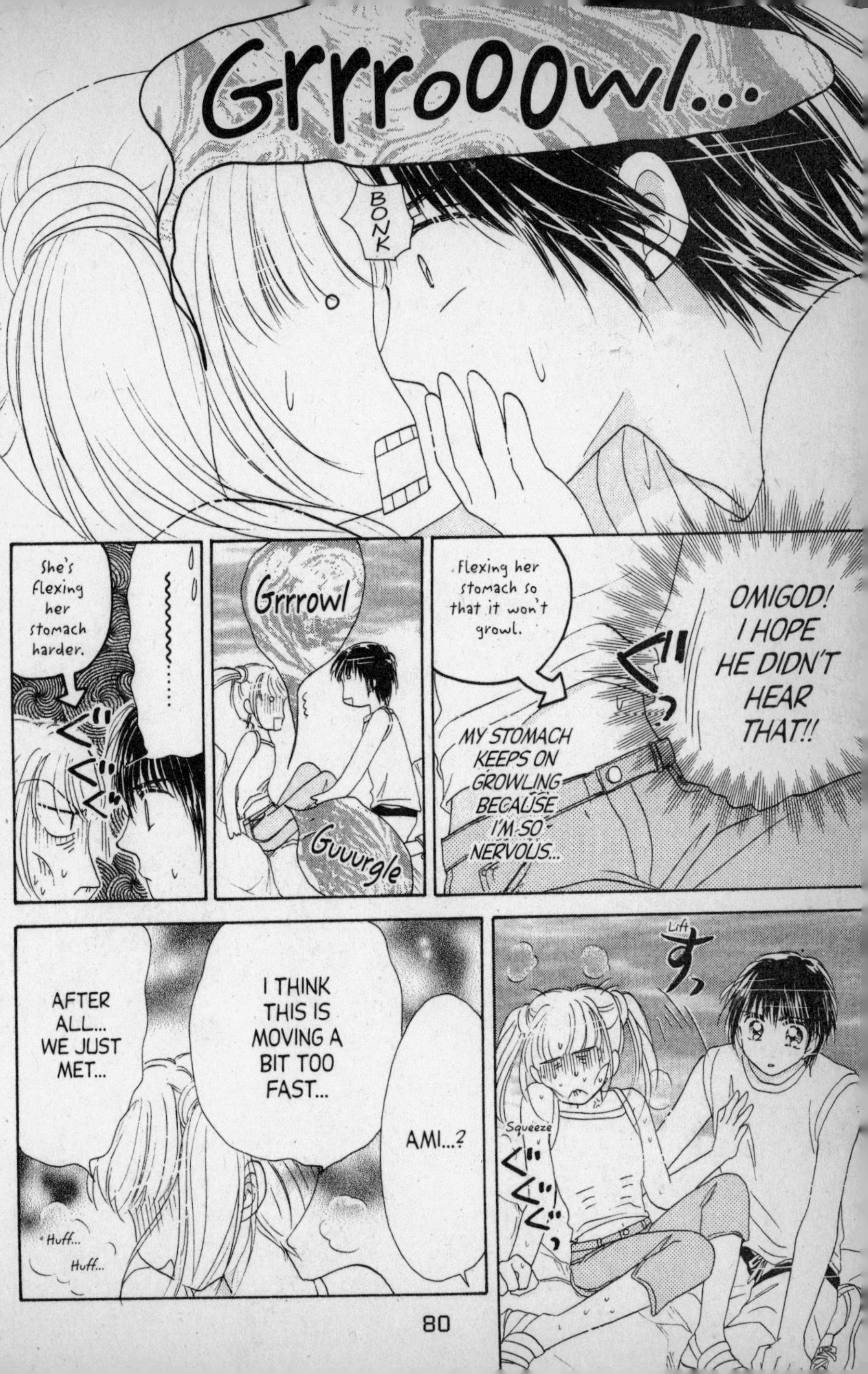
Grrroooowl...
BONK
OMIGOD! I HOPE HE DIDN'T HEAR THAT!!
MY STOMACH KEEPS ON GROWLING BECAUSE I'M SO NERVOUS...
Flexing her stomach so that it won't growl.
Grrrowl
Guuurgle
She's flexing her stomach harder.
Lift
Squeeze
AMI...?
I THINK THIS IS MOVING A BIT TOO FAST...
AFTER ALL... WE JUST MET...
Huff... Huff...

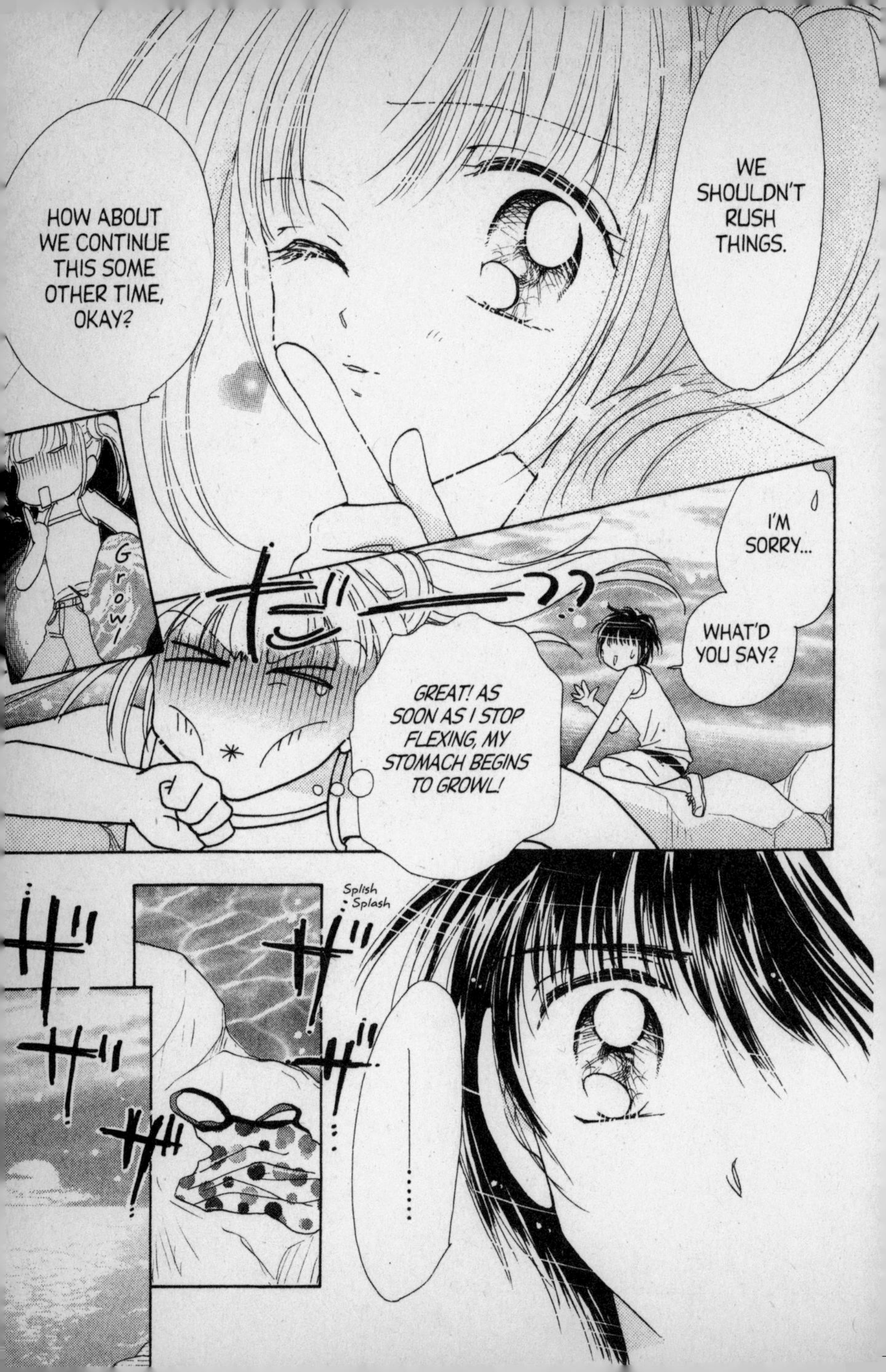
WE SHOULDN'T RUSH THINGS.
HOW ABOUT WE CONTINUE THIS SOME OTHER TIME, OKAY?
I'M SORRY...
WHAT'D YOU SAY?
GREAT! AS SOON AS I STOP FLEXING, MY STOMACH BEGINS TO GROWL!
Growl
Splish Splash
......

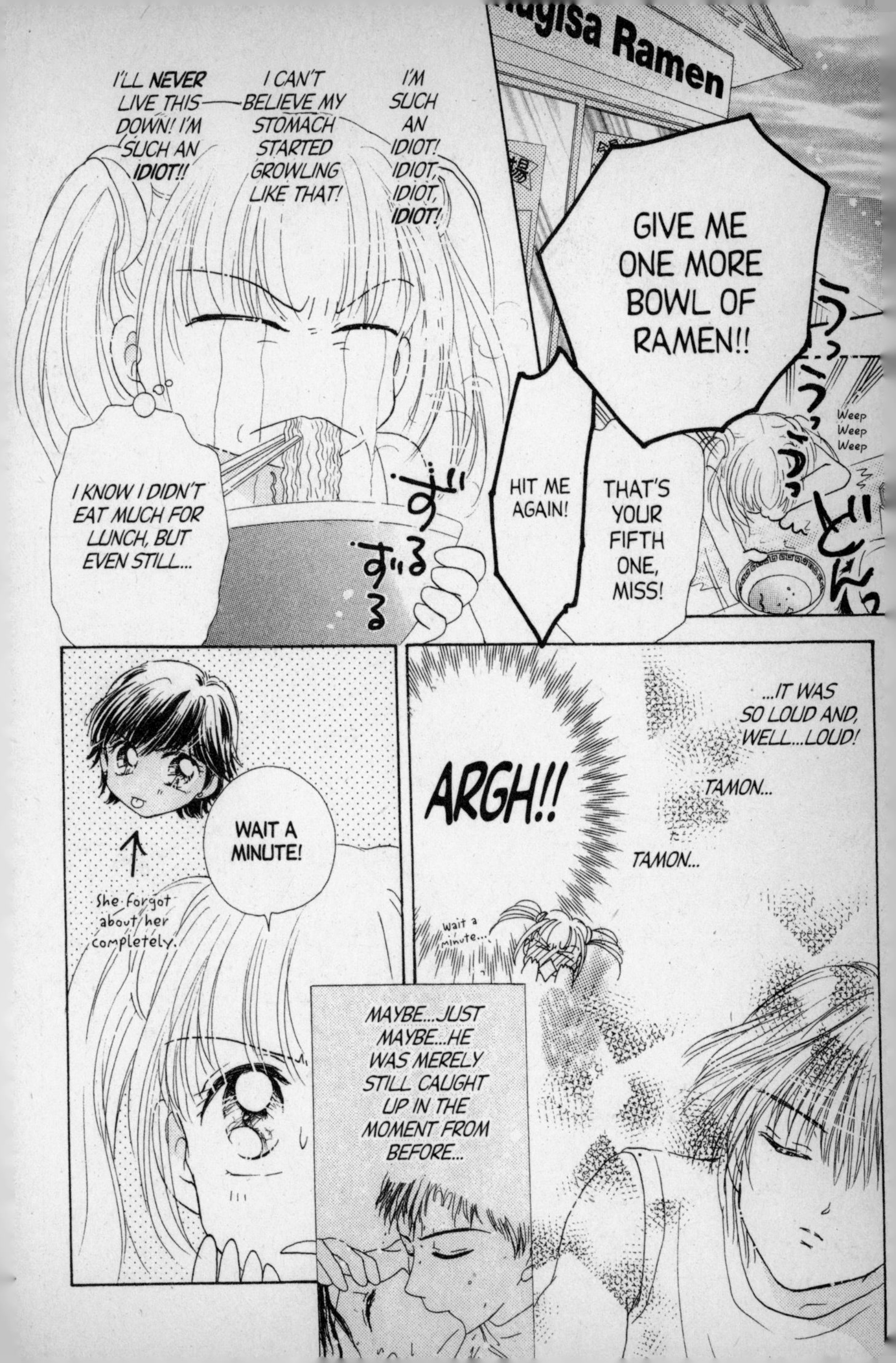
agisa Ramen
GIVE ME ONE MORE BOWL OF RAMEN!!
THAT'S YOUR FIFTH ONE, MISS!
HIT ME AGAIN!
Weep Weep Weep
I'M SUCH AN IDIOT! IDIOT, IDIOT, IDIOT!
I CAN'T BELIEVE MY STOMACH STARTED GROWLING LIKE THAT!
I'LL NEVER LIVE THIS DOWN! I'M SUCH AN IDIOT!!
ずるずる
I KNOW I DIDN'T EAT MUCH FOR LUNCH, BUT EVEN STILL...
...IT WAS SO LOUD AND, WELL...LOUD!
TAMON...
TAMON...
ARGH!!
Wait a minute...
WAIT A MINUTE!
She forgot about her completely.
MAYBE...JUST MAYBE...HE WAS MERELY STILL CAUGHT UP IN THE MOMENT FROM BEFORE...

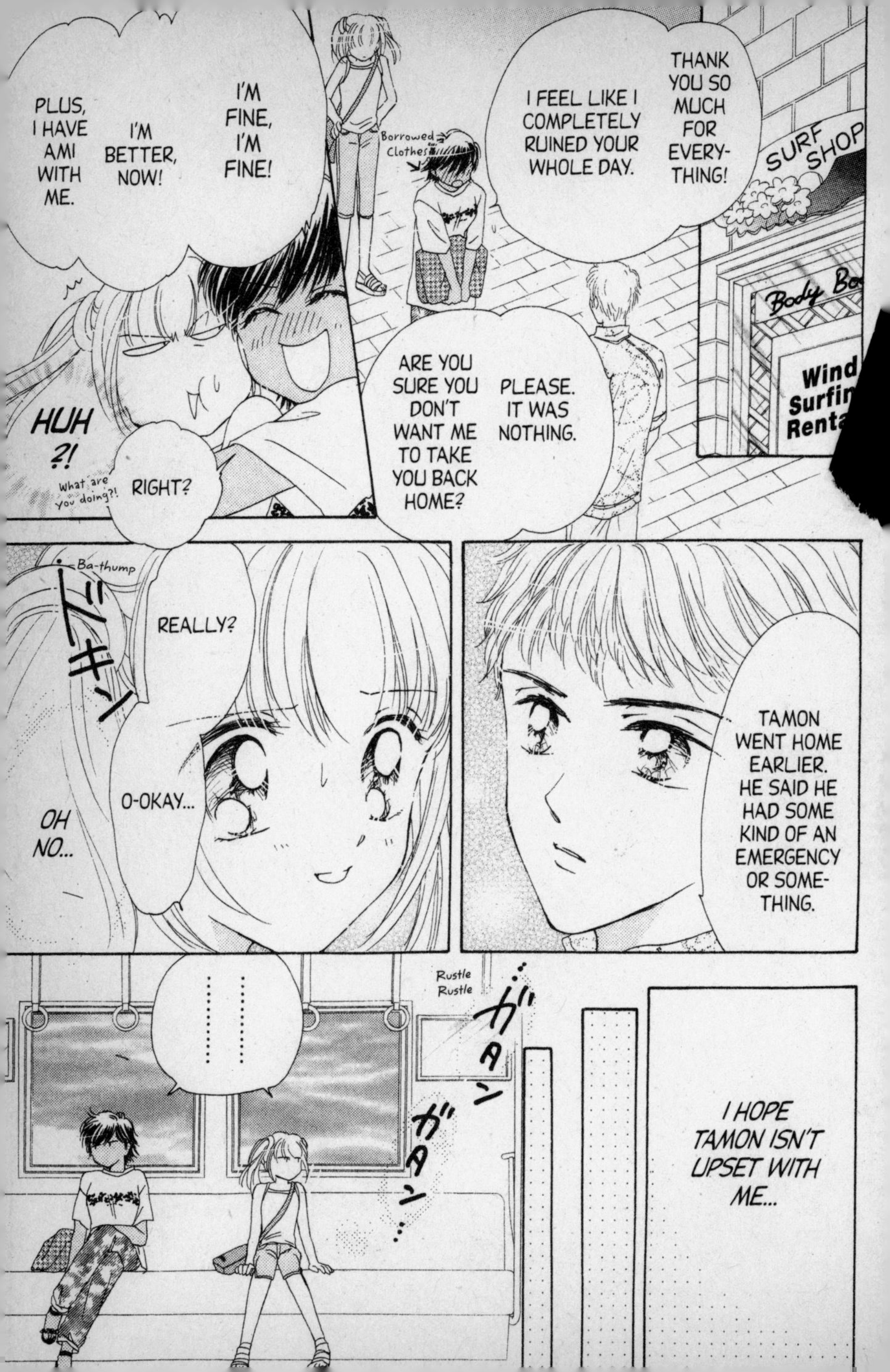
THANK YOU SO MUCH FOR EVERY-THING!
I FEEL LIKE I COMPLETELY RUINED YOUR WHOLE DAY.
Borrowed Clothes
SURF SHOP
PLEASE. IT WAS NOTHING.
ARE YOU SURE YOU DON'T WANT ME TO TAKE YOU BACK HOME?
I'M FINE, I'M FINE!
I'M BETTER, NOW!
PLUS, I HAVE AMI WITH ME.
RIGHT?
HUH ?!
What are you doing?!
TAMON WENT HOME EARLIER. HE SAID HE HAD SOME KIND OF AN EMERGENCY OR SOME-THING.
Ba-thump
REALLY?
O-OKAY...
OH NO...
I HOPE TAMON ISN'T UPSET WITH ME...
Rustle Rustle
ガタン
ガタン
......

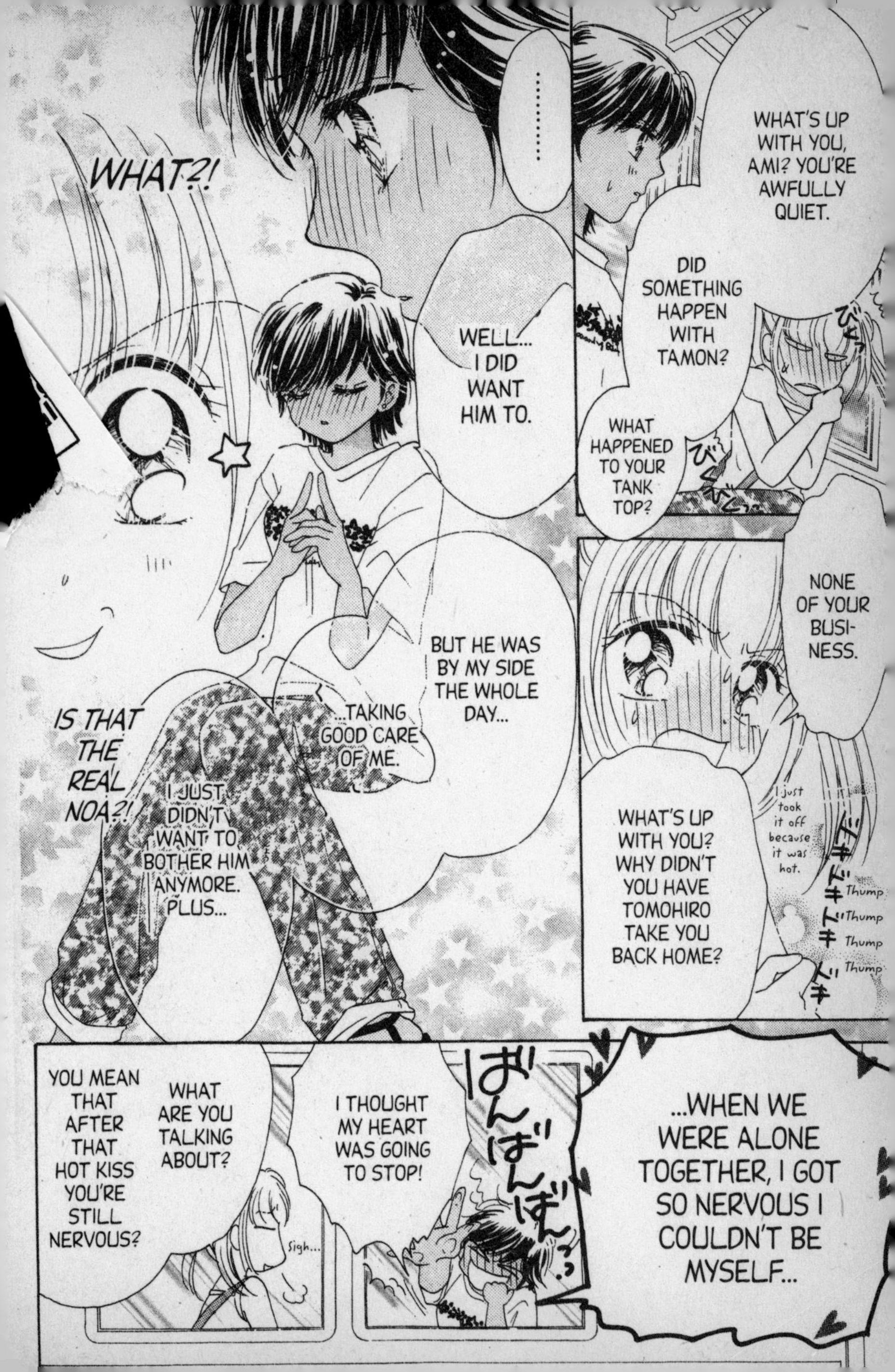
WHAT'S UP WITH YOU, AMI? YOU'RE AWFULLY QUIET.
DID SOMETHING HAPPEN WITH TAMON?
WHAT HAPPENED TO YOUR TANK TOP?
NONE OF YOUR BUSINESS.
I just took it off because it was hot.
Thump Thump Thump Thump
WHAT'S UP WITH YOU? WHY DIDN'T YOU HAVE TOMOHIRO TAKE YOU BACK HOME?
......
WELL... I DID WANT HIM TO.
BUT HE WAS BY MY SIDE THE WHOLE DAY...
...TAKING GOOD CARE OF ME.
I JUST DIDN'T WANT TO BOTHER HIM ANYMORE. PLUS...
WHAT?!
IS THAT THE REAL NOA?!
...WHEN WE WERE ALONE TOGETHER, I GOT SO NERVOUS I COULDN'T BE MYSELF...
I THOUGHT MY HEART WAS GOING TO STOP!
WHAT ARE YOU TALKING ABOUT?
YOU MEAN THAT AFTER THAT HOT KISS YOU'RE STILL NERVOUS?
Sigh...

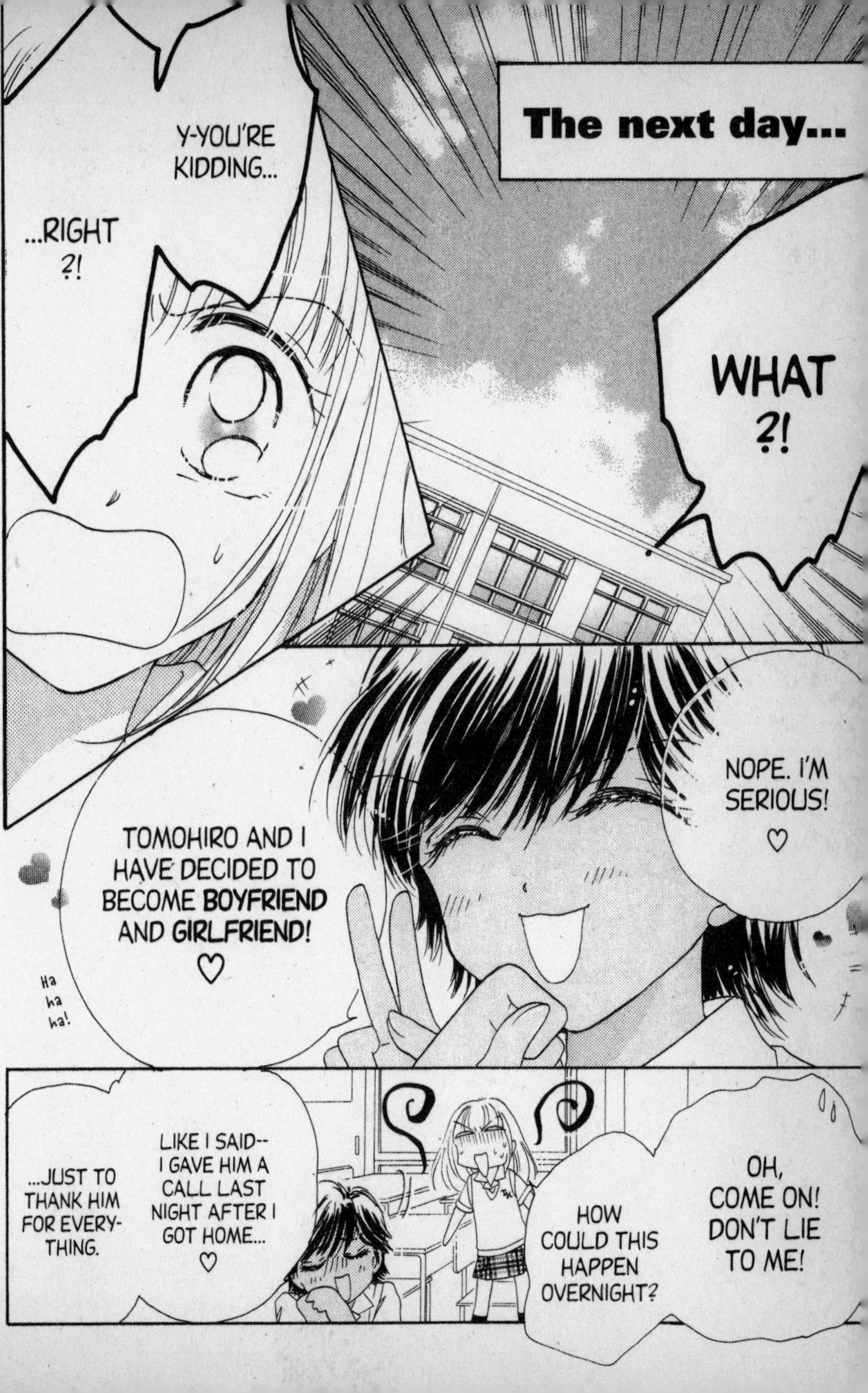
The next day...
WHAT?!
Y-YOU'RE KIDDING... ...RIGHT?!
NOPE. I'M SERIOUS! ♡
TOMOHIRO AND I HAVE DECIDED TO BECOME BOYFRIEND AND GIRLFRIEND! ♡
Ha ha ha!
OH, COME ON! DON'T LIE TO ME!
HOW COULD THIS HAPPEN OVERNIGHT?
LIKE I SAID-- I GAVE HIM A CALL LAST NIGHT AFTER I GOT HOME... ♡
...JUST TO THANK HIM FOR EVERY-THING.

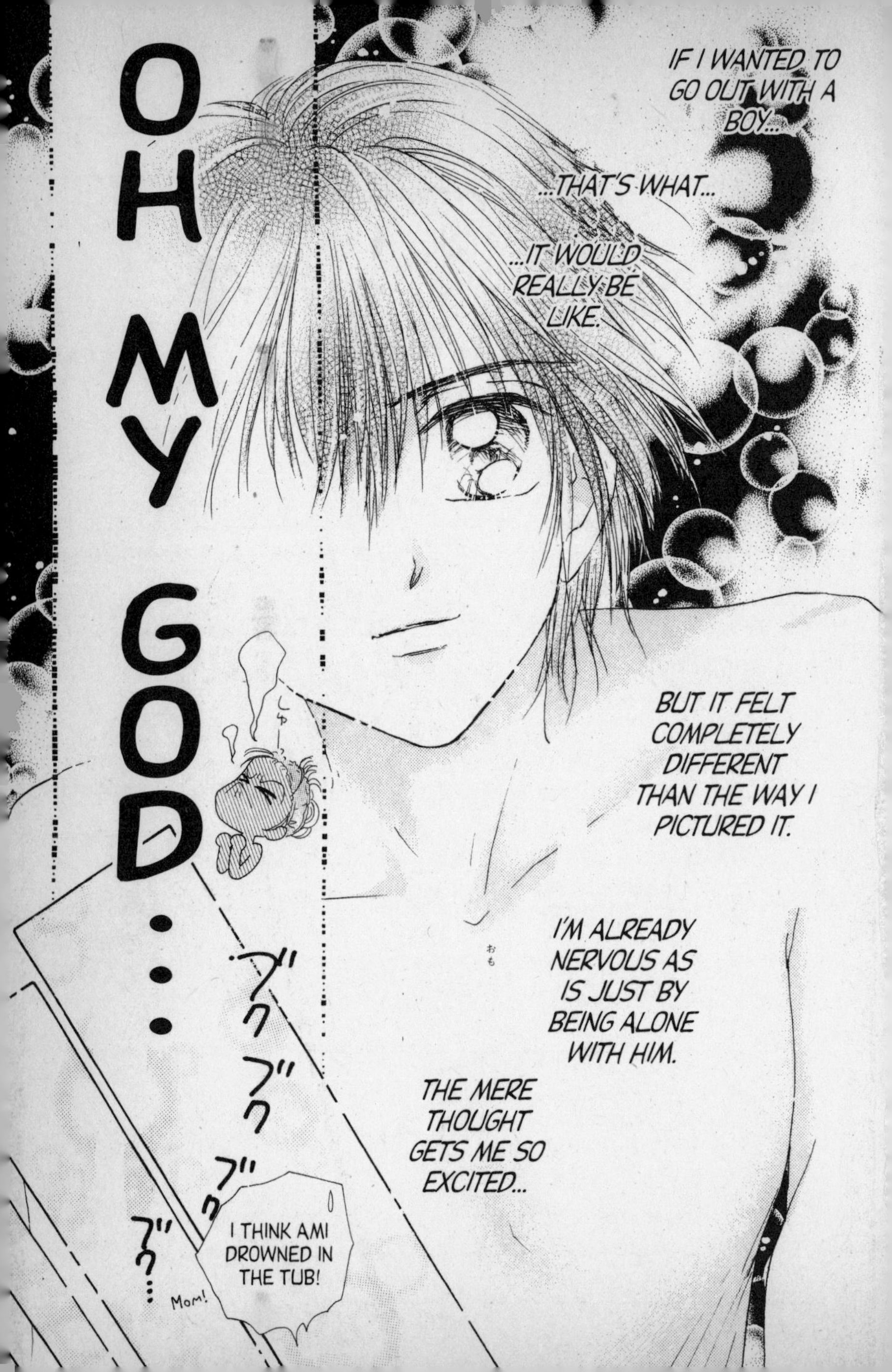
IF I WANTED TO GO OUT WITH A BOY...
...THAT'S WHAT...
...IT WOULD REALLY BE LIKE.
BUT IT FELT COMPLETELY DIFFERENT THAN THE WAY I PICTURED IT.
I'M ALREADY NERVOUS AS IS JUST BY BEING ALONE WITH HIM.
THE MERE THOUGHT GETS ME SO EXCITED...
OH MY GOD...
ブク ブク ブク ブク...
I THINK AMI DROWNED IN THE TUB!
Mom!

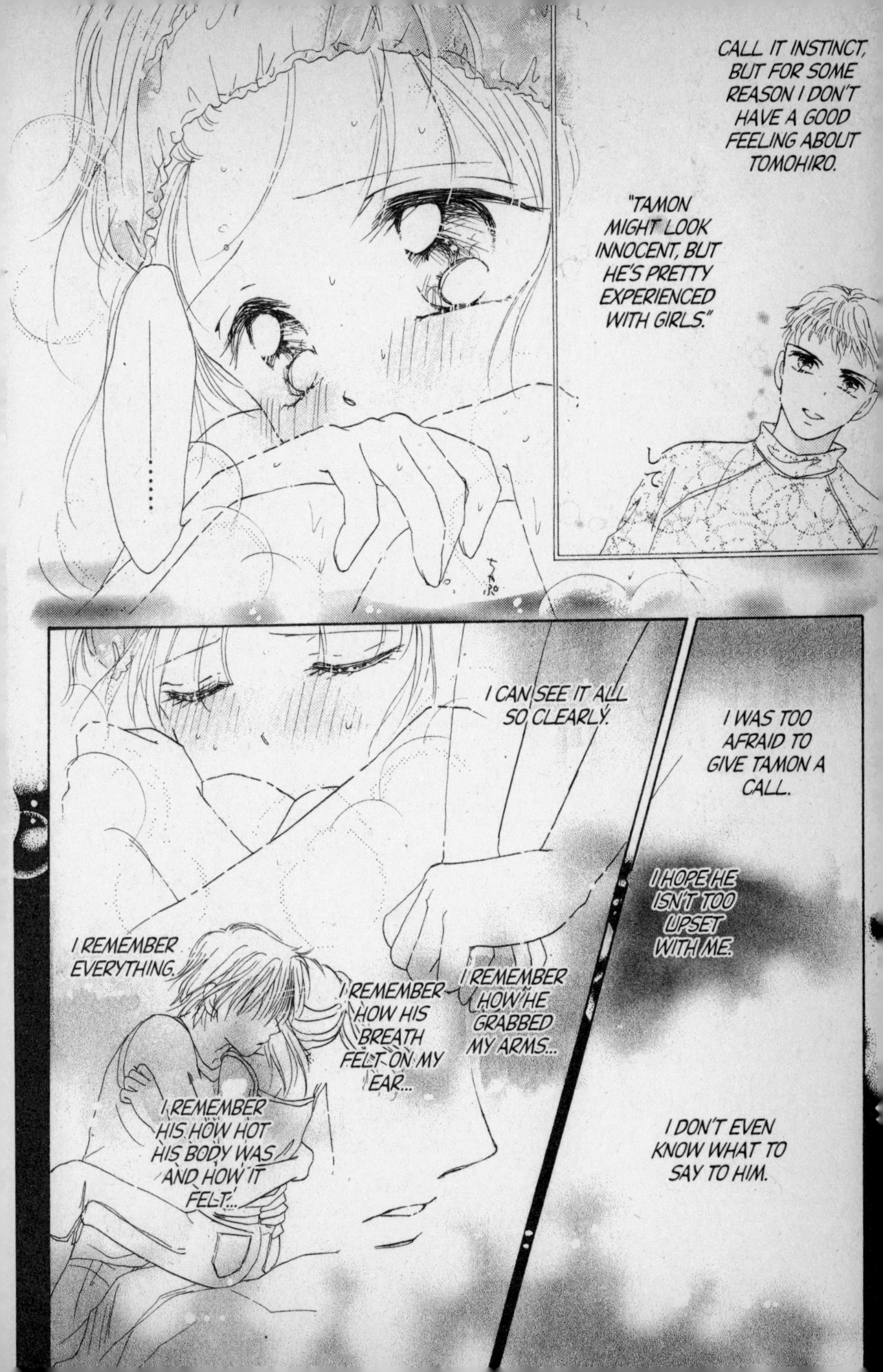
CALL IT INSTINCT, BUT FOR SOME REASON I DON'T HAVE A GOOD FEELING ABOUT TOMOHIRO.
"TAMON MIGHT LOOK INNOCENT, BUT HE'S PRETTY EXPERIENCED WITH GIRLS."
I WAS TOO AFRAID TO GIVE TAMON A CALL.
I HOPE HE ISN'T TOO UPSET WITH ME.
I DON'T EVEN KNOW WHAT TO SAY TO HIM.
I CAN SEE IT ALL SO CLEARLY.
I REMEMBER HOW HE GRABBED MY ARMS...
I REMEMBER HOW HIS BREATH FELT ON MY EAR...
I REMEMBER EVERYTHING.
I REMEMBER HIS HOW HOT HIS BODY WAS AND HOW IT FELT...

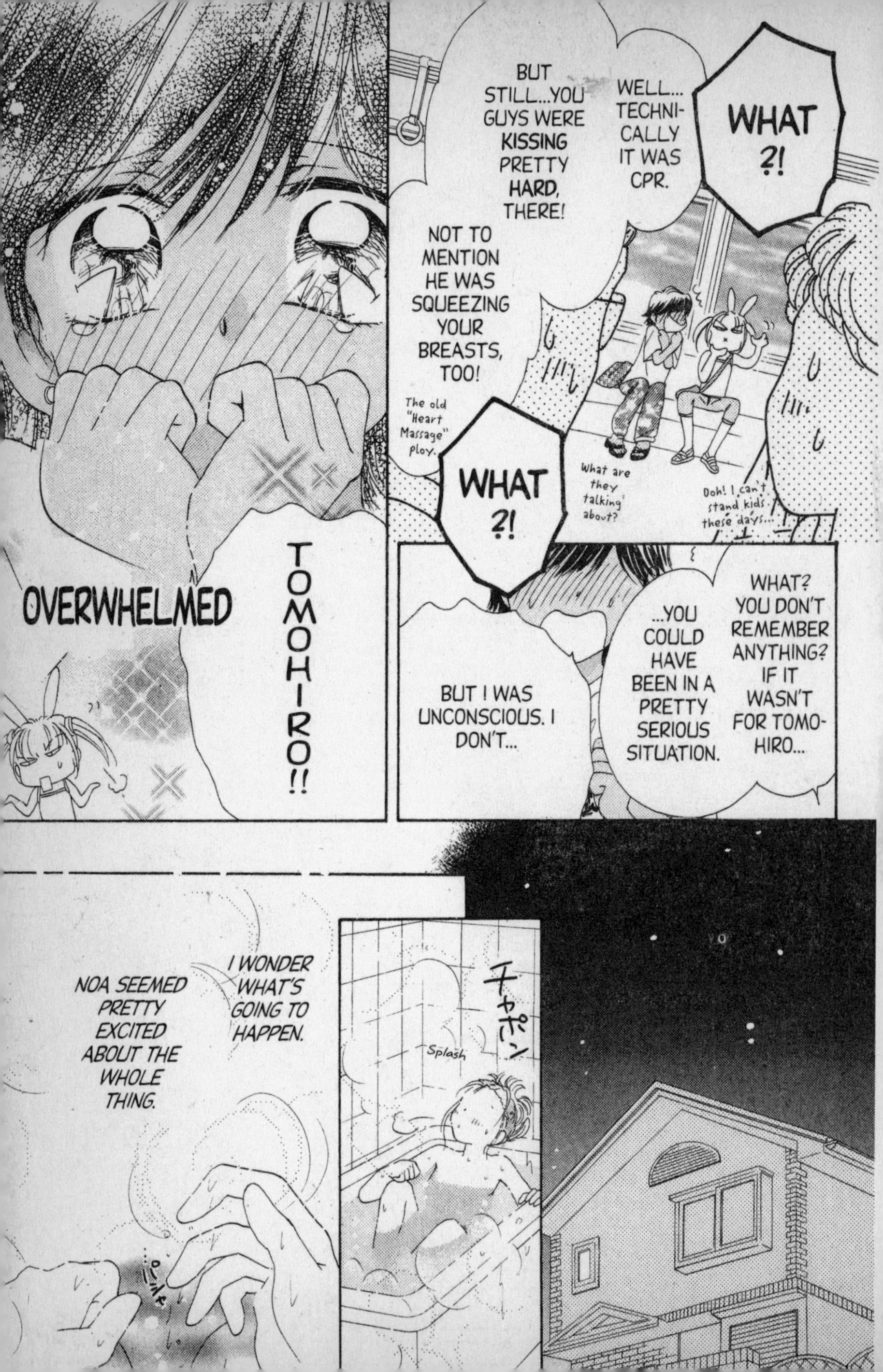
WHAT?!
WELL... TECHNICALLY IT WAS CPR.
BUT STILL...YOU GUYS WERE KISSING PRETTY HARD, THERE!
NOT TO MENTION HE WAS SQUEEZING YOUR BREASTS, TOO!
The old "Heart Massage" ploy.
WHAT?!
What are they talking about?
Ooh! I can't stand kids these days...
WHAT? YOU DON'T REMEMBER ANYTHING? IF IT WASN'T FOR TOMOHIRO...
...YOU COULD HAVE BEEN IN A PRETTY SERIOUS SITUATION.
BUT I WAS UNCONSCIOUS. I DON'T...
TOMOHIRO!!
OVERWHELMED
チャポン
Splash
I WONDER WHAT'S GOING TO HAPPEN.
NOA SEEMED PRETTY EXCITED ABOUT THE WHOLE THING.

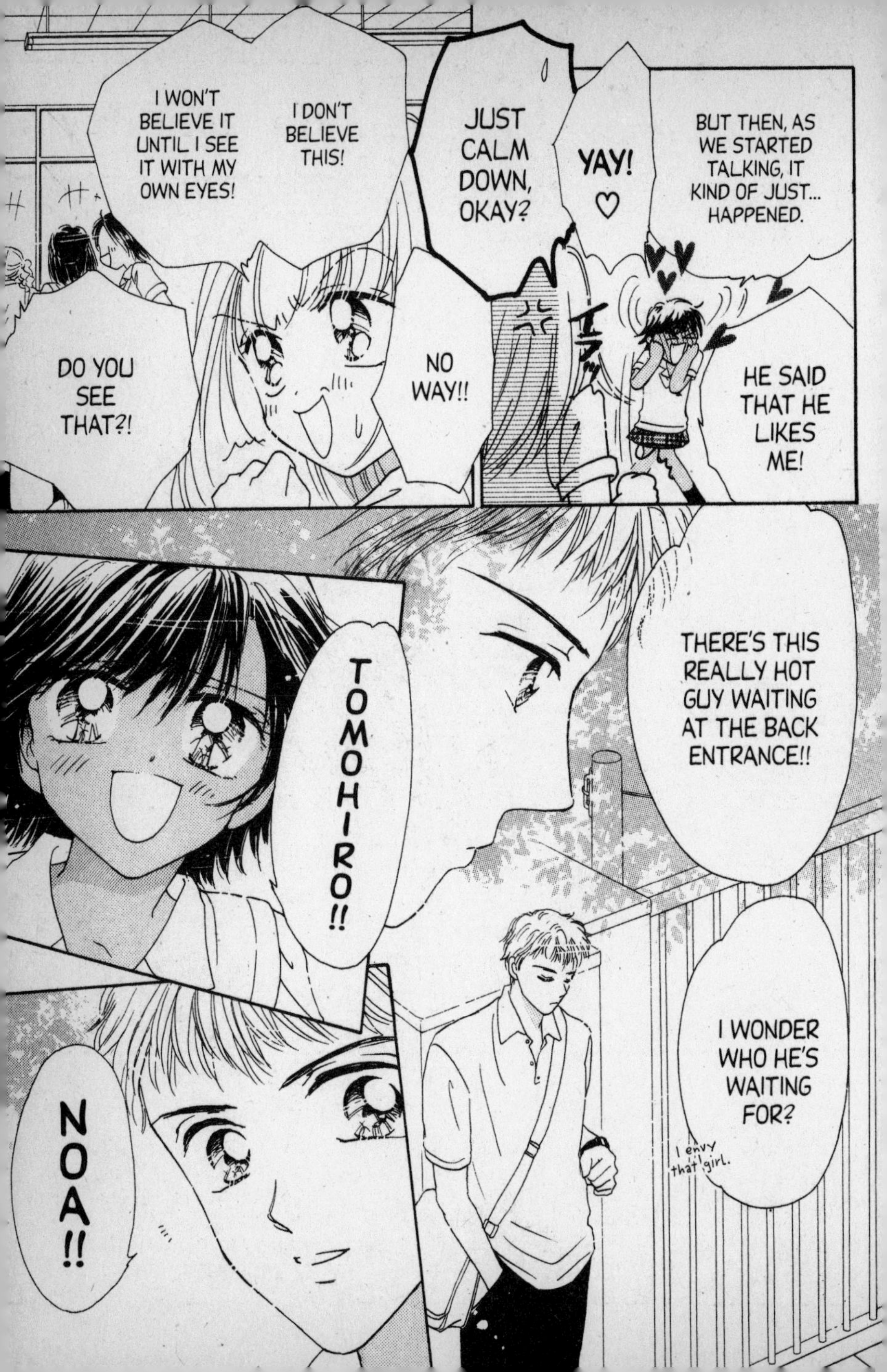
BUT THEN, AS WE STARTED TALKING, IT KIND OF JUST... HAPPENED.
YAY! ♡
HE SAID THAT HE LIKES ME!
JUST CALM DOWN, OKAY?
I DON'T BELIEVE THIS!
I WON'T BELIEVE IT UNTIL I SEE IT WITH MY OWN EYES!
NO WAY!!
DO YOU SEE THAT?!
THERE'S THIS REALLY HOT GUY WAITING AT THE BACK ENTRANCE!!
I WONDER WHO HE'S WAITING FOR?
I envy that girl.
TOMOHIRO!!
NOA!!

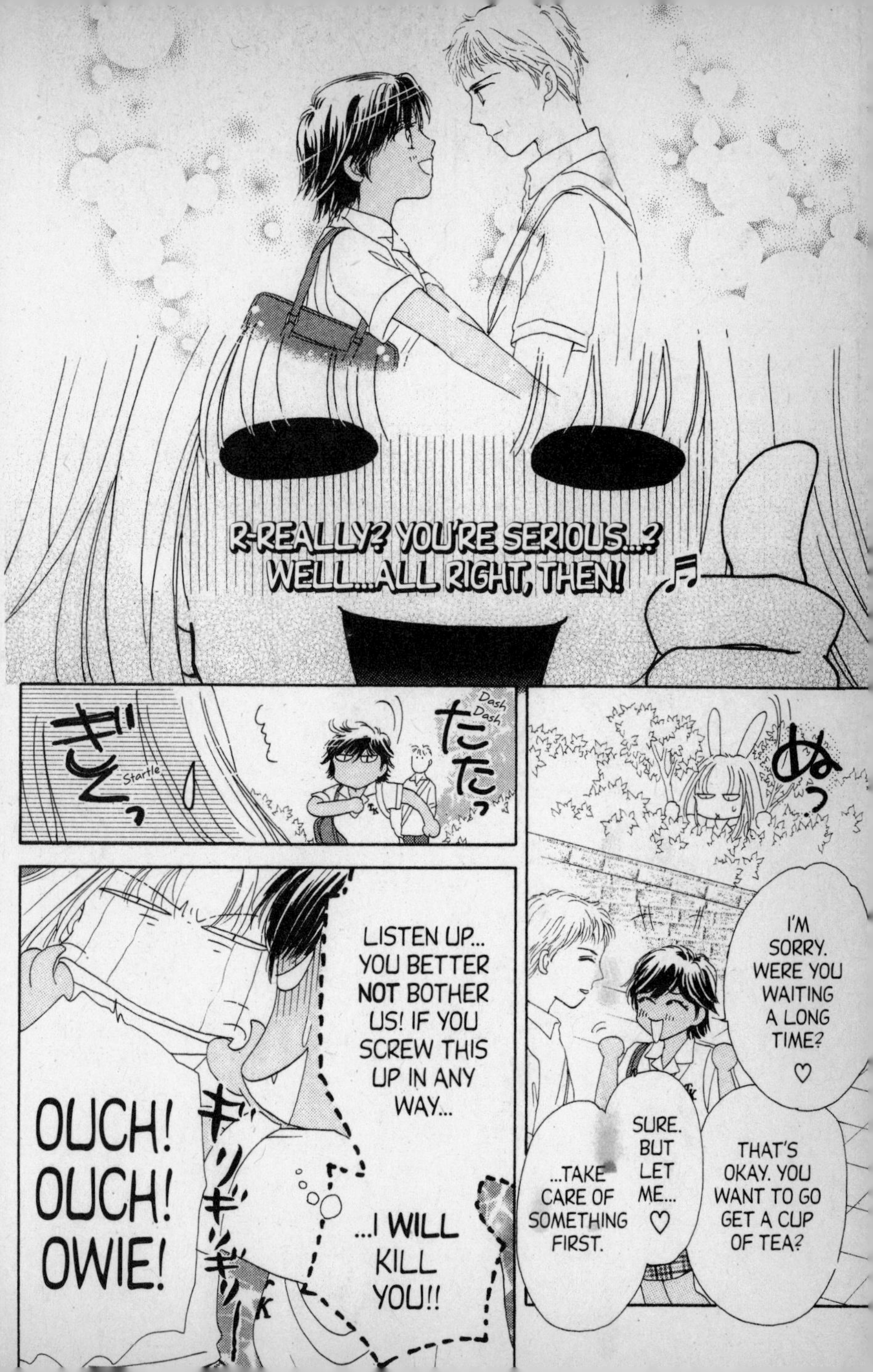
R-REALLY? YOU'RE SERIOUS...? WELL...ALL RIGHT, THEN! ♬
ぬっ
I'M SORRY. WERE YOU WAITING A LONG TIME? ♡
THAT'S OKAY. YOU WANT TO GO GET A CUP OF TEA?
SURE. BUT LET ME... ♡
...TAKE CARE OF SOMETHING FIRST.
たたっ
Dash Dash
ぎくっ
Startle
LISTEN UP... YOU BETTER NOT BOTHER US! IF YOU SCREW THIS UP IN ANY WAY...
...I WILL KILL YOU!!
ギリギリ
OUCH! OUCH! OWIE!

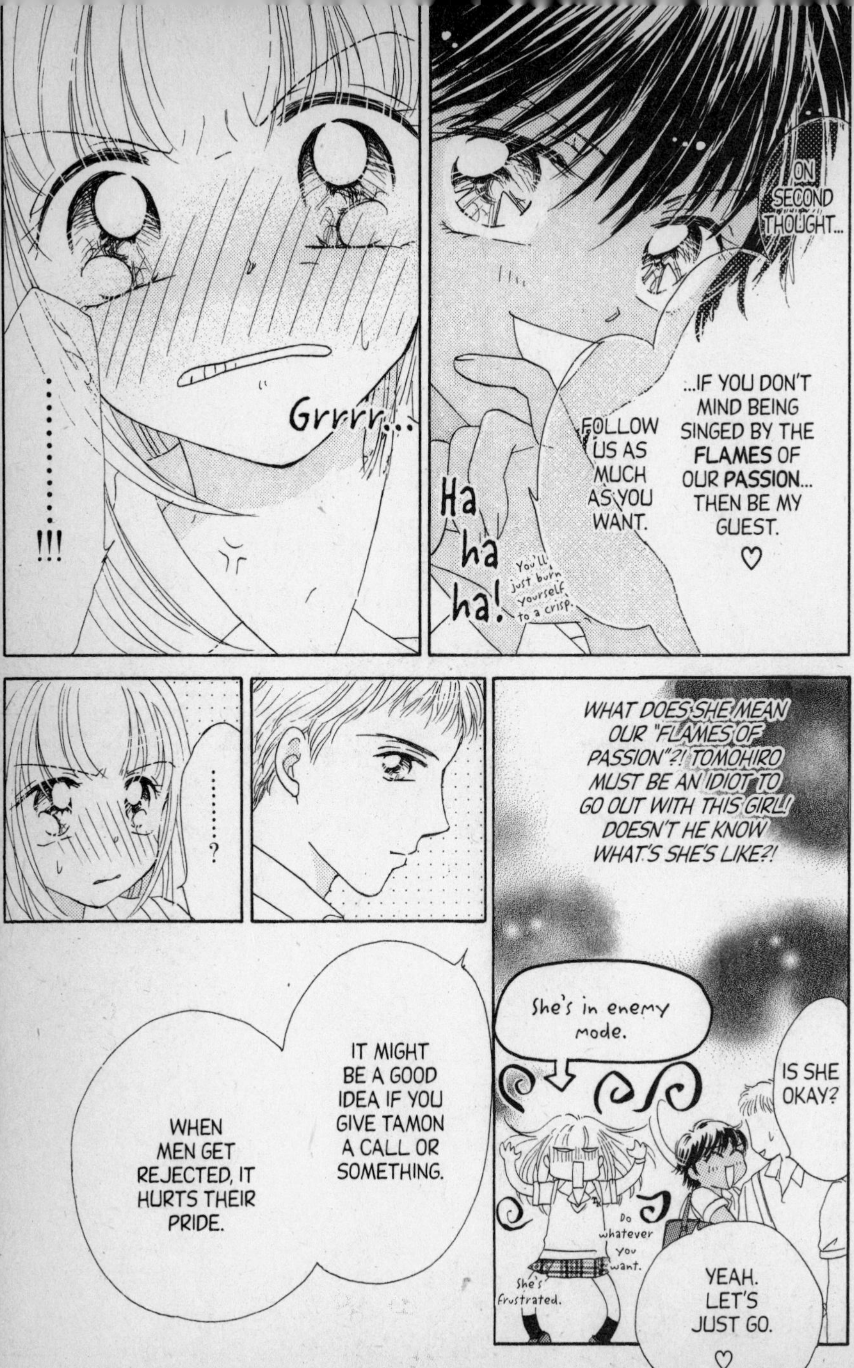
ON SECOND THOUGHT...
...IF YOU DON'T MIND BEING SINGED BY THE **FLAMES** OF OUR **PASSION**... THEN BE MY GUEST. ♡
FOLLOW US AS MUCH AS YOU WANT.
Ha ha ha!
You'll just burn yourself to a crisp.
Grrrr...
.......!!!
WHAT DOES SHE MEAN OUR "FLAMES OF PASSION"?! TOMOHIRO MUST BE AN IDIOT TO GO OUT WITH THIS GIRL! DOESN'T HE KNOW WHAT'S SHE'S LIKE?!
She's in enemy mode.
IS SHE OKAY?
Do whatever you want.
She's frustrated.
YEAH. LET'S JUST GO. ♡
.......?
IT MIGHT BE A GOOD IDEA IF YOU GIVE TAMON A CALL OR SOMETHING.
WHEN MEN GET REJECTED, IT HURTS THEIR PRIDE.

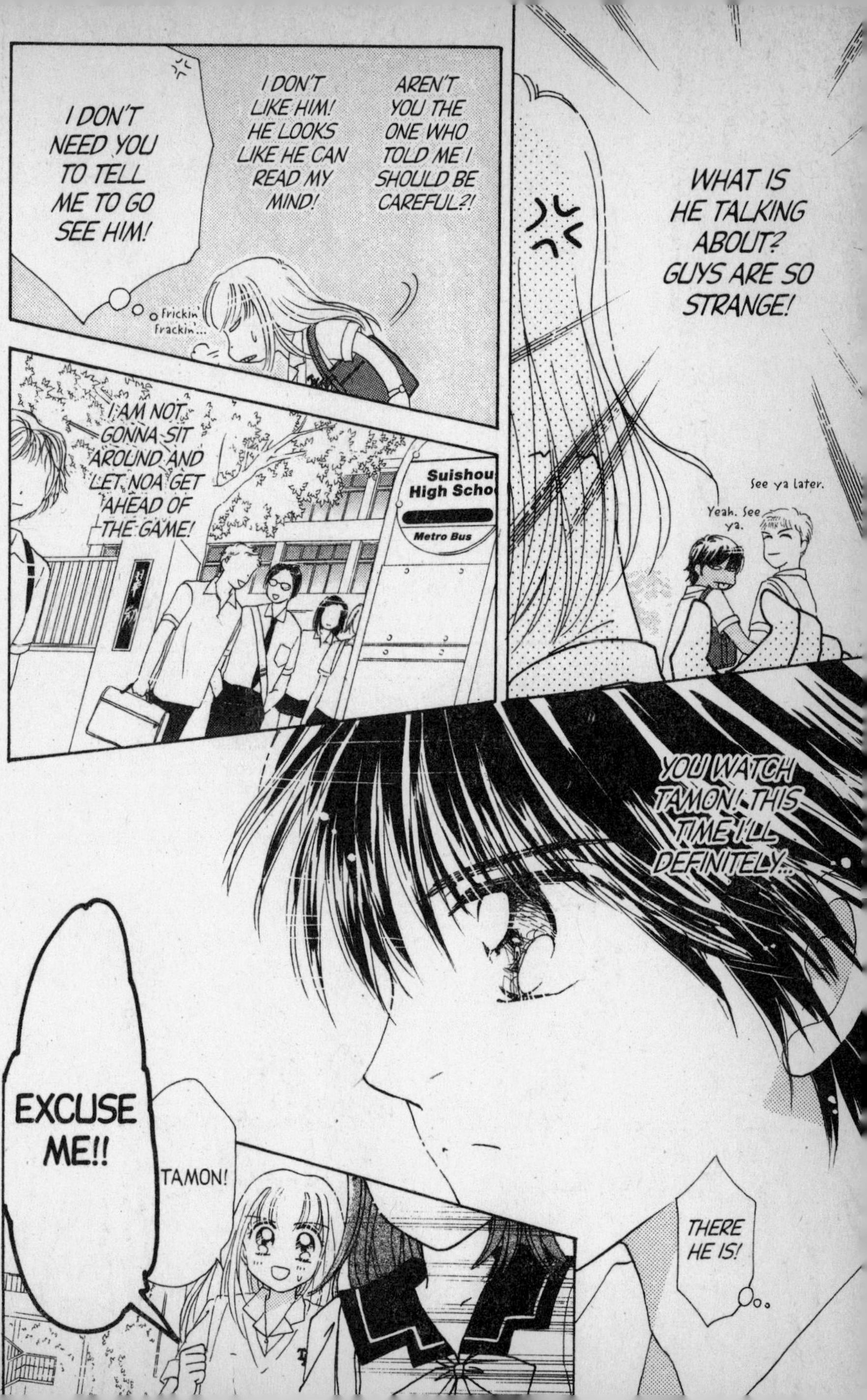
WHAT IS HE TALKING ABOUT? GUYS ARE SO STRANGE!
See ya later.
Yeah. See ya.
AREN'T YOU THE ONE WHO TOLD ME I SHOULD BE CAREFUL?!
I DON'T LIKE HIM! HE LOOKS LIKE HE CAN READ MY MIND!
I DON'T NEED YOU TO TELL ME TO GO SEE HIM!
Frickin' Frackin'...
Suishou High Schoo
Metro Bus
I AM NOT GONNA SIT AROUND AND LET NOA GET AHEAD OF THE GAME!
YOU WATCH TAMON! THIS TIME I'LL DEFINITELY...
THERE HE IS!
TAMON!
EXCUSE ME!!

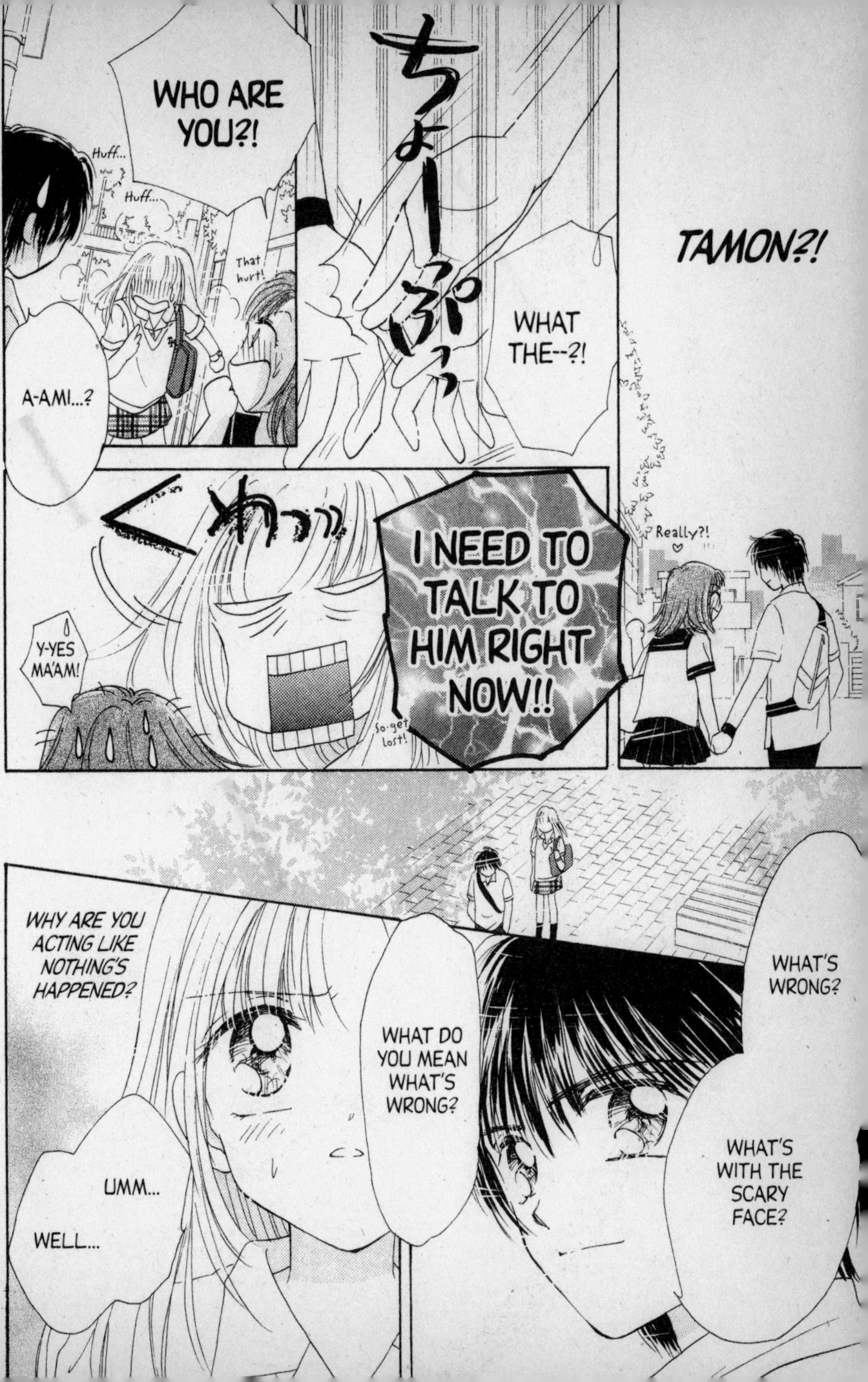
TAMON?!
Really?!
ちょーっぷっ
WHAT THE--?!
WHO ARE YOU?!
Huff...
Huff...
That hurt!
A-AMI...?
I NEED TO TALK TO HIM RIGHT NOW!!
So get lost!
くわっっ
Y-YES MA'AM!
WHAT'S WRONG?
WHAT'S WITH THE SCARY FACE?
WHAT DO YOU MEAN WHAT'S WRONG?
WHY ARE YOU ACTING LIKE NOTHING'S HAPPENED?
UMM...
WELL...

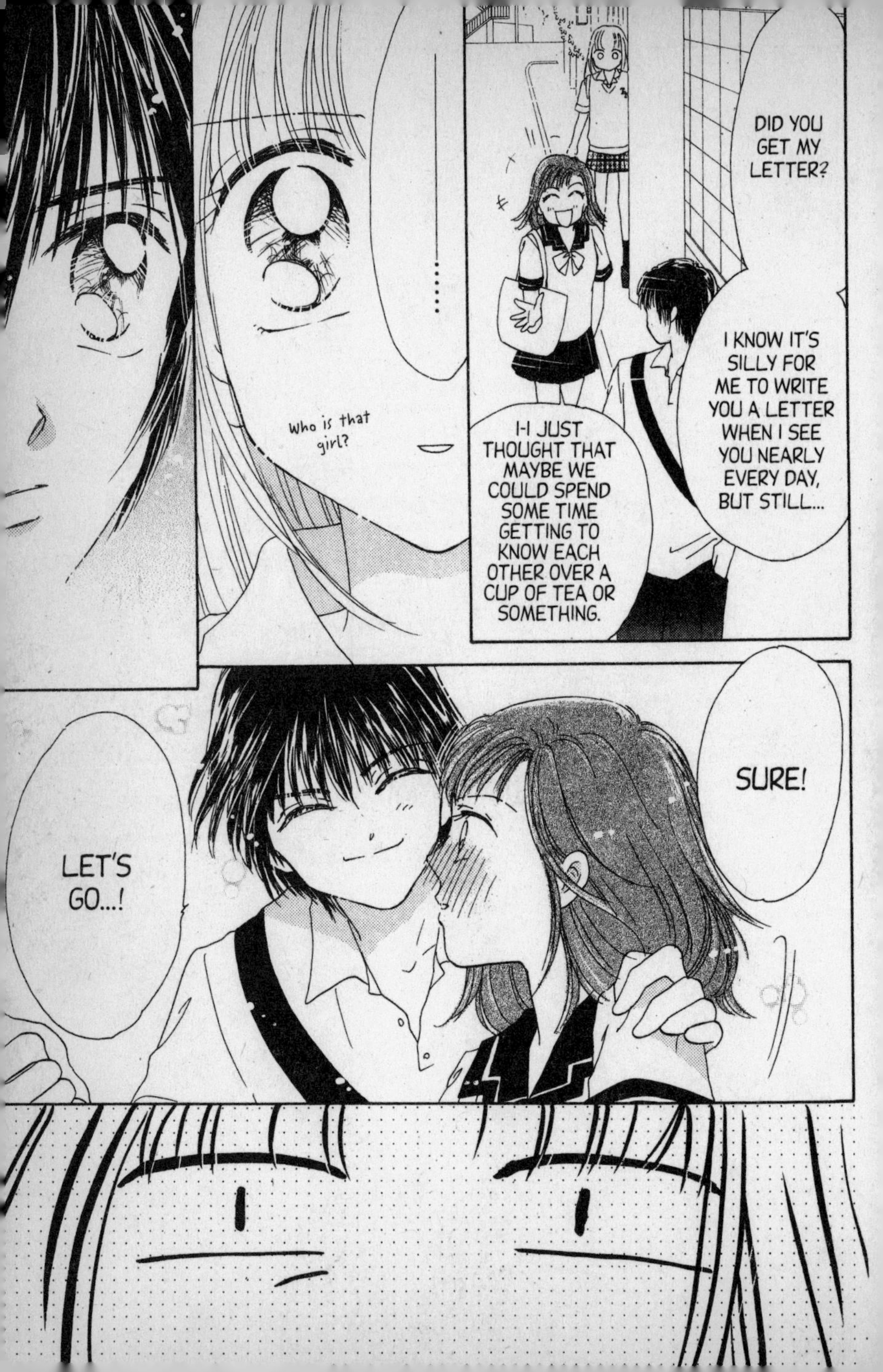
DID YOU GET MY LETTER?
I KNOW IT'S SILLY FOR ME TO WRITE YOU A LETTER WHEN I SEE YOU NEARLY EVERY DAY, BUT STILL...
I-I JUST THOUGHT THAT MAYBE WE COULD SPEND SOME TIME GETTING TO KNOW EACH OTHER OVER A CUP OF TEA OR SOMETHING.
......
Who is that girl?
SURE!
LET'S GO...!

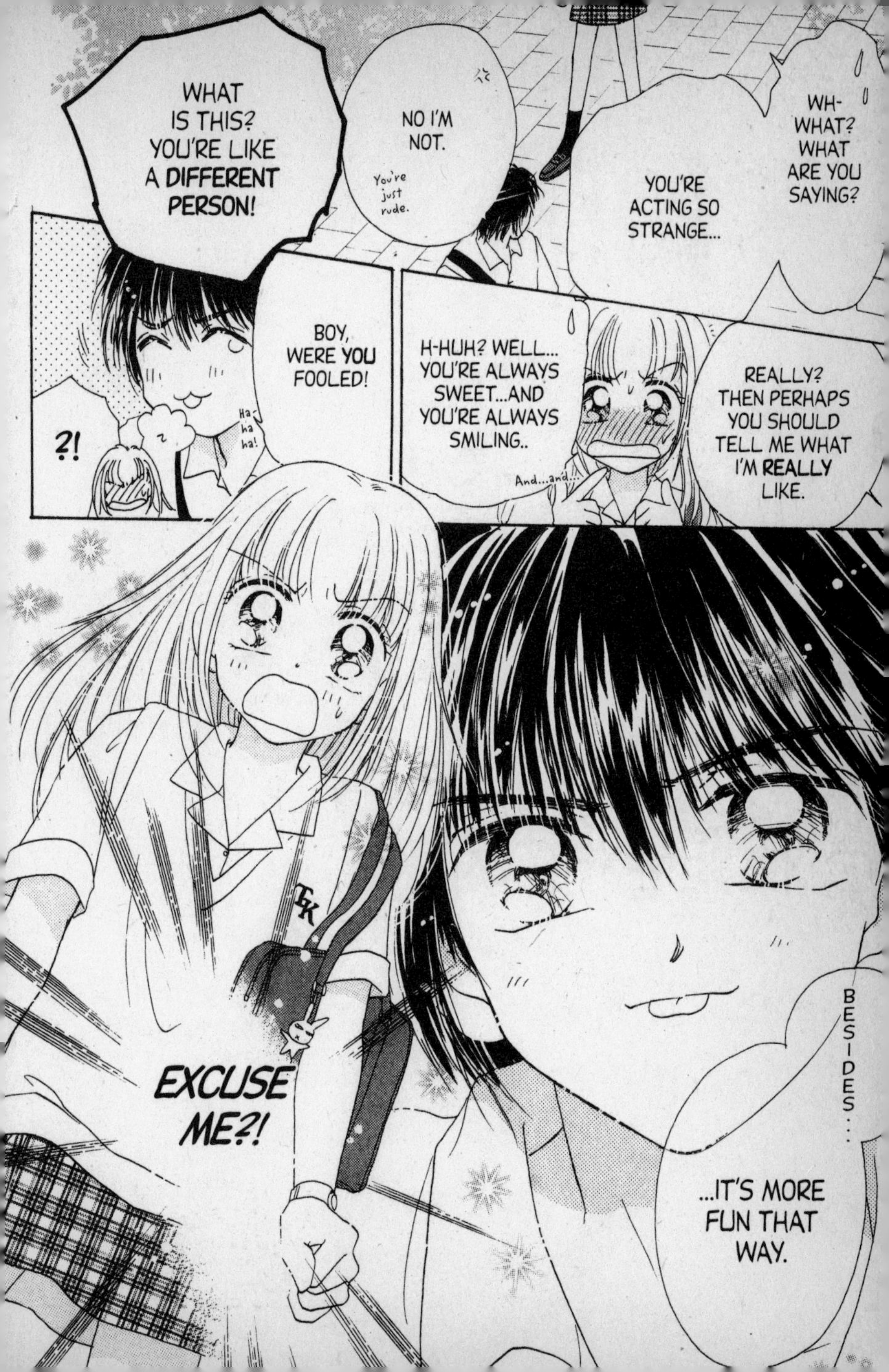
WH- WHAT? WHAT ARE YOU SAYING?
YOU'RE ACTING SO STRANGE...
NO I'M NOT.
You're just rude.
WHAT IS THIS? YOU'RE LIKE A DIFFERENT PERSON!
REALLY? THEN PERHAPS YOU SHOULD TELL ME WHAT I'M REALLY LIKE.
H-HUH? WELL... YOU'RE ALWAYS SWEET...AND YOU'RE ALWAYS SMILING..
And...and...
BOY, WERE YOU FOOLED!
Ha ha ha!
?!
BESIDES...
...IT'S MORE FUN THAT WAY.
EXCUSE ME?!

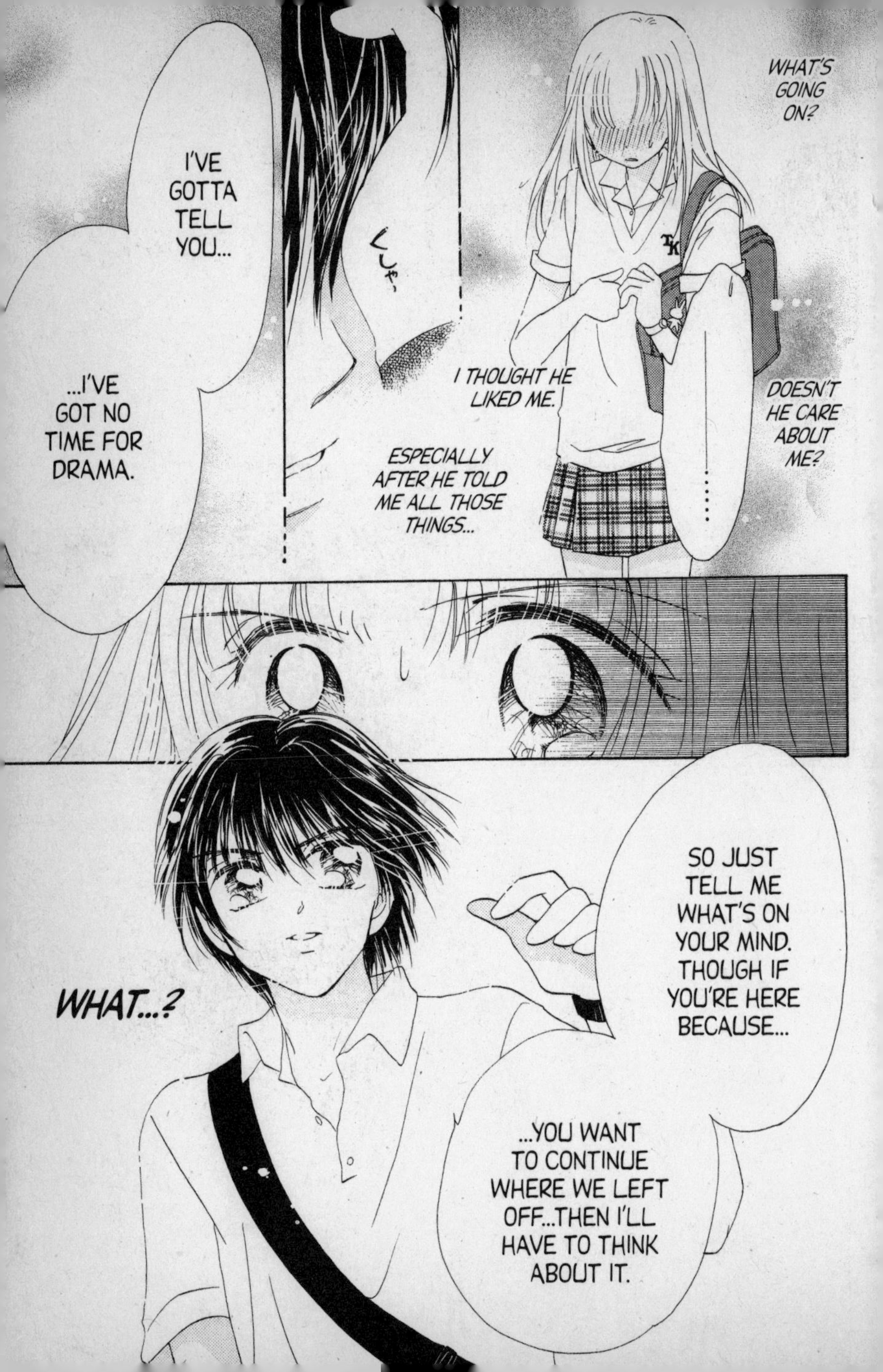
WHAT'S GOING ON?
DOESN'T HE CARE ABOUT ME?
I THOUGHT HE LIKED ME.
ESPECIALLY AFTER HE TOLD ME ALL THOSE THINGS...
くしゃ
I'VE GOTTA TELL YOU...
...I'VE GOT NO TIME FOR DRAMA.
SO JUST TELL ME WHAT'S ON YOUR MIND. THOUGH IF YOU'RE HERE BECAUSE...
...YOU WANT TO CONTINUE WHERE WE LEFT OFF...THEN I'LL HAVE TO THINK ABOUT IT.
WHAT...?

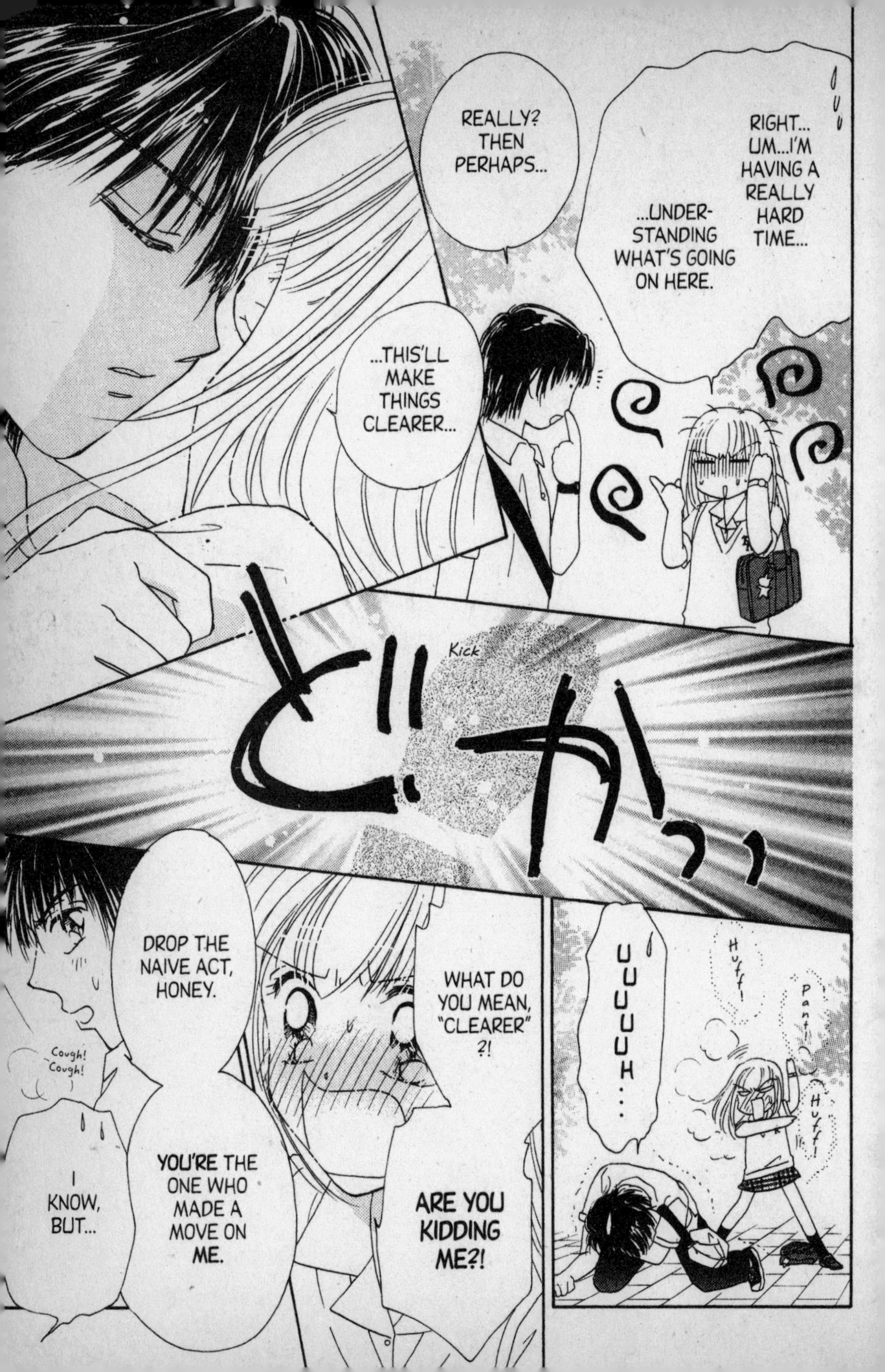
RIGHT... UM...I'M HAVING A REALLY HARD TIME...
...UNDER-STANDING WHAT'S GOING ON HERE.
REALLY? THEN PERHAPS...
...THIS'LL MAKE THINGS CLEARER...
どかっ
Kick
UUUUUH...
Huff!
Pant!
Huff!
WHAT DO YOU MEAN, "CLEARER"?!
ARE YOU KIDDING ME?!
DROP THE NAIVE ACT, HONEY.
YOU'RE THE ONE WHO MADE A MOVE ON ME.
Cough! Cough!
I KNOW, BUT...

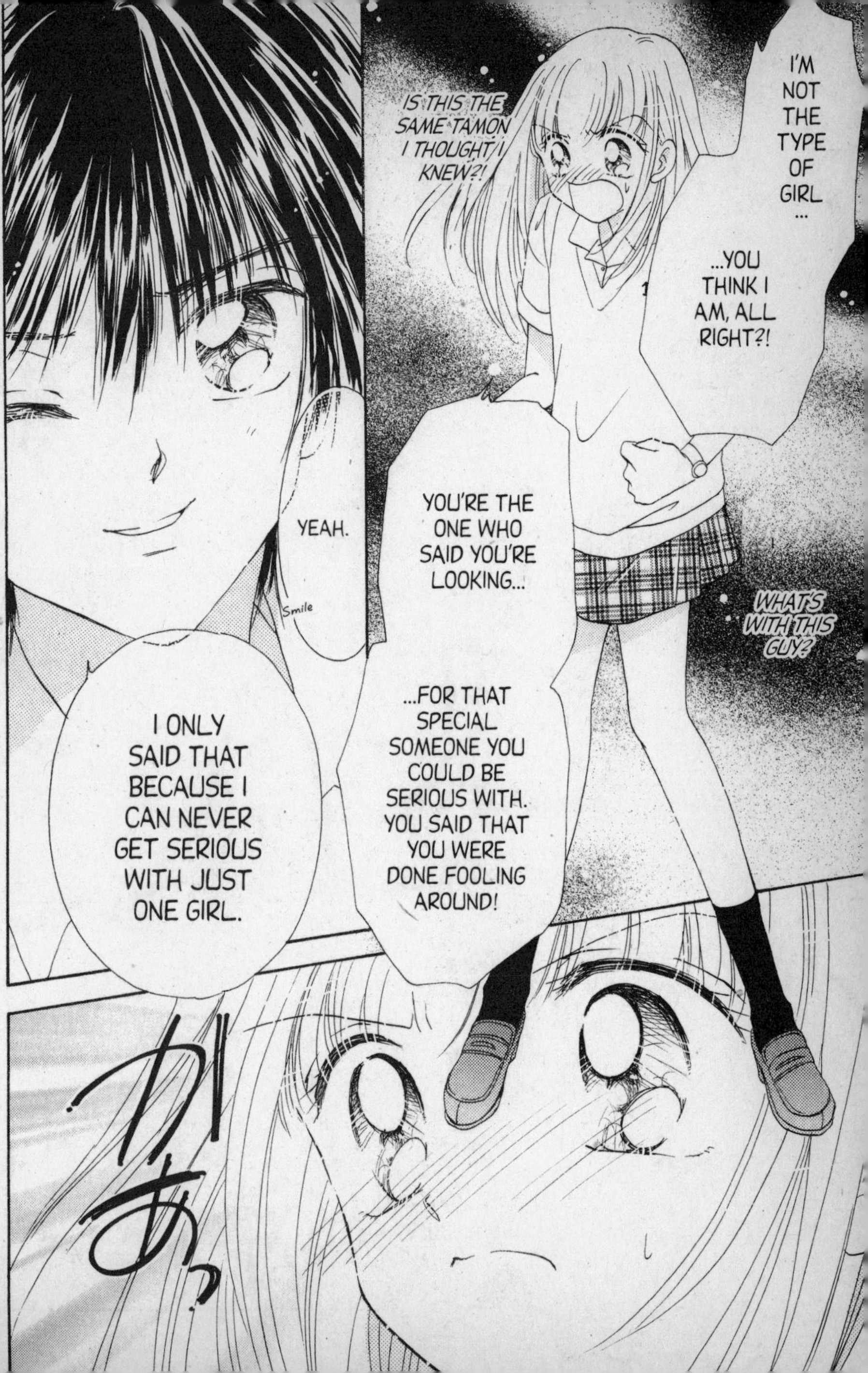
I'M NOT THE TYPE OF GIRL ...
IS THIS THE SAME TAMON I THOUGHT I KNEW?!
...YOU THINK I AM, ALL RIGHT?!
WHAT'S WITH THIS GUY?
YOU'RE THE ONE WHO SAID YOU'RE LOOKING...
...FOR THAT SPECIAL SOMEONE YOU COULD BE SERIOUS WITH. YOU SAID THAT YOU WERE DONE FOOLING AROUND!
YEAH.
Smile
I ONLY SAID THAT BECAUSE I CAN NEVER GET SERIOUS WITH JUST ONE GIRL.
かあっ

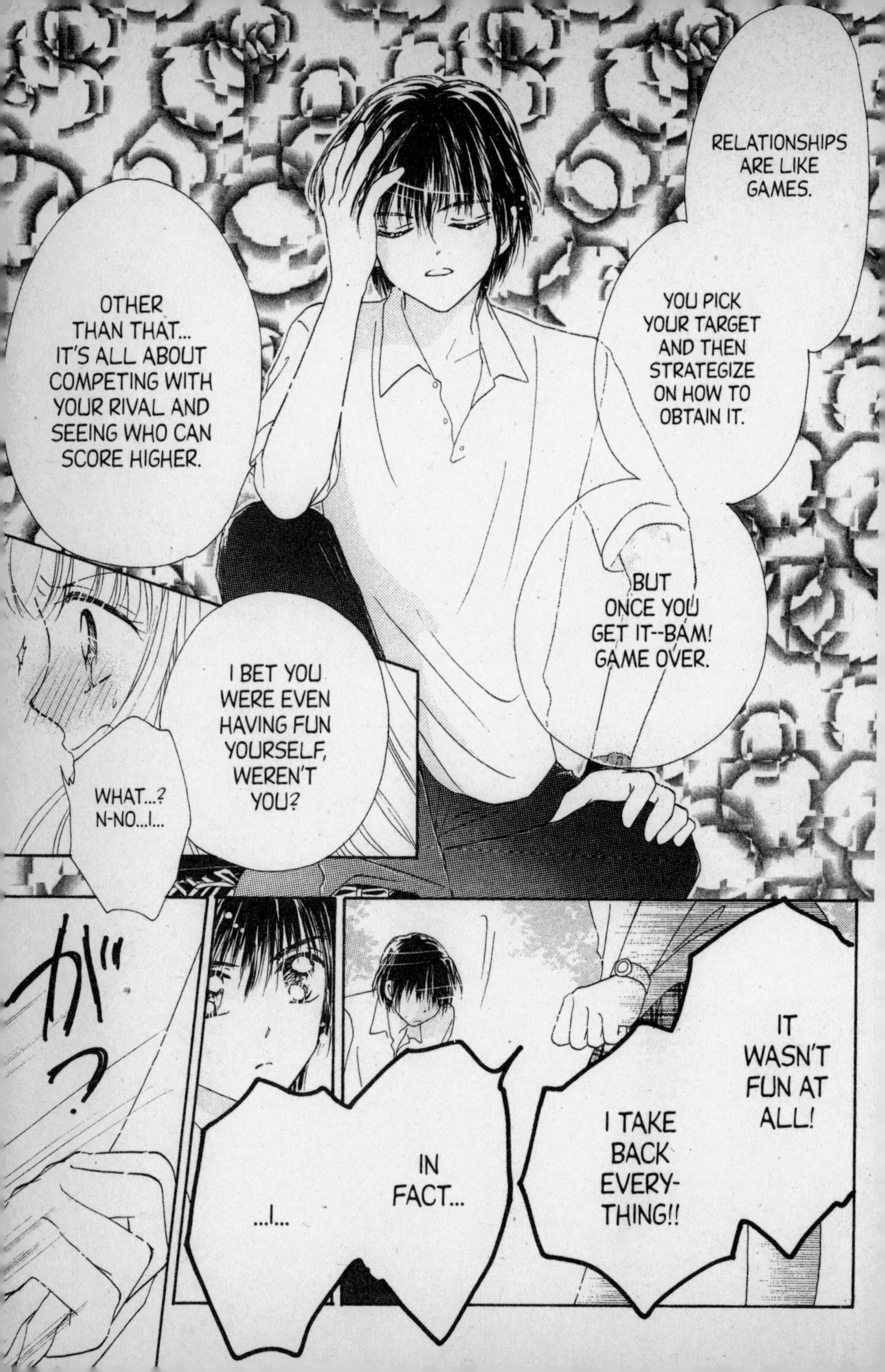
RELATIONSHIPS ARE LIKE GAMES.
YOU PICK YOUR TARGET AND THEN STRATEGIZE ON HOW TO OBTAIN IT.
BUT ONCE YOU GET IT--BAM! GAME OVER.
OTHER THAN THAT... IT'S ALL ABOUT COMPETING WITH YOUR RIVAL AND SEEING WHO CAN SCORE HIGHER.
I BET YOU WERE EVEN HAVING FUN YOURSELF, WEREN'T YOU?
WHAT...? N-NO...I...
IT WASN'T FUN AT ALL!
I TAKE BACK EVERY-THING!!
IN FACT...
...I...
がっ

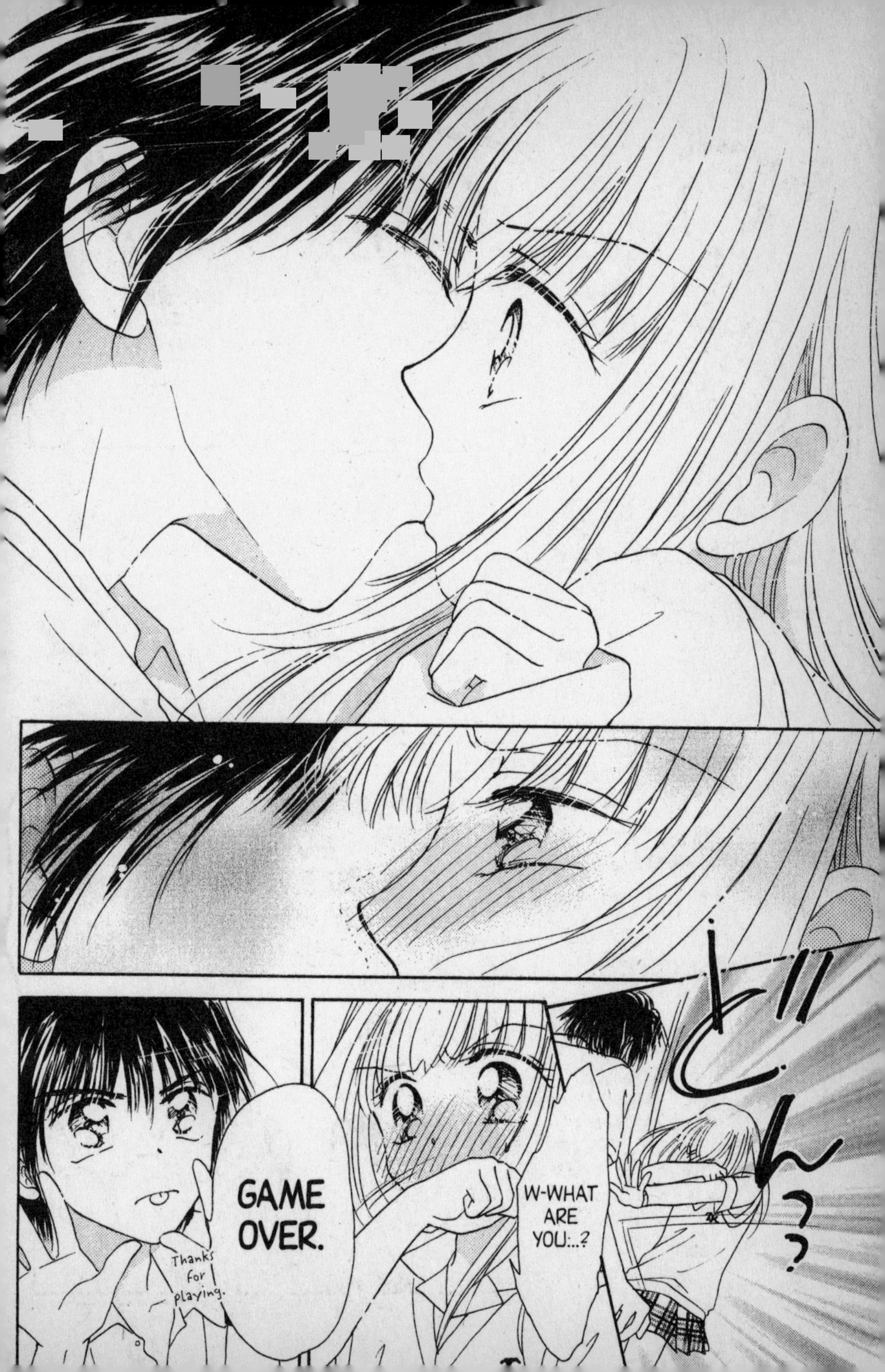
どん??
W-WHAT ARE YOU...?
GAME OVER.
Thanks for playing.

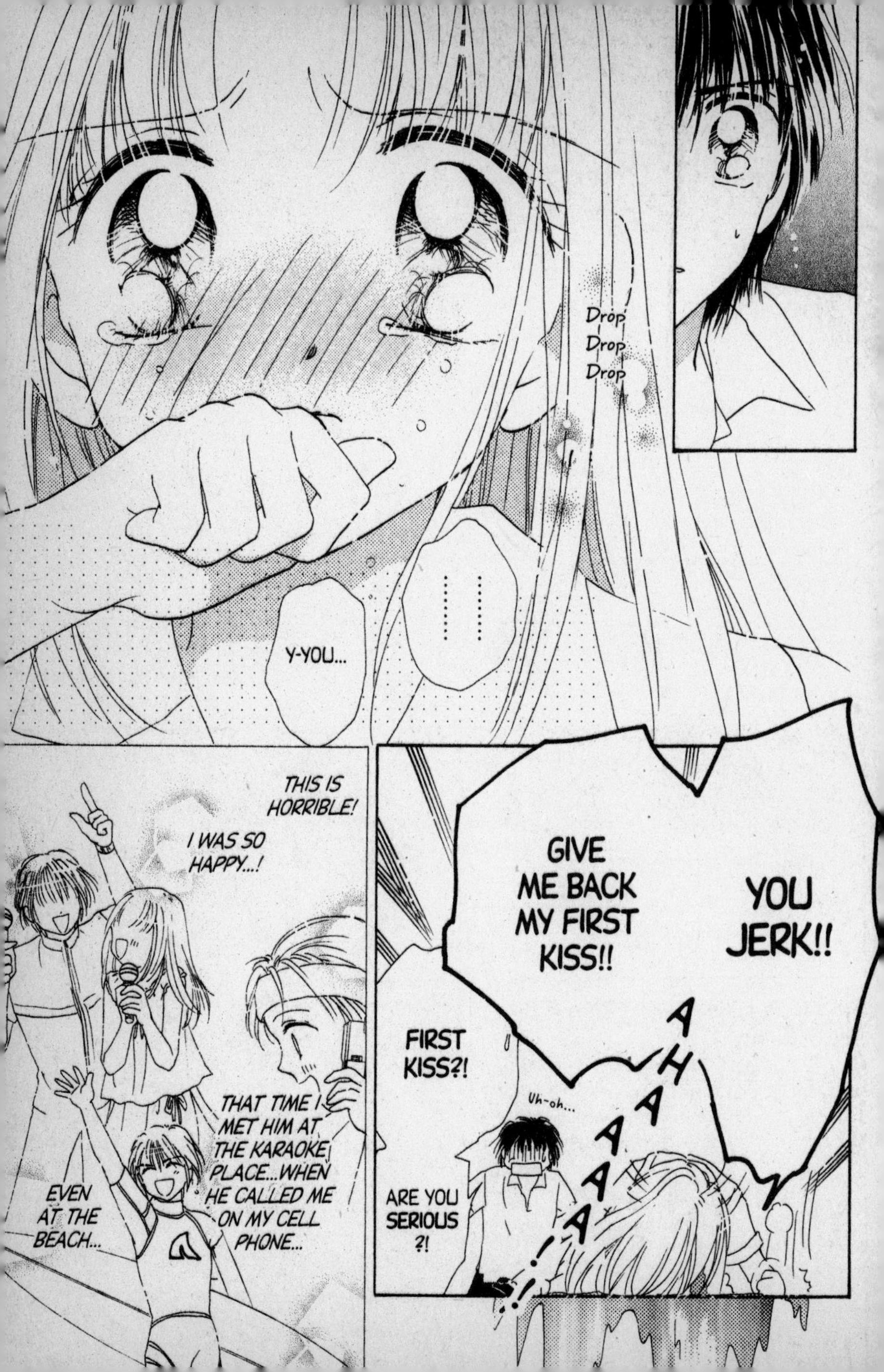
Drop
Drop
Drop
……
Y-YOU...
GIVE ME BACK MY FIRST KISS!!
YOU JERK!!
AHAAAAA!!
FIRST KISS?!
Uh-oh...
ARE YOU SERIOUS?!
THIS IS HORRIBLE!
I WAS SO HAPPY...!
THAT TIME I MET HIM AT THE KARAOKE PLACE...WHEN HE CALLED ME ON MY CELL PHONE...
EVEN AT THE BEACH...

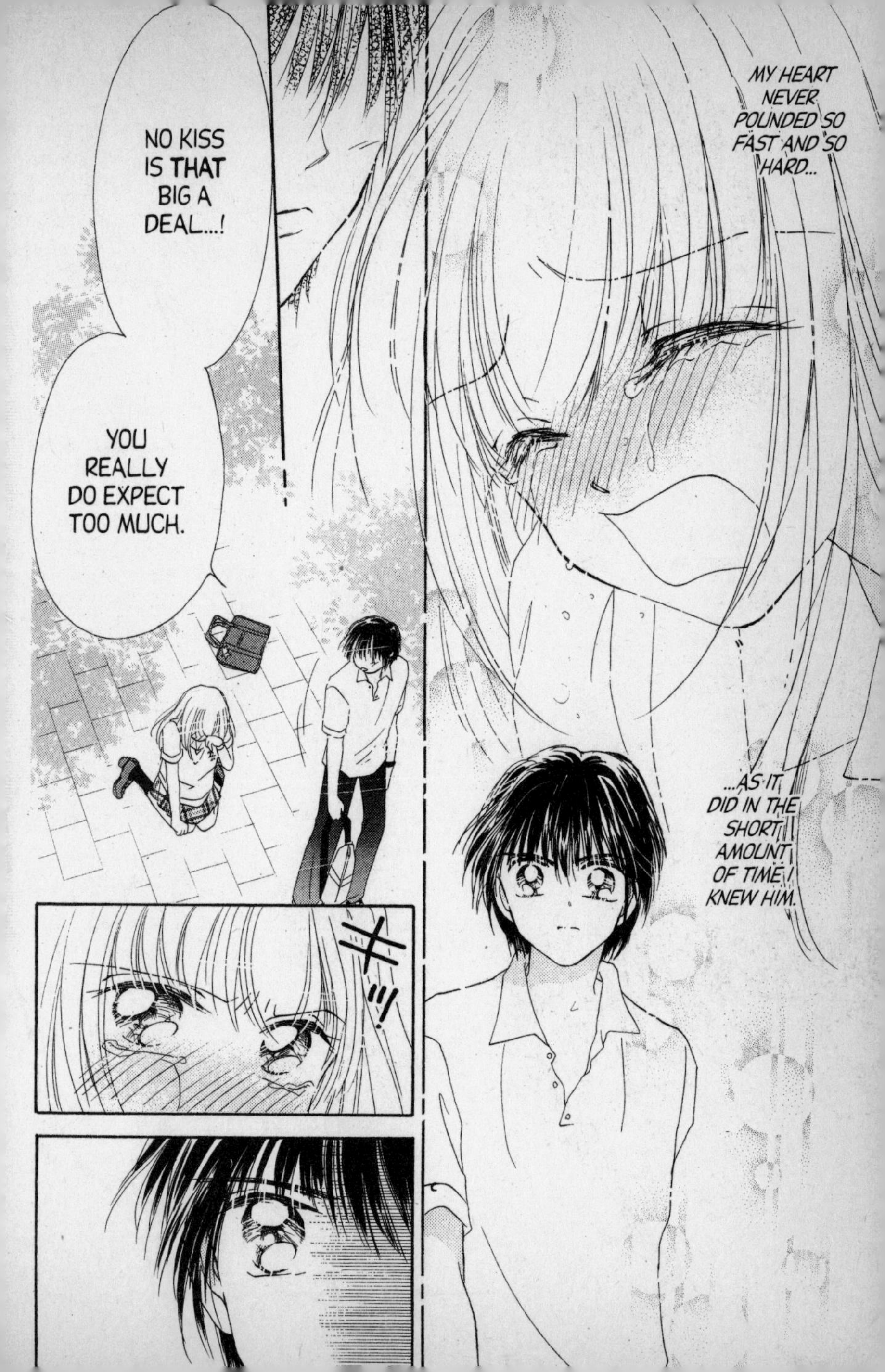
MY HEART NEVER POUNDED SO FAST AND SO HARD...
...AS IT DID IN THE SHORT AMOUNT OF TIME I KNEW HIM.
NO KISS IS THAT BIG A DEAL...!
YOU REALLY DO EXPECT TOO MUCH.

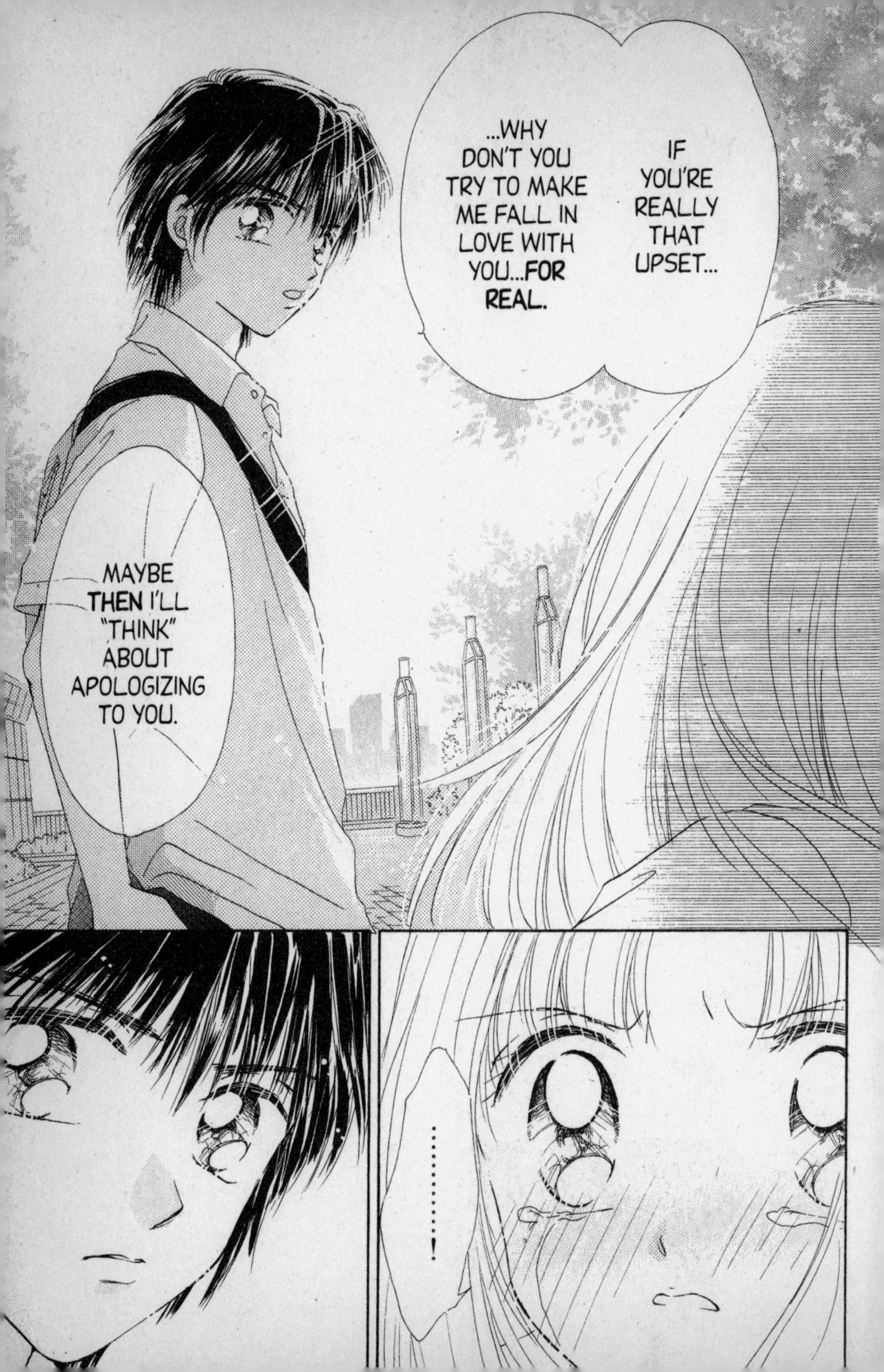
IF YOU'RE REALLY THAT UPSET...
...WHY DON'T YOU TRY TO MAKE ME FALL IN LOVE WITH YOU...**FOR REAL.**
MAYBE **THEN** I'LL "THINK" ABOUT APOLOGIZING TO YOU.
......!

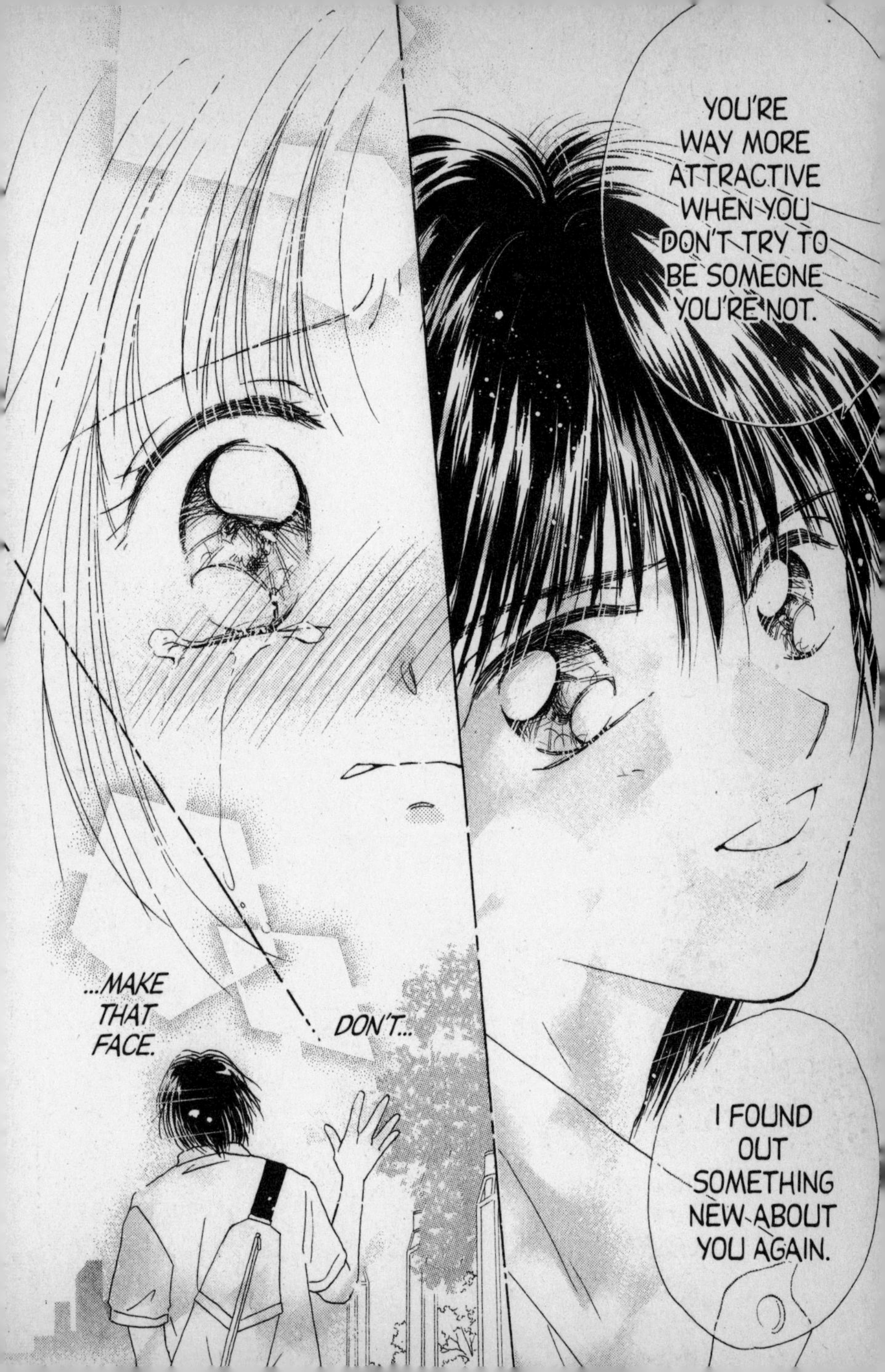
YOU'RE WAY MORE ATTRACTIVE WHEN YOU DON'T TRY TO BE SOMEONE YOU'RE NOT.
I FOUND OUT SOMETHING NEW ABOUT YOU AGAIN.
DON'T...
...MAKE THAT FACE.

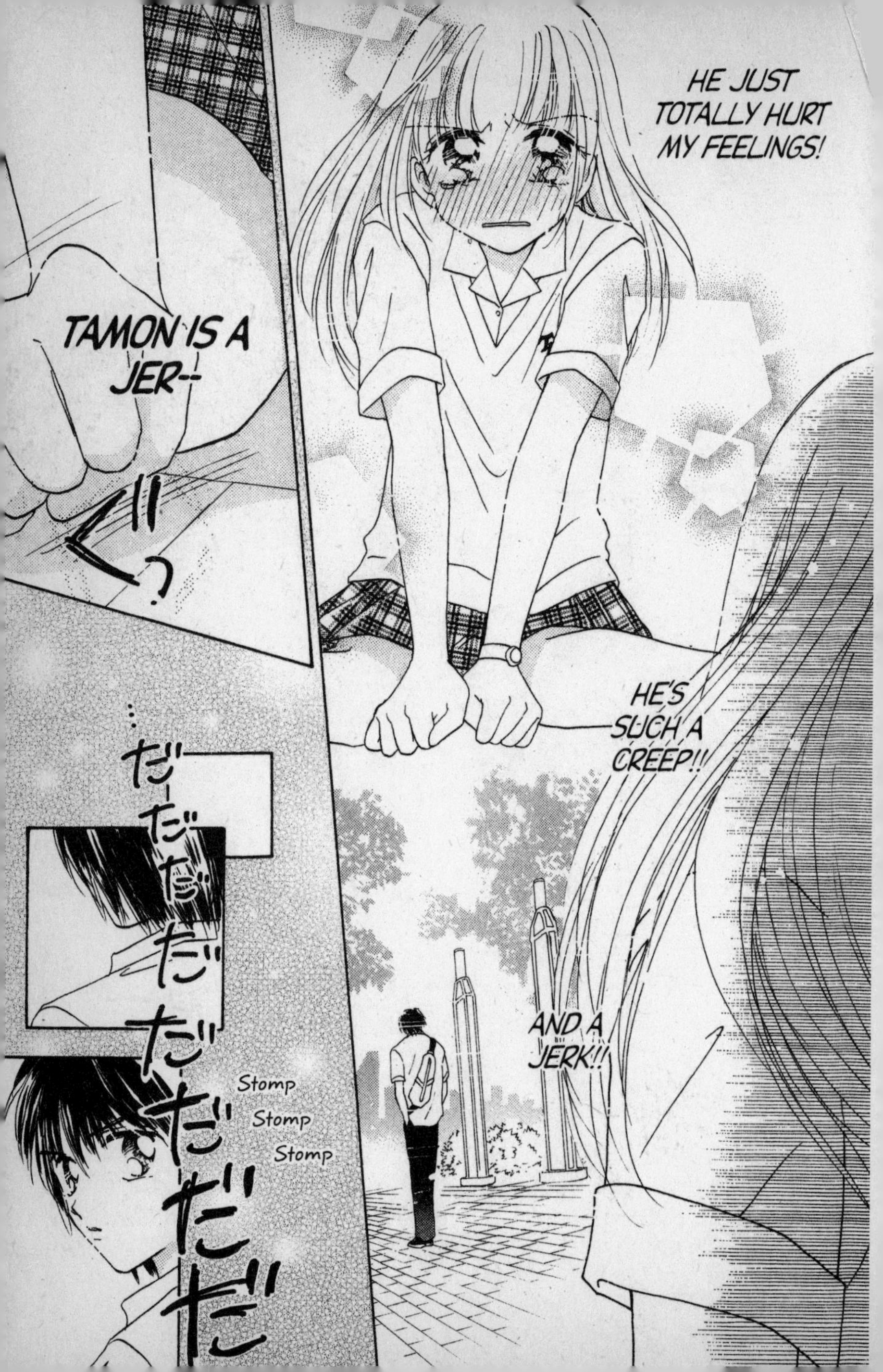
HE JUST TOTALLY HURT MY FEELINGS!
HE'S SUCH A CREEP!!
AND A JERK!!
TAMON IS A JER--
くっ
...だだだだだだ
Stomp
Stomp
Stomp

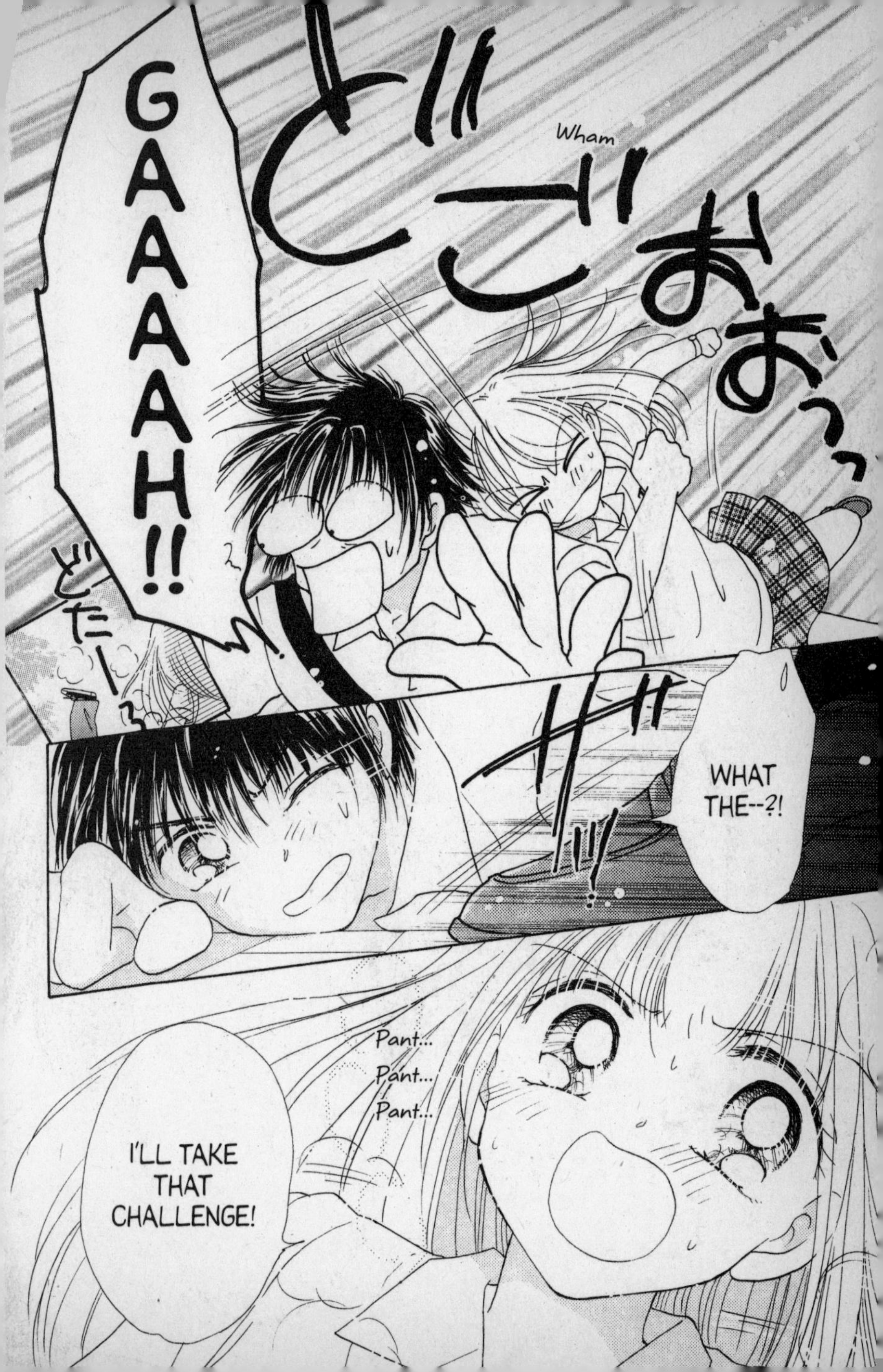
どごおおっ
Wham
GAAAAH!!
どたーっ
WHAT THE--?!
Pant...
Pant...
Pant...
I'LL TAKE THAT CHALLENGE!

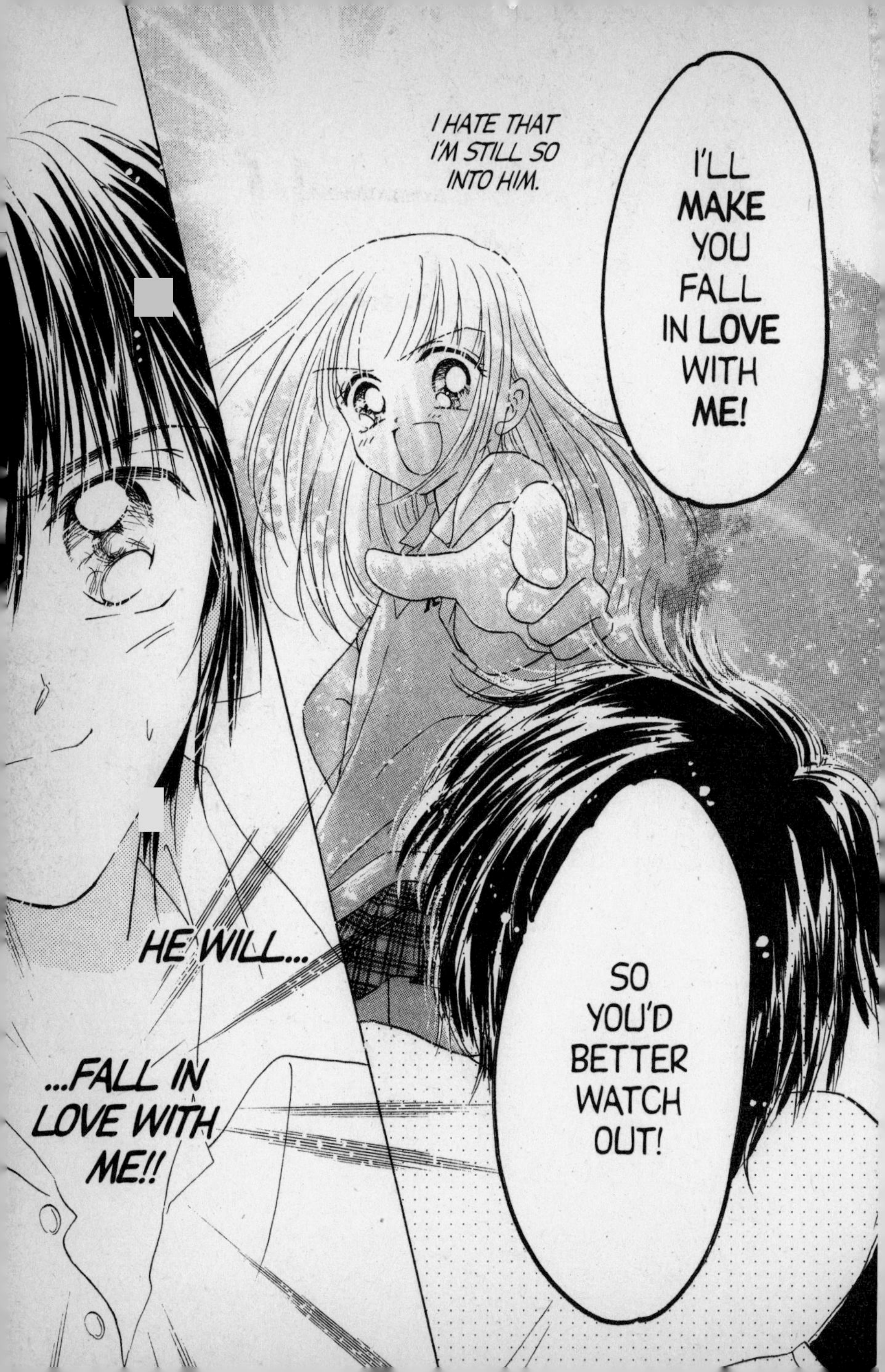
I'LL MAKE YOU FALL IN LOVE WITH ME!
I HATE THAT I'M STILL SO INTO HIM.
SO YOU'D BETTER WATCH OUT!
HE WILL...
...FALL IN LOVE WITH ME!!

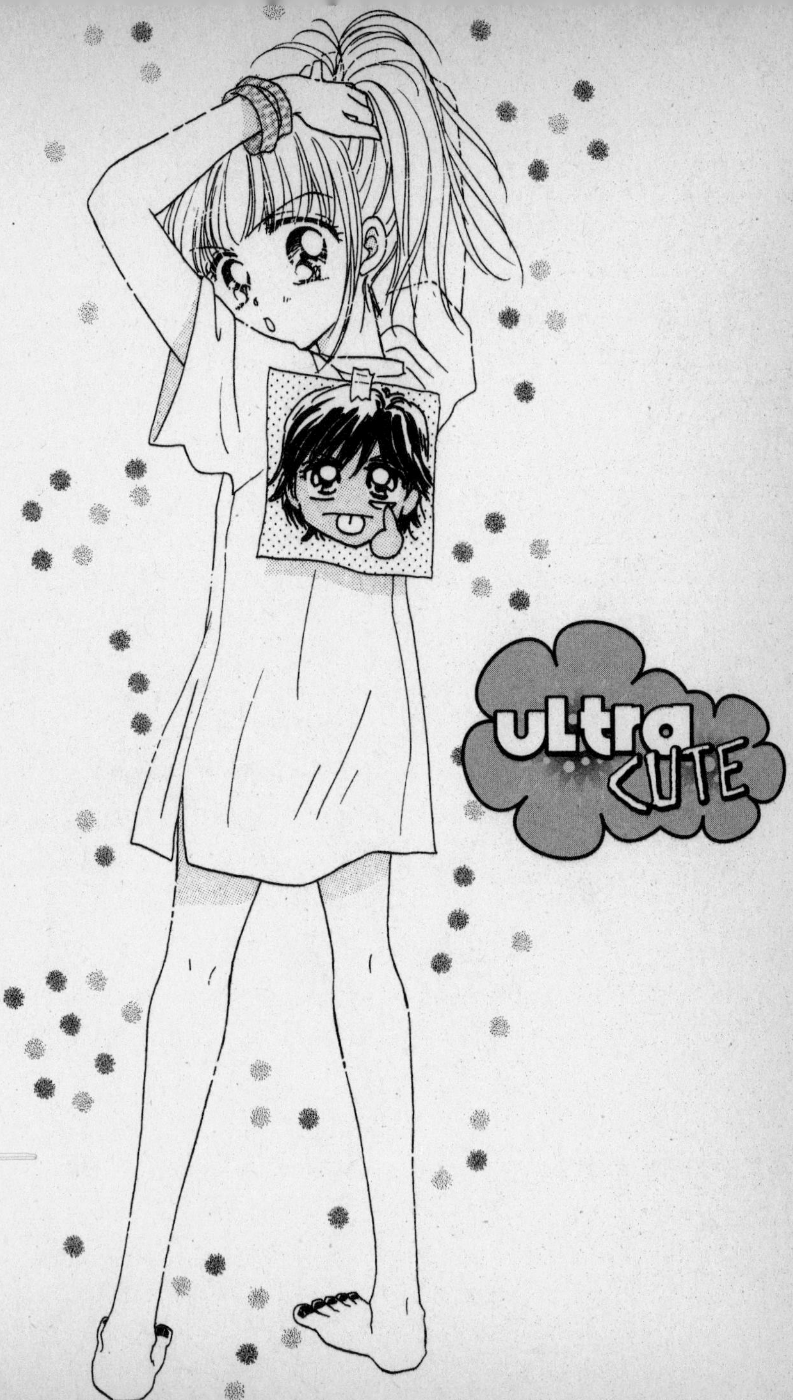
ultra
CUTE

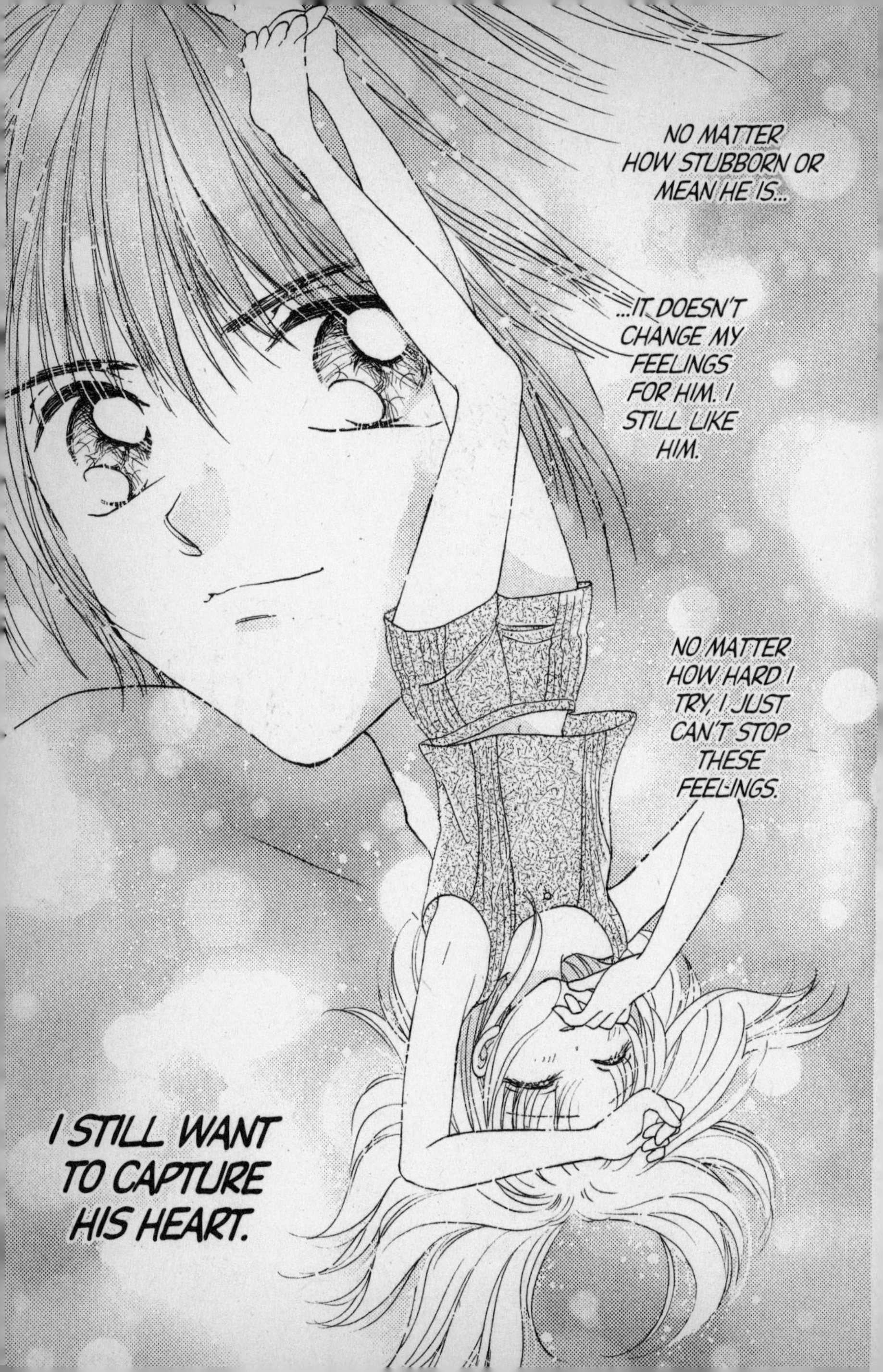
NO MATTER HOW STUBBORN OR MEAN HE IS...
...IT DOESN'T CHANGE MY FEELINGS FOR HIM. I STILL LIKE HIM.
NO MATTER HOW HARD I TRY, I JUST CAN'T STOP THESE FEELINGS.
I STILL WANT TO CAPTURE HIS HEART.

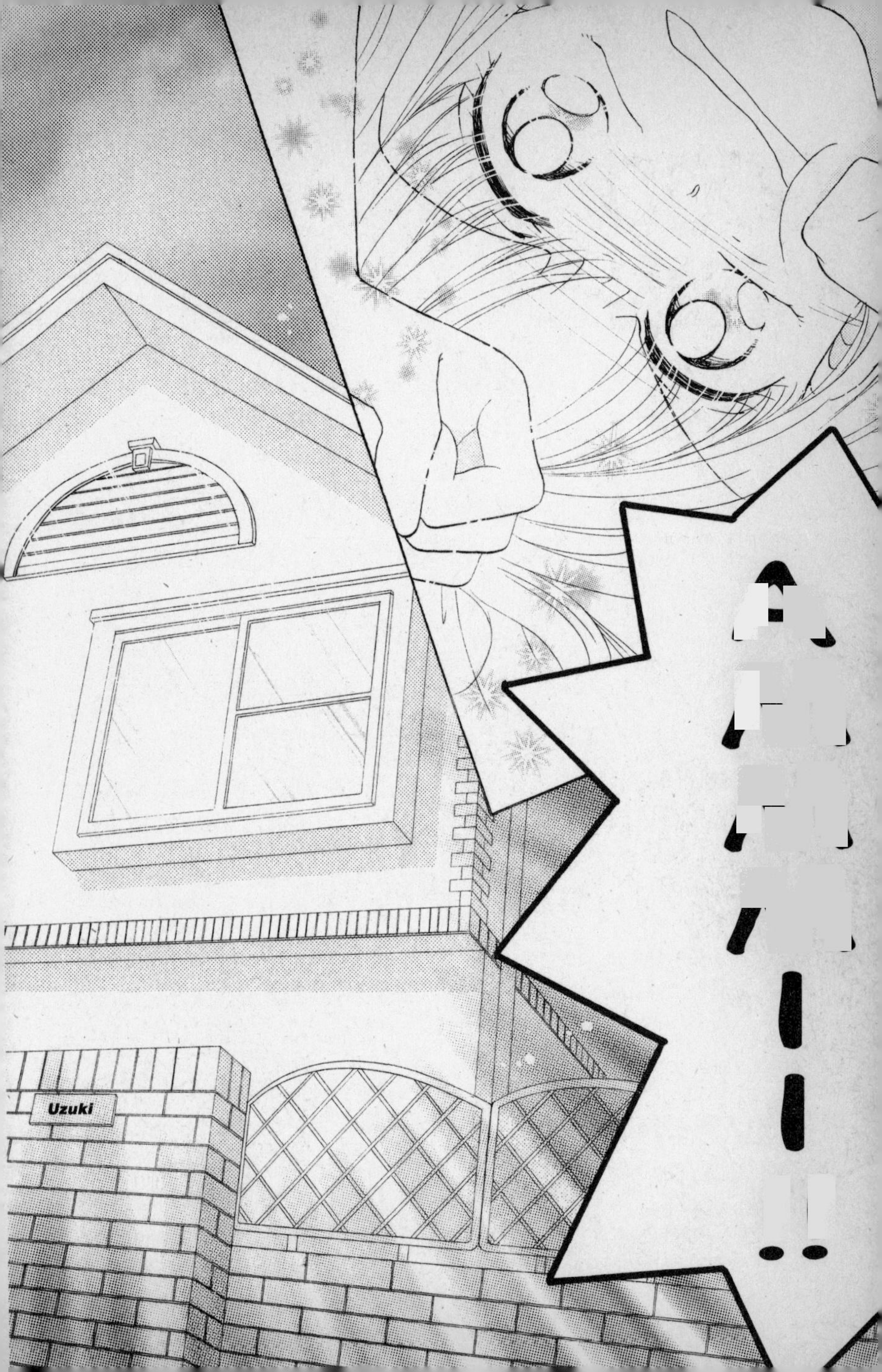
Uzuki

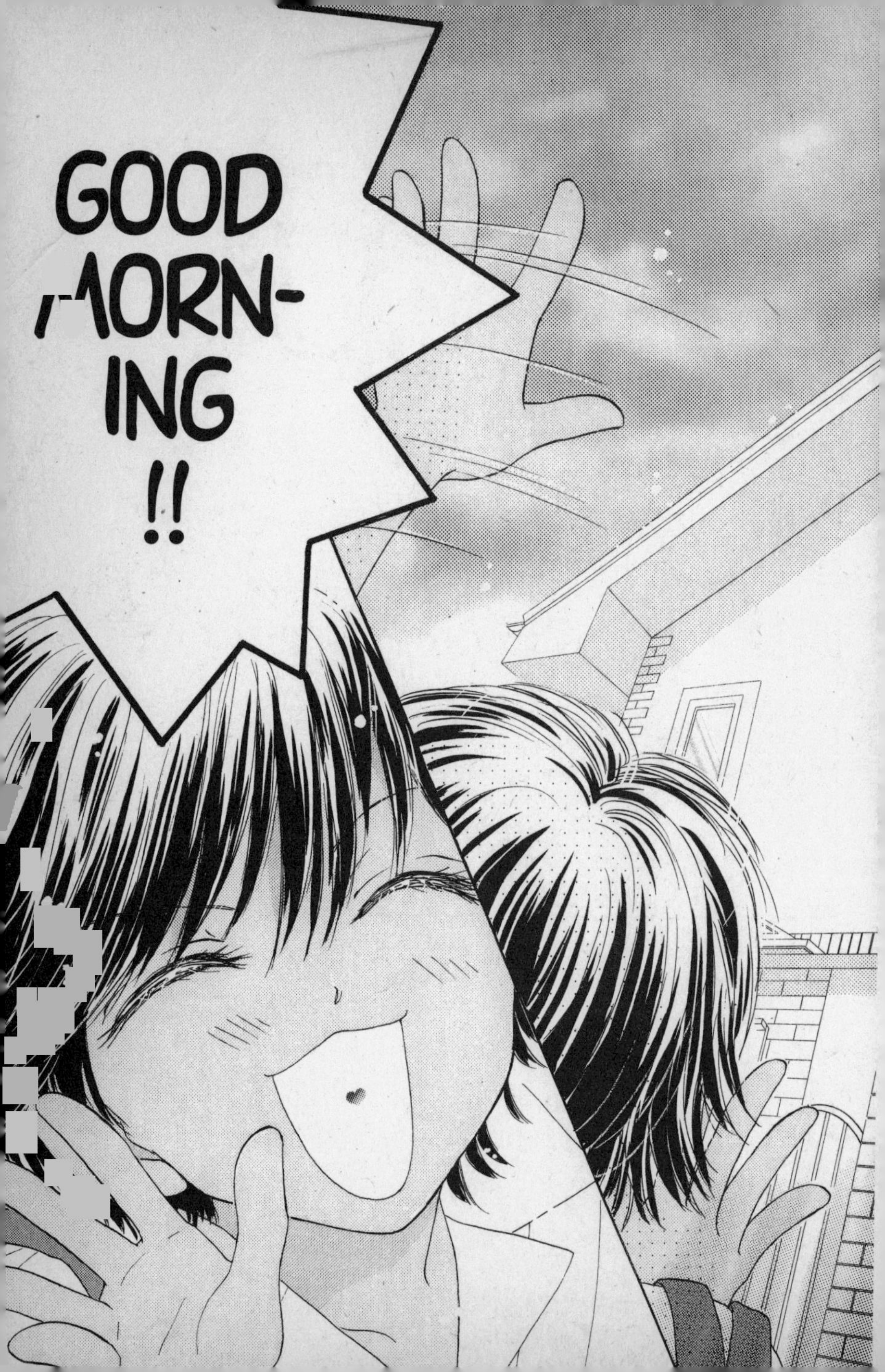
GOOD MORN-ING !!

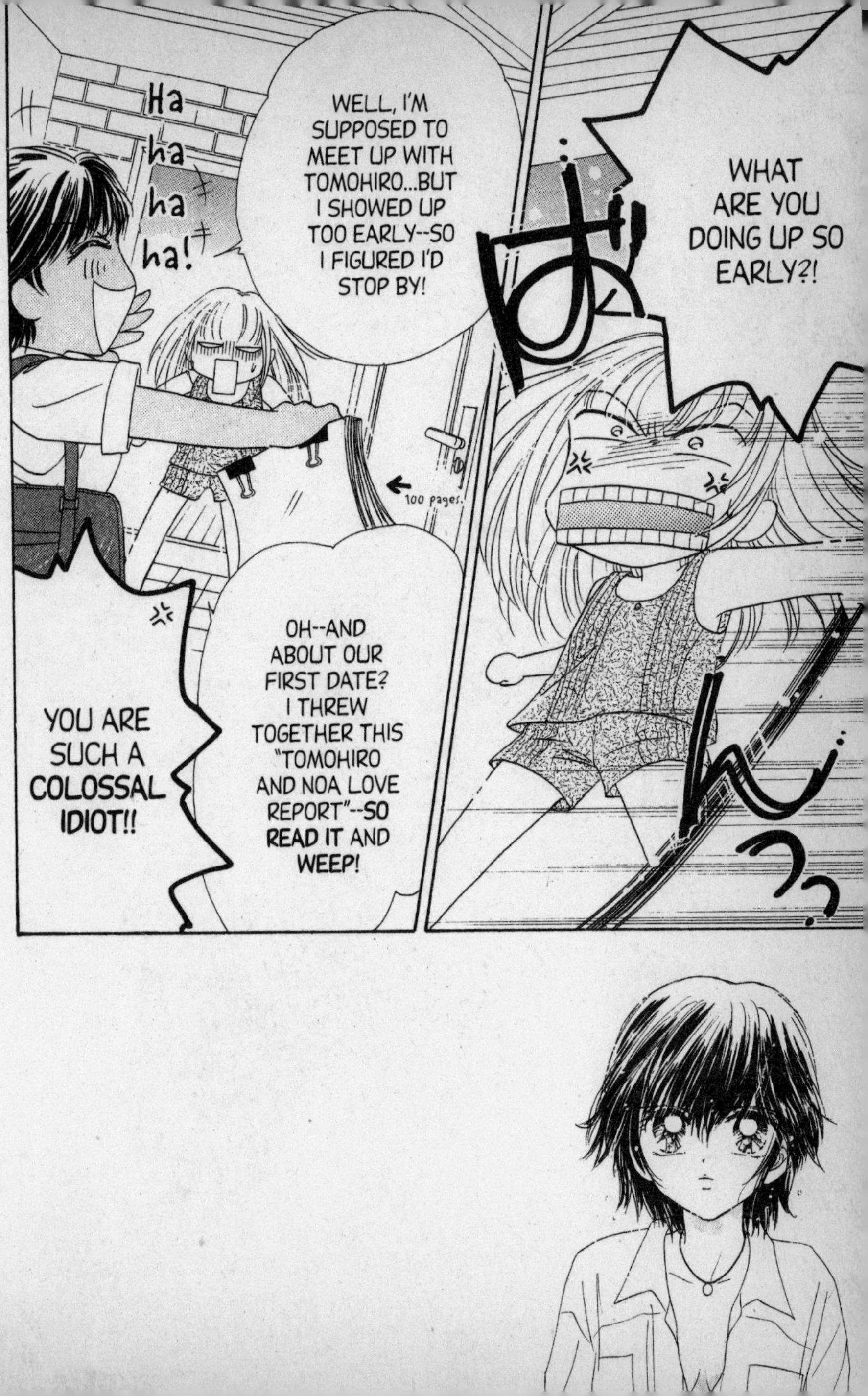
WHAT ARE YOU DOING UP SO EARLY?!
WELL, I'M SUPPOSED TO MEET UP WITH TOMOHIRO...BUT I SHOWED UP TOO EARLY--SO I FIGURED I'D STOP BY!
Ha ha ha ha!
100 pages.
OH--AND ABOUT OUR FIRST DATE? I THREW TOGETHER THIS "TOMOHIRO AND NOA LOVE REPORT"--SO READ IT AND WEEP!
YOU ARE SUCH A COLOSSAL IDIOT!!

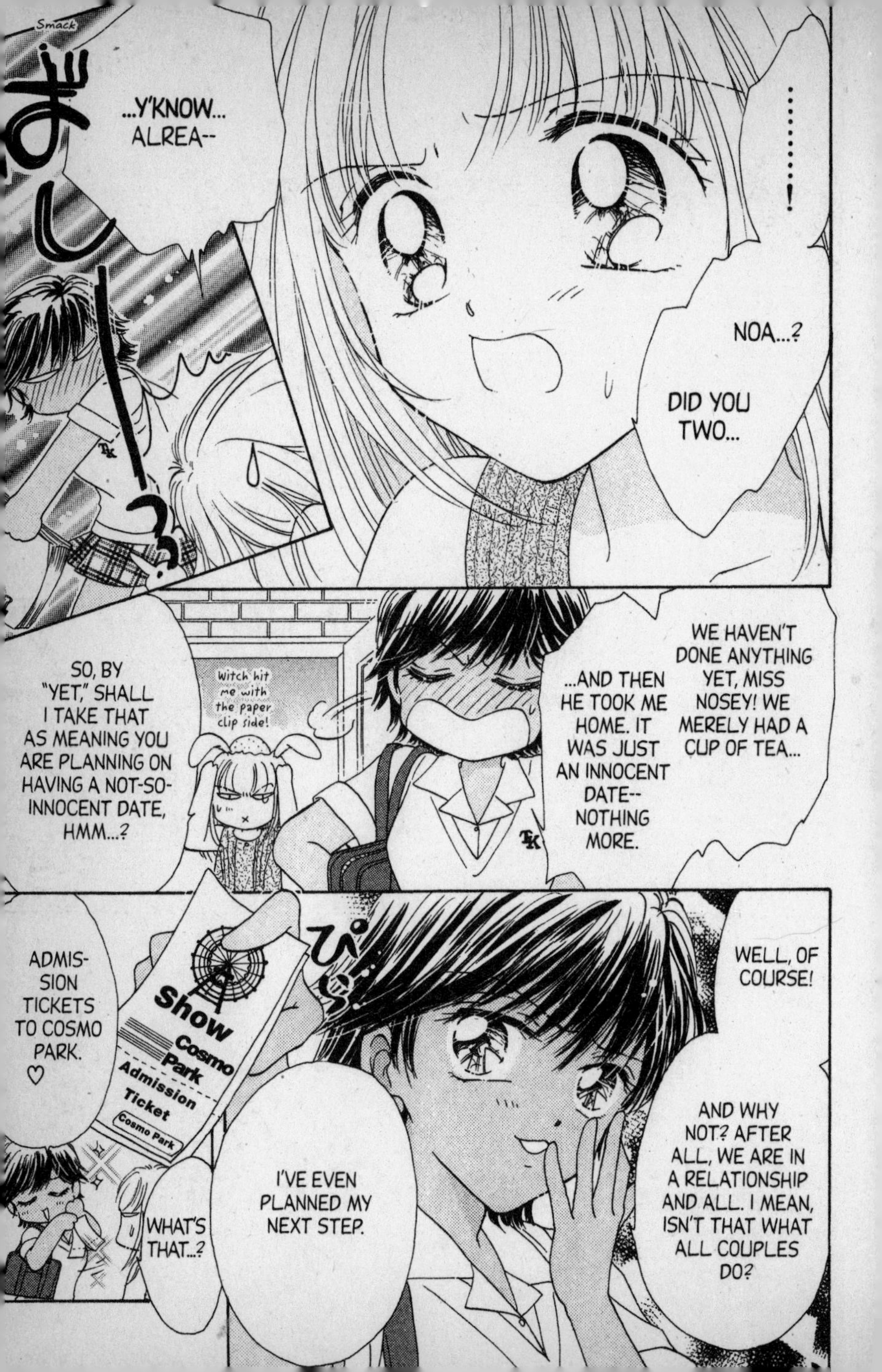
......!
NOA...? DID YOU TWO...
...Y'KNOW... ALREA--
Smack
WE HAVEN'T DONE ANYTHING YET, MISS NOSEY! WE MERELY HAD A CUP OF TEA...
...AND THEN HE TOOK ME HOME. IT WAS JUST AN INNOCENT DATE-- NOTHING MORE.
Witch hit me with the paper clip side!
SO, BY "YET," SHALL I TAKE THAT AS MEANING YOU ARE PLANNING ON HAVING A NOT-SO-INNOCENT DATE, HMM...?
WELL, OF COURSE!
AND WHY NOT? AFTER ALL, WE ARE IN A RELATIONSHIP AND ALL. I MEAN, ISN'T THAT WHAT ALL COUPLES DO?
I'VE EVEN PLANNED MY NEXT STEP.
WHAT'S THAT...?
ADMISSION TICKETS TO COSMO PARK. ♡
Show
Cosmo Park
Admission Ticket
Cosmo Park

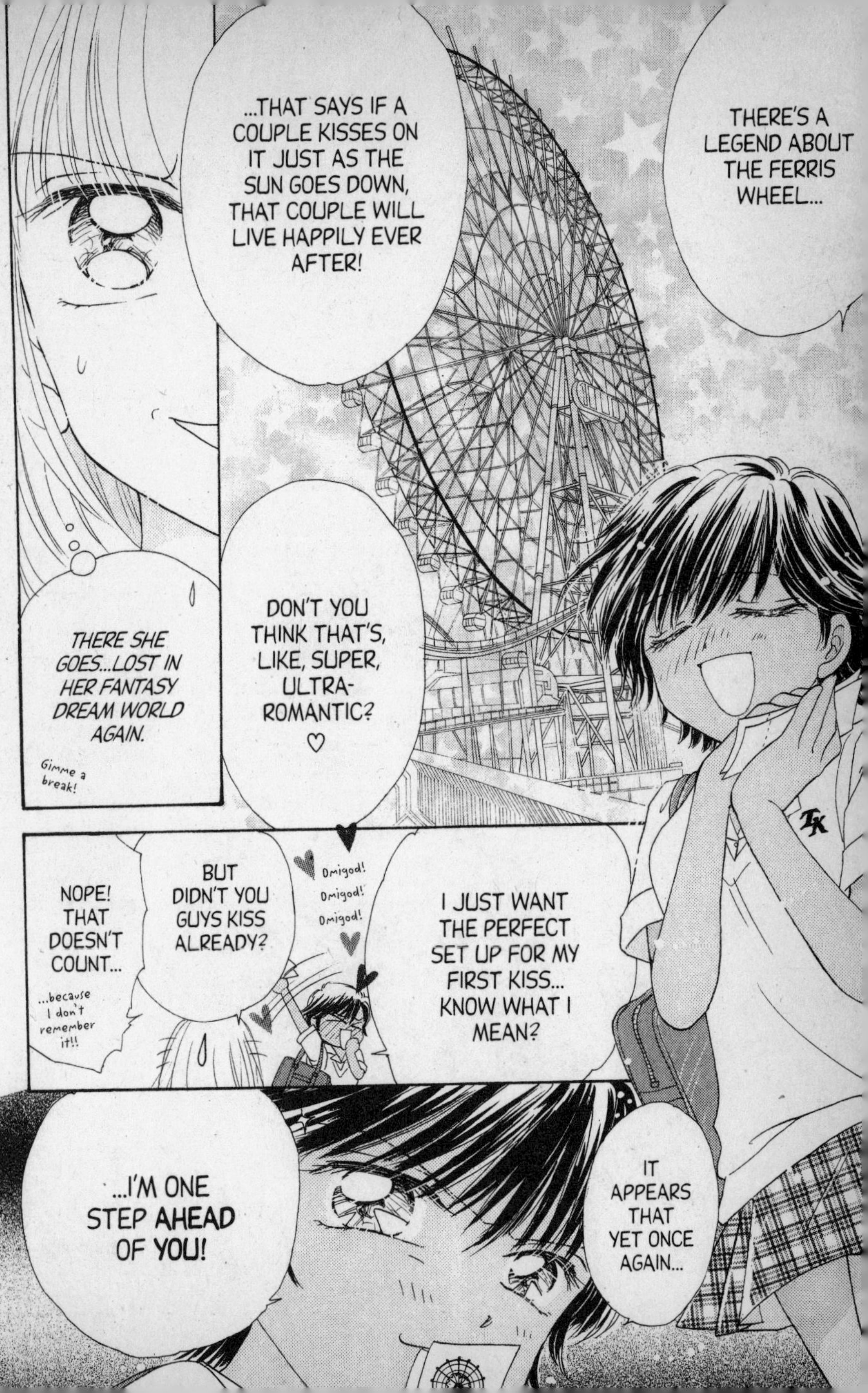
THERE'S A LEGEND ABOUT THE FERRIS WHEEL...
...THAT SAYS IF A COUPLE KISSES ON IT JUST AS THE SUN GOES DOWN, THAT COUPLE WILL LIVE HAPPILY EVER AFTER!
DON'T YOU THINK THAT'S, LIKE, SUPER, ULTRA-ROMANTIC? ♡
THERE SHE GOES...LOST IN HER FANTASY DREAM WORLD AGAIN.
Gimme a break!
I JUST WANT THE PERFECT SET UP FOR MY FIRST KISS... KNOW WHAT I MEAN?
Omigod! Omigod! Omigod!
BUT DIDN'T YOU GUYS KISS ALREADY?
NOPE! THAT DOESN'T COUNT...
...because I don't remember it!!
IT APPEARS THAT YET ONCE AGAIN...
...I'M ONE STEP AHEAD OF YOU!

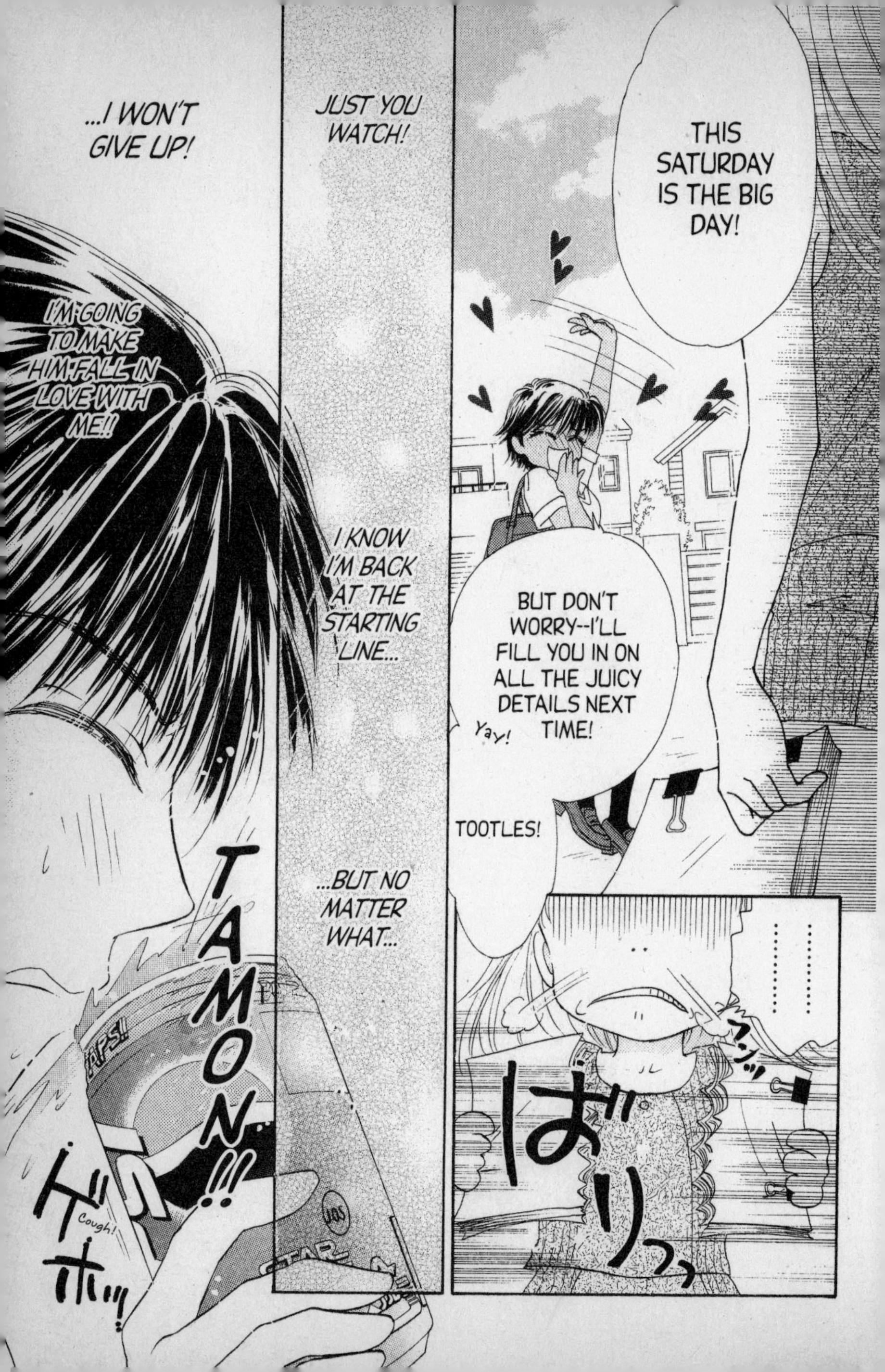
THIS SATURDAY IS THE BIG DAY!
BUT DON'T WORRY--I'LL FILL YOU IN ON ALL THE JUICY DETAILS NEXT TIME!
Yay!
TOOTLES!
......
ぱりっ
JUST YOU WATCH!
I KNOW I'M BACK AT THE STARTING LINE...
...BUT NO MATTER WHAT...
...I WON'T GIVE UP!
I'M GOING TO MAKE HIM FALL IN LOVE WITH ME!!
TAMON!!
Cough!

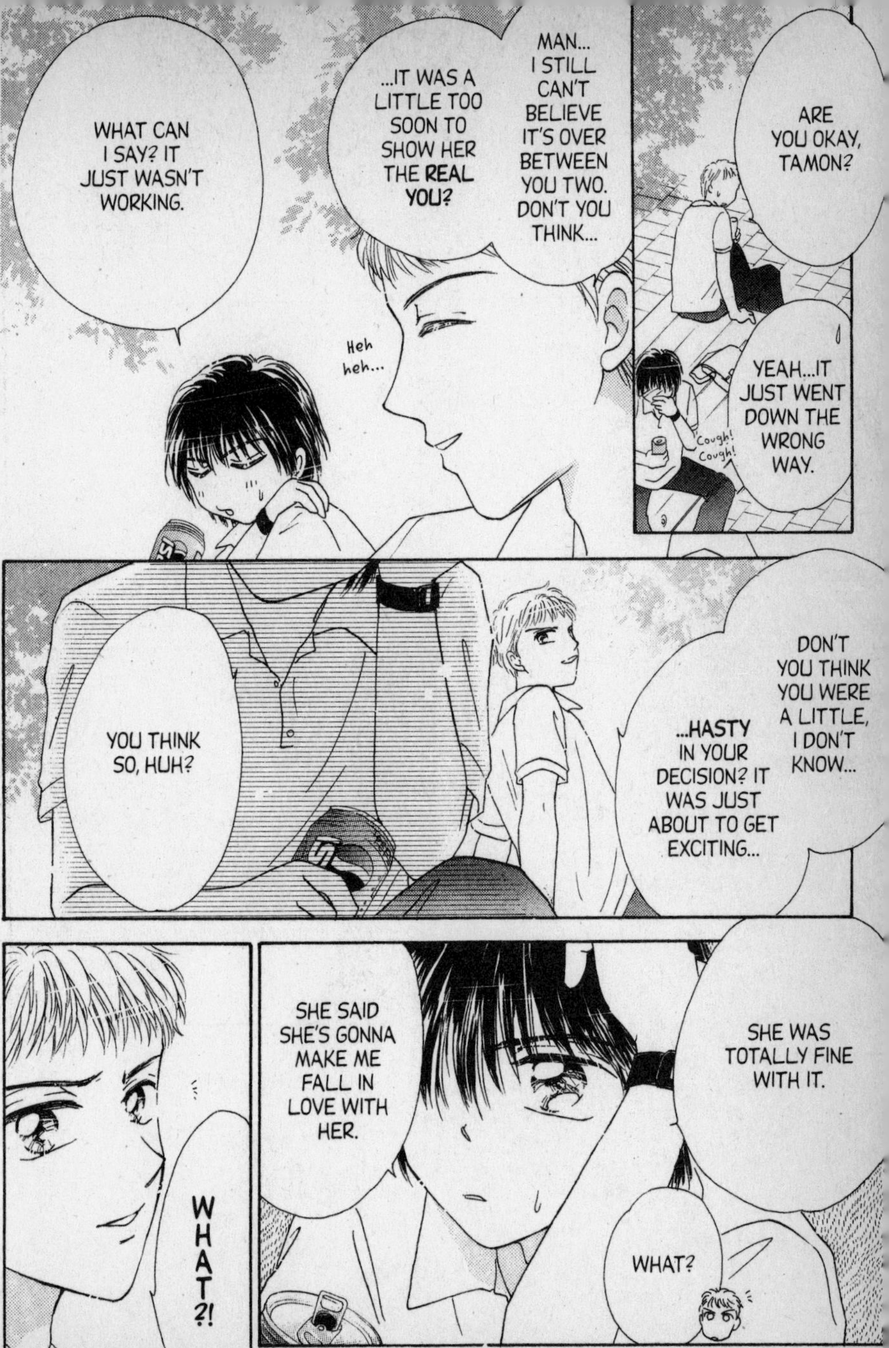
ARE YOU OKAY, TAMON?
Cough! Cough!
YEAH...IT JUST WENT DOWN THE WRONG WAY.
MAN... I STILL CAN'T BELIEVE IT'S OVER BETWEEN YOU TWO. DON'T YOU THINK...
...IT WAS A LITTLE TOO SOON TO SHOW HER THE **REAL YOU?**
Heh heh...
WHAT CAN I SAY? IT JUST WASN'T WORKING.
DON'T YOU THINK YOU WERE A LITTLE, I DON'T KNOW...
...HASTY IN YOUR DECISION? IT WAS JUST ABOUT TO GET EXCITING...
YOU THINK SO, HUH?
SHE WAS TOTALLY FINE WITH IT.
SHE SAID SHE'S GONNA MAKE ME FALL IN LOVE WITH HER.
WHAT?
WHAT?!

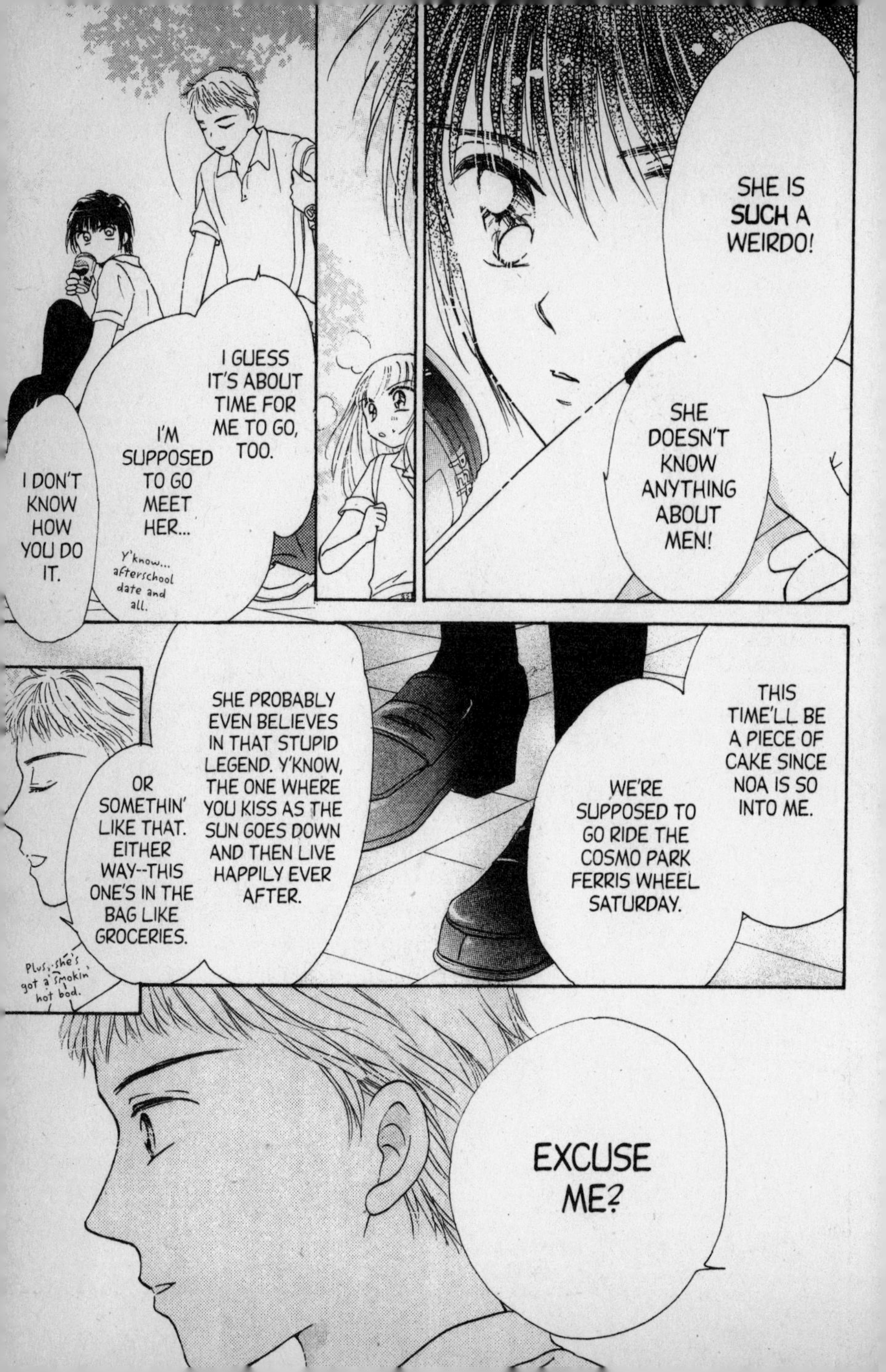
SHE IS SUCH A WEIRDO!
SHE DOESN'T KNOW ANYTHING ABOUT MEN!
I GUESS IT'S ABOUT TIME FOR ME TO GO, TOO.
I'M SUPPOSED TO GO MEET HER...
Y'know... afterschool date and all.
I DON'T KNOW HOW YOU DO IT.
THIS TIME'LL BE A PIECE OF CAKE SINCE NOA IS SO INTO ME.
WE'RE SUPPOSED TO GO RIDE THE COSMO PARK FERRIS WHEEL SATURDAY.
SHE PROBABLY EVEN BELIEVES IN THAT STUPID LEGEND. Y'KNOW, THE ONE WHERE YOU KISS AS THE SUN GOES DOWN AND THEN LIVE HAPPILY EVER AFTER.
OR SOMETHIN' LIKE THAT. EITHER WAY--THIS ONE'S IN THE BAG LIKE GROCERIES.
Plus, she's got a smokin' hot bod.
EXCUSE ME?

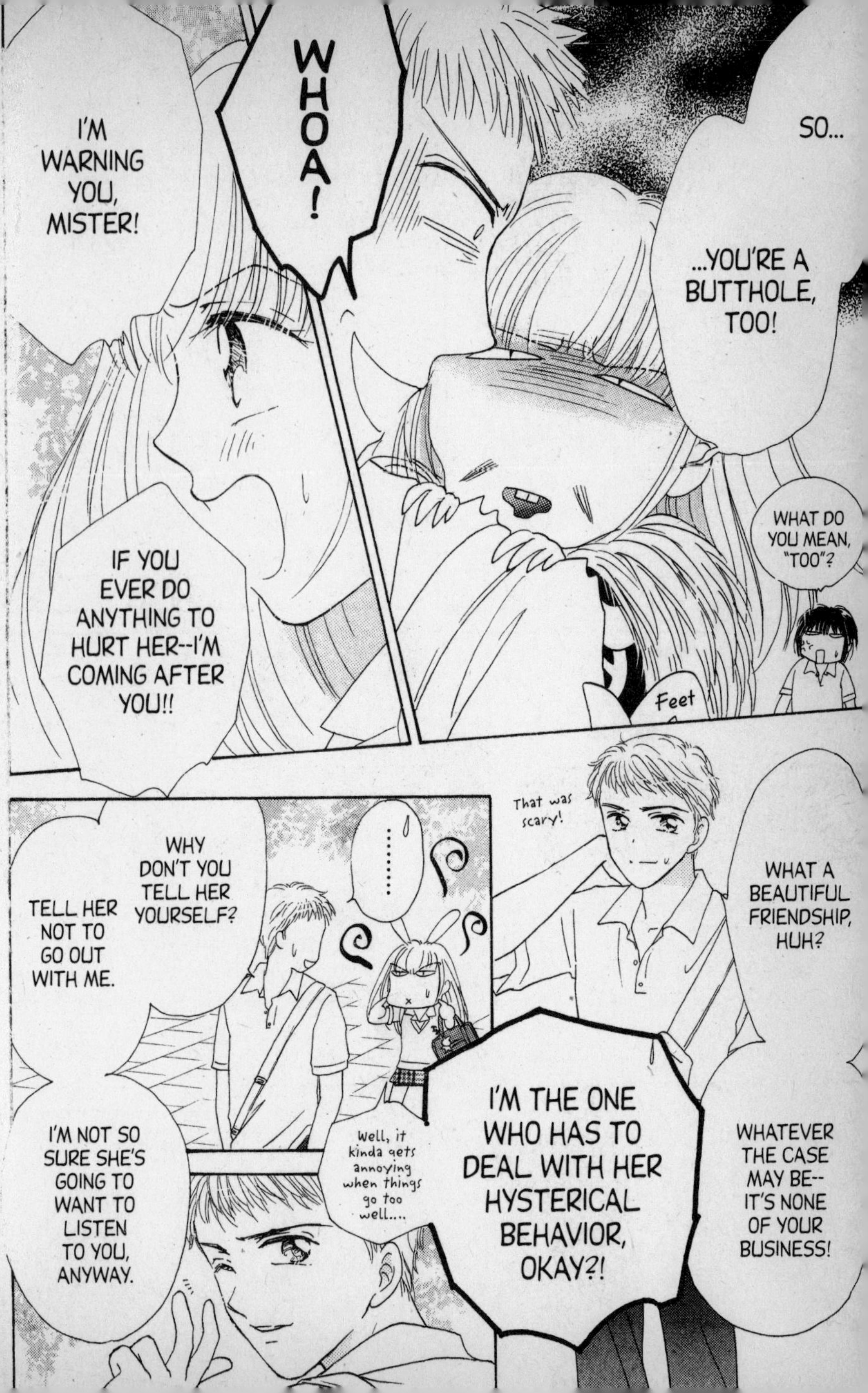
SO...
...YOU'RE A BUTTHOLE, TOO!
WHOA!
I'M WARNING YOU, MISTER!
WHAT DO YOU MEAN, "TOO"?
IF YOU EVER DO ANYTHING TO HURT HER--I'M COMING AFTER YOU!!
Feet
That was scary!
WHAT A BEAUTIFUL FRIENDSHIP, HUH?
......
WHY DON'T YOU TELL HER YOURSELF?
TELL HER NOT TO GO OUT WITH ME.
WHATEVER THE CASE MAY BE-- IT'S NONE OF YOUR BUSINESS!
I'M THE ONE WHO HAS TO DEAL WITH HER HYSTERICAL BEHAVIOR, OKAY?!
Well, it kinda gets annoying when things go too well....
I'M NOT SO SURE SHE'S GOING TO WANT TO LISTEN TO YOU, ANYWAY.

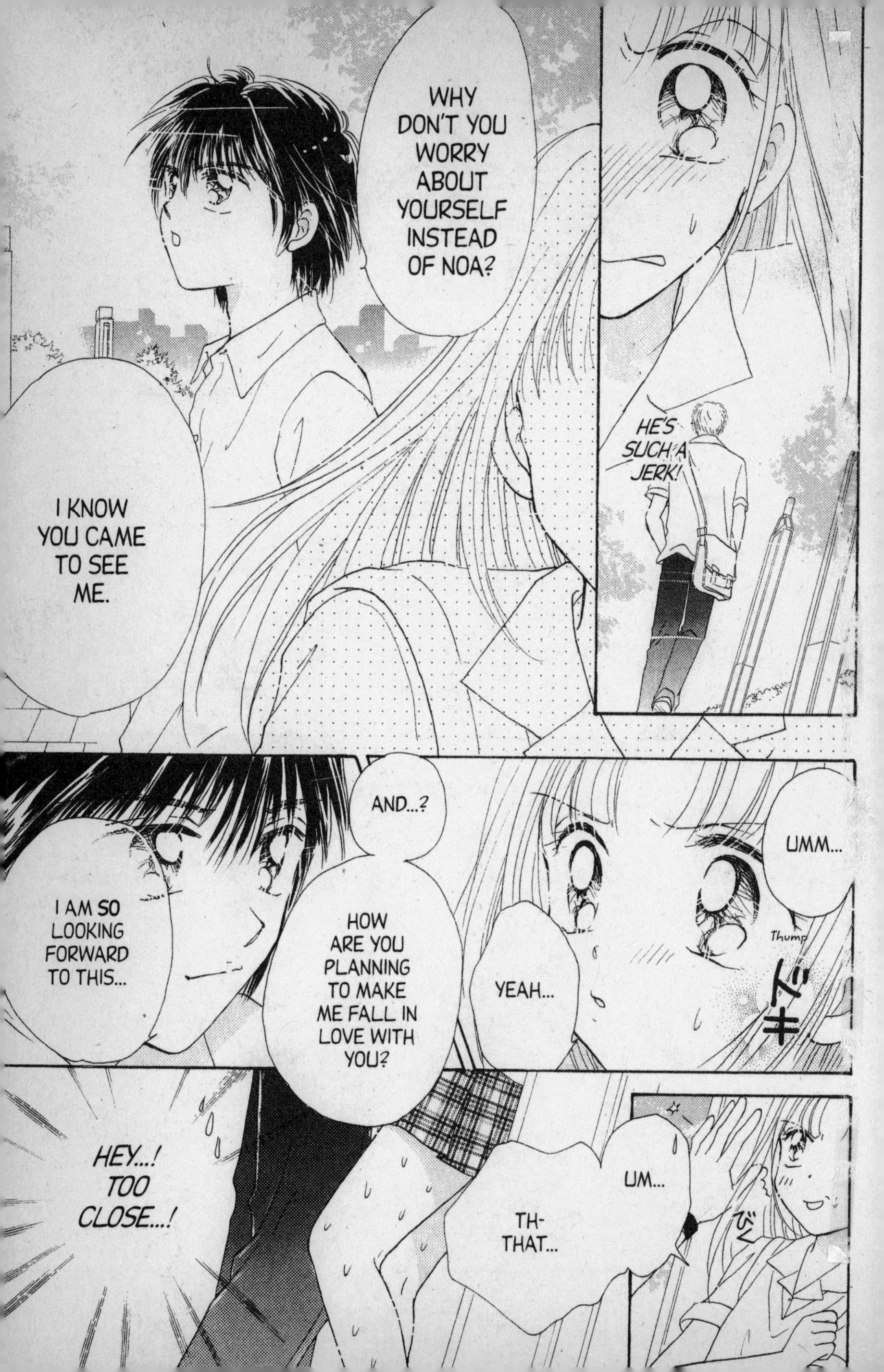
HE'S SUCH A JERK!
WHY DON'T YOU WORRY ABOUT YOURSELF INSTEAD OF NOA?
I KNOW YOU CAME TO SEE ME.
UMM...
Thump
ドキ
YEAH...
AND...?
HOW ARE YOU PLANNING TO MAKE ME FALL IN LOVE WITH YOU?
I AM SO LOOKING FORWARD TO THIS...
UM...
TH- THAT...
びく
HEY...! TOO CLOSE...!

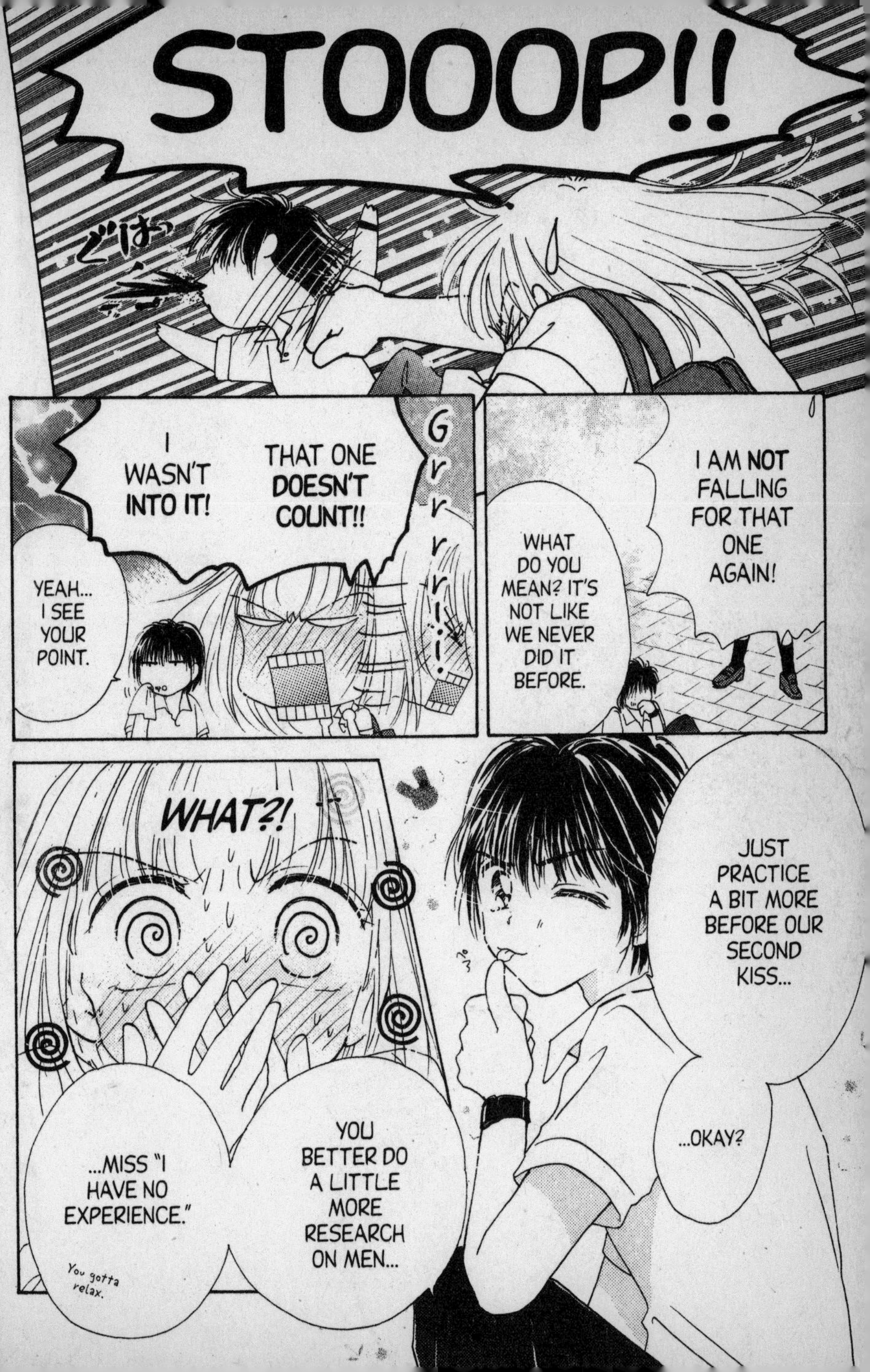
STOOOP!!
ごはっ
I AM NOT FALLING FOR THAT ONE AGAIN!
WHAT DO YOU MEAN? IT'S NOT LIKE WE NEVER DID IT BEFORE.
THAT ONE DOESN'T COUNT!!
I WASN'T INTO IT!
Grrrr!!
YEAH... I SEE YOUR POINT.
JUST PRACTICE A BIT MORE BEFORE OUR SECOND KISS...
...OKAY?
WHAT?!
YOU BETTER DO A LITTLE MORE RESEARCH ON MEN...
...MISS "I HAVE NO EXPERIENCE."
You gotta relax.

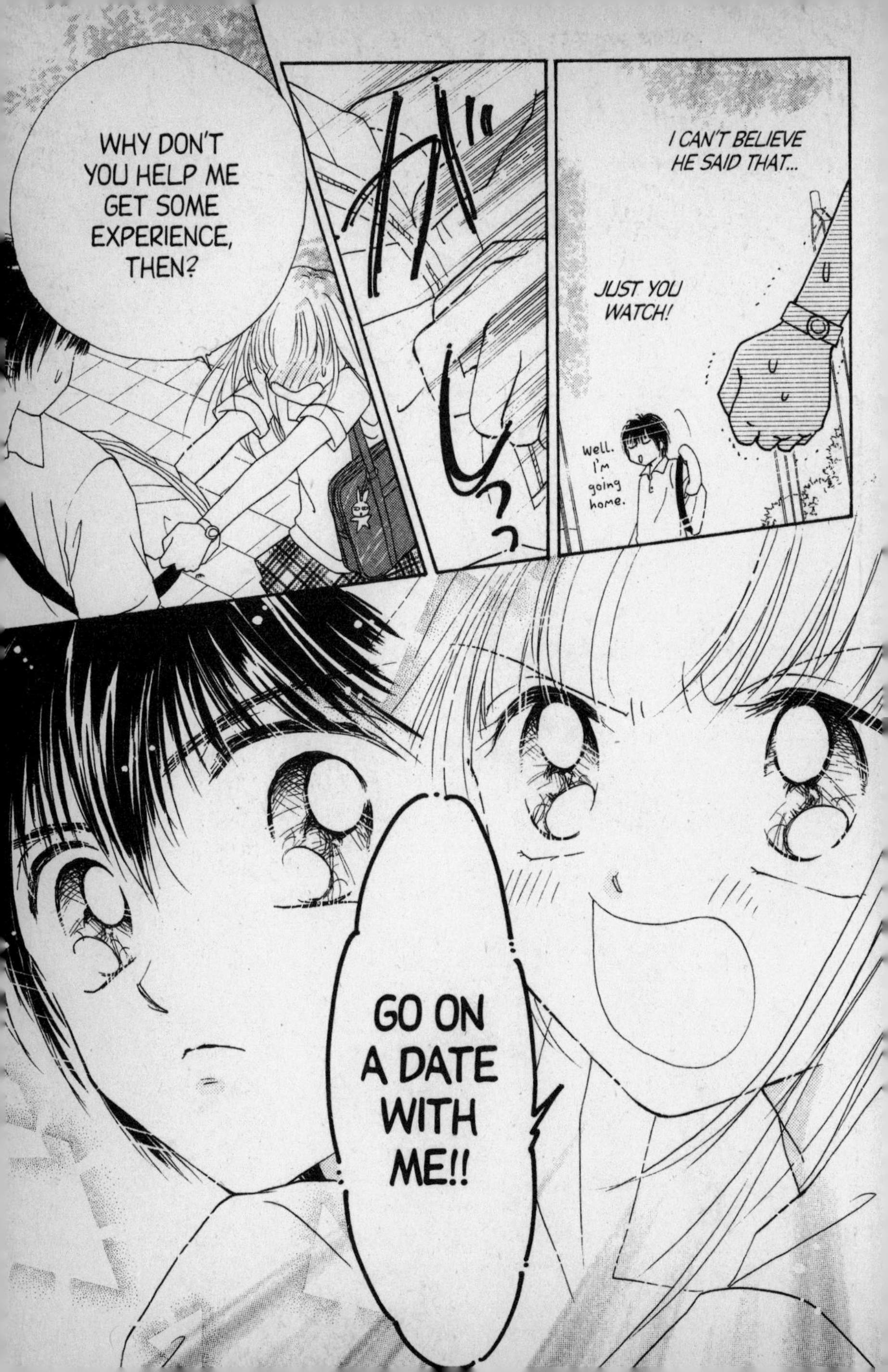
I CAN'T BELIEVE HE SAID THAT...
JUST YOU WATCH!
Well. I'm going home.
WHY DON'T YOU HELP ME GET SOME EXPERIENCE, THEN?
GO ON A DATE WITH ME!!

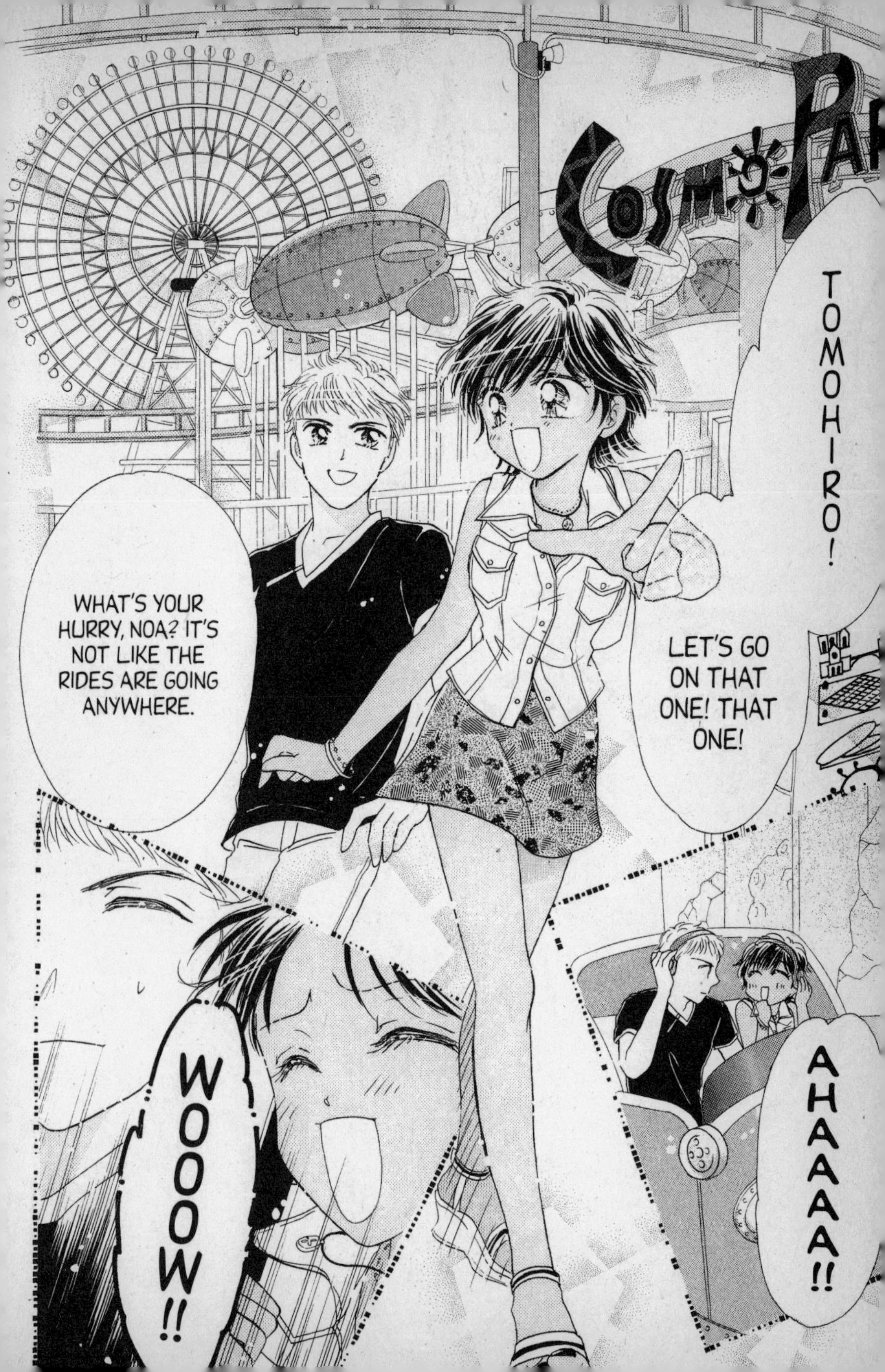
COSMO
TOMOHIRO!
LET'S GO ON THAT ONE! THAT ONE!
WHAT'S YOUR HURRY, NOA? IT'S NOT LIKE THE RIDES ARE GOING ANYWHERE.
AHAAAA!!
WOOOW!!

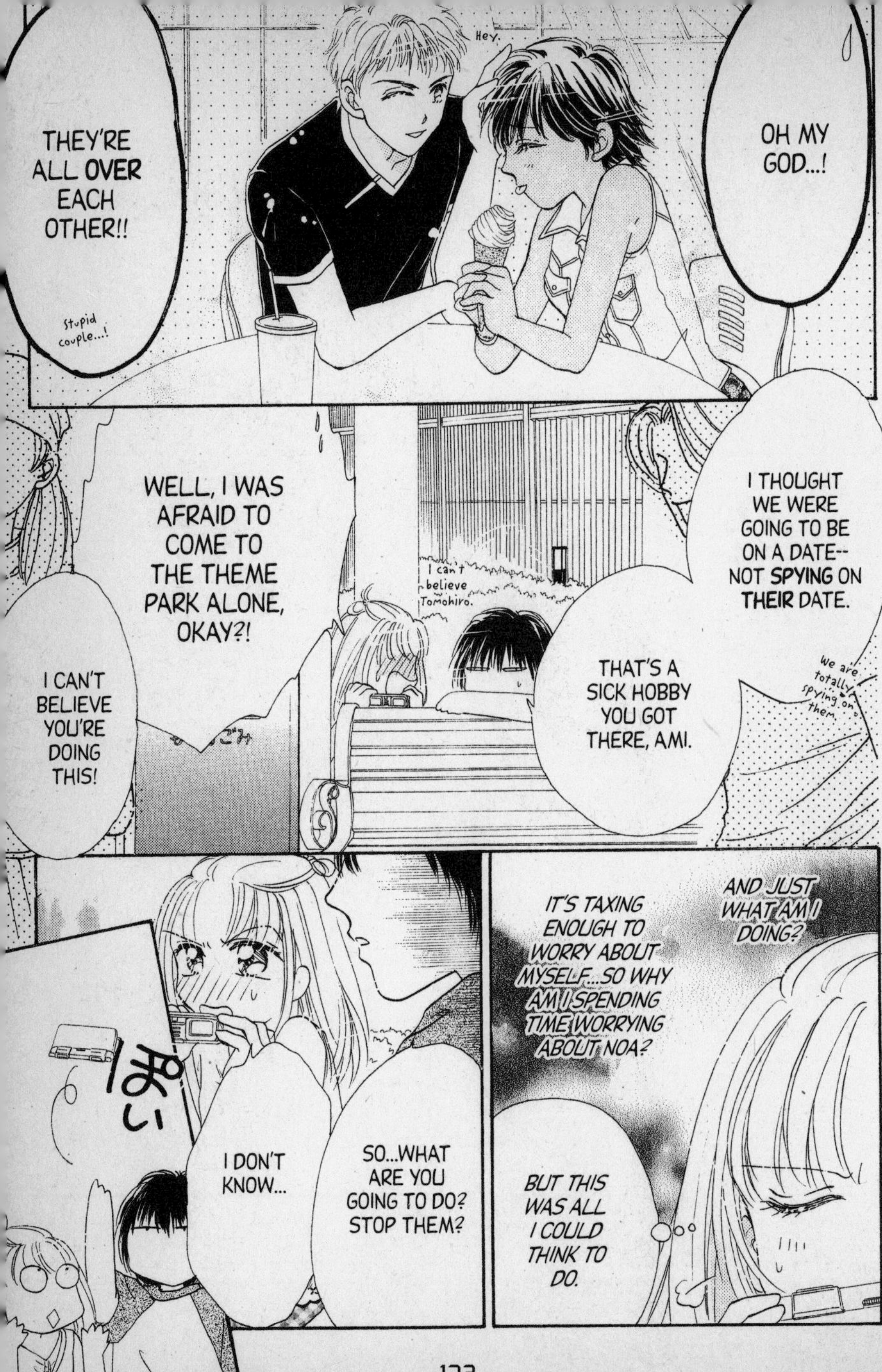
OH MY GOD...!
Hey.
THEY'RE ALL OVER EACH OTHER!!
Stupid couple...!
I THOUGHT WE WERE GOING TO BE ON A DATE-- NOT SPYING ON THEIR DATE.
We are totally spying on them.
THAT'S A SICK HOBBY YOU GOT THERE, AMI.
I can't believe Tomohiro.
WELL, I WAS AFRAID TO COME TO THE THEME PARK ALONE, OKAY?!
I CAN'T BELIEVE YOU'RE DOING THIS!
AND JUST WHAT AM I DOING?
IT'S TAXING ENOUGH TO WORRY ABOUT MYSELF...SO WHY AM I SPENDING TIME WORRYING ABOUT NOA?
BUT THIS WAS ALL I COULD THINK TO DO.
ぽい
SO...WHAT ARE YOU GOING TO DO? STOP THEM?
I DON'T KNOW...

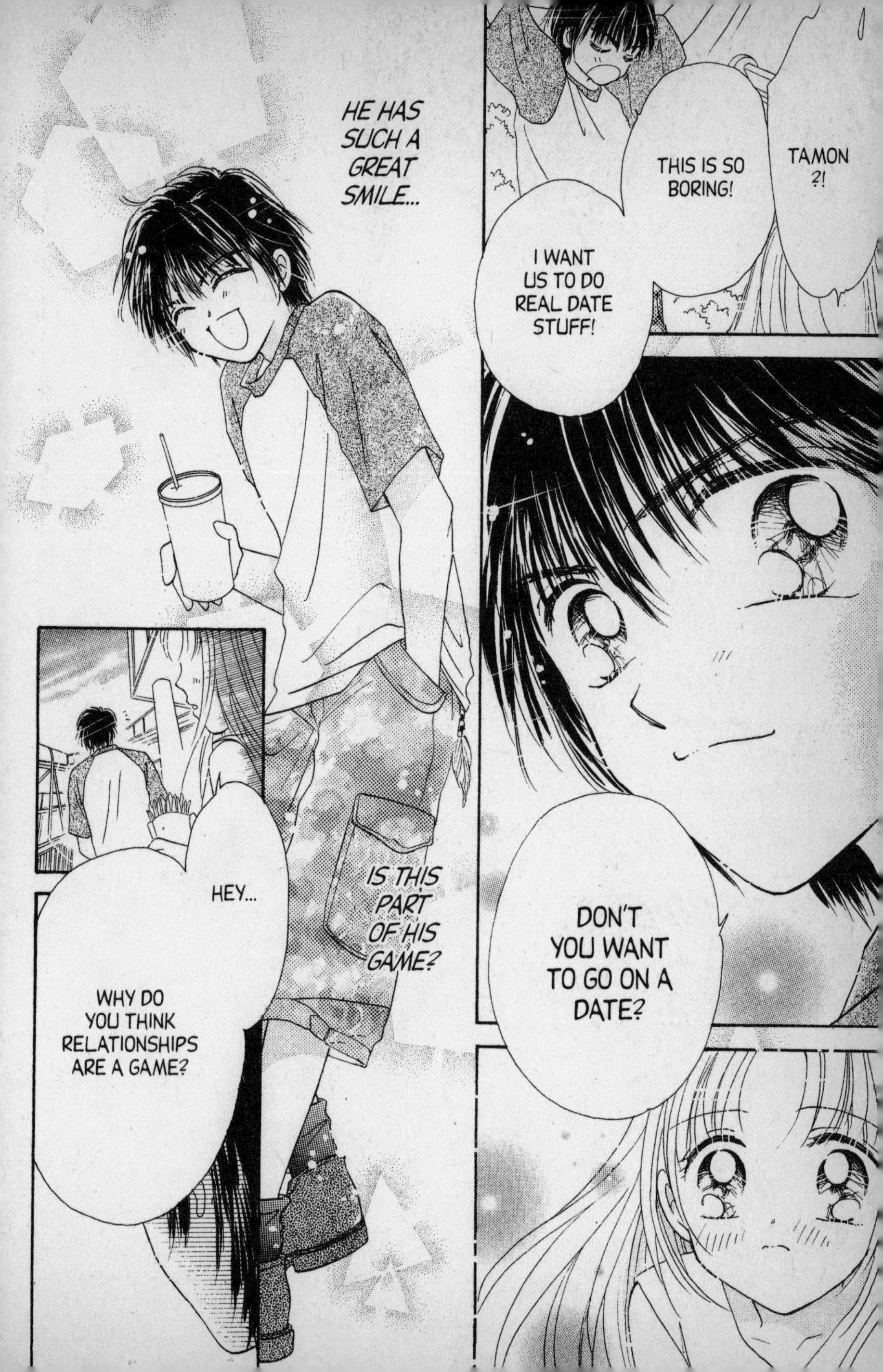
TAMON ?!
THIS IS SO BORING!
I WANT US TO DO REAL DATE STUFF!
DON'T YOU WANT TO GO ON A DATE?
HE HAS SUCH A GREAT SMILE...
IS THIS PART OF HIS GAME?
HEY...
WHY DO YOU THINK RELATIONSHIPS ARE A GAME?

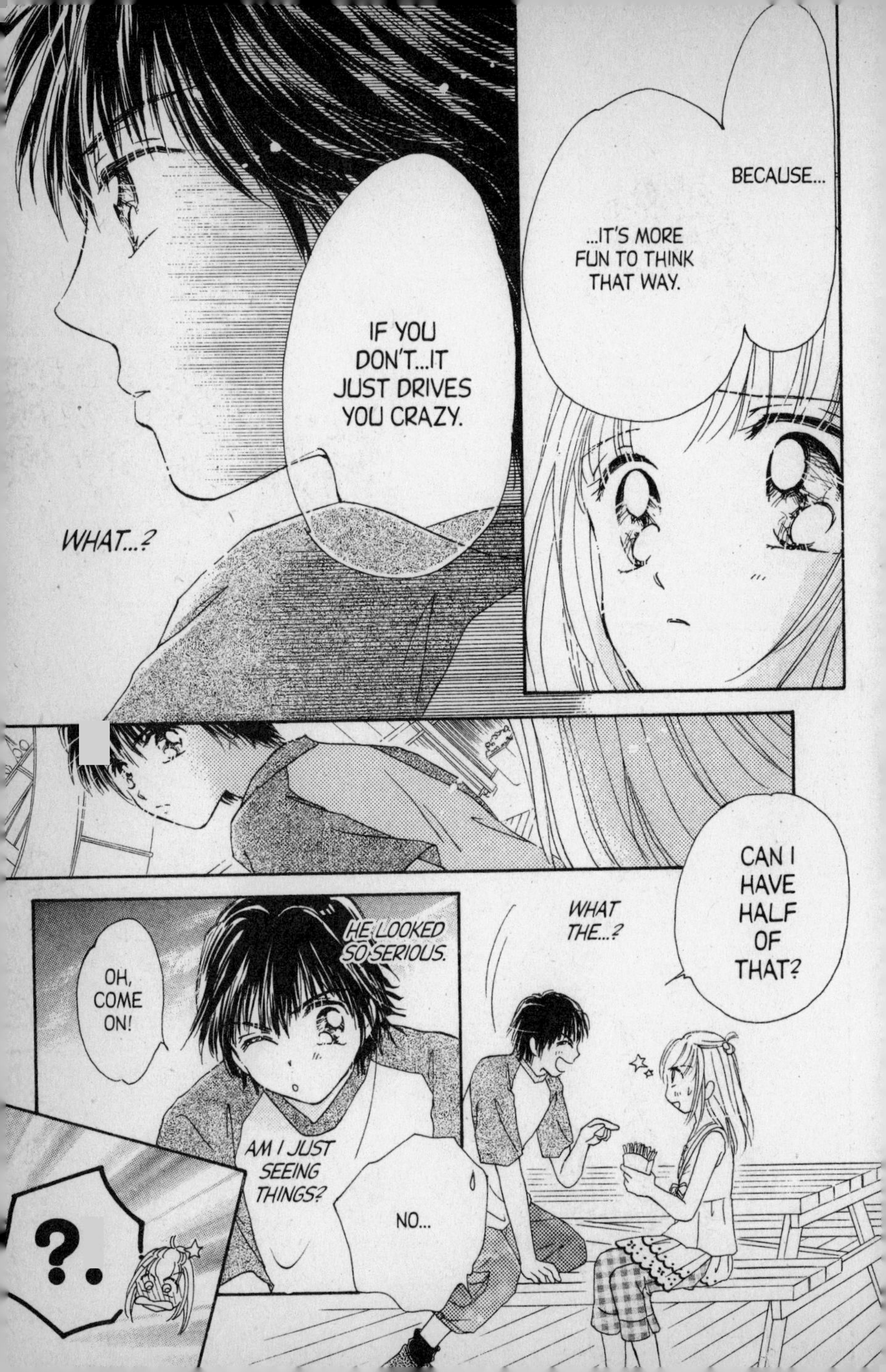
BECAUSE...
...IT'S MORE FUN TO THINK THAT WAY.
IF YOU DON'T...IT JUST DRIVES YOU CRAZY.
WHAT...?
CAN I HAVE HALF OF THAT?
WHAT THE...?
HE LOOKED SO SERIOUS.
OH, COME ON!
AM I JUST SEEING THINGS?
NO...
?.

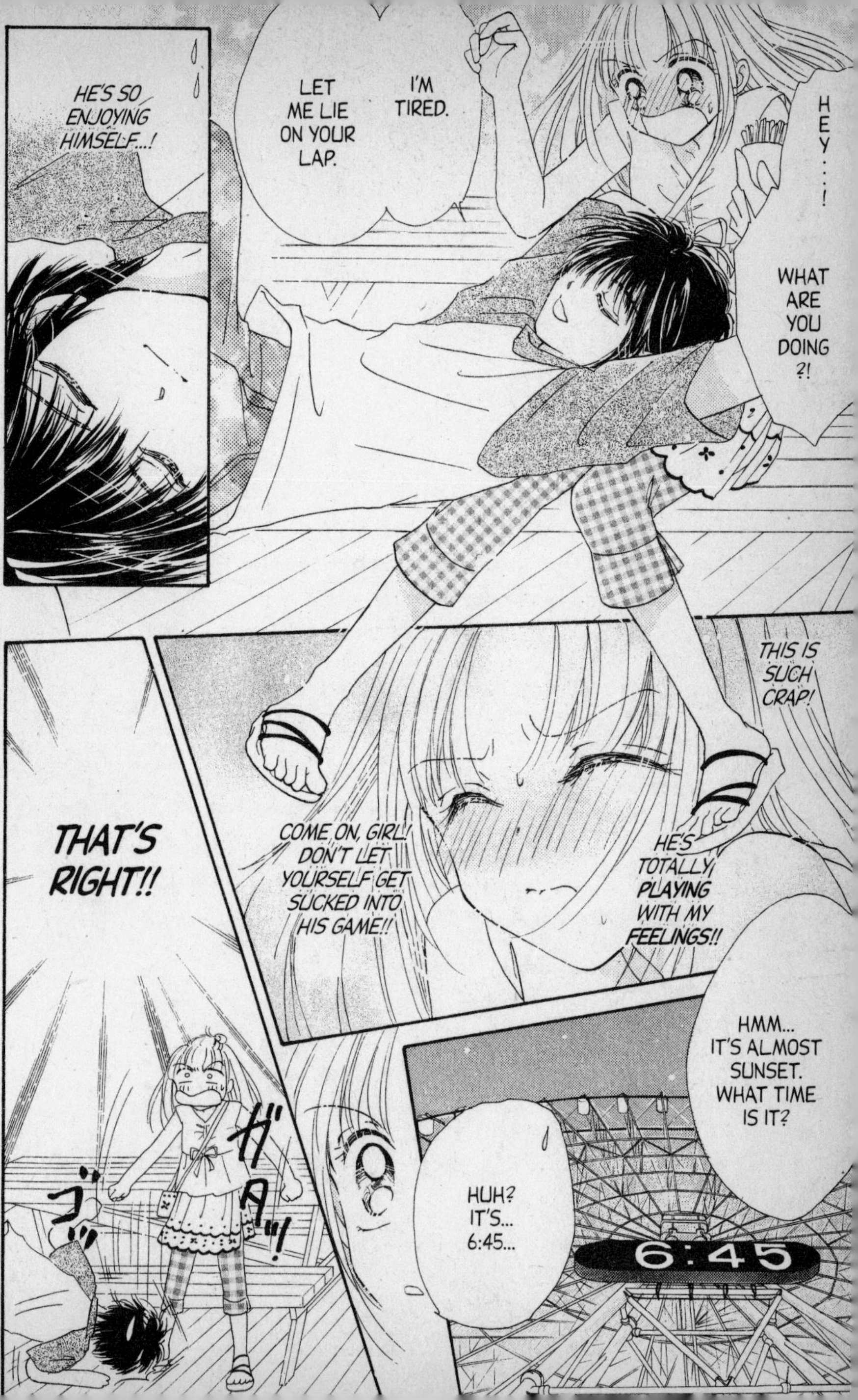
HEY...!
WHAT ARE YOU DOING?!
I'M TIRED.
LET ME LIE ON YOUR LAP.
HE'S SO ENJOYING HIMSELF...!
THIS IS SUCH CRAP!
HE'S TOTALLY PLAYING WITH MY FEELINGS!!
COME ON, GIRL! DON'T LET YOURSELF GET SUCKED INTO HIS GAME!!
HMM... IT'S ALMOST SUNSET. WHAT TIME IS IT?
HUH? IT'S... 6:45...
6:45
THAT'S RIGHT!!

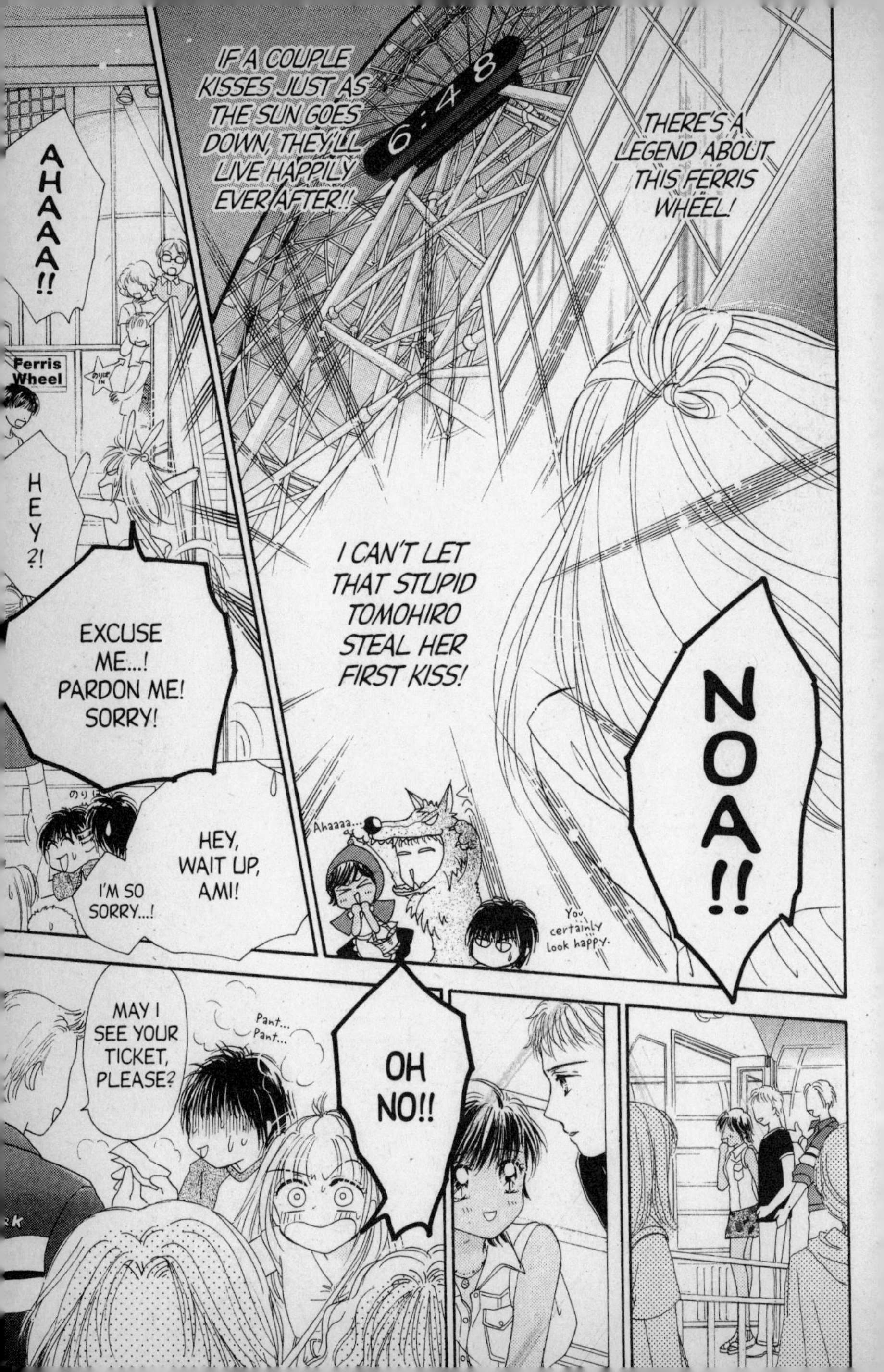
THERE'S A LEGEND ABOUT THIS FERRIS WHEEL!
6:48
IF A COUPLE KISSES JUST AS THE SUN GOES DOWN, THEY'LL LIVE HAPPILY EVER AFTER!!
I CAN'T LET THAT STUPID TOMOHIRO STEAL HER FIRST KISS!
NOA!!
You certainly look happy.
Ahaaaa...
AHAAAA!!
Ferris Wheel
HEY?!
EXCUSE ME...! PARDON ME! SORRY!
HEY, WAIT UP, AMI!
I'M SO SORRY...!
OH NO!!
Pant... Pant...
MAY I SEE YOUR TICKET, PLEASE?

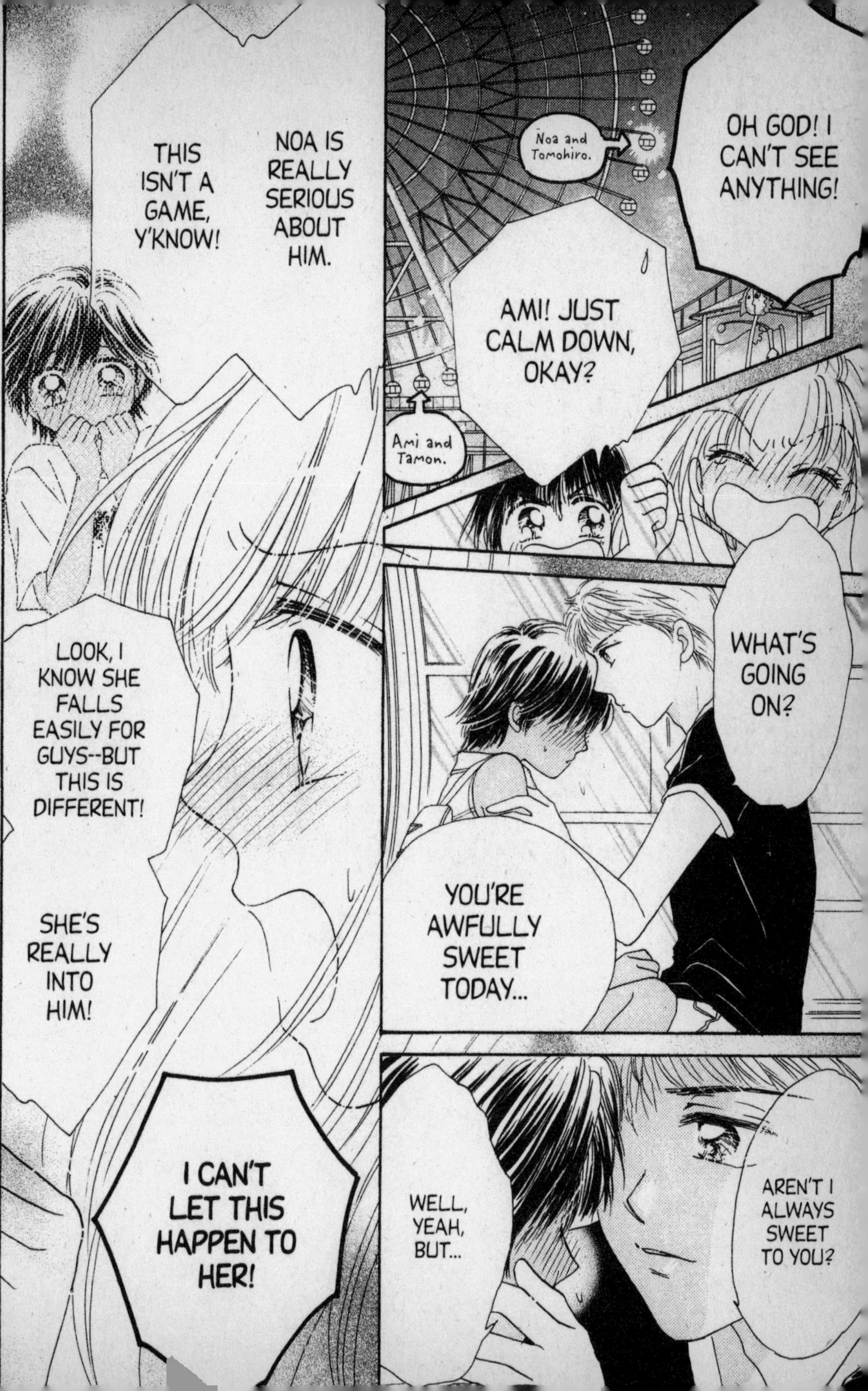
OH GOD! I CAN'T SEE ANYTHING!
Noa and Tomohiro.
AMI! JUST CALM DOWN, OKAY?
Ami and Tamon.
WHAT'S GOING ON?
YOU'RE AWFULLY SWEET TODAY...
AREN'T I ALWAYS SWEET TO YOU?
WELL, YEAH, BUT...
NOA IS REALLY SERIOUS ABOUT HIM.
THIS ISN'T A GAME, Y'KNOW!
LOOK, I KNOW SHE FALLS EASILY FOR GUYS--BUT THIS IS DIFFERENT!
SHE'S REALLY INTO HIM!
I CAN'T LET THIS HAPPEN TO HER!

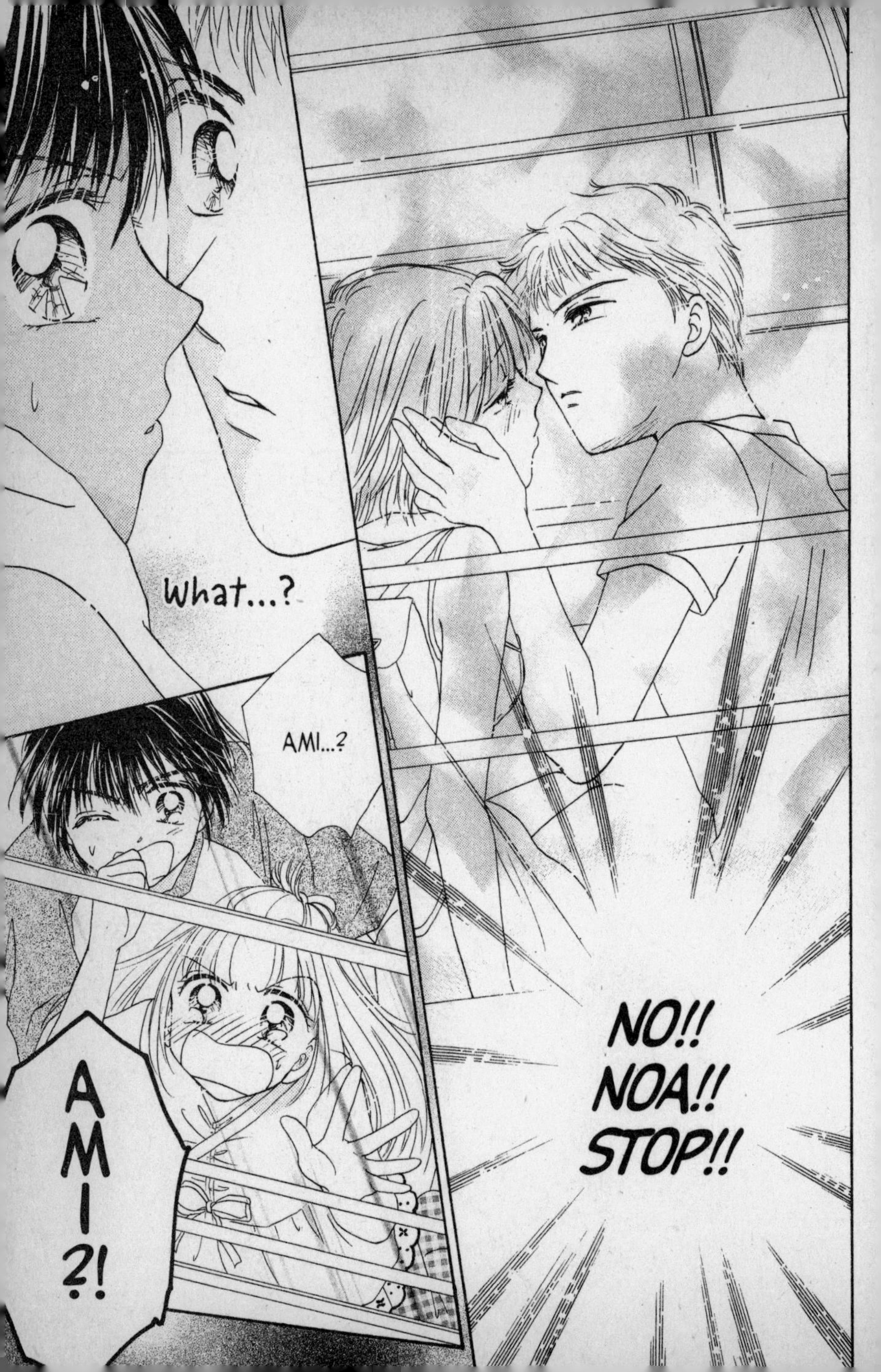
NO!! NOA!! STOP!!
What...?
AMI...?
AMI?!

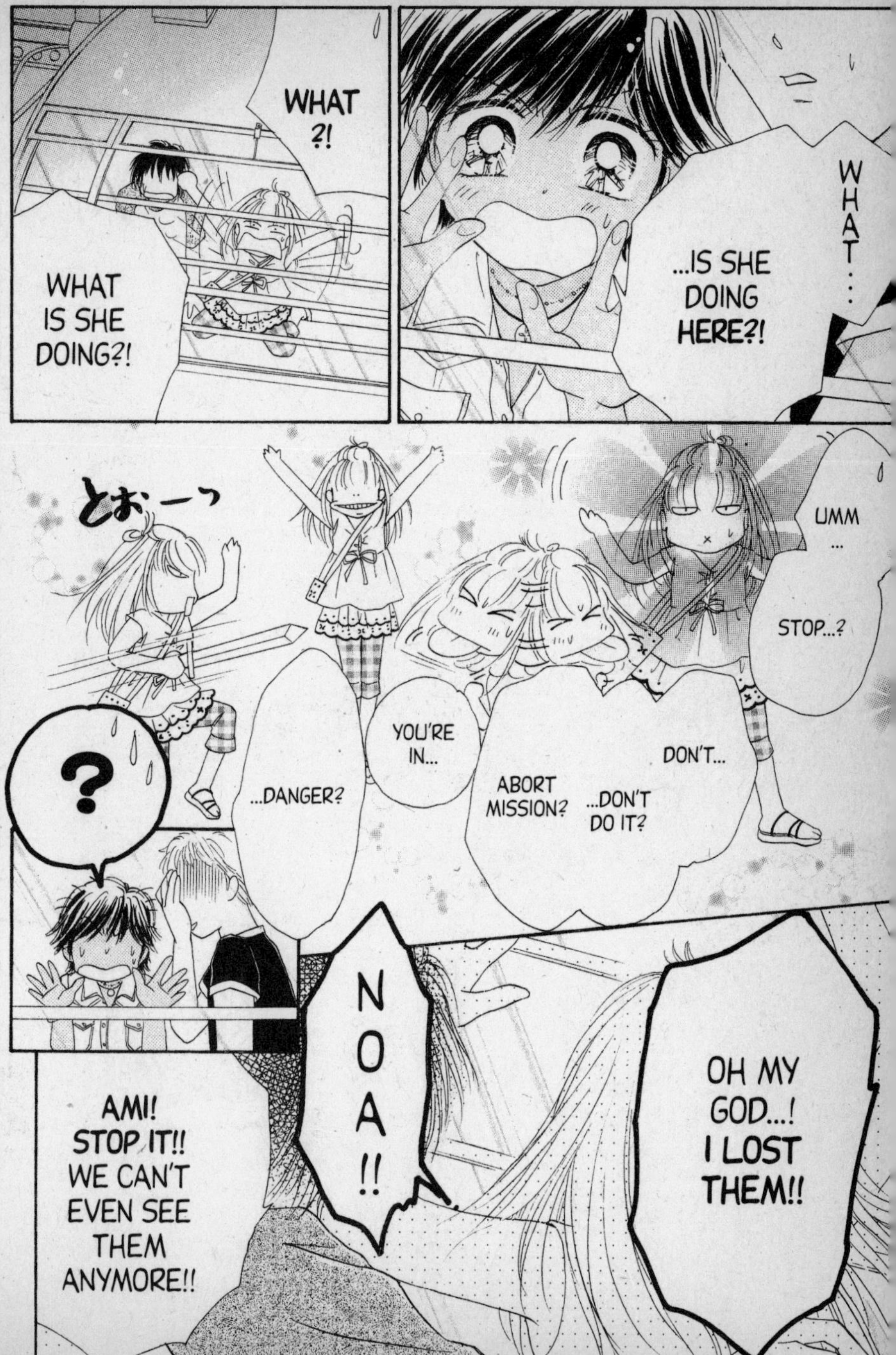
WHAT...
...IS SHE DOING HERE?!
WHAT?!
WHAT IS SHE DOING?!
UMM... STOP...?
DON'T...
...DON'T DO IT?
ABORT MISSION?
YOU'RE IN...
...DANGER?
とおーっ
OH MY GOD...! I LOST THEM!!
NOA!!
?
AMI! STOP IT!! WE CAN'T EVEN SEE THEM ANYMORE!!

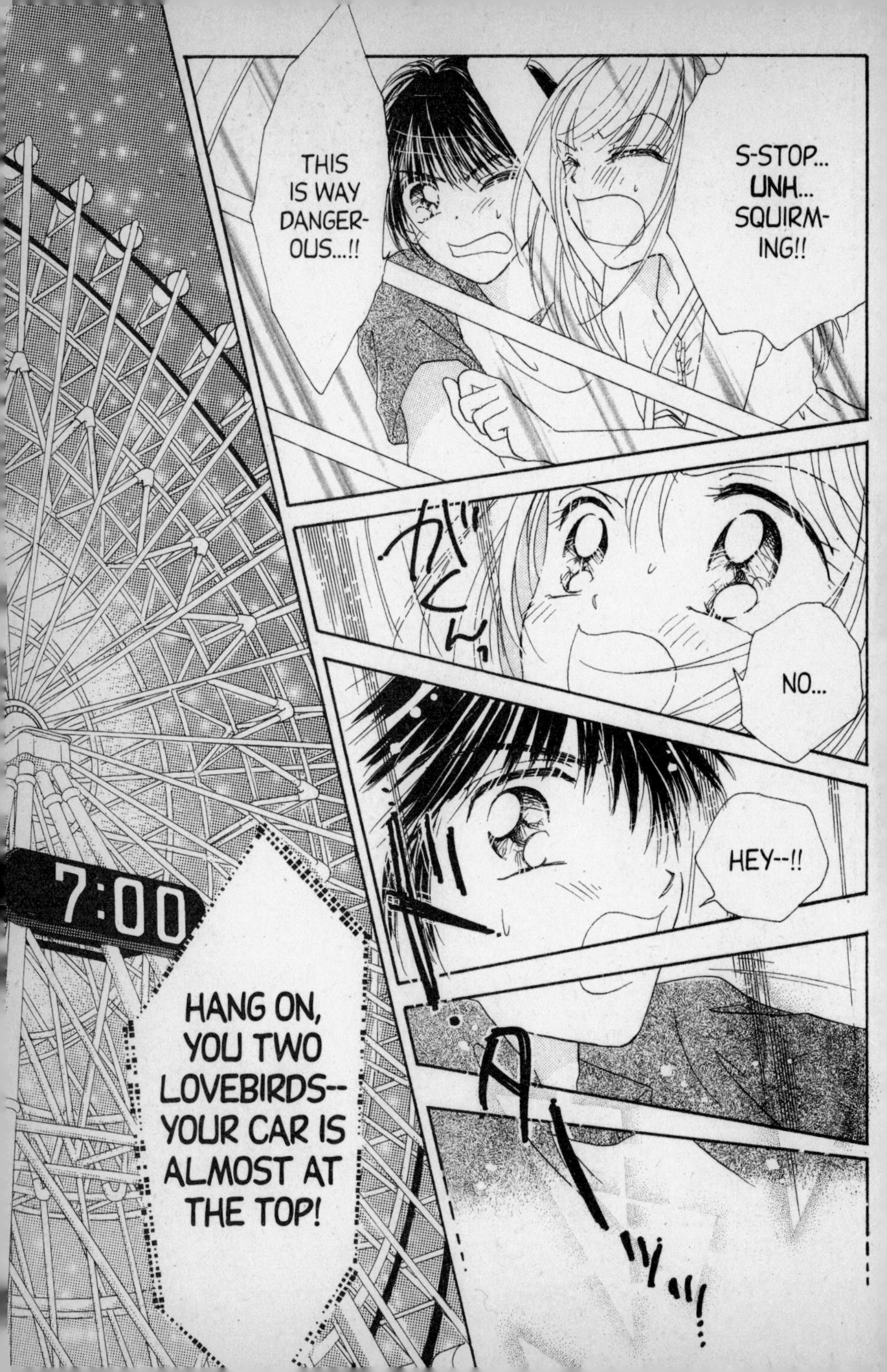
S-STOP... UNH... SQUIRMING!!
THIS IS WAY DANGEROUS...!!
がくん
NO...
HEY--!!
7:00
HANG ON, YOU TWO LOVEBIRDS-- YOUR CAR IS ALMOST AT THE TOP!

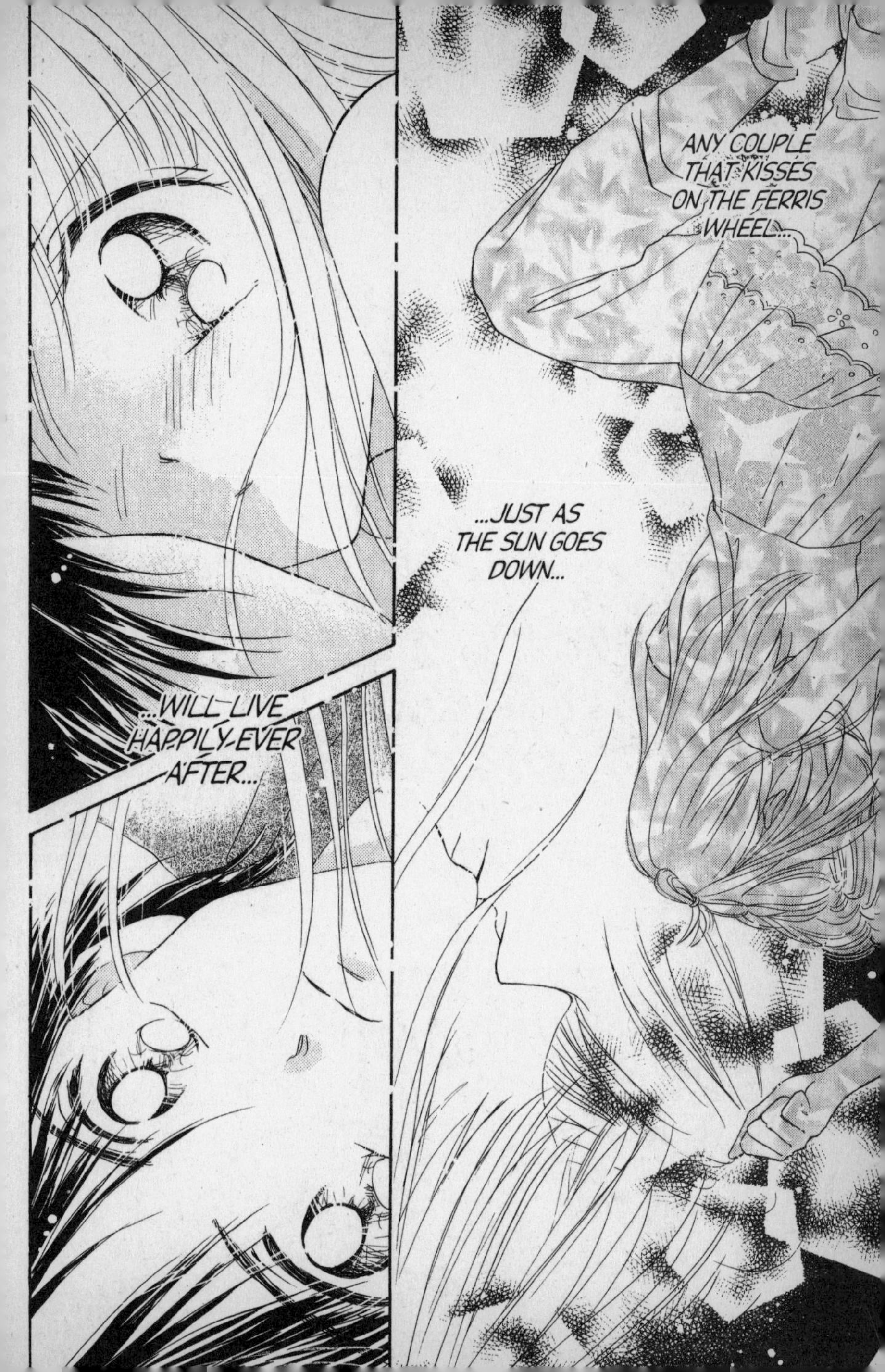
ANY COUPLE THAT KISSES ON THE FERRIS WHEEL...
...JUST AS THE SUN GOES DOWN...
...WILL LIVE HAPPILY EVER AFTER...

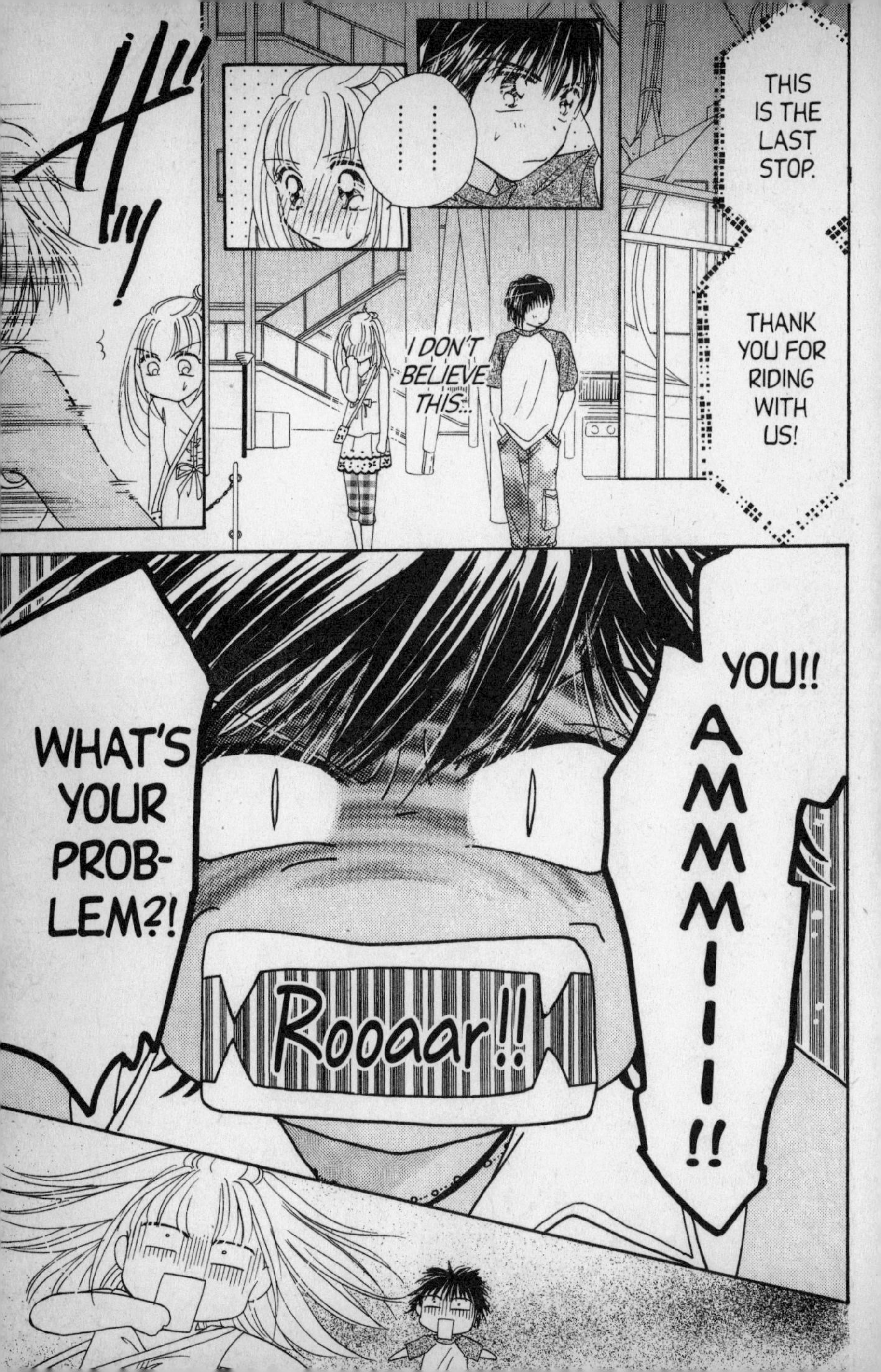

THIS IS THE LAST STOP.
THANK YOU FOR RIDING WITH US!
......
I DON'T BELIEVE THIS...
YOU!!
AMMMIII!!
WHAT'S YOUR PROB-LEM?!
Rooaar!!

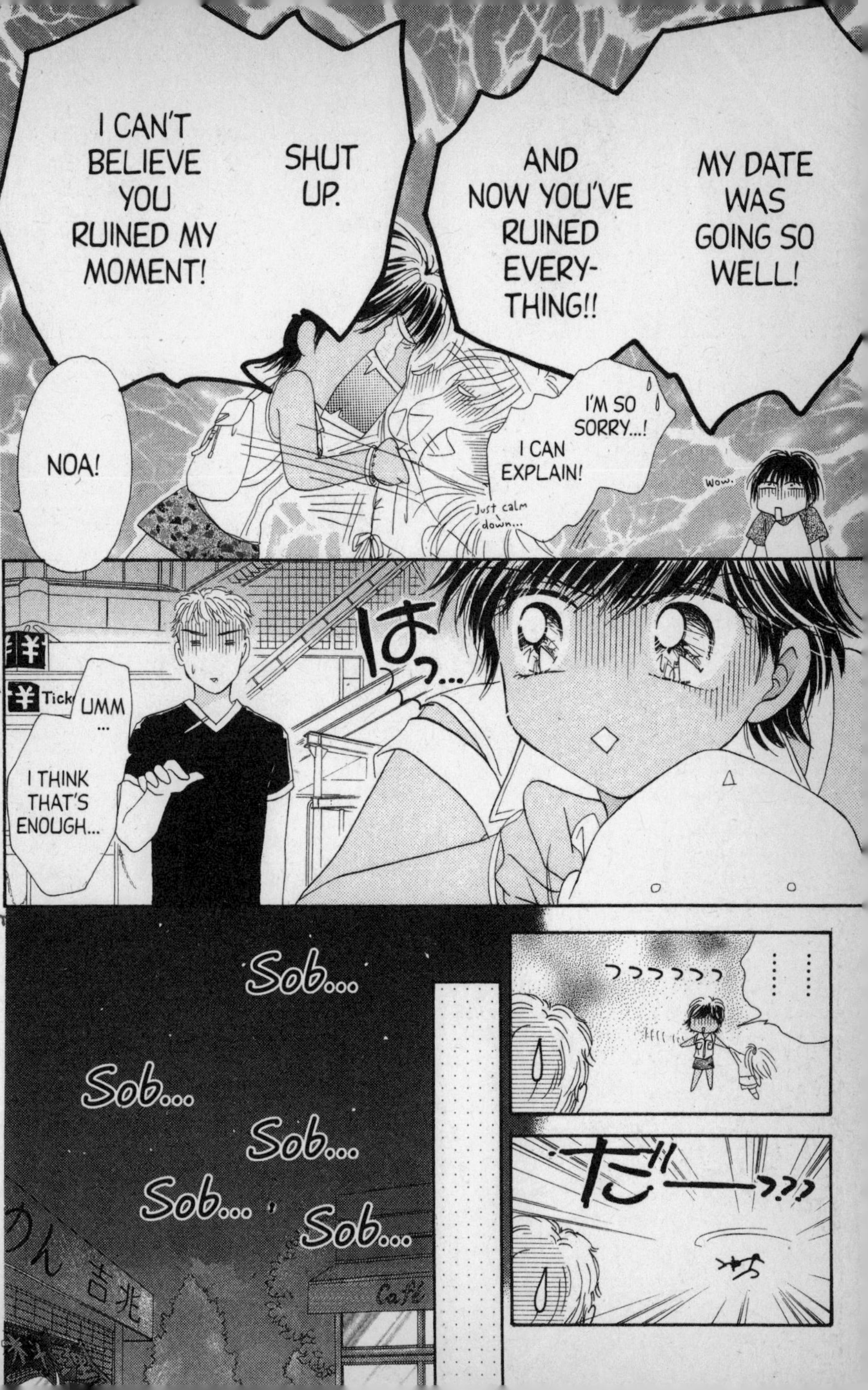
MY DATE WAS GOING SO WELL!
AND NOW YOU'VE RUINED EVERY-THING!!
SHUT UP.
I CAN'T BELIEVE YOU RUINED MY MOMENT!
I'M SO SORRY...!
I CAN EXPLAIN!
Wow.
Just calm down...
NOA!
はっ...
UMM ...
I THINK THAT'S ENOUGH...
......
......
つつつつつつ
だーっっっ
Sob...
Sob...
Sob...
Sob...
Sob...
Café

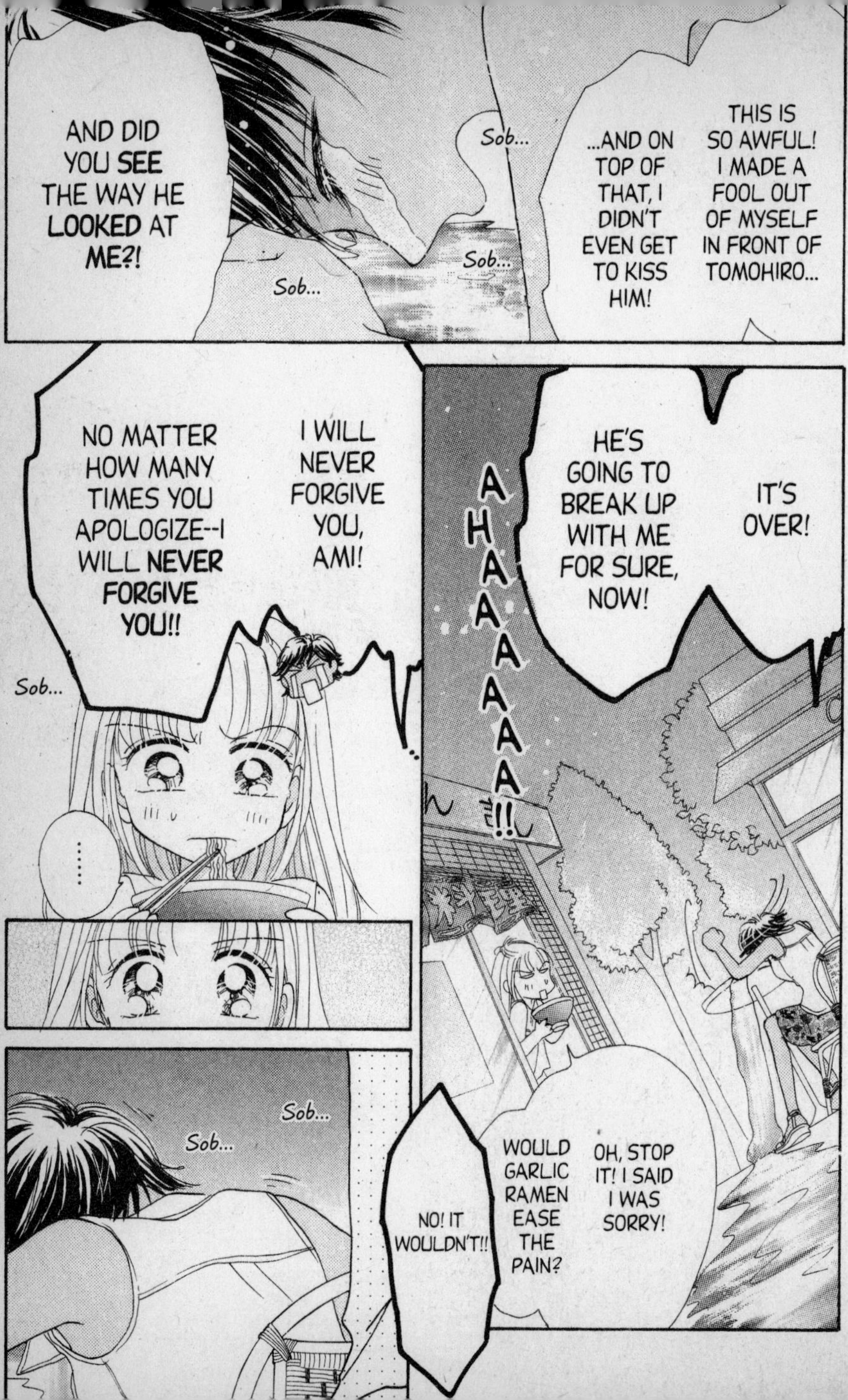
THIS IS SO AWFUL! I MADE A FOOL OUT OF MYSELF IN FRONT OF TOMOHIRO...
...AND ON TOP OF THAT, I DIDN'T EVEN GET TO KISS HIM!
Sob...
Sob...
Sob...
AND DID YOU SEE THE WAY HE LOOKED AT ME?!
IT'S OVER!
HE'S GOING TO BREAK UP WITH ME FOR SURE, NOW!
AHAAAAAAA!!
OH, STOP IT! I SAID I WAS SORRY!
WOULD GARLIC RAMEN EASE THE PAIN?
NO! IT WOULDN'T!!
I WILL NEVER FORGIVE YOU, AMI!
NO MATTER HOW MANY TIMES YOU APOLOGIZE--I WILL NEVER FORGIVE YOU!!
Sob...
......
Sob...
Sob...

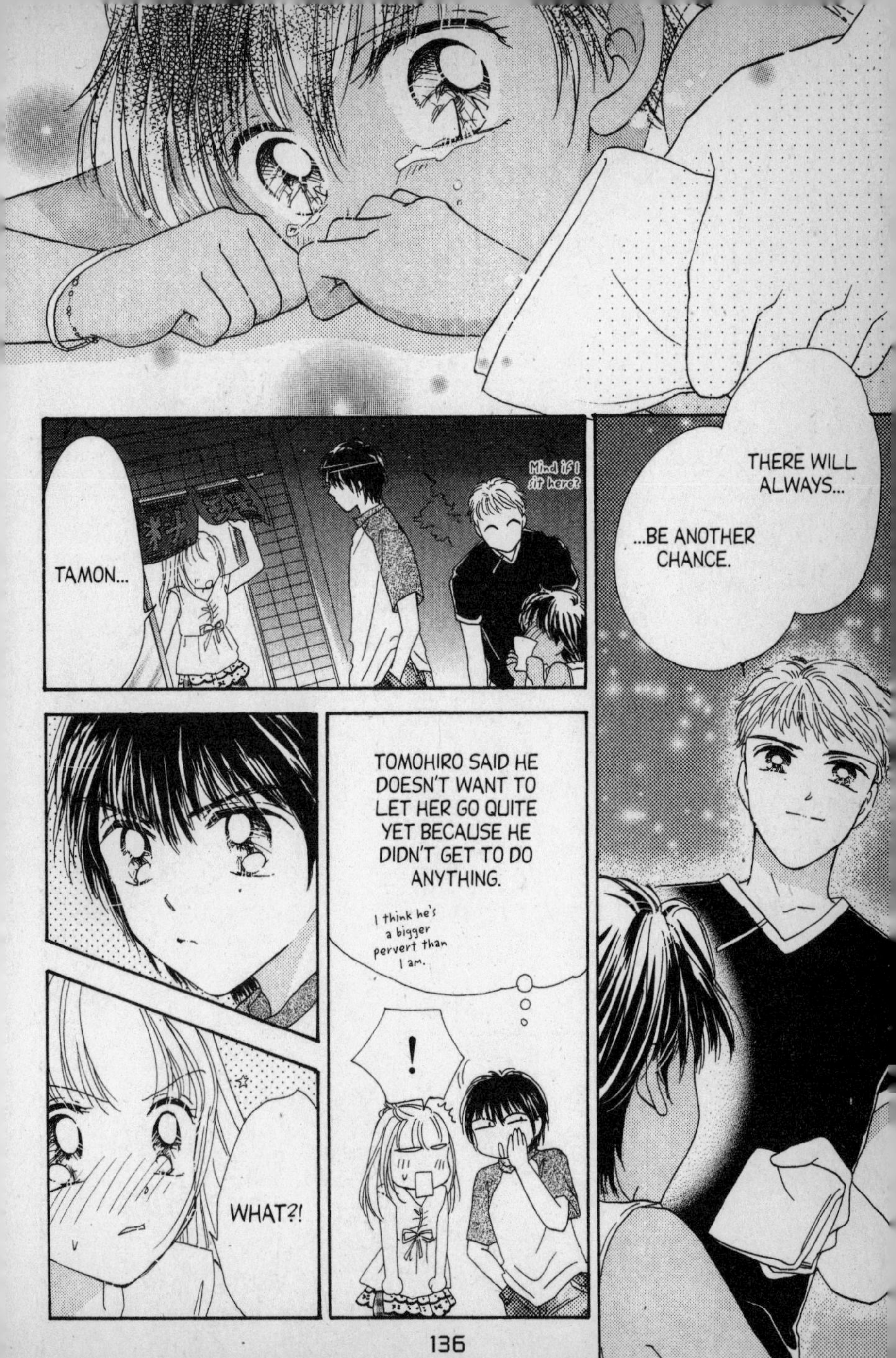
THERE WILL ALWAYS...
...BE ANOTHER CHANCE.
Mind if I sit here?
TAMON...
TOMOHIRO SAID HE DOESN'T WANT TO LET HER GO QUITE YET BECAUSE HE DIDN'T GET TO DO ANYTHING.
I think he's a bigger pervert than I am.
!
WHAT?!

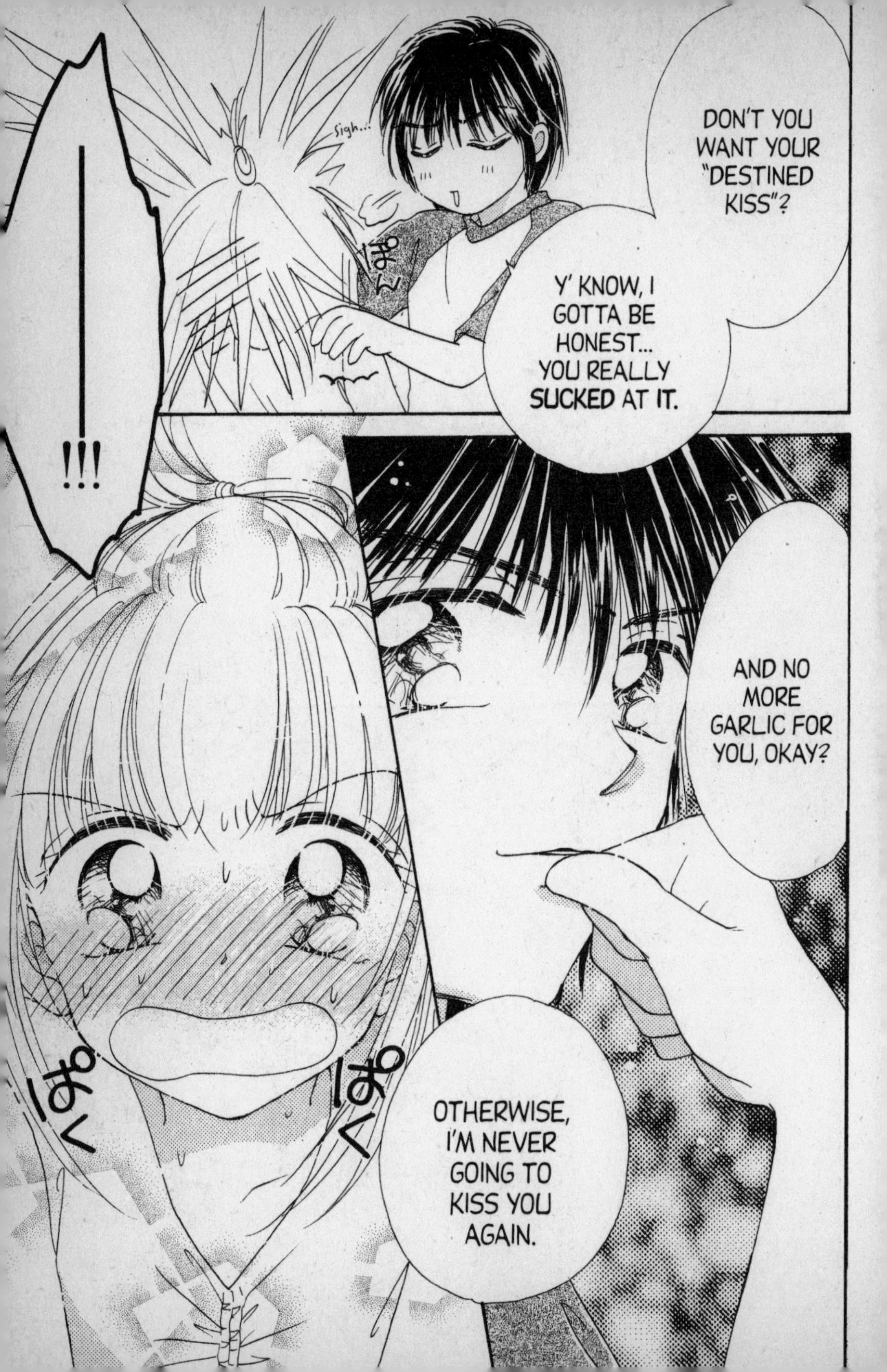
DON'T YOU WANT YOUR "DESTINED KISS"?
Y' KNOW, I GOTTA BE HONEST... YOU REALLY **SUCKED** AT IT.
Sigh...
ぽん
AND NO MORE GARLIC FOR YOU, OKAY?
OTHERWISE, I'M NEVER GOING TO KISS YOU AGAIN.
!!!
ぱく
ぱく

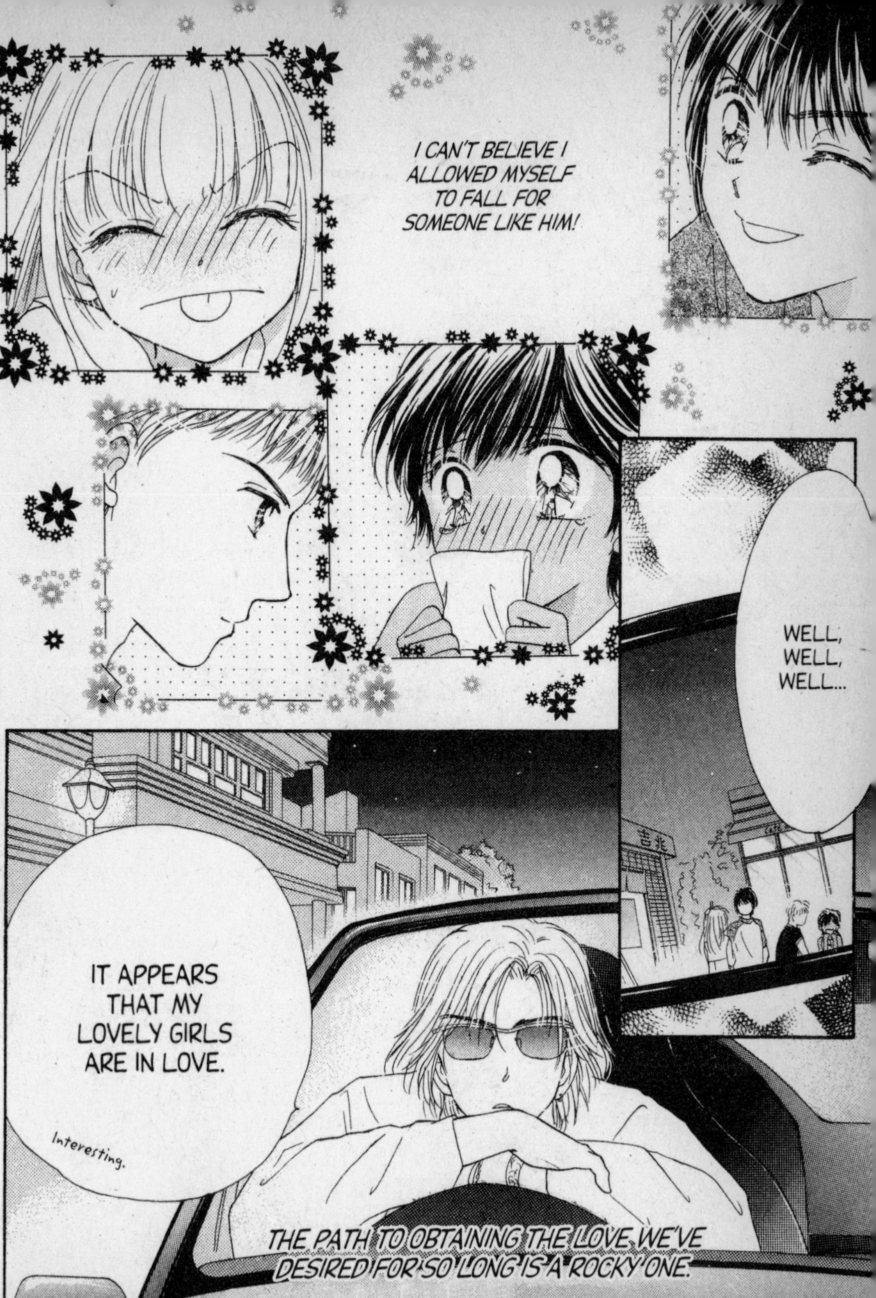
I CAN'T BELIEVE I ALLOWED MYSELF TO FALL FOR SOMEONE LIKE HIM!
WELL, WELL, WELL...
IT APPEARS THAT MY LOVELY GIRLS ARE IN LOVE.
Interesting.
THE PATH TO OBTAINING THE LOVE WE'VE DESIRED FOR SO LONG IS A ROCKY ONE.

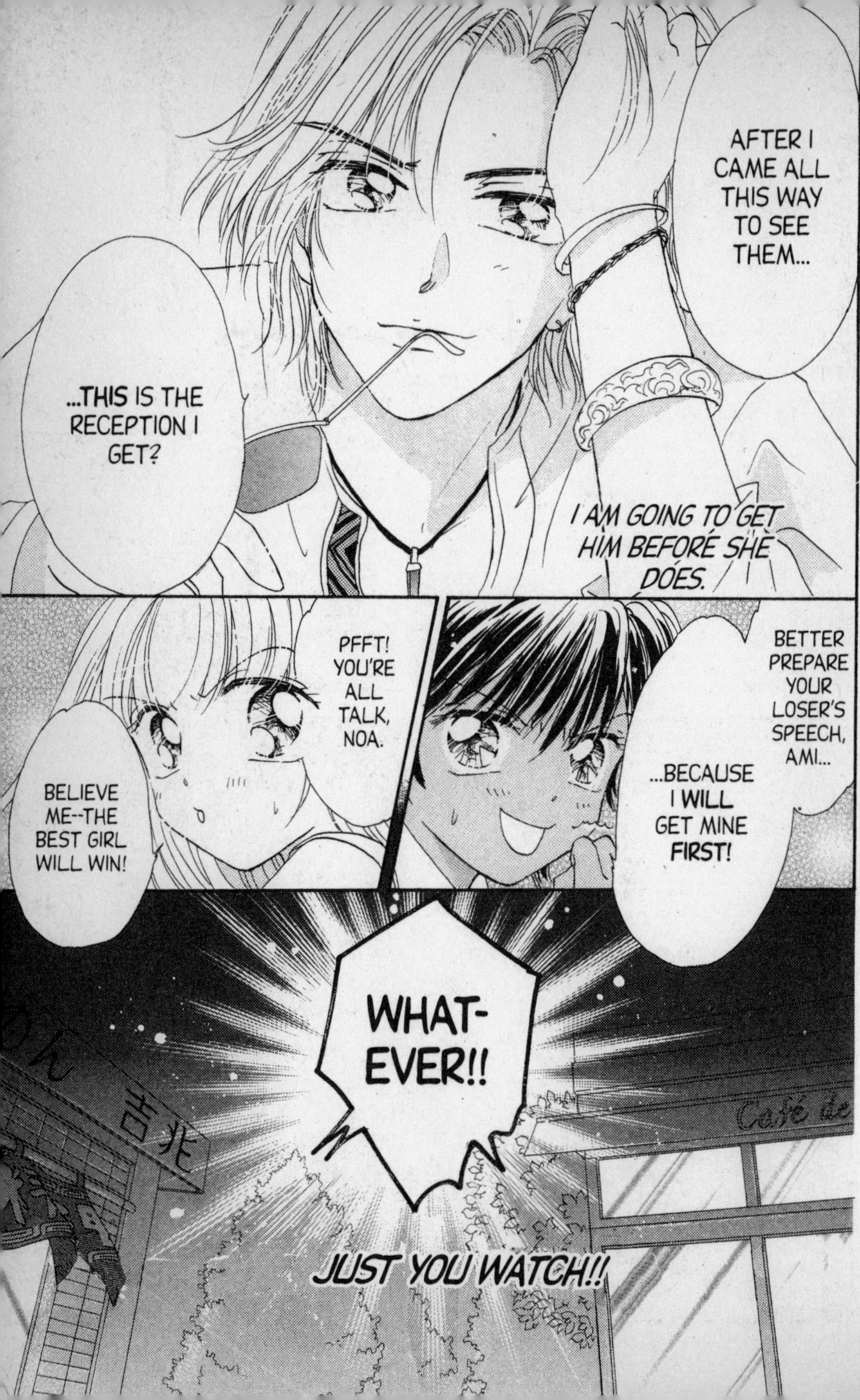
AFTER I CAME ALL THIS WAY TO SEE THEM...
...THIS IS THE RECEPTION I GET?
I AM GOING TO GET HIM BEFORE SHE DOES.
BETTER PREPARE YOUR LOSER'S SPEECH, AMI...
...BECAUSE I WILL GET MINE FIRST!
PFFT! YOU'RE ALL TALK, NOA.
BELIEVE ME--THE BEST GIRL WILL WIN!
WHAT-EVER!!
Café de
JUST YOU WATCH!!

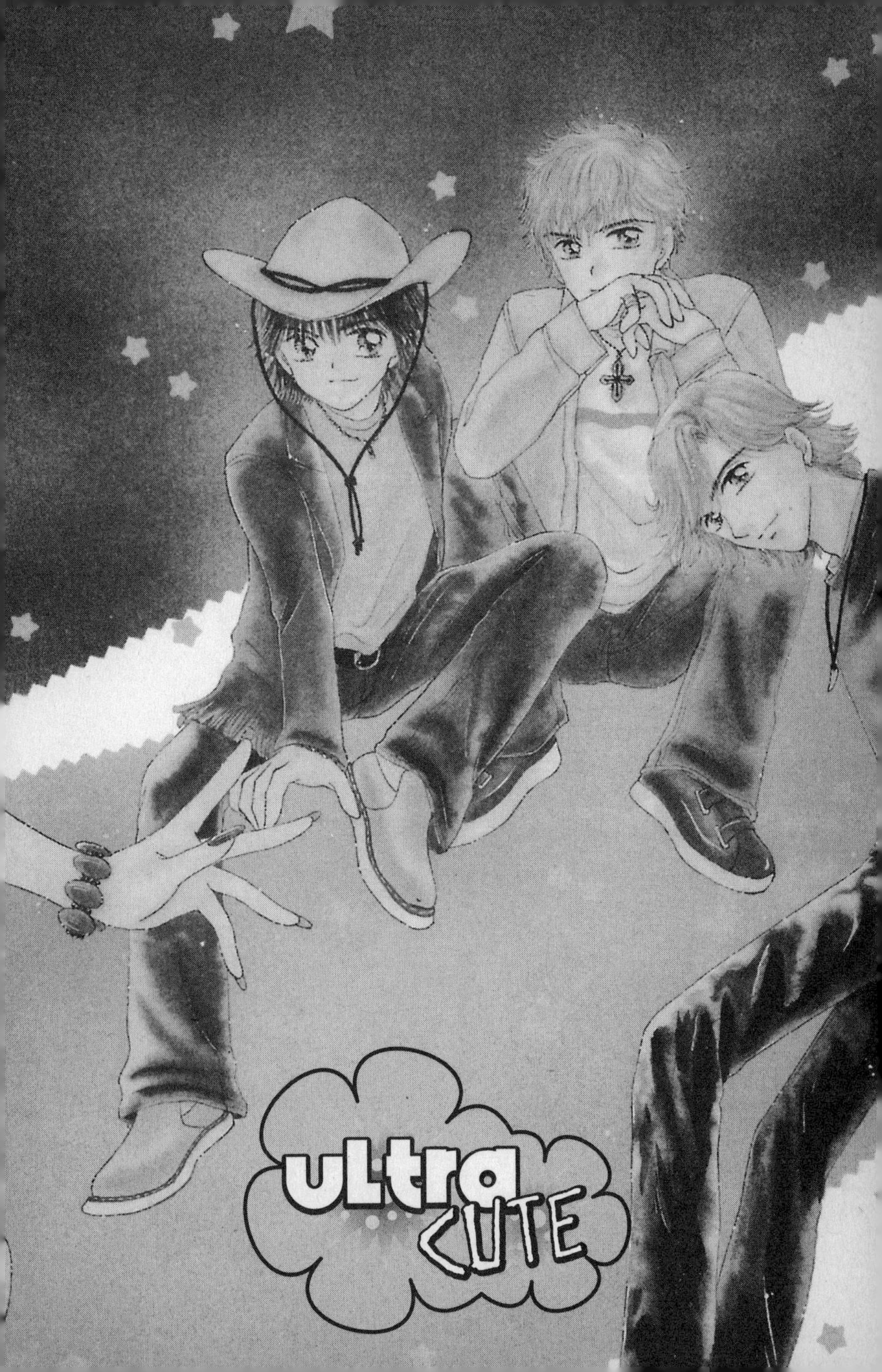
ultra
CUTE

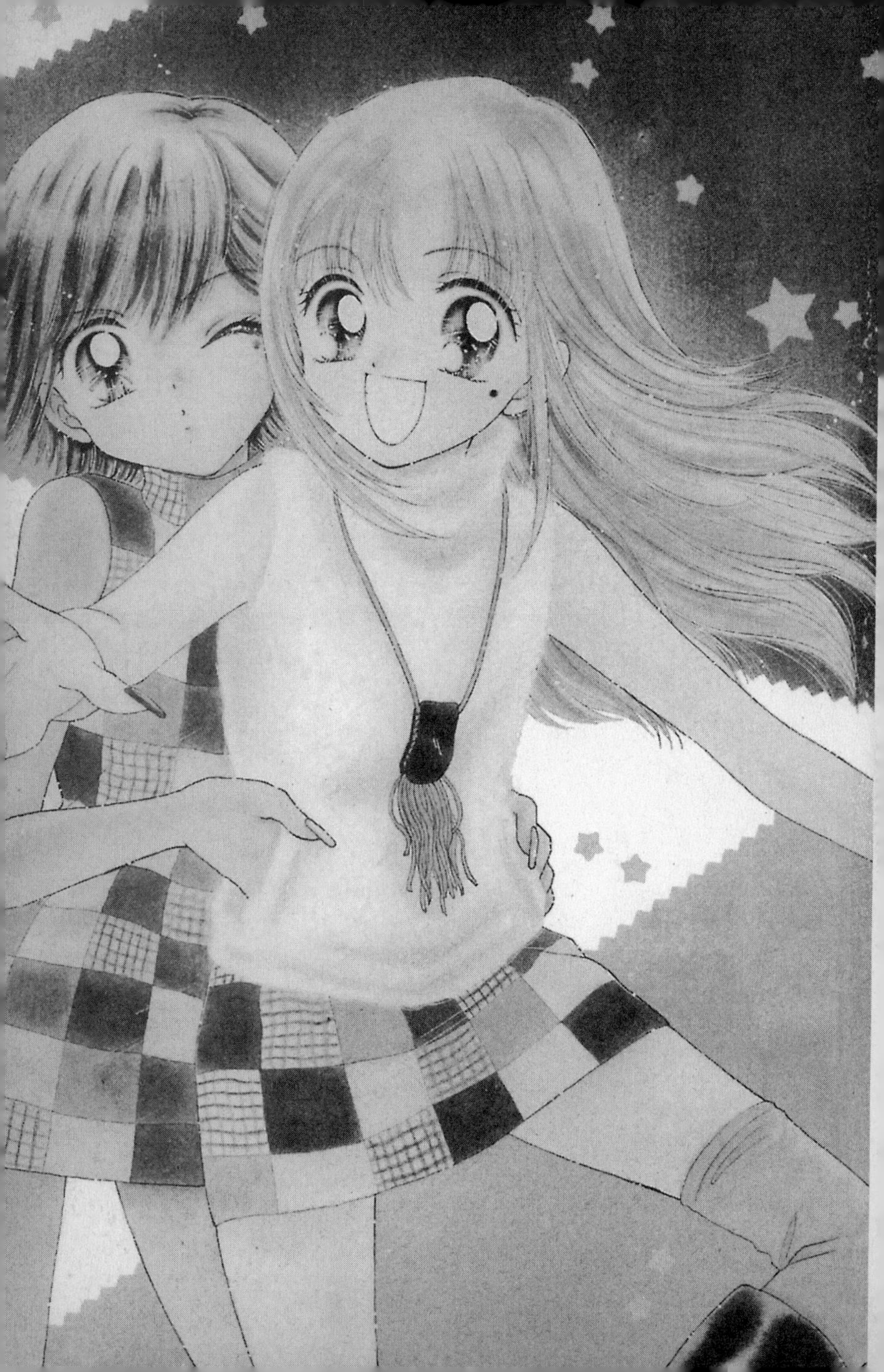

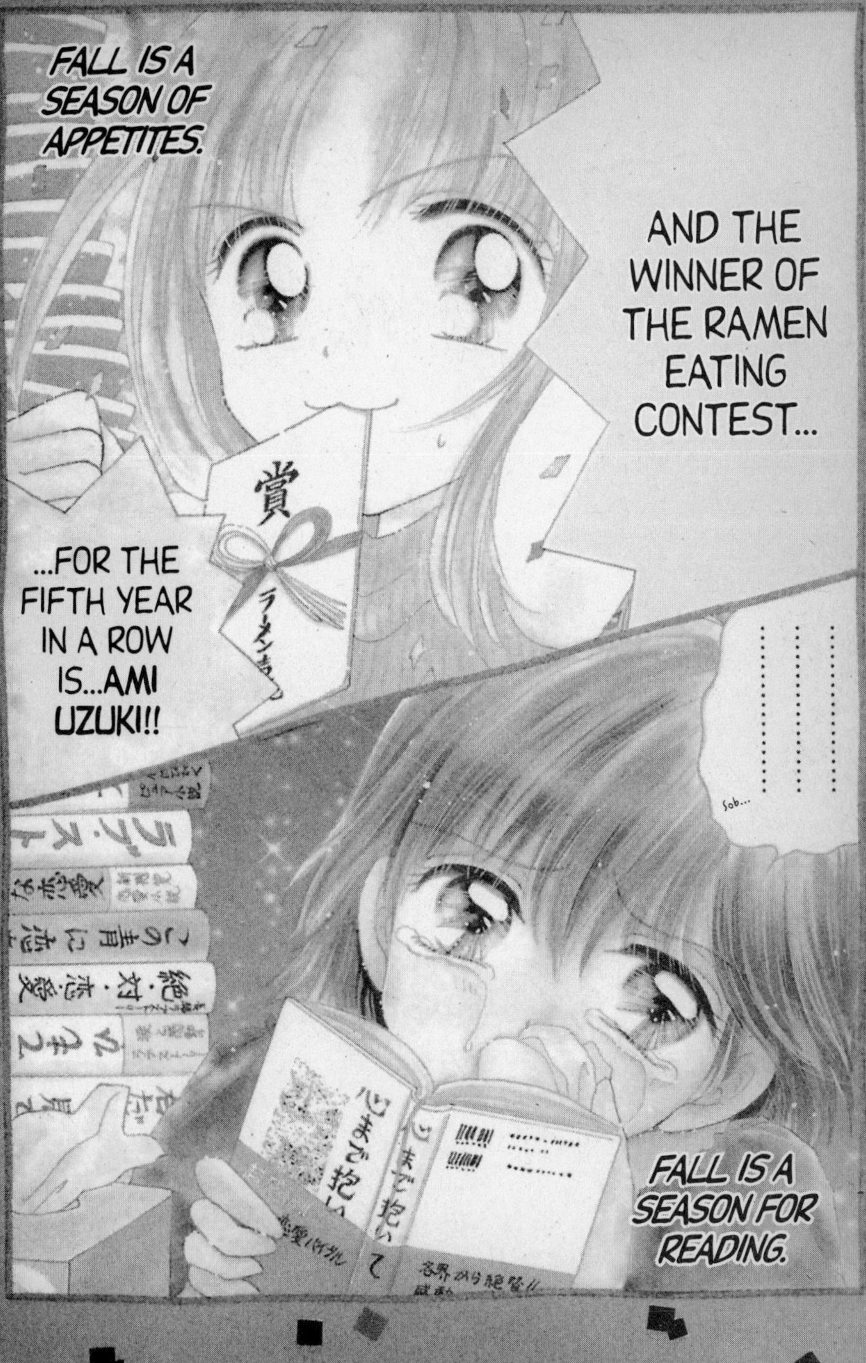
FALL IS A SEASON OF APPETITES.
AND THE WINNER OF THE RAMEN EATING CONTEST...
賞
...FOR THE FIFTH YEAR IN A ROW IS...AMI UZUKI!!
......
Sob...
FALL IS A SEASON FOR READING.

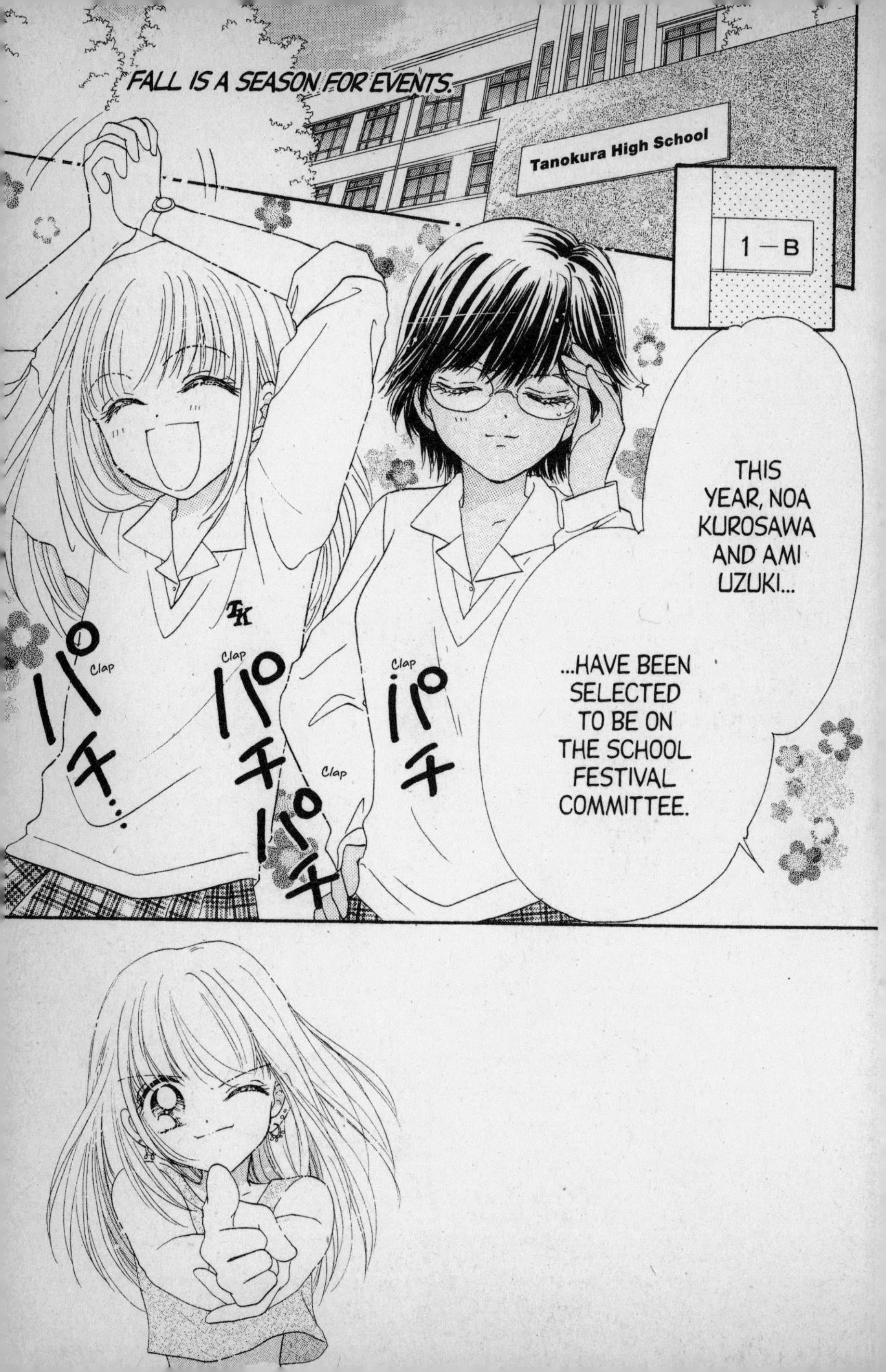
FALL IS A SEASON FOR EVENTS.
Tanokura High School
1—B
THIS YEAR, NOA KUROSAWA AND AMI UZUKI...
...HAVE BEEN SELECTED TO BE ON THE SCHOOL FESTIVAL COMMITTEE.
パチ Clap
パチパチ Clap Clap
パチ… Clap

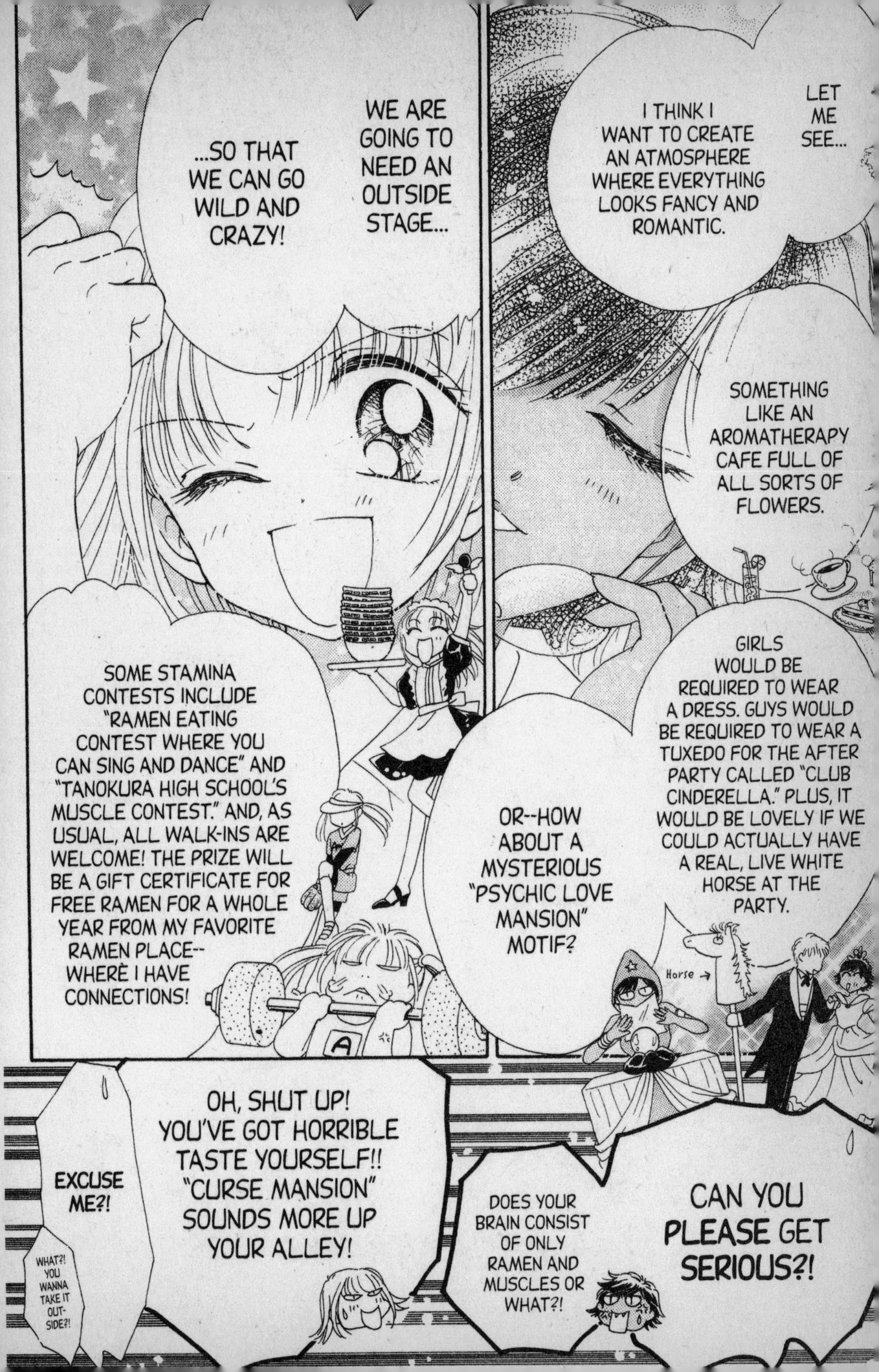
LET ME SEE...
I THINK I WANT TO CREATE AN ATMOSPHERE WHERE EVERYTHING LOOKS FANCY AND ROMANTIC.
SOMETHING LIKE AN AROMATHERAPY CAFE FULL OF ALL SORTS OF FLOWERS.
GIRLS WOULD BE REQUIRED TO WEAR A DRESS. GUYS WOULD BE REQUIRED TO WEAR A TUXEDO FOR THE AFTER PARTY CALLED "CLUB CINDERELLA." PLUS, IT WOULD BE LOVELY IF WE COULD ACTUALLY HAVE A REAL, LIVE WHITE HORSE AT THE PARTY.
OR--HOW ABOUT A MYSTERIOUS "PSYCHIC LOVE MANSION" MOTIF?
Horse →
WE ARE GOING TO NEED AN OUTSIDE STAGE...
...SO THAT WE CAN GO WILD AND CRAZY!
SOME STAMINA CONTESTS INCLUDE "RAMEN EATING CONTEST WHERE YOU CAN SING AND DANCE" AND "TANOKURA HIGH SCHOOL'S MUSCLE CONTEST." AND, AS USUAL, ALL WALK-INS ARE WELCOME! THE PRIZE WILL BE A GIFT CERTIFICATE FOR FREE RAMEN FOR A WHOLE YEAR FROM MY FAVORITE RAMEN PLACE--WHERE I HAVE CONNECTIONS!
A
CAN YOU PLEASE GET SERIOUS?!
DOES YOUR BRAIN CONSIST OF ONLY RAMEN AND MUSCLES OR WHAT?!
OH, SHUT UP! YOU'VE GOT HORRIBLE TASTE YOURSELF!! "CURSE MANSION" SOUNDS MORE UP YOUR ALLEY!
EXCUSE ME?!
WHAT?! YOU WANNA TAKE IT OUT-SIDE?!

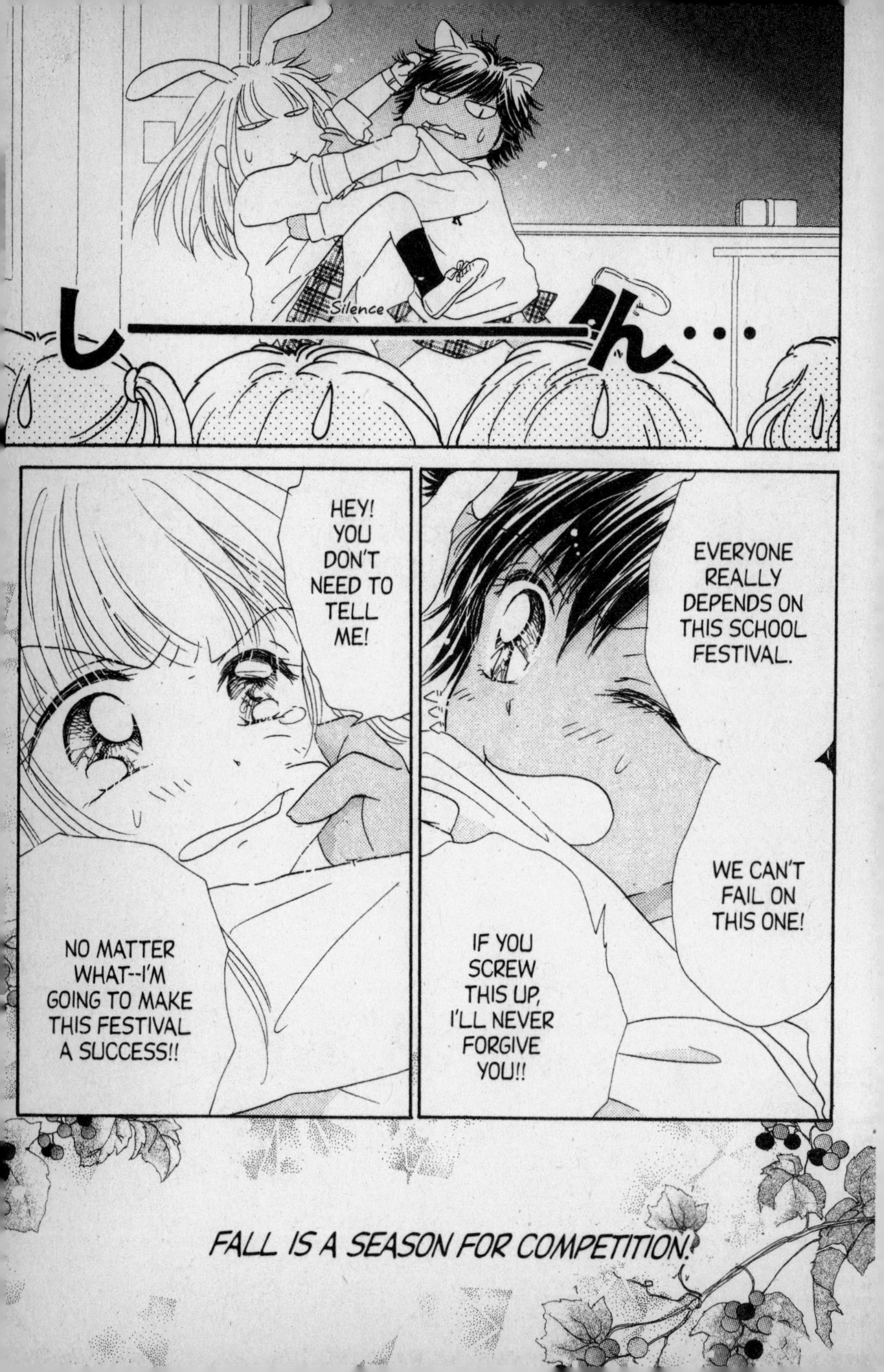

Silence
し––––ん…
EVERYONE REALLY DEPENDS ON THIS SCHOOL FESTIVAL.
WE CAN'T FAIL ON THIS ONE!
IF YOU SCREW THIS UP, I'LL NEVER FORGIVE YOU!!
HEY! YOU DON'T NEED TO TELL ME!
NO MATTER WHAT--I'M GOING TO MAKE THIS FESTIVAL A SUCCESS!!
FALL IS A SEASON FOR COMPETITION!

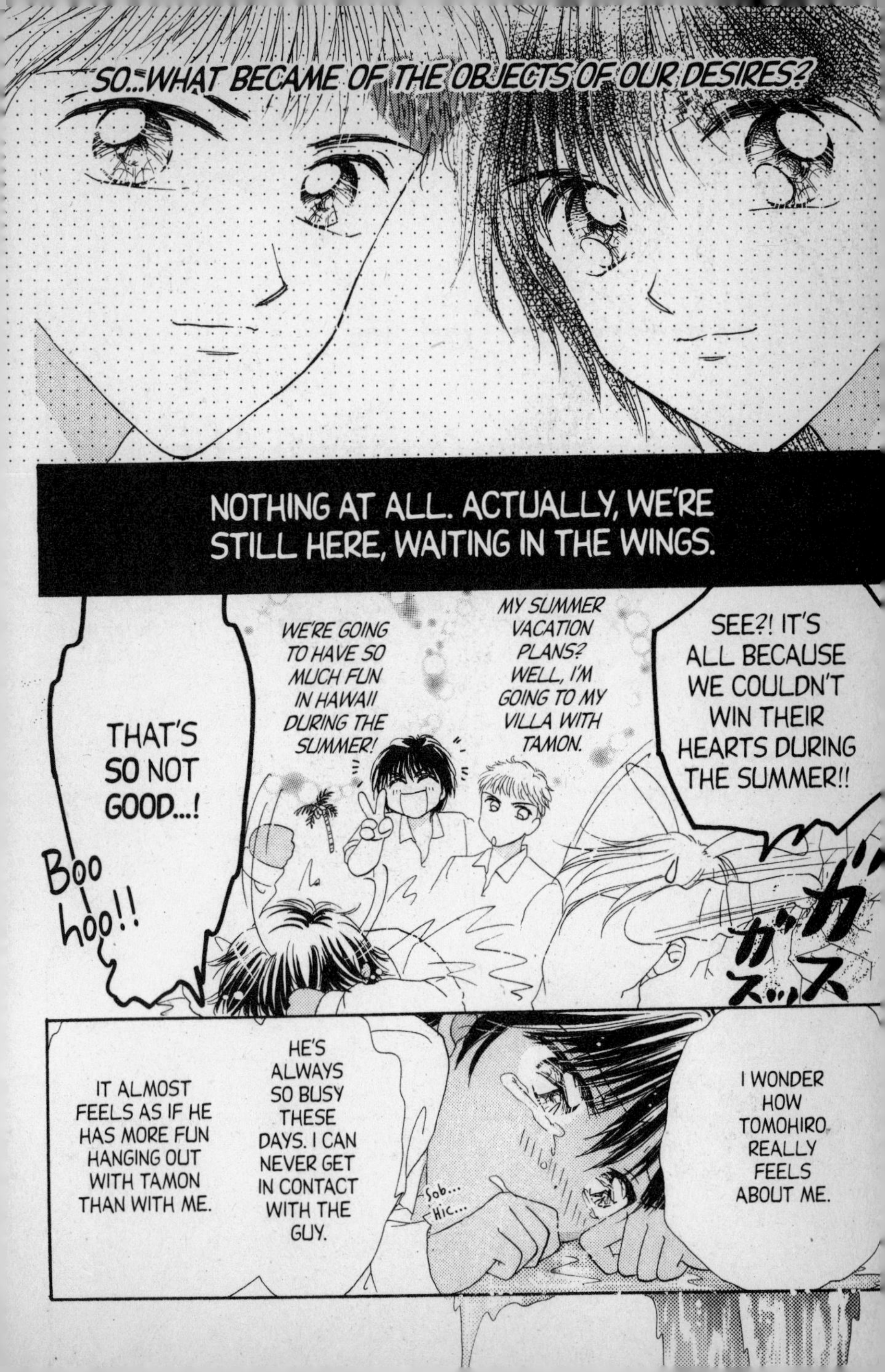
SO...WHAT BECAME OF THE OBJECTS OF OUR DESIRES?
NOTHING AT ALL. ACTUALLY, WE'RE STILL HERE, WAITING IN THE WINGS.
SEE?! IT'S ALL BECAUSE WE COULDN'T WIN THEIR HEARTS DURING THE SUMMER!!
MY SUMMER VACATION PLANS? WELL, I'M GOING TO MY VILLA WITH TAMON.
WE'RE GOING TO HAVE SO MUCH FUN IN HAWAII DURING THE SUMMER!
THAT'S SO NOT GOOD...!
Boo hoo!!
I WONDER HOW TOMOHIRO REALLY FEELS ABOUT ME.
HE'S ALWAYS SO BUSY THESE DAYS. I CAN NEVER GET IN CONTACT WITH THE GUY.
Sob...
Hic...
IT ALMOST FEELS AS IF HE HAS MORE FUN HANGING OUT WITH TAMON THAN WITH ME.

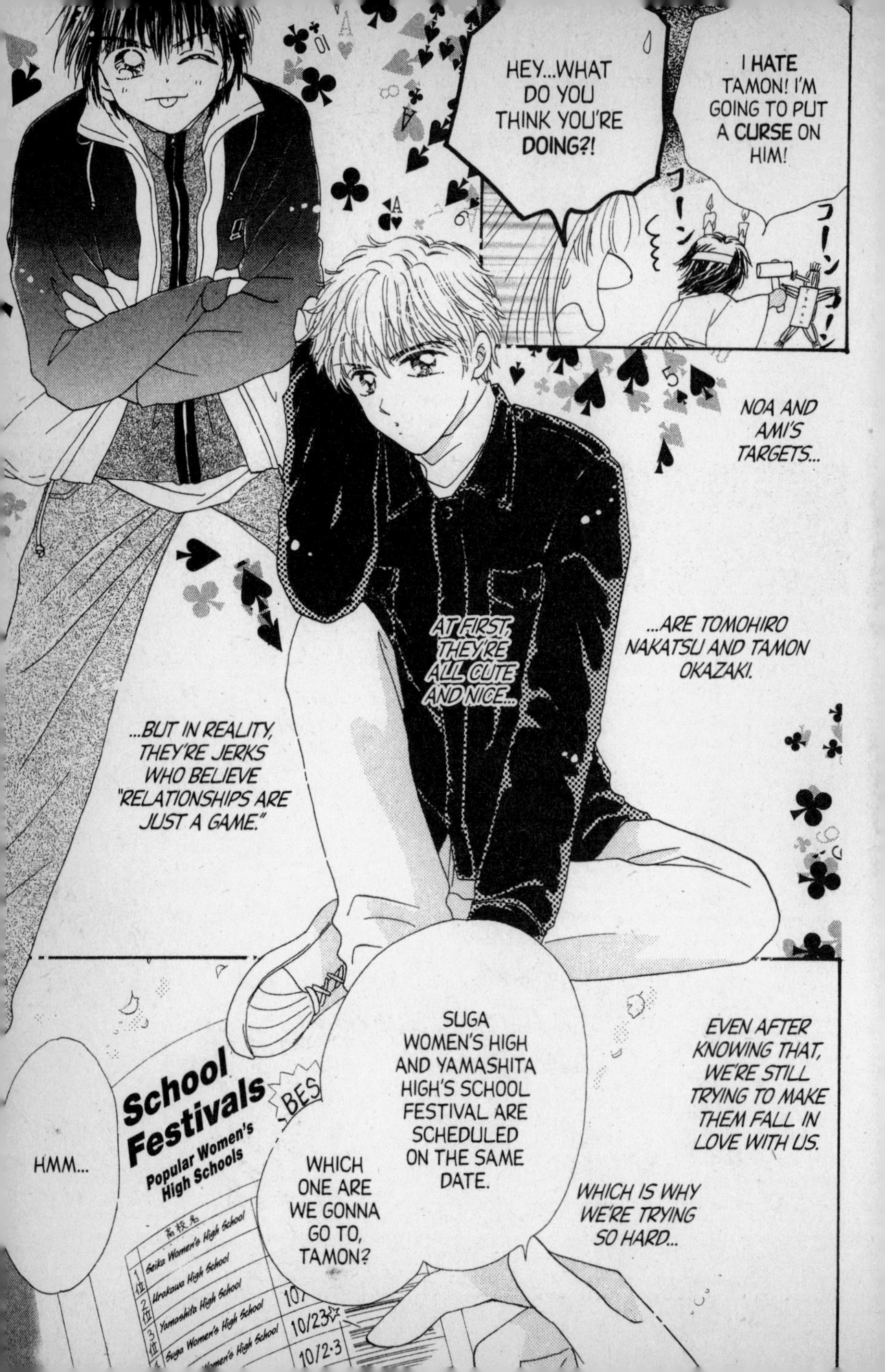
I HATE TAMON! I'M GOING TO PUT A CURSE ON HIM!
HEY...WHAT DO YOU THINK YOU'RE DOING?!
NOA AND AMI'S TARGETS...
...ARE TOMOHIRO NAKATSU AND TAMON OKAZAKI.
AT FIRST, THEY'RE ALL CUTE AND NICE...
...BUT IN REALITY, THEY'RE JERKS WHO BELIEVE "RELATIONSHIPS ARE JUST A GAME."
EVEN AFTER KNOWING THAT, WE'RE STILL TRYING TO MAKE THEM FALL IN LOVE WITH US.
WHICH IS WHY WE'RE TRYING SO HARD...
SUGA WOMEN'S HIGH AND YAMASHITA HIGH'S SCHOOL FESTIVAL ARE SCHEDULED ON THE SAME DATE.
WHICH ONE ARE WE GONNA GO TO, TAMON?
HMM...
School Festivals
Popular Women's High Schools
Seika Women's High School
Urakawa High School
Yamashita High School
Suga Women's High School
10/23
10/2·3

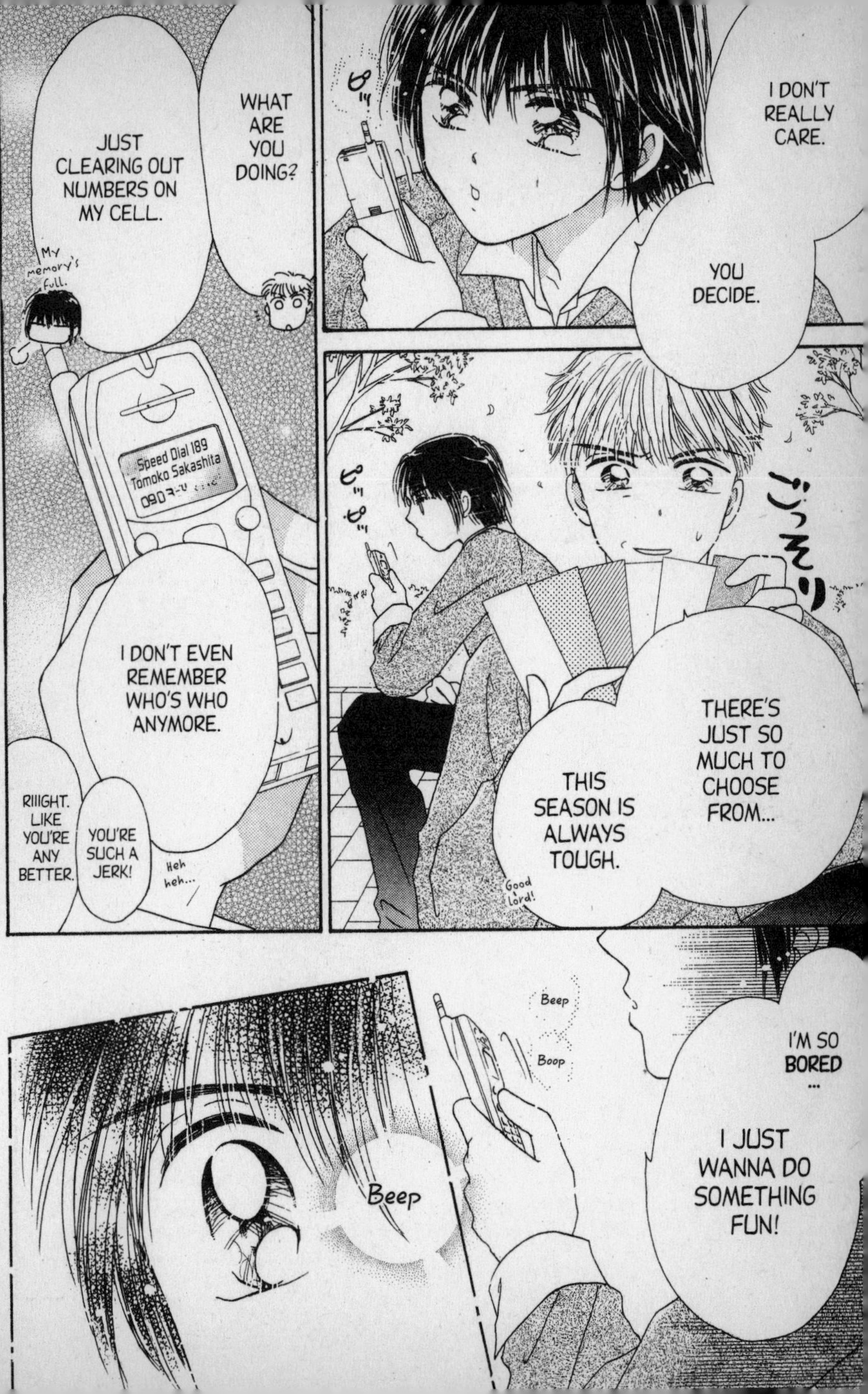
I DON'T REALLY CARE.
YOU DECIDE.
THERE'S JUST SO MUCH TO CHOOSE FROM...
THIS SEASON IS ALWAYS TOUGH.
ごっそり
Good lord!
WHAT ARE YOU DOING?
JUST CLEARING OUT NUMBERS ON MY CELL.
My memory's full.
Speed Dial 189
Tomoko Sakashita
I DON'T EVEN REMEMBER WHO'S WHO ANYMORE.
Heh heh...
YOU'RE SUCH A JERK!
RIIIGHT. LIKE YOU'RE ANY BETTER.
I'M SO BORED...
I JUST WANNA DO SOMETHING FUN!
Beep
Boop
Beep

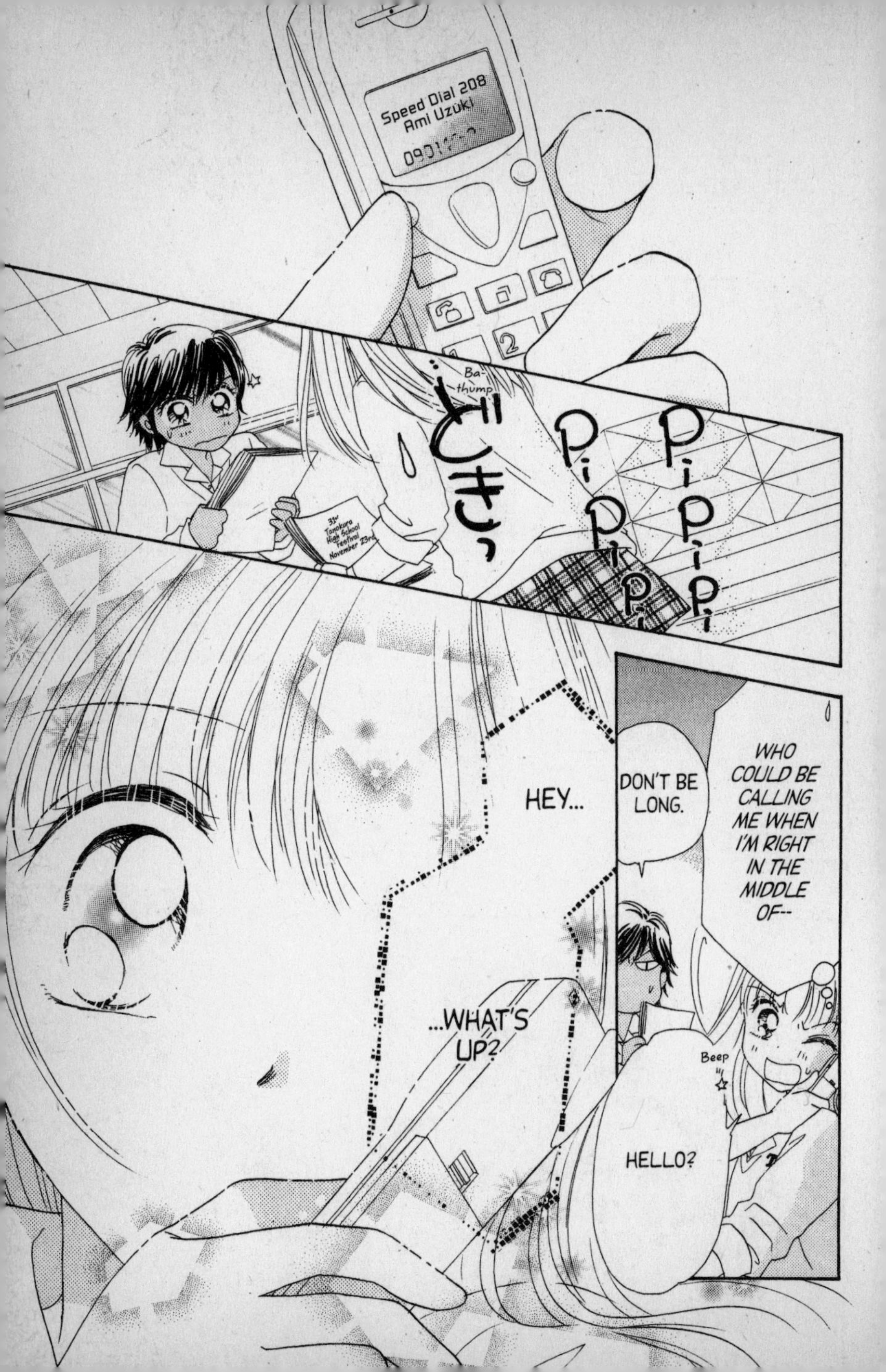
Speed Dial 208
Ami Uzuki
Pi Pi Pi
Pi Pi Pi
Ba-thump
どき
33rd Tanokura High School Festival November 23rd
WHO COULD BE CALLING ME WHEN I'M RIGHT IN THE MIDDLE OF--
DON'T BE LONG.
Beep
HELLO?
HEY...
...WHAT'S UP?

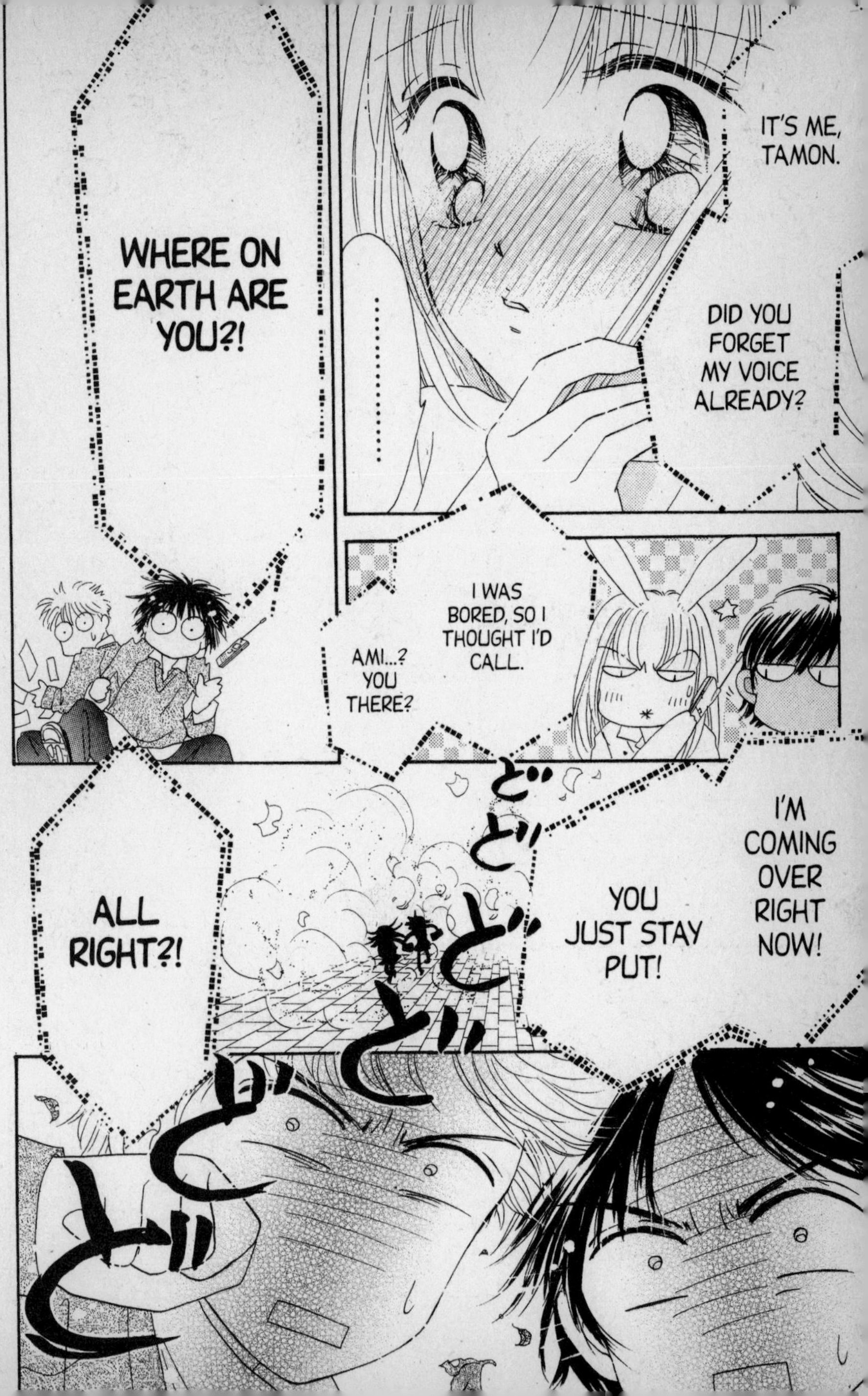
IT'S ME, TAMON.
DID YOU FORGET MY VOICE ALREADY?
I WAS BORED, SO I THOUGHT I'D CALL.
AMI...? YOU THERE?
WHERE ON EARTH ARE YOU?!
I'M COMING OVER RIGHT NOW!
YOU JUST STAY PUT!
ALL RIGHT?!
どどどどどど

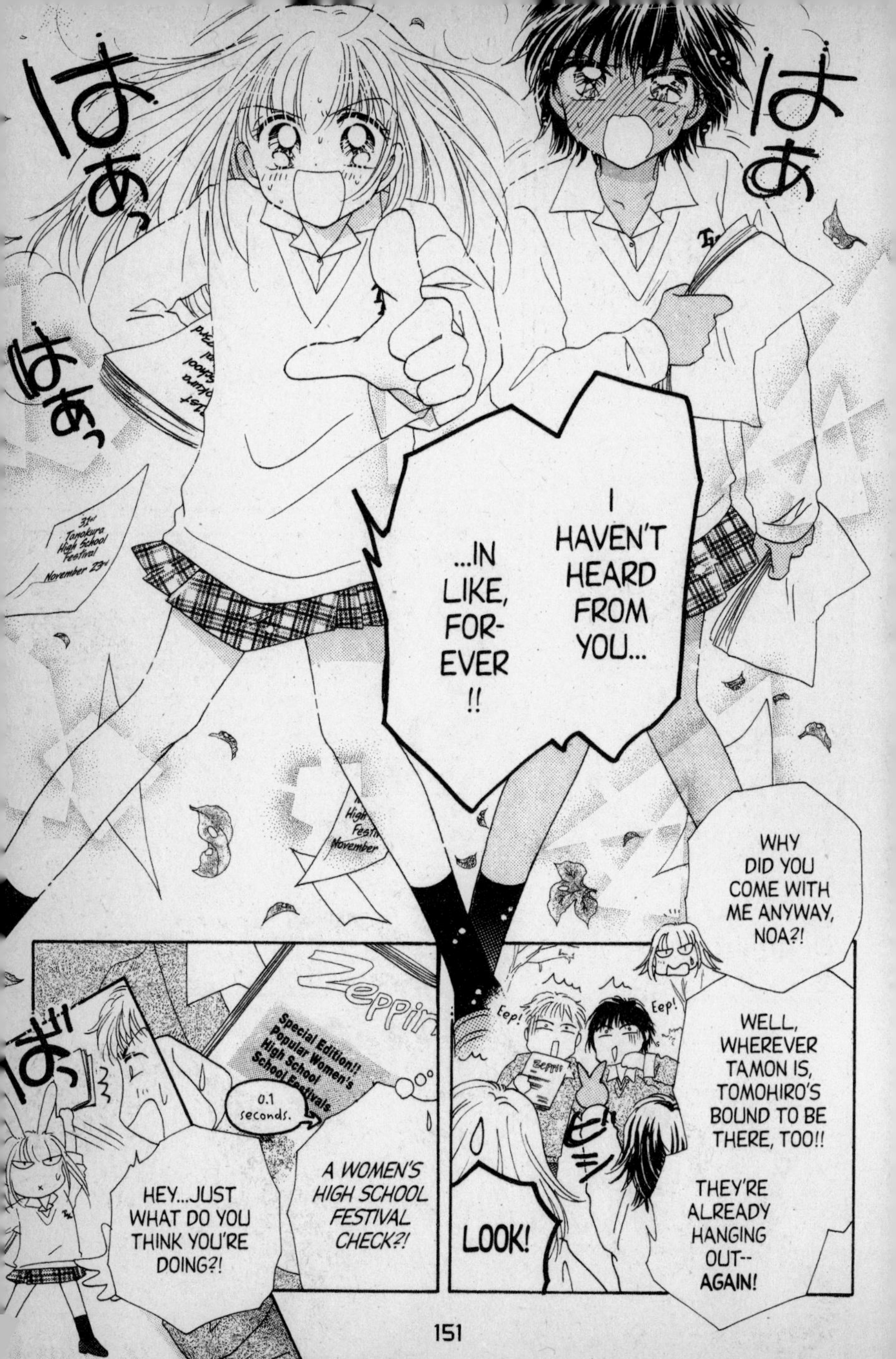
はぁ
はぁっ
はぁっ
I HAVEN'T HEARD FROM YOU...
...IN LIKE, FOREVER!!
31st Tanokura High School Festival November 23rd
WHY DID YOU COME WITH ME ANYWAY, NOA?!
Eep!
Eep!
WELL, WHEREVER TAMON IS, TOMOHIRO'S BOUND TO BE THERE, TOO!!
THEY'RE ALREADY HANGING OUT-- AGAIN!
LOOK!
Zeppin
Special Edition!! Popular Women's High School School Festivals
0.1 seconds.
A WOMEN'S HIGH SCHOOL FESTIVAL CHECK?!
ばっ
HEY...JUST WHAT DO YOU THINK YOU'RE DOING?!

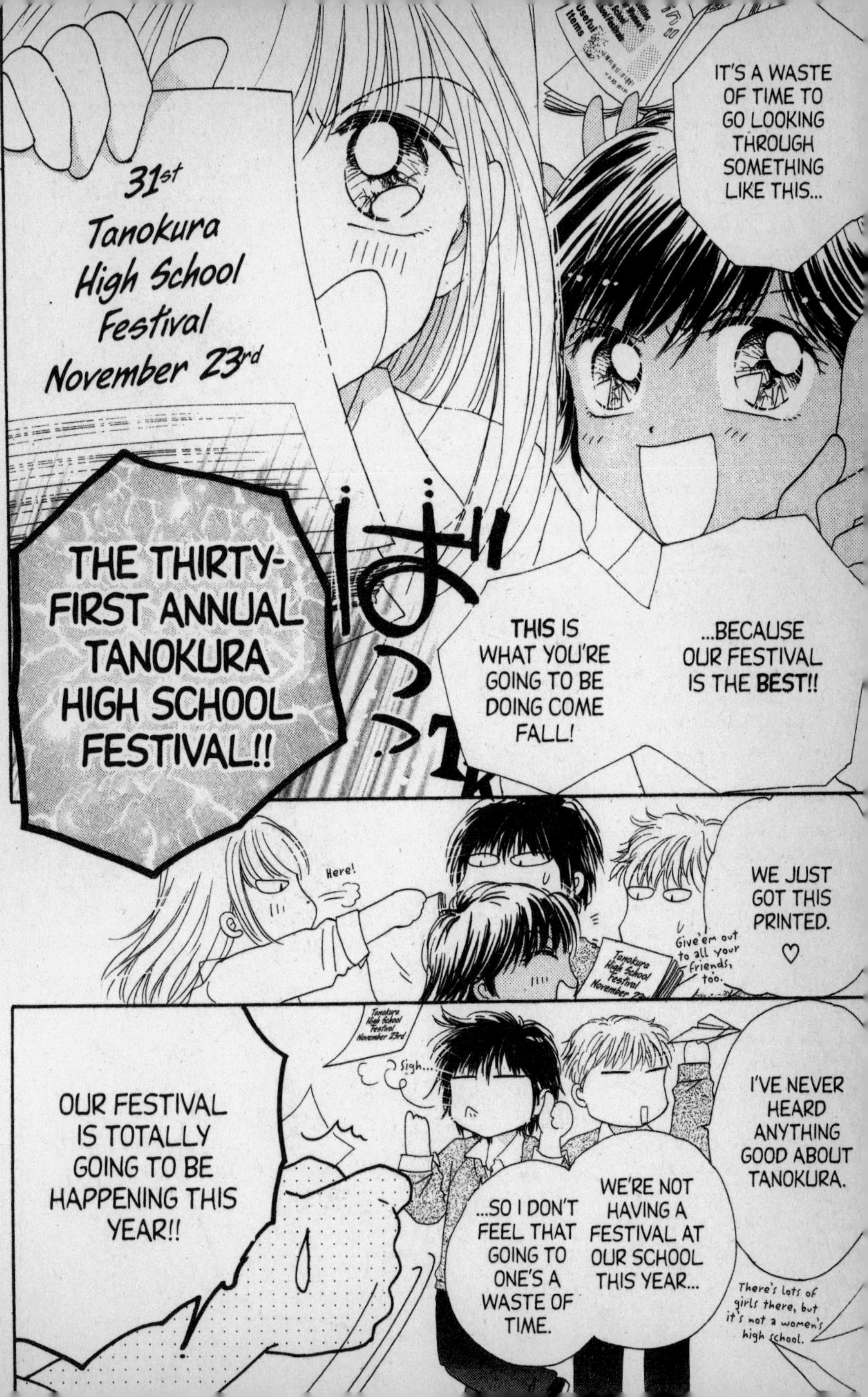
Useful Items
IT'S A WASTE OF TIME TO GO LOOKING THROUGH SOMETHING LIKE THIS...
...BECAUSE OUR FESTIVAL IS THE BEST!!
THIS IS WHAT YOU'RE GOING TO BE DOING COME FALL!
31st Tanokura High School Festival November 23rd
THE THIRTY-FIRST ANNUAL TANOKURA HIGH SCHOOL FESTIVAL!!
ばっ
WE JUST GOT THIS PRINTED. ♡
Give'em out to all your friends, too.
Tanokura High School Festival November 23
Here!
I'VE NEVER HEARD ANYTHING GOOD ABOUT TANOKURA.
There's lots of girls there, but it's not a women's high school.
WE'RE NOT HAVING A FESTIVAL AT OUR SCHOOL THIS YEAR...
...SO I DON'T FEEL THAT GOING TO ONE'S A WASTE OF TIME.
Sigh...
Tanokura High School Festival November 23rd
OUR FESTIVAL IS TOTALLY GOING TO BE HAPPENING THIS YEAR!!

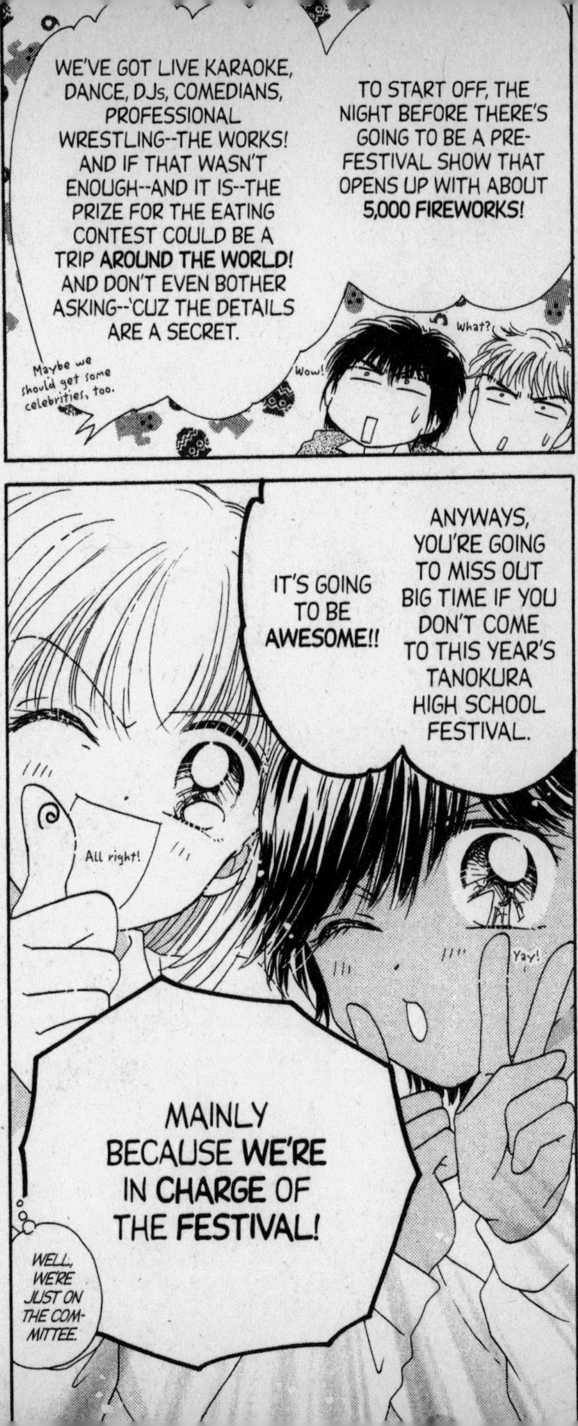
TO START OFF, THE NIGHT BEFORE THERE'S GOING TO BE A PRE-FESTIVAL SHOW THAT OPENS UP WITH ABOUT **5,000 FIREWORKS!**
WE'VE GOT LIVE KARAOKE, DANCE, DJs, COMEDIANS, PROFESSIONAL WRESTLING--THE WORKS! AND IF THAT WASN'T ENOUGH--AND IT IS--THE PRIZE FOR THE EATING CONTEST COULD BE A TRIP **AROUND THE WORLD!** AND DON'T EVEN BOTHER ASKING--'CUZ THE DETAILS ARE A SECRET.
What?
Wow!
Maybe we should get some celebrities, too.
ANYWAYS, YOU'RE GOING TO MISS OUT BIG TIME IF YOU DON'T COME TO THIS YEAR'S TANOKURA HIGH SCHOOL FESTIVAL.
IT'S GOING TO BE **AWESOME!!**
Yay!
All right!
MAINLY BECAUSE **WE'RE** IN **CHARGE** OF THE **FESTIVAL!**
WELL, WE'RE JUST ON THE COM-MITTEE.

From Akimoto--
Hey, everybody! Can you believe it's been an entire year since we last spoke? Time sure does fly!
This volume is coming out in 2000. There is also going to be a serious love story coming out called "Hold Me Tight." Definitely a must read for those who are into more adult love stories!

So, let me tell you what's been going on in my life. First of all, by the time this volume comes out, I should be already be enrolled in tea ceremony classes. I'm still continuing with my wine tasting class--and I was even able to lose some weight! Now I am working out a lot in order to get in shape. I lost more than 10kg...but that just brought me back down to my average weight! It's scary how much I used to weigh! I've got to make sure I don't gain it all back. My goal is to fit into my Jill Saunders dress and my favorite shoes (If that's even possible).

You could say I'm like a firecracker about to explode! Ha ha ha!

What? Concentrate on my work? Oh...right.

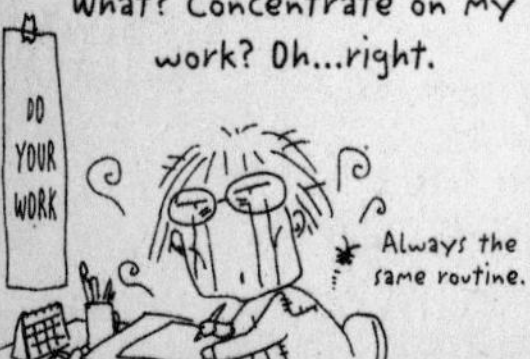
DO YOUR WORK
Always the same routine.

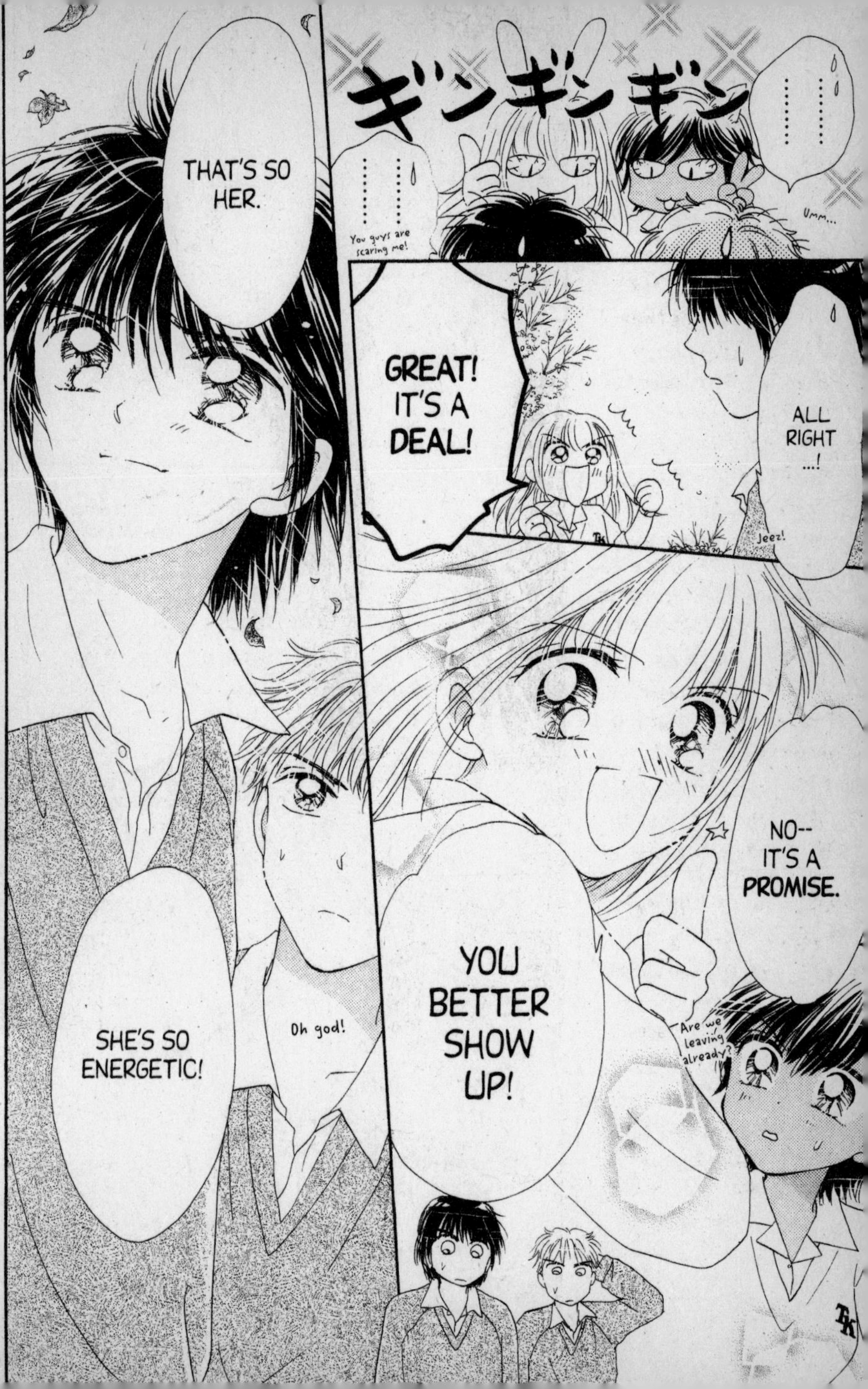
......
Umm...
ギンギンギン
......
You guys are scaring me!
ALL RIGHT ...!
Jeez!
GREAT! IT'S A DEAL!
NO-- IT'S A PROMISE.
Are we leaving already?
YOU BETTER SHOW UP!
THAT'S SO HER.
Oh god!
SHE'S SO ENERGETIC!

Let's talk about the new series, "Urukyu." So many people ask what the title means. Urukyu is short for Ultra Cute. Whether this is a real word or not, I don't know. I basically made it up on my own. Apparently, this series is supposed to continue for a while, but the particulars are somewhat unknown to me. A new character already came out and I don't quite even know what's going to happen to the story yet. Everybody tells me, "This series is a bit different from your other stuff." What do you think? I don't think so...I'm just writing whatever comes to mind. Whatever the case may be, I hope you'll enjoy this series. Oh-- and check out the additional pages at the end!

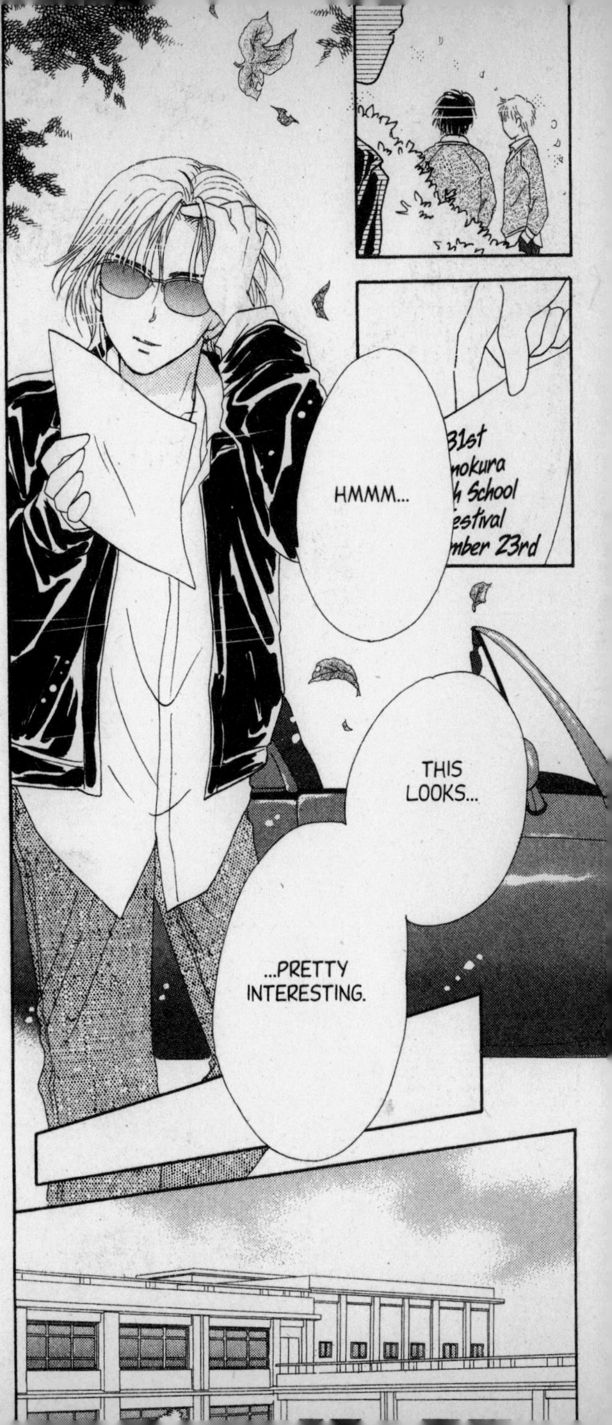
31st
nokura
h School
estival
mber 23rd
HMMM...
THIS LOOKS...
...PRETTY INTERESTING.

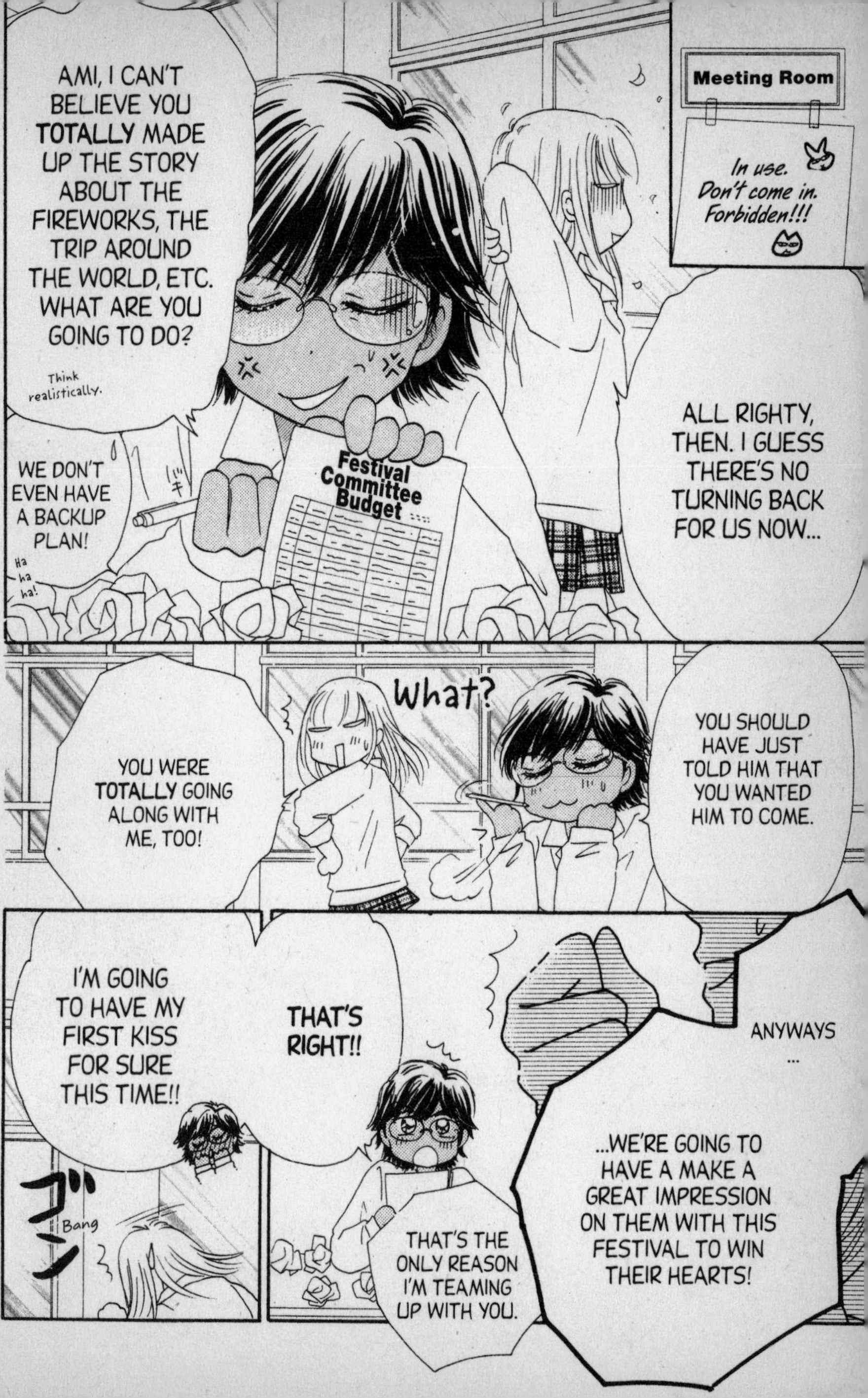
Meeting Room
In use. Don't come in. Forbidden!!!
ALL RIGHTY, THEN. I GUESS THERE'S NO TURNING BACK FOR US NOW...
AMI, I CAN'T BELIEVE YOU TOTALLY MADE UP THE STORY ABOUT THE FIREWORKS, THE TRIP AROUND THE WORLD, ETC. WHAT ARE YOU GOING TO DO?
Think realistically.
Festival Committee Budget
WE DON'T EVEN HAVE A BACKUP PLAN!
Ha ha ha!
YOU SHOULD HAVE JUST TOLD HIM THAT YOU WANTED HIM TO COME.
What?
YOU WERE TOTALLY GOING ALONG WITH ME, TOO!
ANYWAYS ...
...WE'RE GOING TO HAVE A MAKE A GREAT IMPRESSION ON THEM WITH THIS FESTIVAL TO WIN THEIR HEARTS!
THAT'S THE ONLY REASON I'M TEAMING UP WITH YOU.
THAT'S RIGHT!!
I'M GOING TO HAVE MY FIRST KISS FOR SURE THIS TIME!!
ゴン
Bang

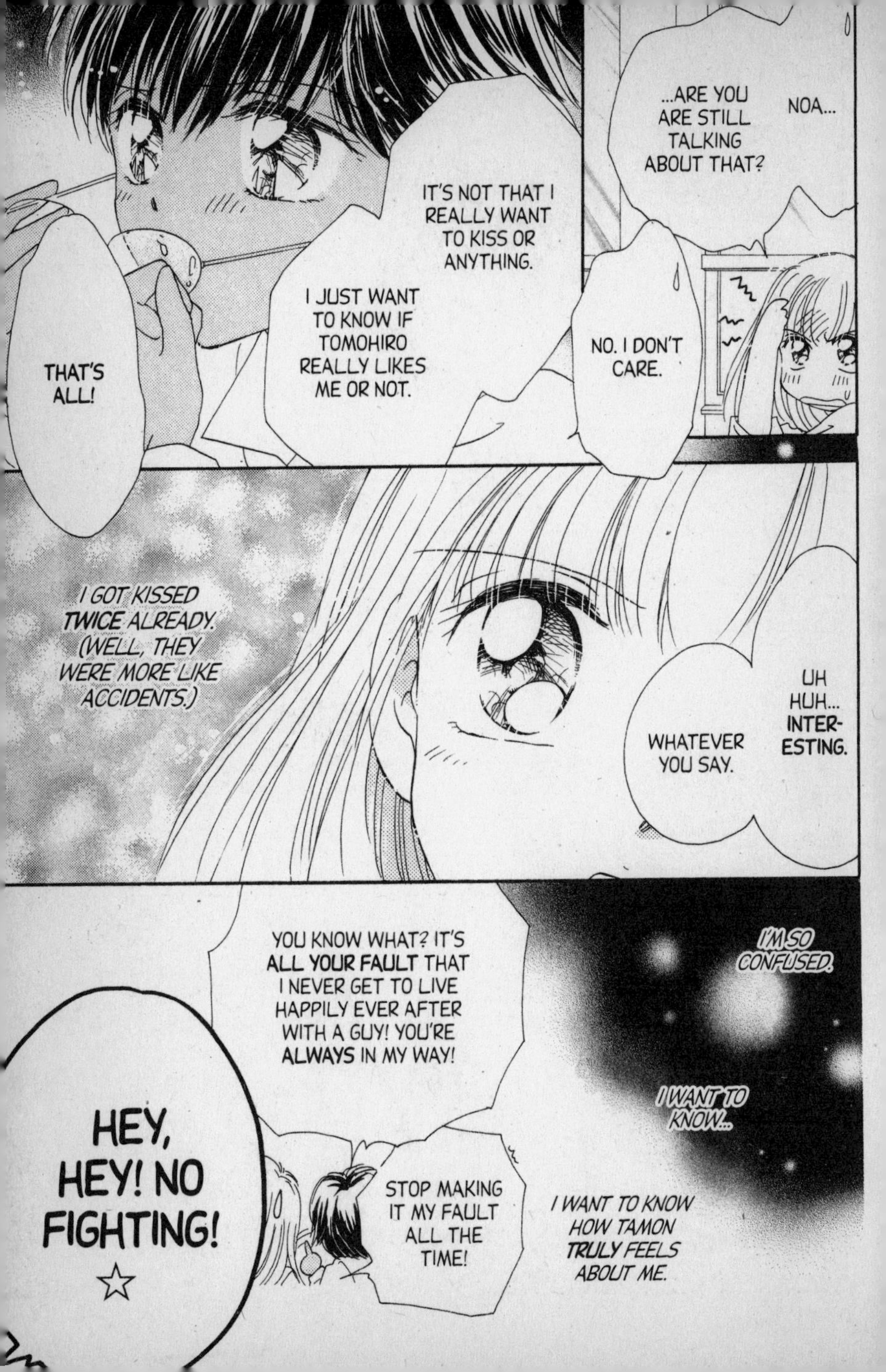
NOA...
...ARE YOU ARE STILL TALKING ABOUT THAT?
NO. I DON'T CARE.
IT'S NOT THAT I REALLY WANT TO KISS OR ANYTHING.
I JUST WANT TO KNOW IF TOMOHIRO REALLY LIKES ME OR NOT.
THAT'S ALL!
UH HUH... INTERESTING.
WHATEVER YOU SAY.
I GOT KISSED TWICE ALREADY. (WELL, THEY WERE MORE LIKE ACCIDENTS.)
I'M SO CONFUSED.
I WANT TO KNOW...
I WANT TO KNOW HOW TAMON TRULY FEELS ABOUT ME.
YOU KNOW WHAT? IT'S ALL YOUR FAULT THAT I NEVER GET TO LIVE HAPPILY EVER AFTER WITH A GUY! YOU'RE ALWAYS IN MY WAY!
STOP MAKING IT MY FAULT ALL THE TIME!
HEY, HEY! NO FIGHTING! ☆

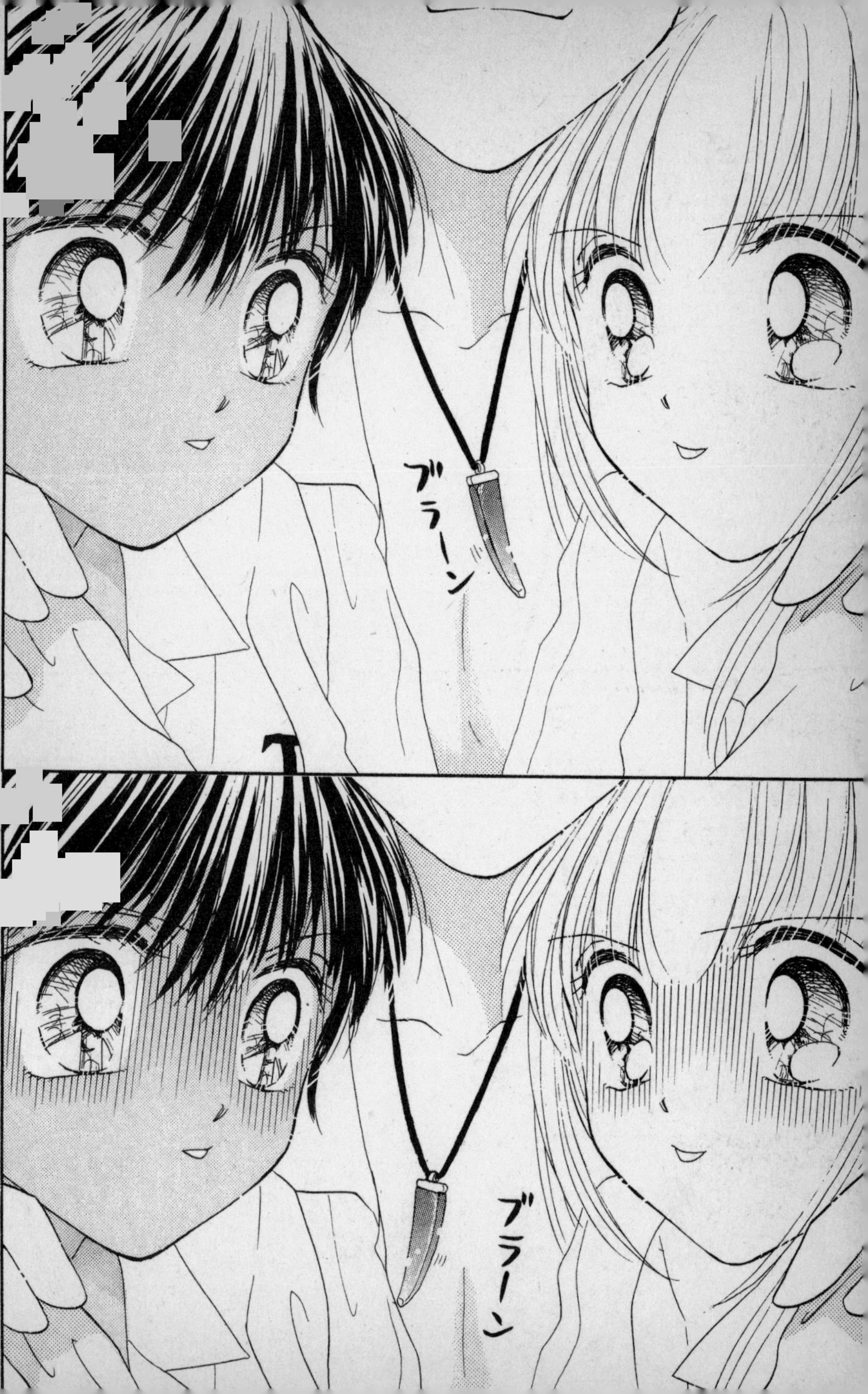
ブラーン
ブラーン

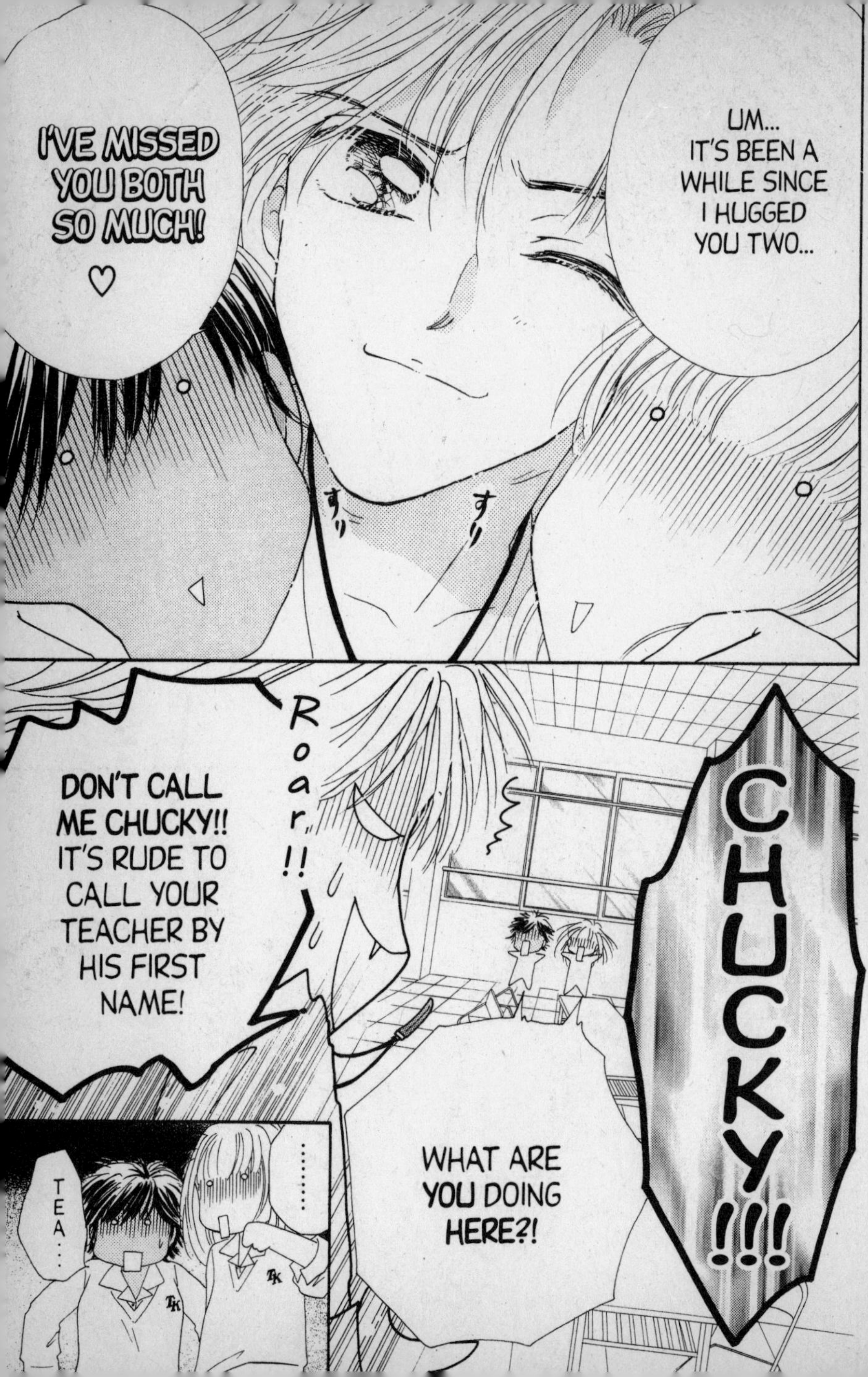
UM... IT'S BEEN A WHILE SINCE I HUGGED YOU TWO...
I'VE MISSED YOU BOTH SO MUCH! ♡
すり
すり
CHUCKY!!!
WHAT ARE YOU DOING HERE?!
Roar!!
DON'T CALL ME CHUCKY!! IT'S RUDE TO CALL YOUR TEACHER BY HIS FIRST NAME!
......
TEA...

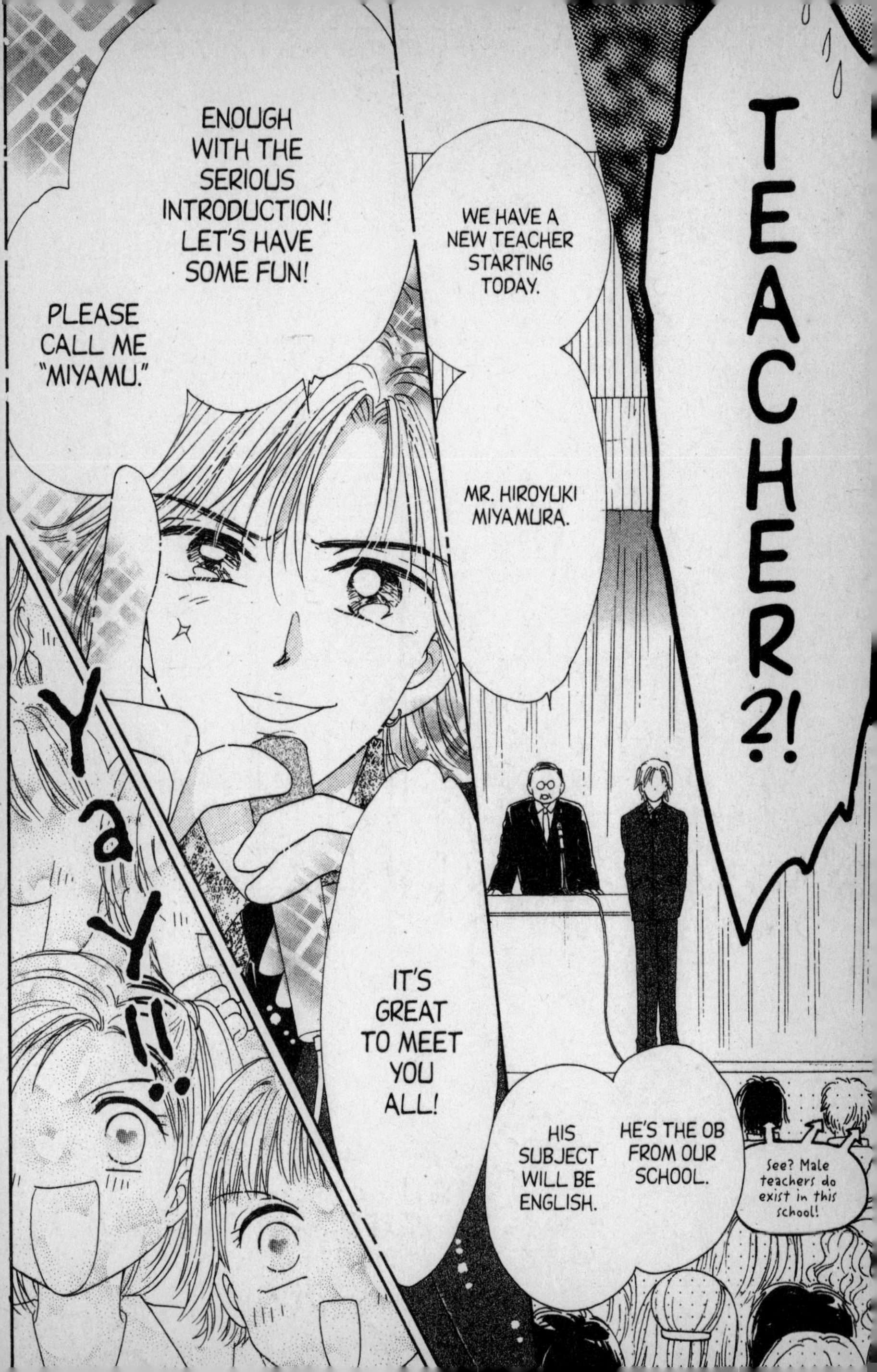
TEACHER?!
WE HAVE A NEW TEACHER STARTING TODAY.
MR. HIROYUKI MIYAMURA.
HE'S THE OB FROM OUR SCHOOL.
HIS SUBJECT WILL BE ENGLISH.
See? Male teachers do exist in this school!
ENOUGH WITH THE SERIOUS INTRODUCTION! LET'S HAVE SOME FUN!
PLEASE CALL ME "MIYAMU."
IT'S GREAT TO MEET YOU ALL!
Yay!!

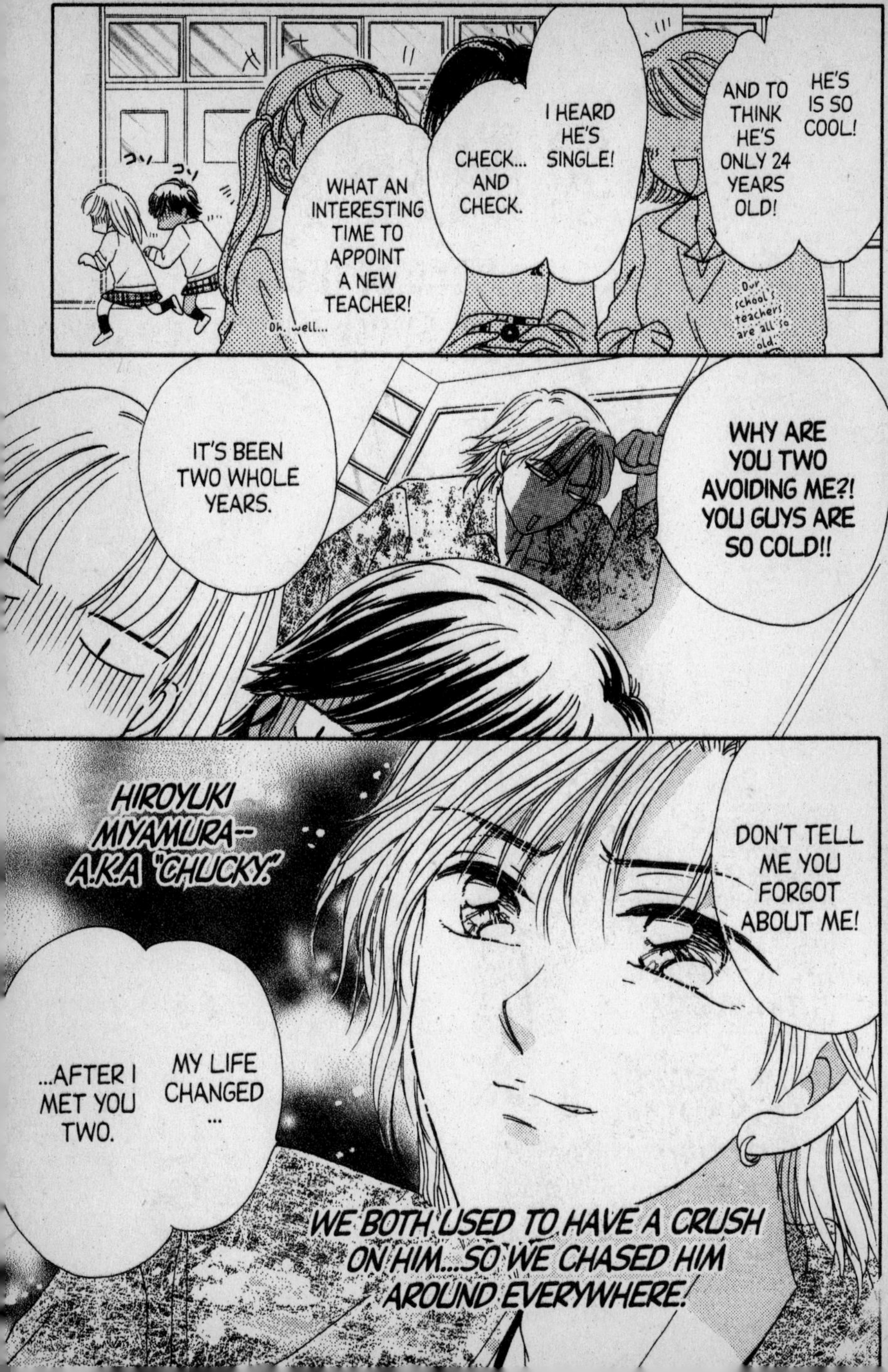
HE'S IS SO COOL!
AND TO THINK HE'S ONLY 24 YEARS OLD!
Our school's teachers are all so old.
I HEARD HE'S SINGLE!
CHECK... AND CHECK.
WHAT AN INTERESTING TIME TO APPOINT A NEW TEACHER!
Oh, well...
WHY ARE YOU TWO AVOIDING ME?! YOU GUYS ARE SO COLD!!
IT'S BEEN TWO WHOLE YEARS.
DON'T TELL ME YOU FORGOT ABOUT ME!
HIROYUKI MIYAMURA-- A.K.A "CHUCKY."
MY LIFE CHANGED ...
...AFTER I MET YOU TWO.
WE BOTH USED TO HAVE A CRUSH ON HIM...SO WE CHASED HIM AROUND EVERYWHERE.

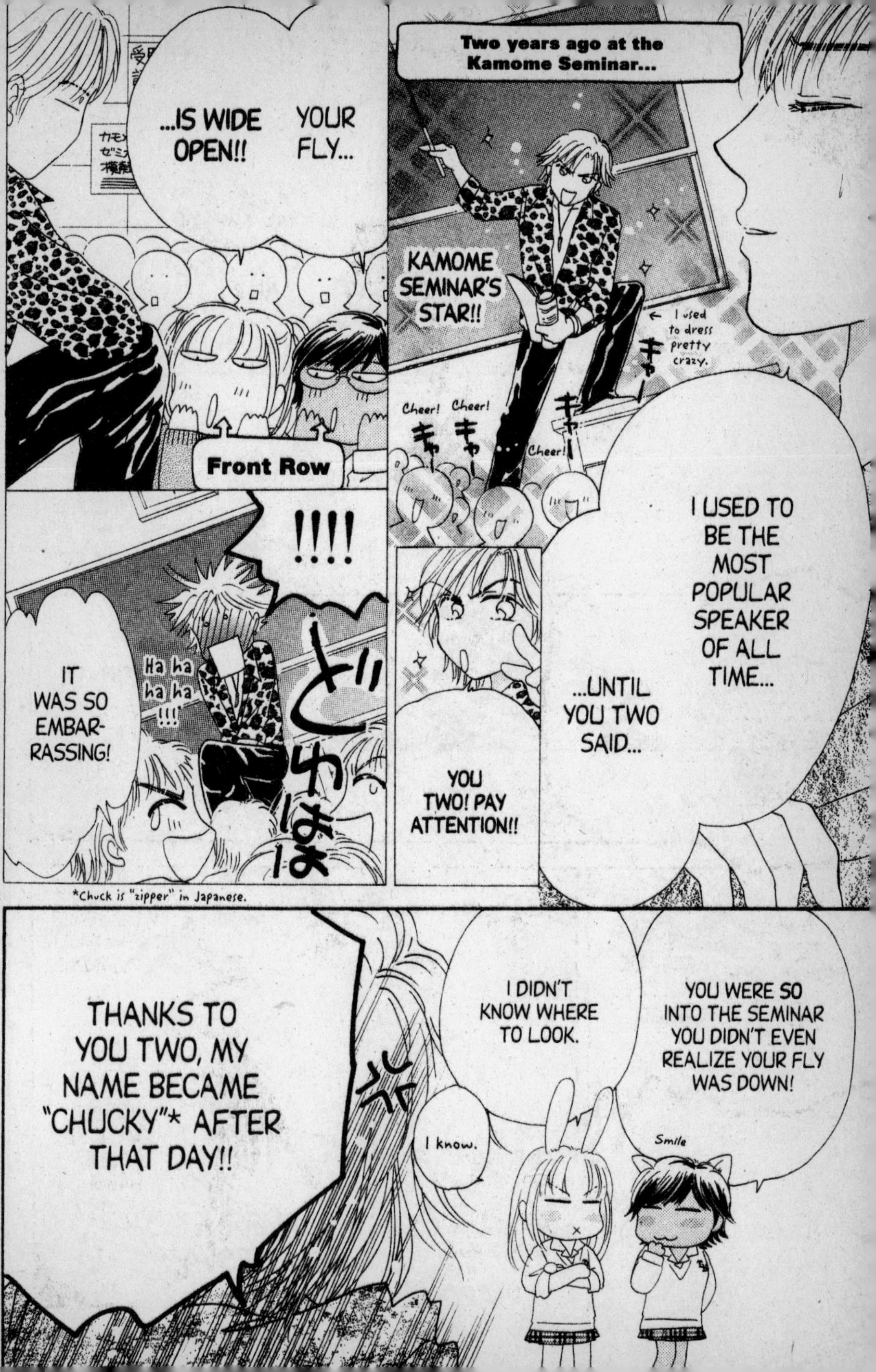
Two years ago at the Kamome Seminar...
KAMOME SEMINAR'S STAR!!
← I used to dress pretty crazy.
キャー
Cheer! Cheer! Cheer!
キャー キャー キャー
I USED TO BE THE MOST POPULAR SPEAKER OF ALL TIME...
...UNTIL YOU TWO SAID...
YOUR FLY...
...IS WIDE OPEN!!
Front Row
!!!!
YOU TWO! PAY ATTENTION!!
どわはは
Ha ha ha ha!!!
IT WAS SO EMBARRASSING!
YOU WERE SO INTO THE SEMINAR YOU DIDN'T EVEN REALIZE YOUR FLY WAS DOWN!
I DIDN'T KNOW WHERE TO LOOK.
Smile
I know.
THANKS TO YOU TWO, MY NAME BECAME "CHUCKY"* AFTER THAT DAY!!

*Chuck is "zipper" in Japanese.

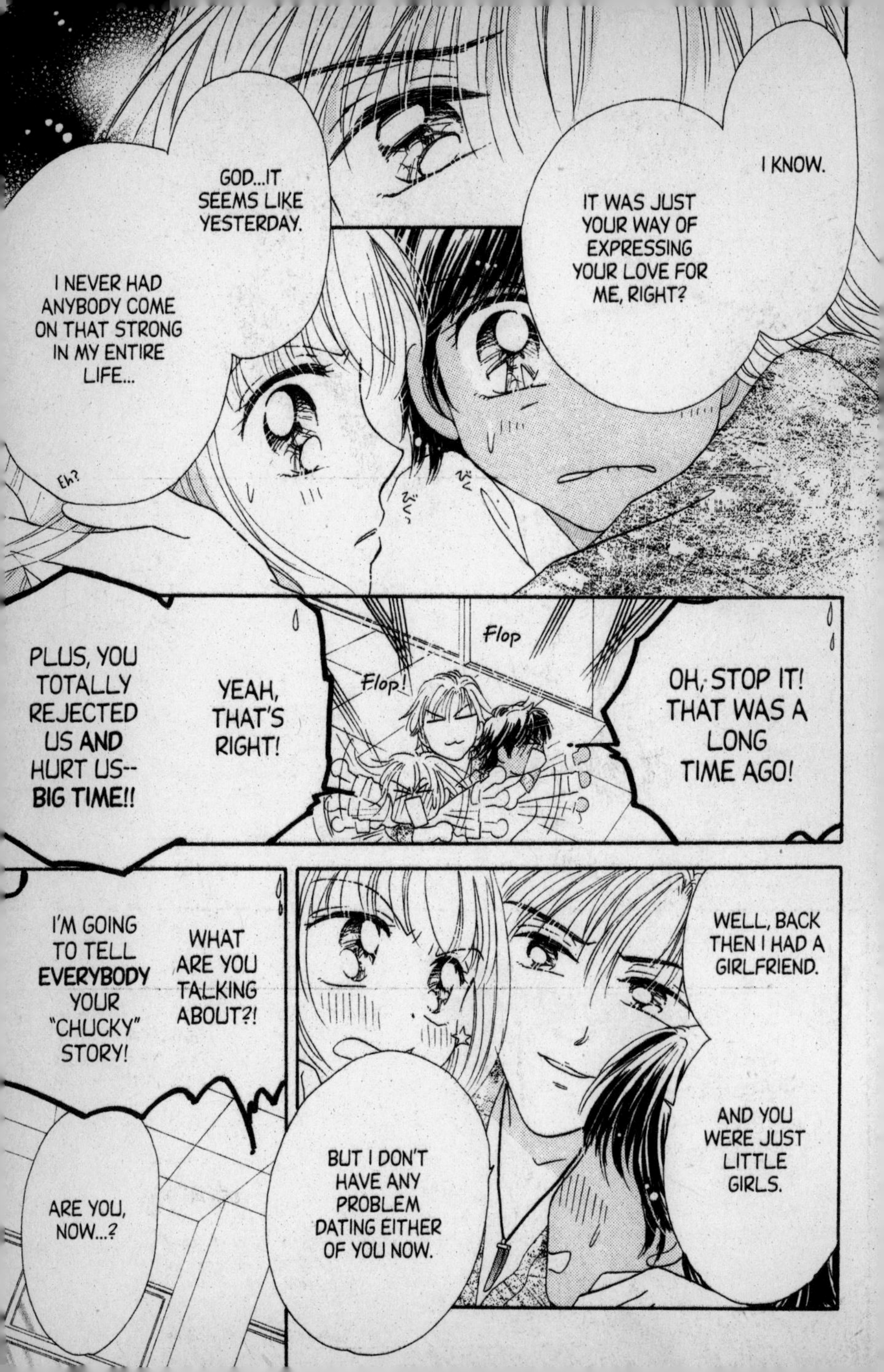
I KNOW.
IT WAS JUST YOUR WAY OF EXPRESSING YOUR LOVE FOR ME, RIGHT?
GOD...IT SEEMS LIKE YESTERDAY.
I NEVER HAD ANYBODY COME ON THAT STRONG IN MY ENTIRE LIFE...
Eh?
OH, STOP IT! THAT WAS A LONG TIME AGO!
Flop
Flop!
YEAH, THAT'S RIGHT!
PLUS, YOU TOTALLY REJECTED US AND HURT US--BIG TIME!!
WELL, BACK THEN I HAD A GIRLFRIEND.
AND YOU WERE JUST LITTLE GIRLS.
BUT I DON'T HAVE ANY PROBLEM DATING EITHER OF YOU NOW.
WHAT ARE YOU TALKING ABOUT?!
I'M GOING TO TELL EVERYBODY YOUR "CHUCKY" STORY!
ARE YOU, NOW...?

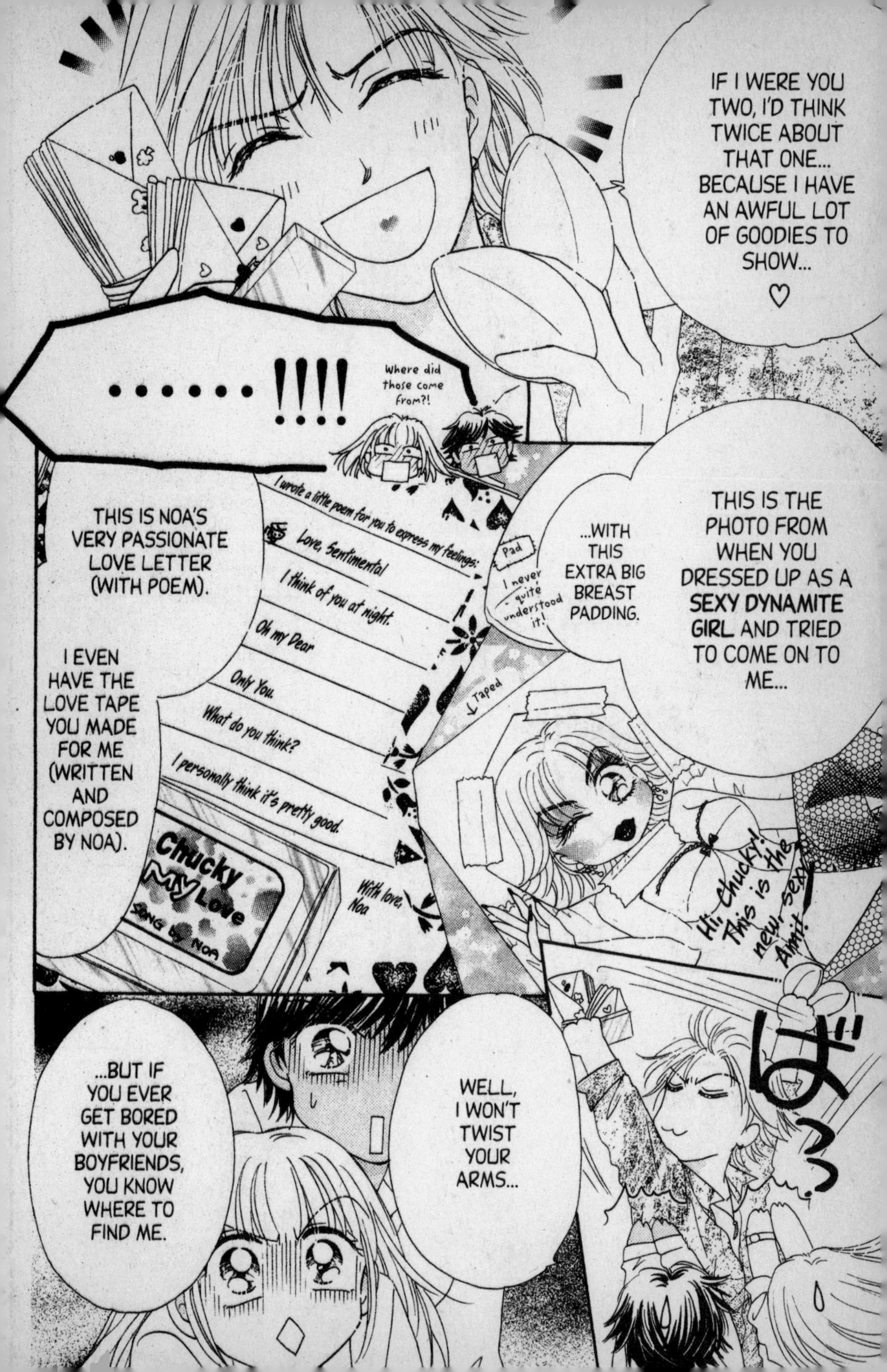
IF I WERE YOU TWO, I'D THINK TWICE ABOUT THAT ONE... BECAUSE I HAVE AN AWFUL LOT OF GOODIES TO SHOW... ♡
......!!!!
Where did those come from?!
THIS IS THE PHOTO FROM WHEN YOU DRESSED UP AS A **SEXY DYNAMITE GIRL** AND TRIED TO COME ON TO ME...
...WITH THIS EXTRA BIG BREAST PADDING.
Pad
I never quite understood it!
Taped
Hi, Chucky! This is the new, sexy Ami!
THIS IS NOA'S VERY PASSIONATE LOVE LETTER (WITH POEM).
I wrote a little poem for you to express my feelings:
Love, Sentimental
I think of you at night.
Oh my Dear
Only You.
What do you think?
I personally think it's pretty good.
With love, Noa
I EVEN HAVE THE LOVE TAPE YOU MADE FOR ME (WRITTEN AND COMPOSED BY NOA).
Chucky My Love
SONG by NOA
ばっ
WELL, I WON'T TWIST YOUR ARMS...
...BUT IF YOU EVER GET BORED WITH YOUR BOYFRIENDS, YOU KNOW WHERE TO FIND ME.

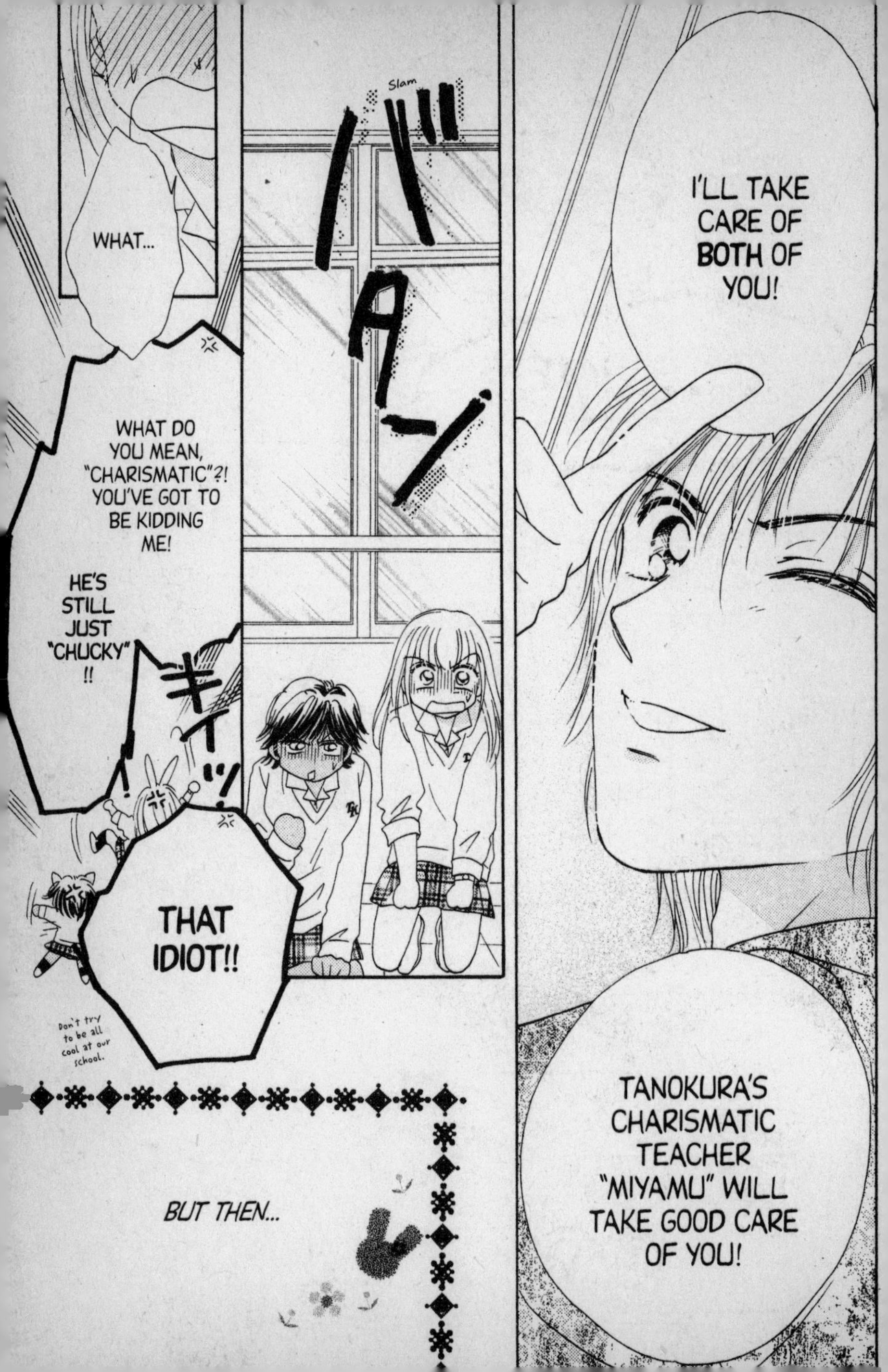
I'LL TAKE CARE OF BOTH OF YOU!
TANOKURA'S CHARISMATIC TEACHER "MIYAMU" WILL TAKE GOOD CARE OF YOU!
Slam
WHAT...
WHAT DO YOU MEAN, "CHARISMATIC"?! YOU'VE GOT TO BE KIDDING ME!
HE'S STILL JUST "CHUCKY" !!
THAT IDIOT!!
Don't try to be all cool at our school.
BUT THEN...

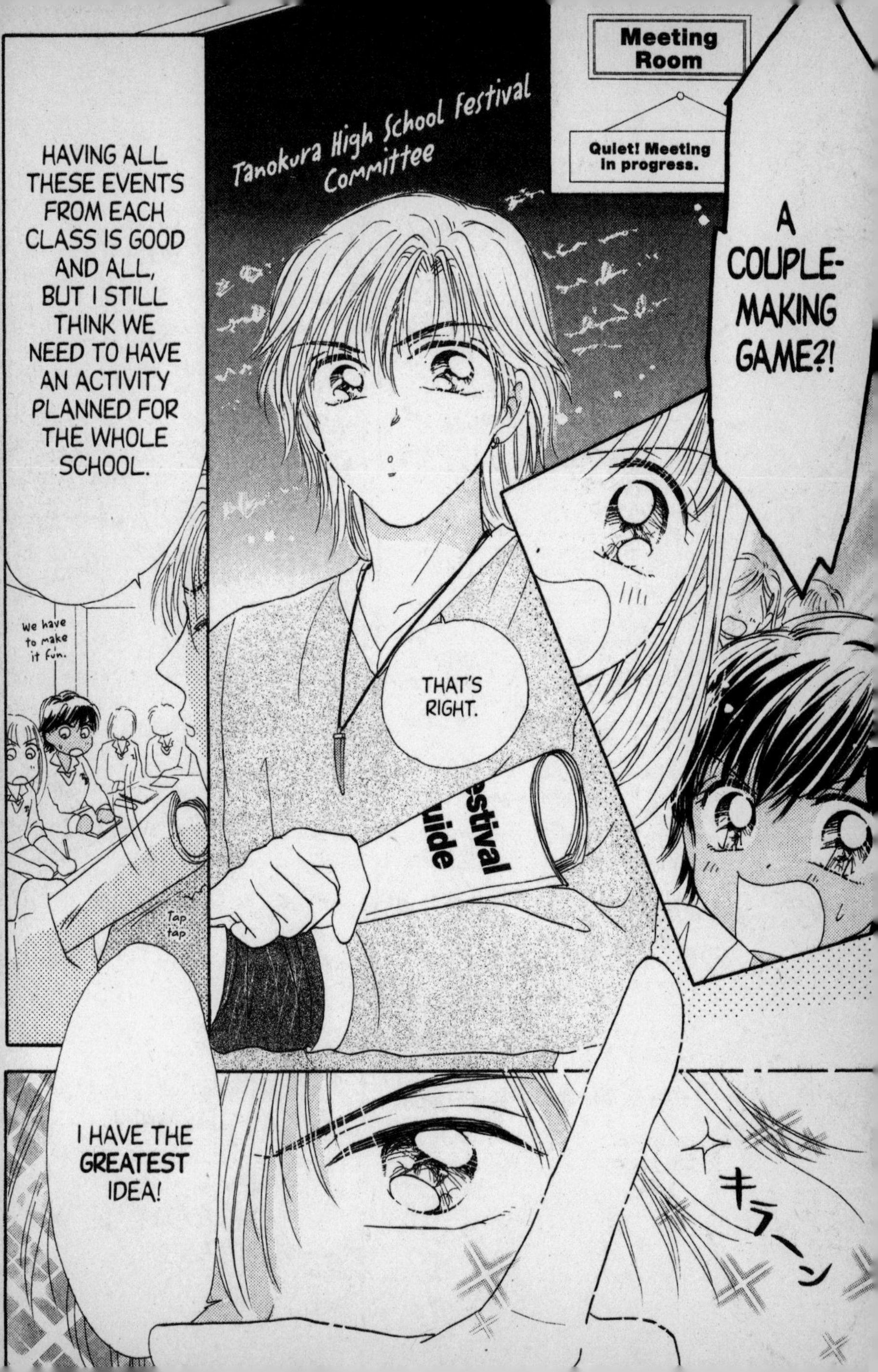
Meeting Room
Quiet! Meeting in progress.
A COUPLE-MAKING GAME?!
Tanokura High School Festival Committee
THAT'S RIGHT.
HAVING ALL THESE EVENTS FROM EACH CLASS IS GOOD AND ALL, BUT I STILL THINK WE NEED TO HAVE AN ACTIVITY PLANNED FOR THE WHOLE SCHOOL.
We have to make it fun.
Tap tap
I HAVE THE GREATEST IDEA!
キラーン

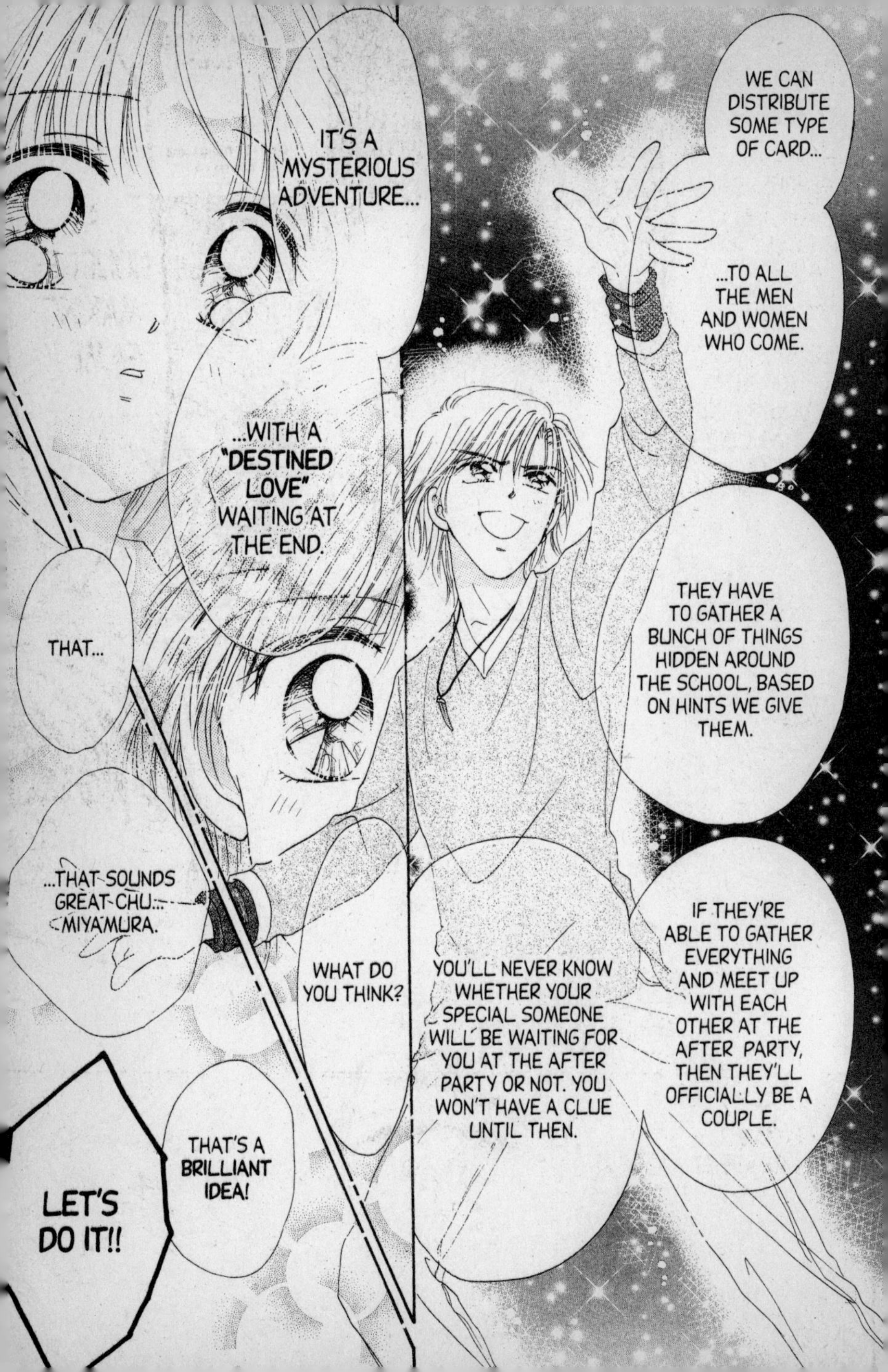
WE CAN DISTRIBUTE SOME TYPE OF CARD...
...TO ALL THE MEN AND WOMEN WHO COME.
THEY HAVE TO GATHER A BUNCH OF THINGS HIDDEN AROUND THE SCHOOL, BASED ON HINTS WE GIVE THEM.
IF THEY'RE ABLE TO GATHER EVERYTHING AND MEET UP WITH EACH OTHER AT THE AFTER PARTY, THEN THEY'LL OFFICIALLY BE A COUPLE.
YOU'LL NEVER KNOW WHETHER YOUR SPECIAL SOMEONE WILL BE WAITING FOR YOU AT THE AFTER PARTY OR NOT. YOU WON'T HAVE A CLUE UNTIL THEN.
IT'S A MYSTERIOUS ADVENTURE...
...WITH A "DESTINED LOVE" WAITING AT THE END.
WHAT DO YOU THINK?
THAT...
...THAT SOUNDS GREAT-CHU... MIYAMURA.
THAT'S A BRILLIANT IDEA!
LET'S DO IT!!

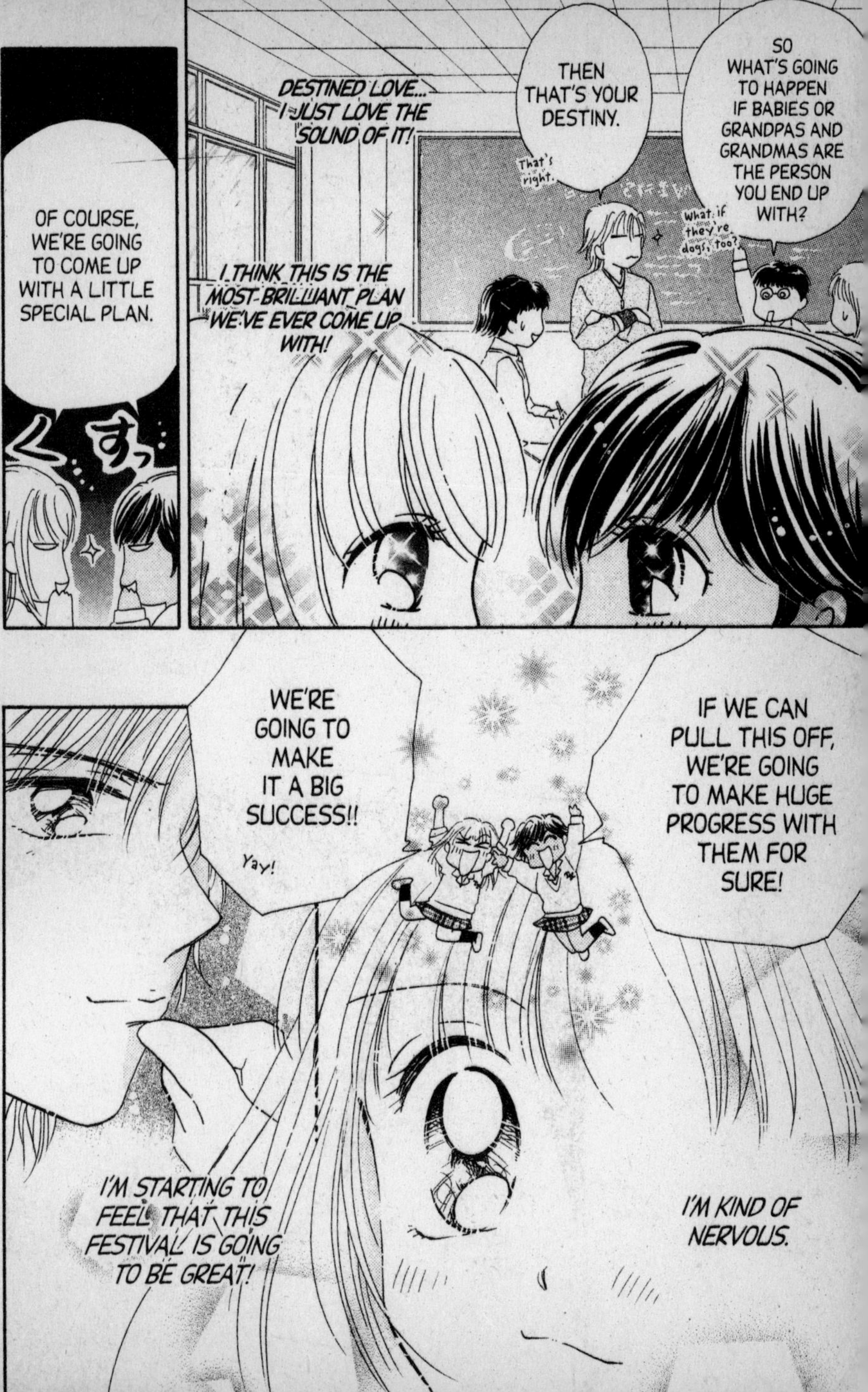
SO WHAT'S GOING TO HAPPEN IF BABIES OR GRANDPAS AND GRANDMAS ARE THE PERSON YOU END UP WITH?
What if they're dogs, too?
THEN THAT'S YOUR DESTINY.
That's right.
DESTINED LOVE... I JUST LOVE THE SOUND OF IT!
I THINK THIS IS THE MOST-BRILLIANT PLAN WE'VE EVER COME UP WITH!
OF COURSE, WE'RE GOING TO COME UP WITH A LITTLE SPECIAL PLAN.
くすっ
IF WE CAN PULL THIS OFF, WE'RE GOING TO MAKE HUGE PROGRESS WITH THEM FOR SURE!
WE'RE GOING TO MAKE IT A BIG SUCCESS!!
Yay!
I'M KIND OF NERVOUS.
I'M STARTING TO FEEL THAT THIS FESTIVAL IS GOING TO BE GREAT!

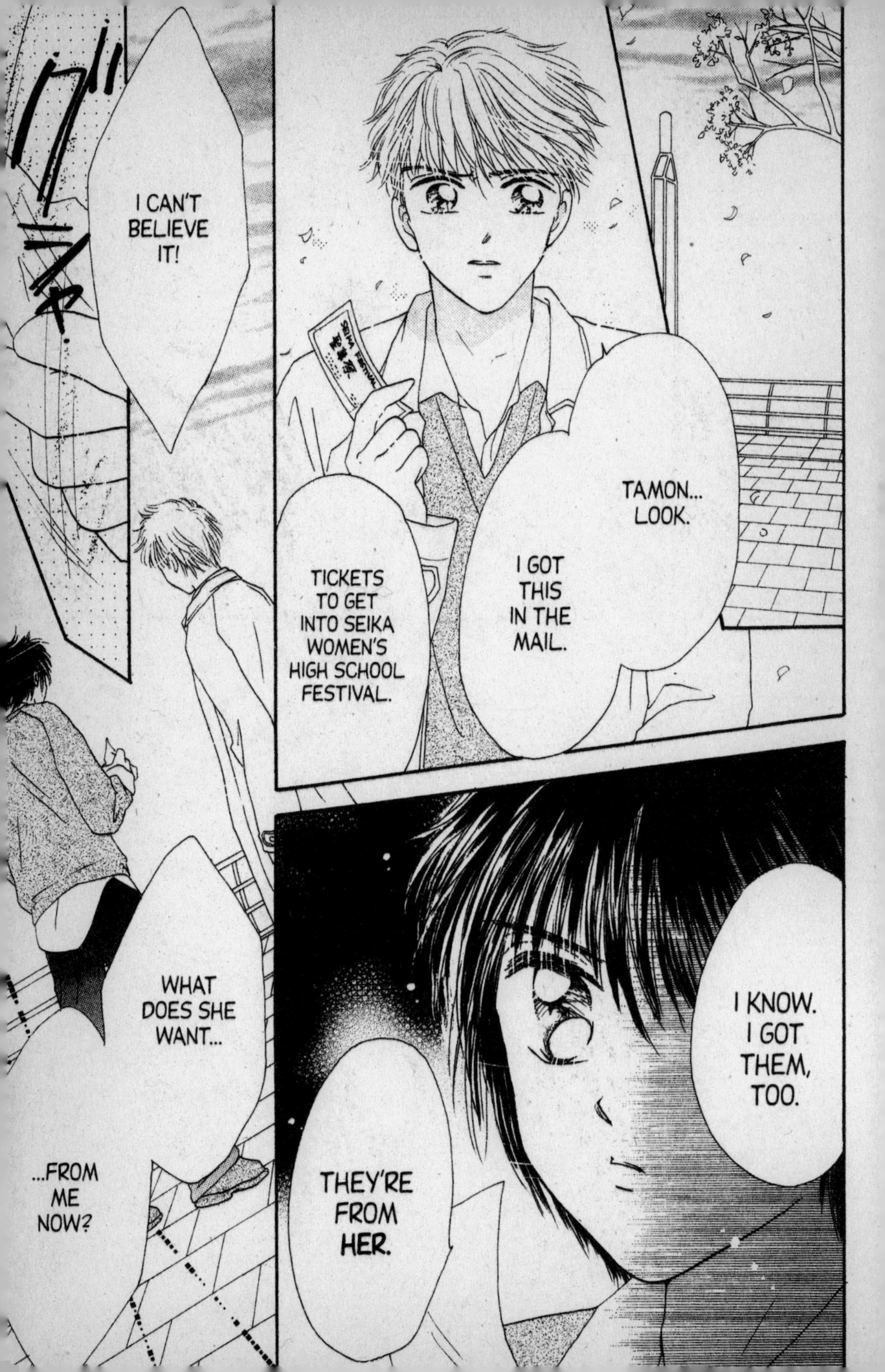
TAMON... LOOK.
I GOT THIS IN THE MAIL.
TICKETS TO GET INTO SEIKA WOMEN'S HIGH SCHOOL FESTIVAL.
I KNOW. I GOT THEM, TOO.
THEY'RE FROM HER.
I CAN'T BELIEVE IT!
WHAT DOES SHE WANT...
...FROM ME NOW?

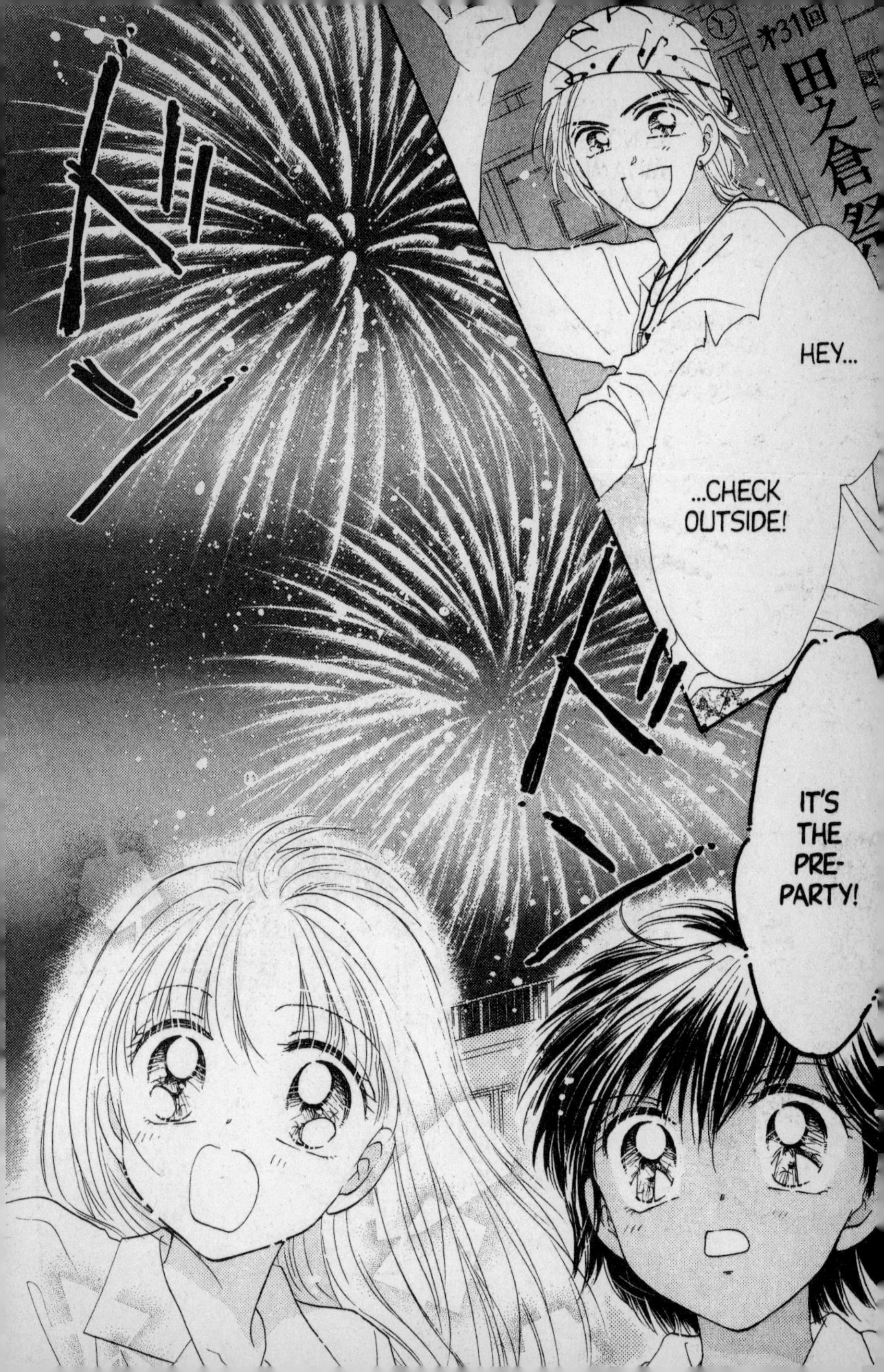
HEY...
...CHECK OUTSIDE!
IT'S THE PRE-PARTY!

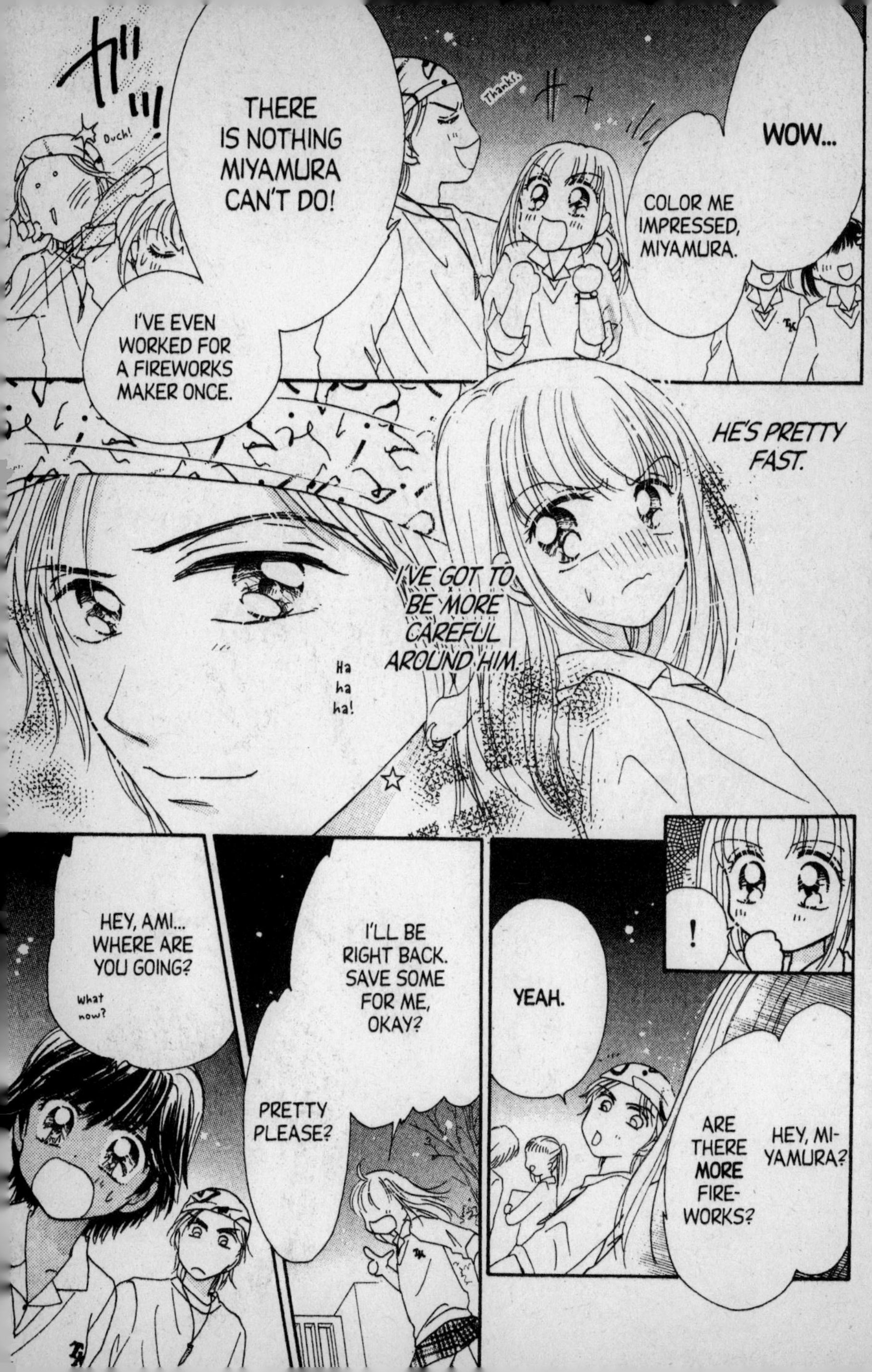
WOW...
COLOR ME IMPRESSED, MIYAMURA.
Thanks.
THERE IS NOTHING MIYAMURA CAN'T DO!
Ouch!
I'VE EVEN WORKED FOR A FIREWORKS MAKER ONCE.
HE'S PRETTY FAST.
I'VE GOT TO BE MORE CAREFUL AROUND HIM.
Ha ha ha!
!
HEY, MI-YAMURA?
ARE THERE MORE FIRE-WORKS?
YEAH.
I'LL BE RIGHT BACK. SAVE SOME FOR ME, OKAY?
PRETTY PLEASE?
HEY, AMI... WHERE ARE YOU GOING?
What now?

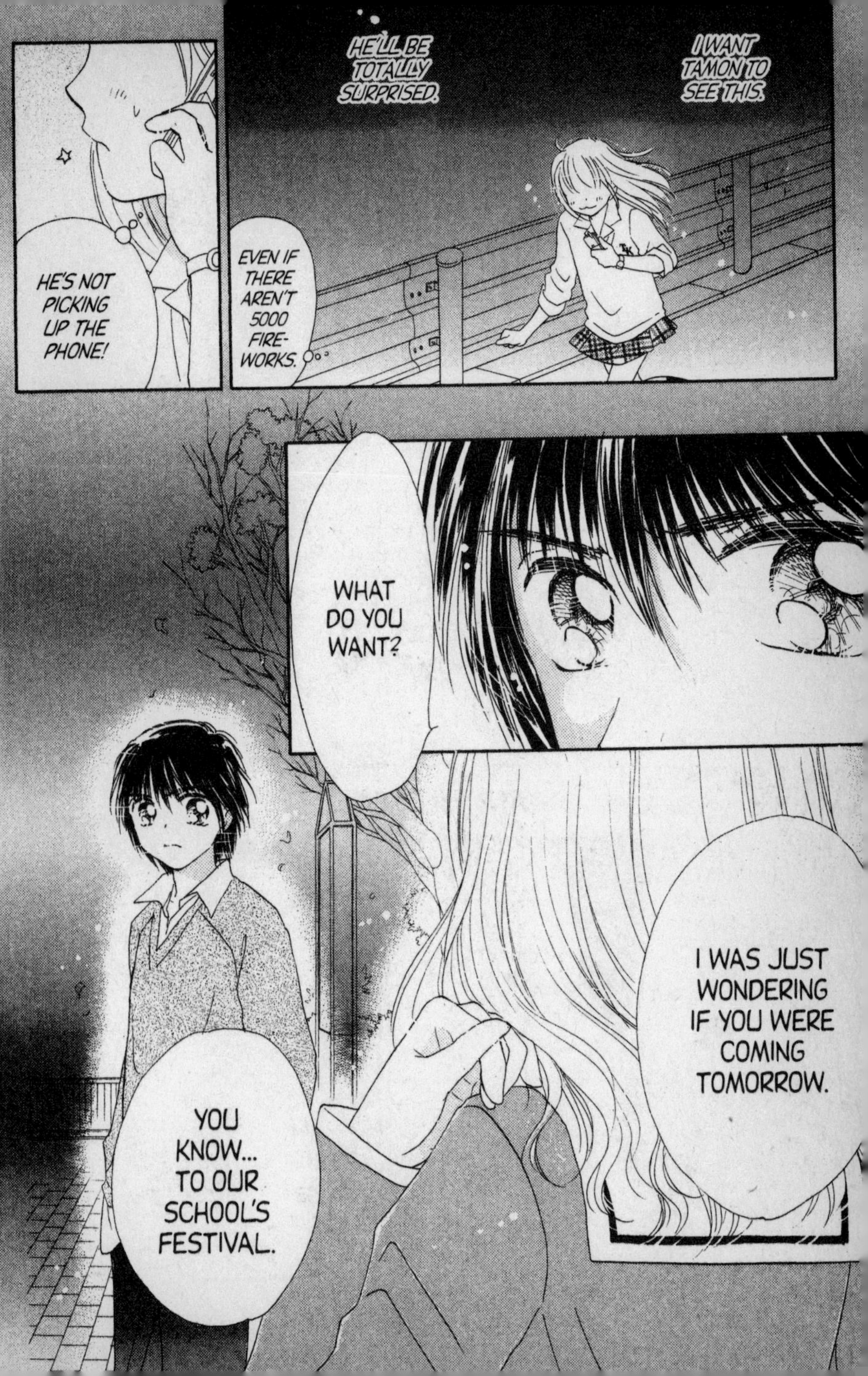
I WANT TAMON TO SEE THIS.
HE'LL BE TOTALLY SURPRISED.
EVEN IF THERE AREN'T 5000 FIRE-WORKS.
HE'S NOT PICKING UP THE PHONE!
WHAT DO YOU WANT?
I WAS JUST WONDERING IF YOU WERE COMING TOMORROW.
YOU KNOW... TO OUR SCHOOL'S FESTIVAL.

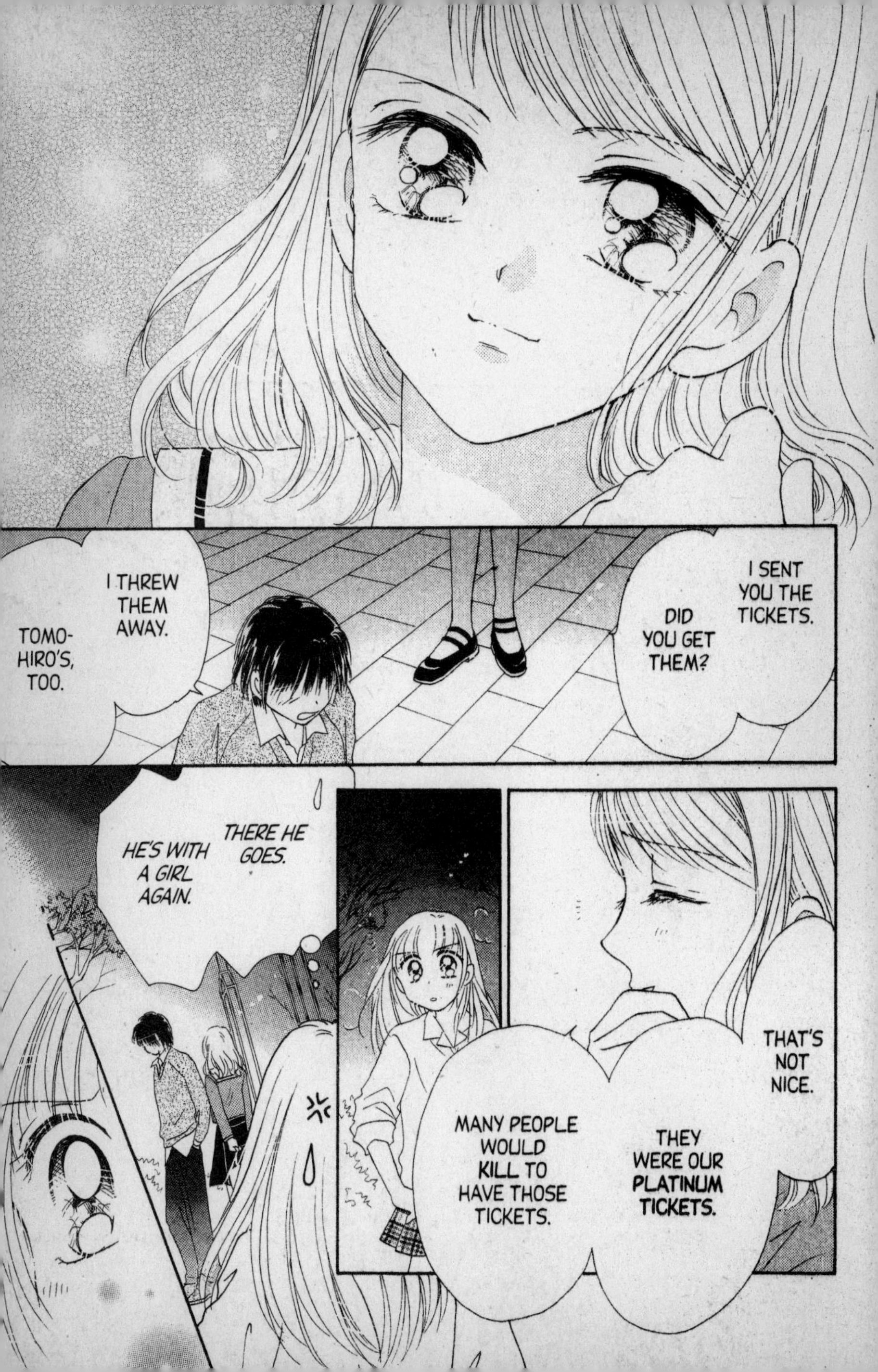
I SENT YOU THE TICKETS.
DID YOU GET THEM?
I THREW THEM AWAY.
TOMO-HIRO'S, TOO.
THAT'S NOT NICE.
THEY WERE OUR PLATINUM TICKETS.
MANY PEOPLE WOULD KILL TO HAVE THOSE TICKETS.
THERE HE GOES.
HE'S WITH A GIRL AGAIN.

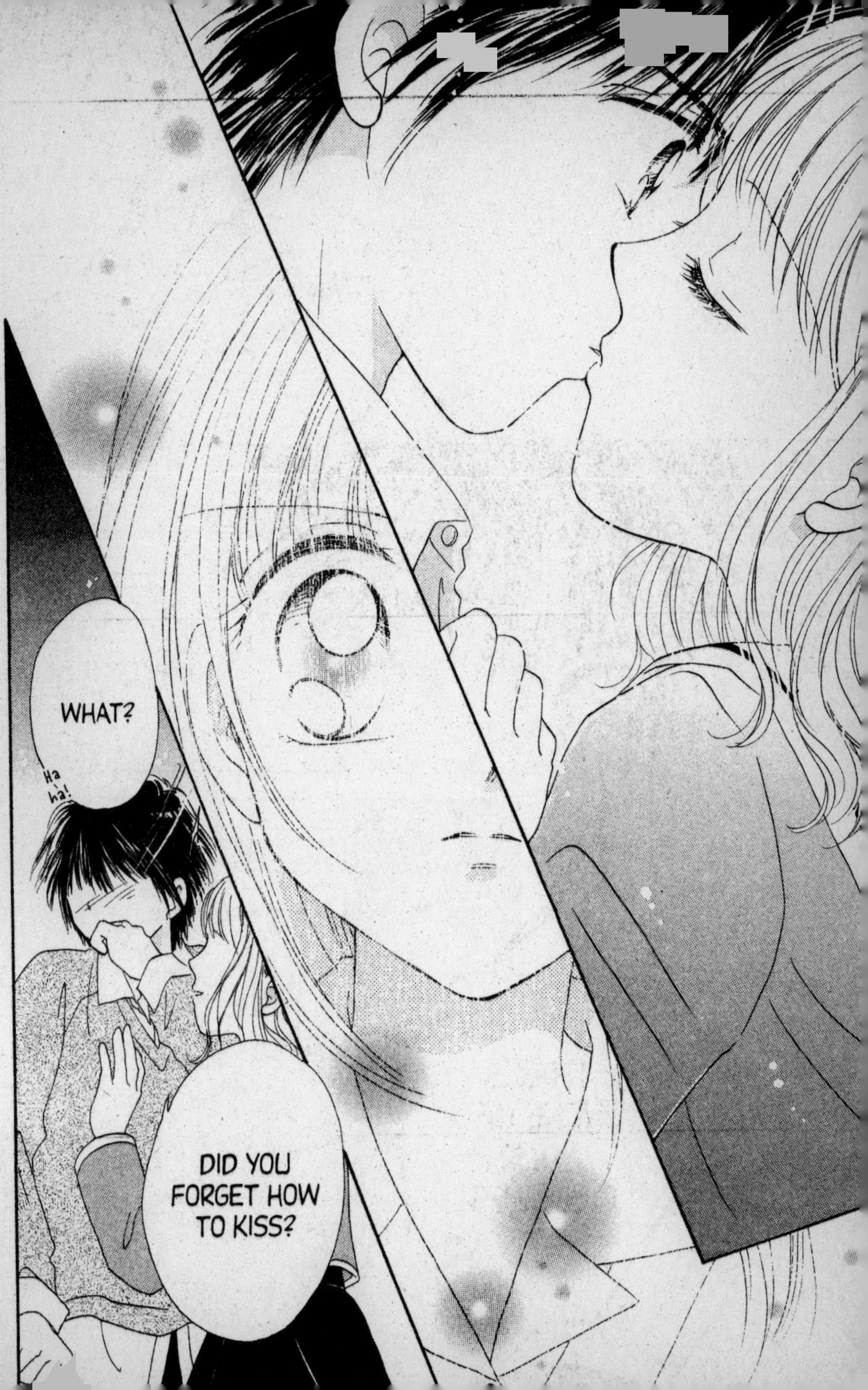
WHAT?
Ha ha!
DID YOU FORGET HOW TO KISS?

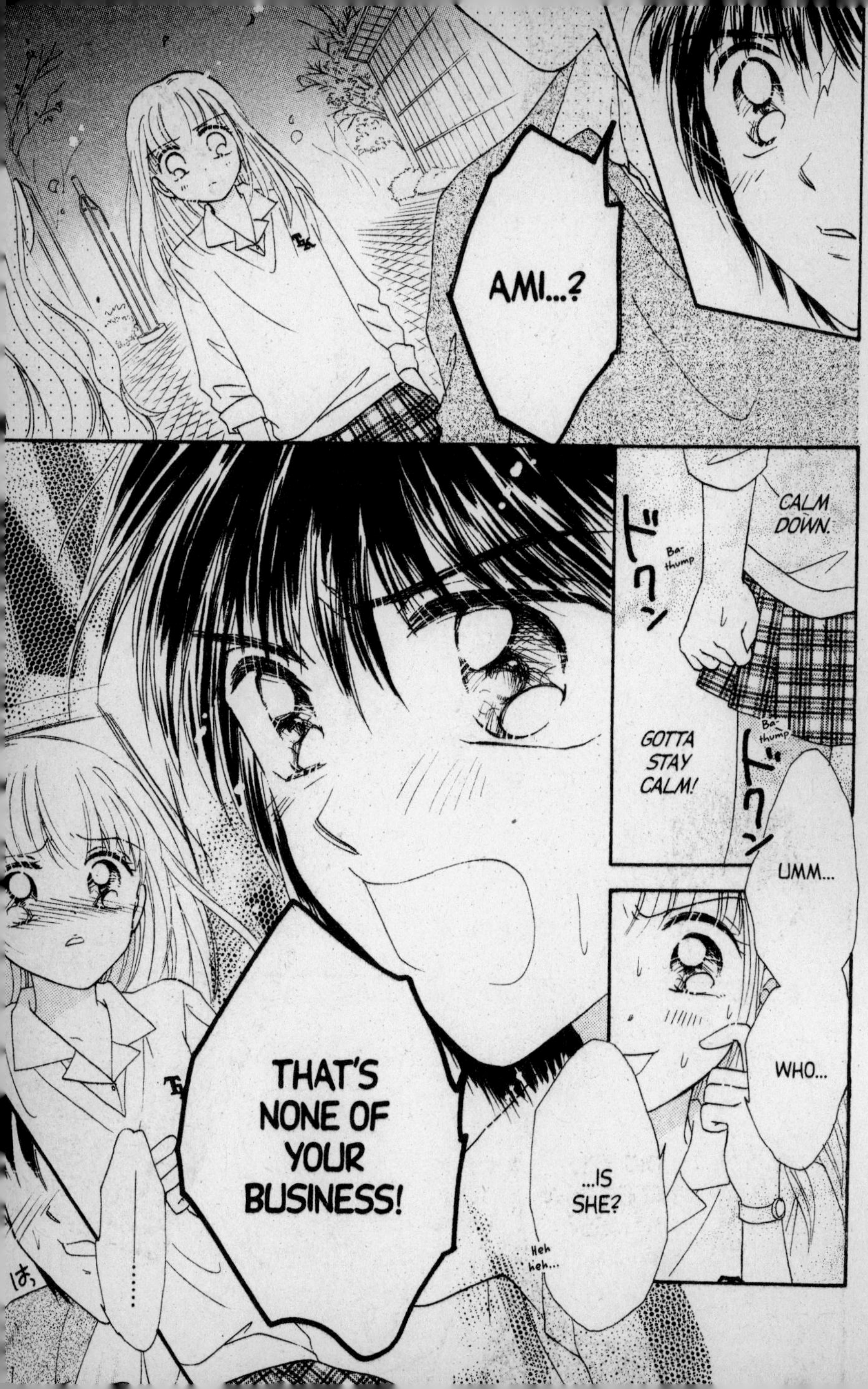
AMI...?
CALM DOWN.
ドクン
Ba-thump
GOTTA STAY CALM!
ドクン
Ba-thump
UMM...
WHO...
...IS SHE?
Heh heh...
THAT'S NONE OF YOUR BUSINESS!
......
は

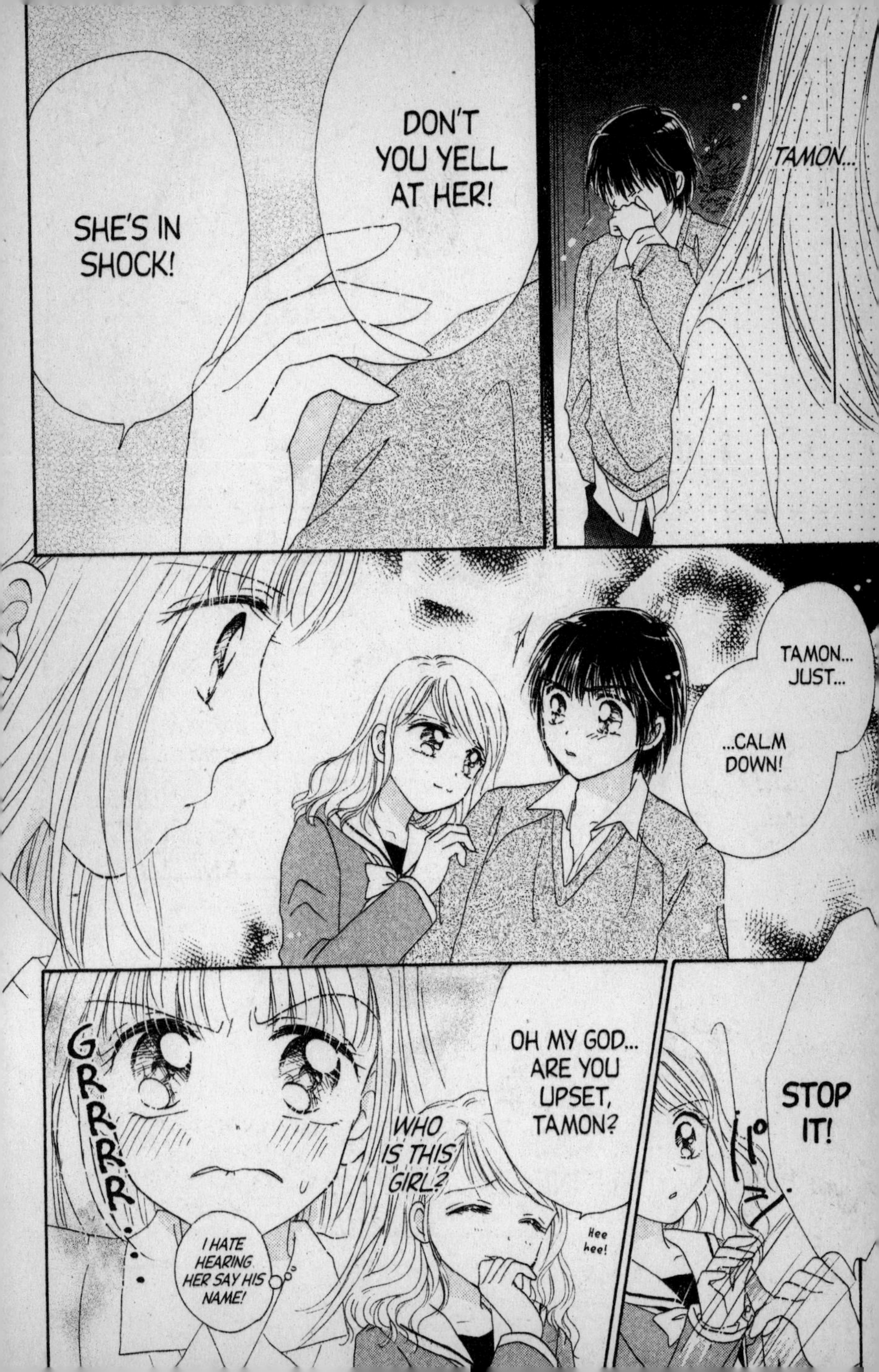
TAMON...
DON'T YOU YELL AT HER!
SHE'S IN SHOCK!
TAMON... JUST...
...CALM DOWN!
STOP IT!
OH MY GOD... ARE YOU UPSET, TAMON?
Hee hee!
WHO IS THIS GIRL?
GRRRR
I HATE HEARING HER SAY HIS NAME!

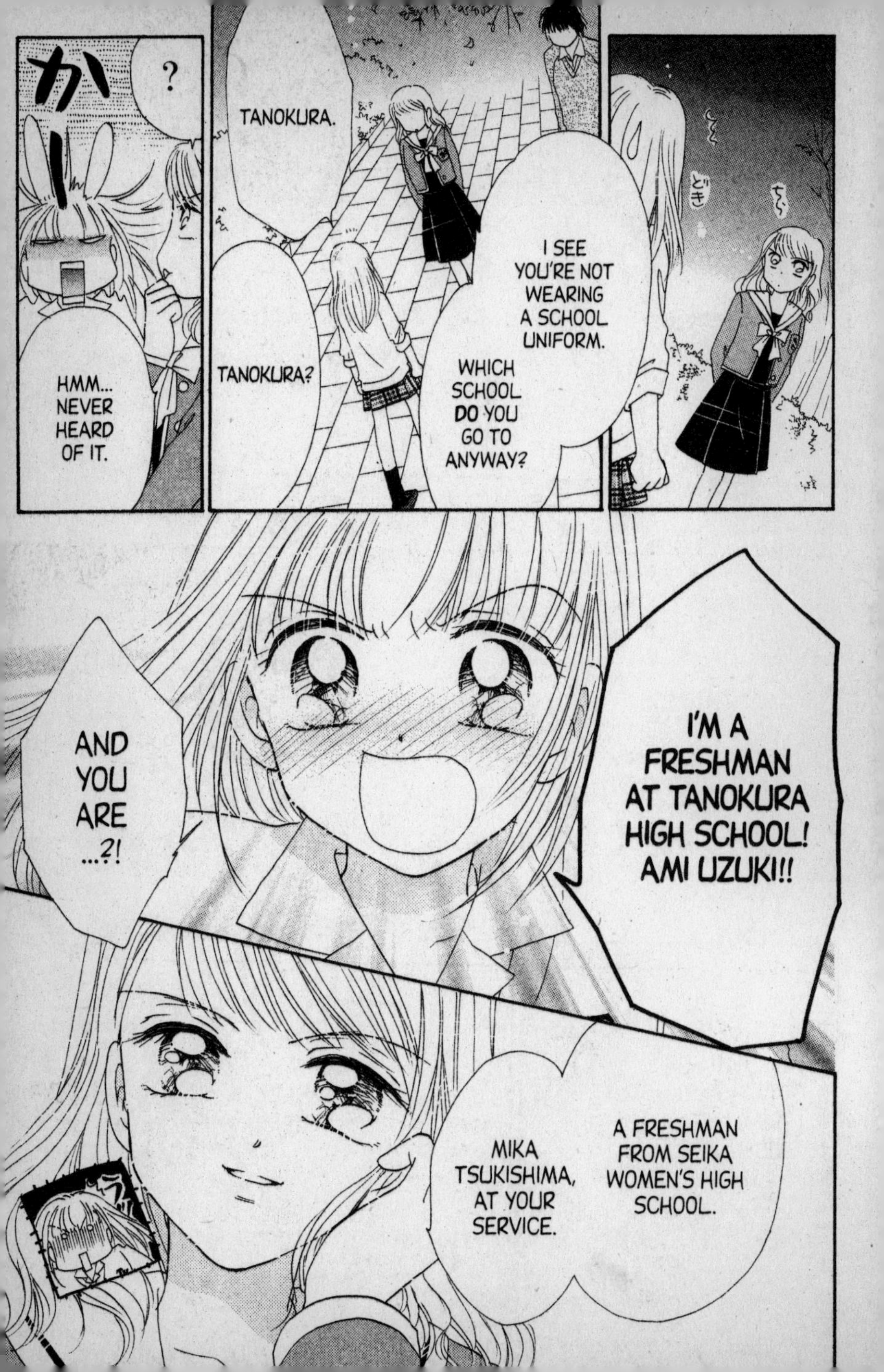
どき
ちら
I SEE YOU'RE NOT WEARING A SCHOOL UNIFORM.
WHICH SCHOOL DO YOU GO TO ANYWAY?
TANOKURA.
TANOKURA?
?
かー
HMM... NEVER HEARD OF IT.
I'M A FRESHMAN AT TANOKURA HIGH SCHOOL! AMI UZUKI!!
AND YOU ARE ...?!
A FRESHMAN FROM SEIKA WOMEN'S HIGH SCHOOL.
MIKA TSUKISHIMA, AT YOUR SERVICE.

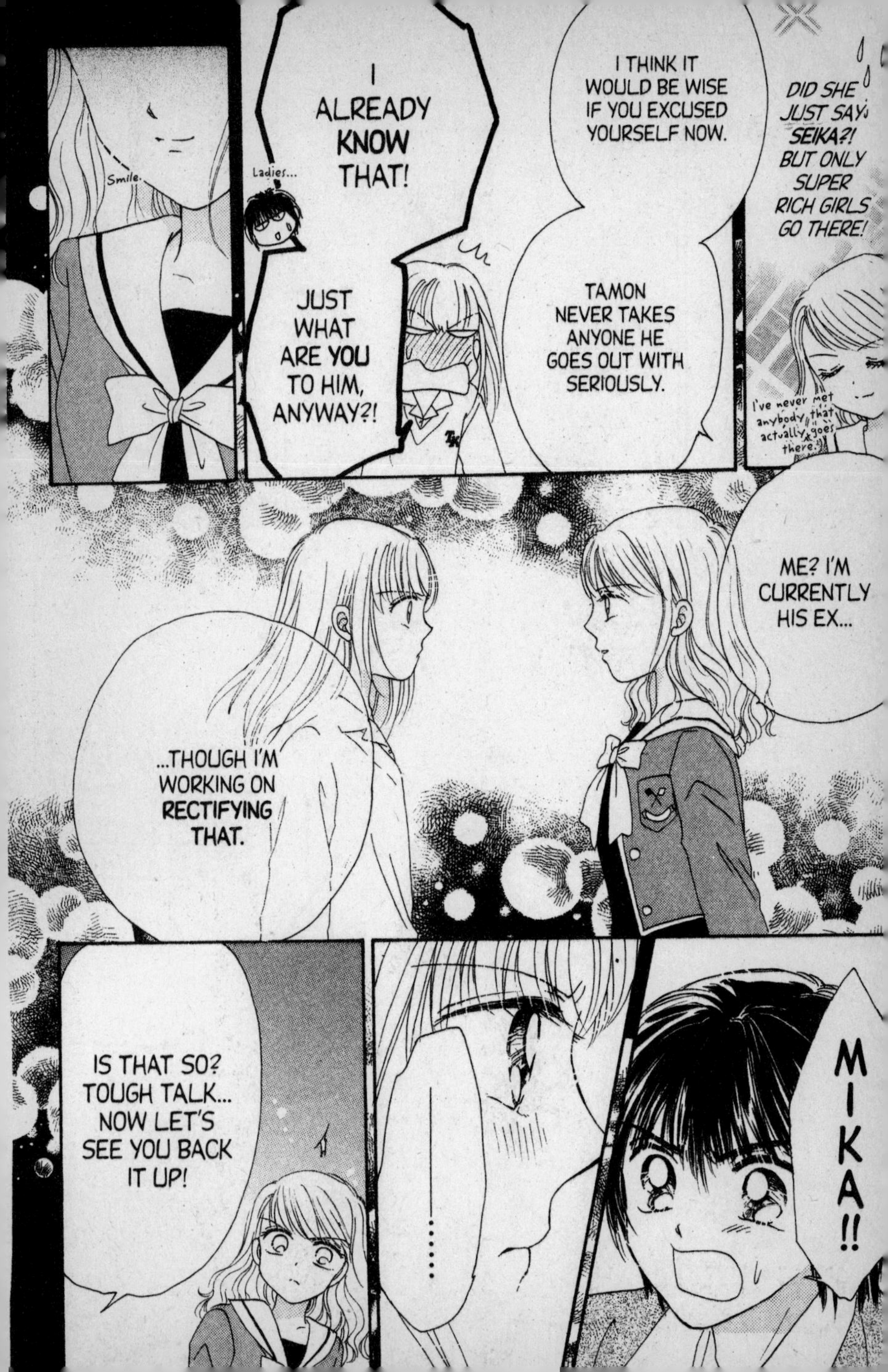
DID SHE JUST SAY SEIKA?! BUT ONLY SUPER RICH GIRLS GO THERE!
I've never met anybody that actually goes there.
I THINK IT WOULD BE WISE IF YOU EXCUSED YOURSELF NOW.
TAMON NEVER TAKES ANYONE HE GOES OUT WITH SERIOUSLY.
I ALREADY KNOW THAT!
Ladies...
JUST WHAT ARE YOU TO HIM, ANYWAY?!
Smile.
ME? I'M CURRENTLY HIS EX...
...THOUGH I'M WORKING ON RECTIFYING THAT.
MIKA!!
......
IS THAT SO? TOUGH TALK... NOW LET'S SEE YOU BACK IT UP!

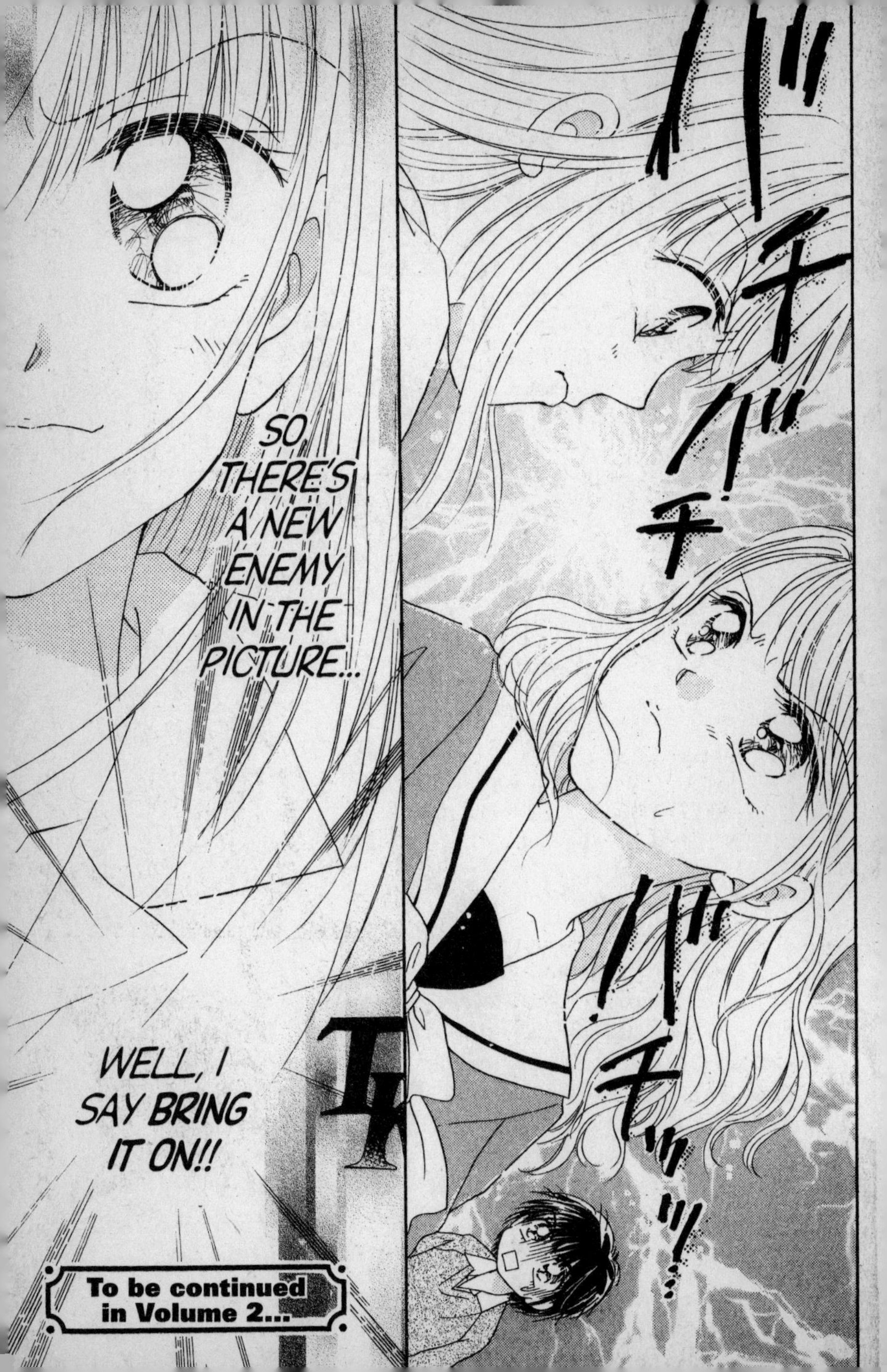
SO, THERE'S A NEW ENEMY IN THE PICTURE...
WELL, I SAY BRING IT ON!!
To be continued in Volume 2...

TOP SECRET!

ultra CUTE

Original Character Designs!

Ultra Cute is a series that was turned down once about a year before it began serialization. After several tweaks here and there, it was finally approved (laugh)! When I first pitched it, the story had lots of characters...but I soon realized the difficulty of keeping the story focused with that many characters. That said, I still think it's fun to tell stories with a ton of characters in there. Oh well...

Their uniforms are slightly different from the standard, simple ones I draw now. I have trouble drawing the long loose socks, so I'll probably never draw them again (non-committal).

(Second Draft)

I actually changed the character's names to "Ami" and "Noa" right before serialization started. There were various reasons for that (laughs).

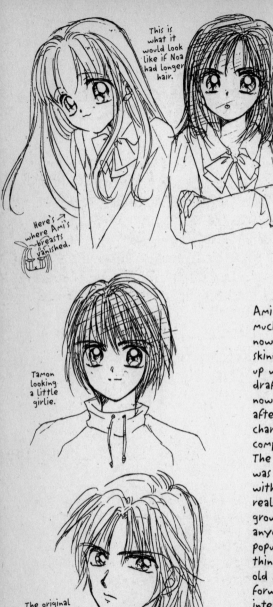

This is what it would look like if Noa had longer hair.
Here's where Ami's breasts vanished.

Ami and Tamon were pretty much the same as they are now. Making Noa darker skinned was something I came up with during the second draft. Because of that I am now in skin-tone hell! And after one more draft, the characters we all know were completed.

The one who changed the most was Tomohiro. I had introduced with short hair...but since it's really hard to draw, I had him grow it out a little bit... Did anyone notice? Tomohiro isn't popular AT ALL! People seem to think he acts like a suspicious old man! Ha ha ha! I look forward to him doing something interesting in the future! Anyway, see you in book two!

Tamon looking a little girlie.

The original Tomohiro. I based Chucky Miyamura off of this design. At the time, I hadn't yet created the Miyamura character.

xxx

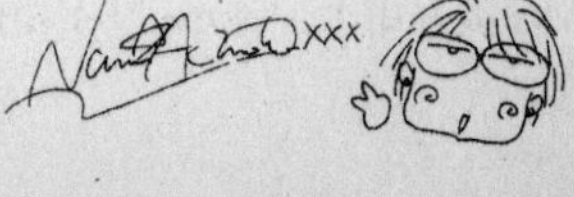

IN THE NEXT VOLUME

AMI'S PLAN TO MELT THE ICE AROUND TAMON'S HEART HITS
A MAJOR ROADBLOCK WITH THE UNEXPECTED ARRIVAL OF
MIKA, TAMON'S CONNIVING EX-GIRLFRIEND. MIKA IS JUST AS
DETERMINED TO WIN BACK TAMON'S HEART AS AMI, AND
WILL DO ANYTHING TO DEFLECT AMI'S ARROWS OF LOVE.
HOWEVER, JUST WHEN ALL LOOKS AS BLEAK AS A FOGGY
DAY IN A CEMETERY, AMI RECEIVES LOVE POINTERS FROM
THE MYSTERIOUS "DR. M"...

**LOVE IS DEFINITELY A BATTLEFIELD IN
ULTRA CUTE VOLUME 2!**

TOKYOPOP PRESENTS
MANGA 漫画
THE NEW SIZZLING HOT
FREE
MAGAZINE
ZELDA AND FRIEND FROM
WAR ON FLESH
© Justin Boring, Greg Hildebrandt and TOKYOPOP Inc.
SIGN UP FOR FREE WWW.TOKYOPOP.COM

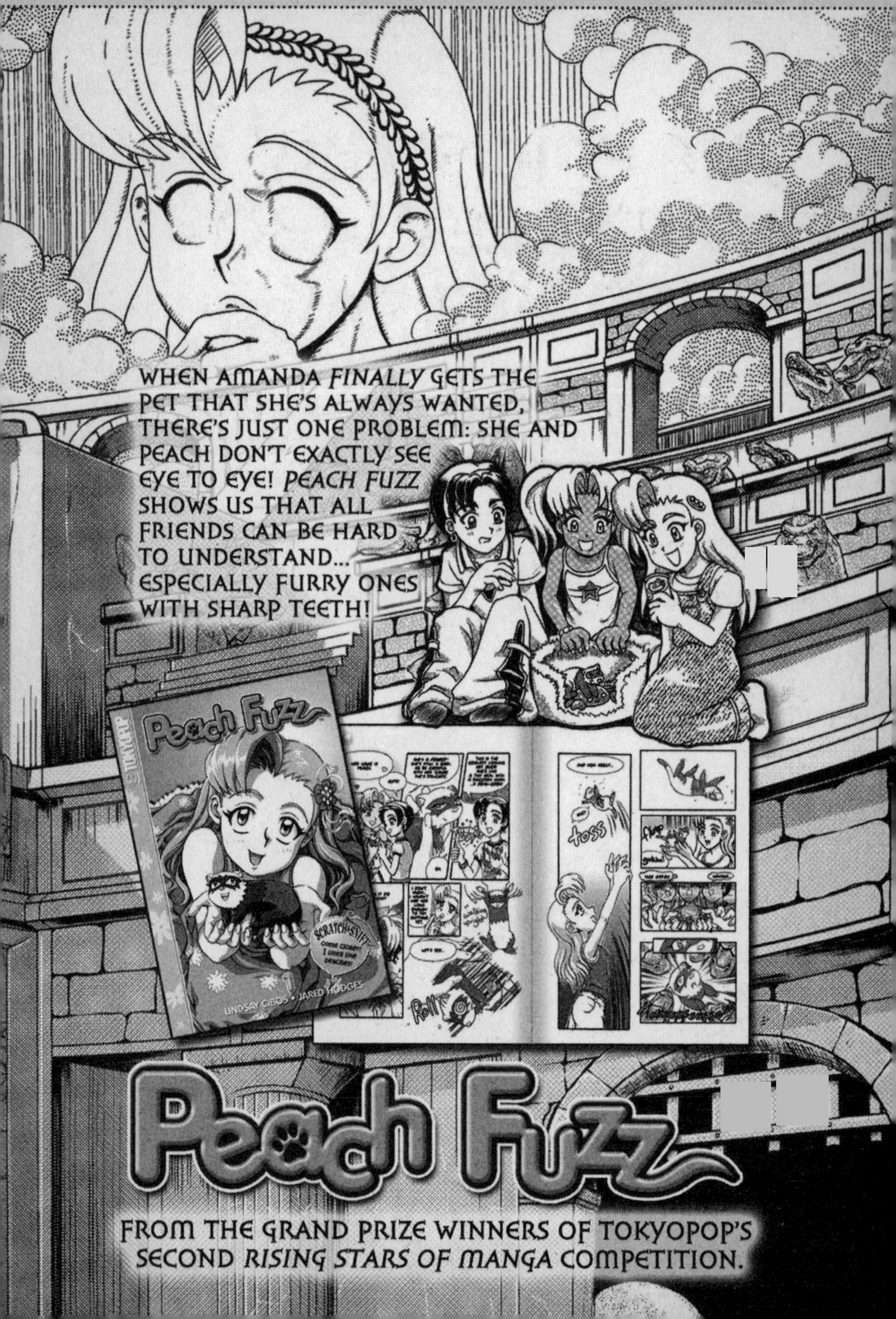
WHEN AMANDA *FINALLY* GETS THE PET THAT SHE'S ALWAYS WANTED, THERE'S JUST ONE PROBLEM: SHE AND PEACH DON'T EXACTLY SEE EYE TO EYE! *PEACH FUZZ* SHOWS US THAT ALL FRIENDS CAN BE HARD TO UNDERSTAND... ESPECIALLY FURRY ONES WITH SHARP TEETH!
Peach Fuzz
LINDSAY CIBOS • JARED HODGES
Peach Fuzz
FROM THE GRAND PRIZE WINNERS OF TOKYOPOP'S SECOND *RISING STARS OF MANGA* COMPETITION.

PEACHFUZZ

THE EPIC STORY OF A FERRET WHO DEFIED HER CAGE.

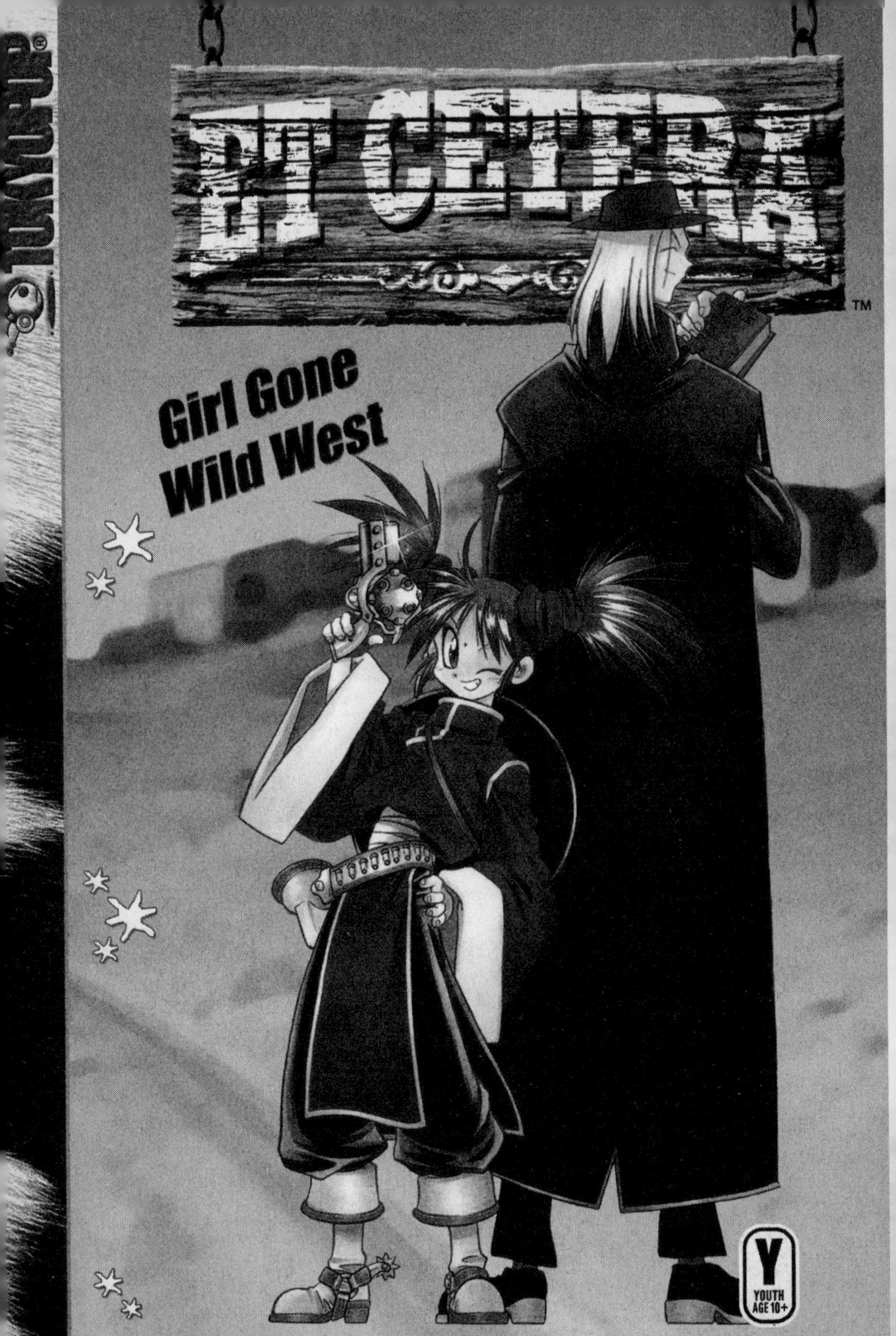
TOKYOPOP
ET CETERA
TM
Girl Gone
Wild West
Y
YOUTH
AGE 10+

The <cyber> world's newest
Pop Idol has just received
an upgrade... ;-)

MiNK™

TOKYOPOP®

Y YOUTH AGE 10+

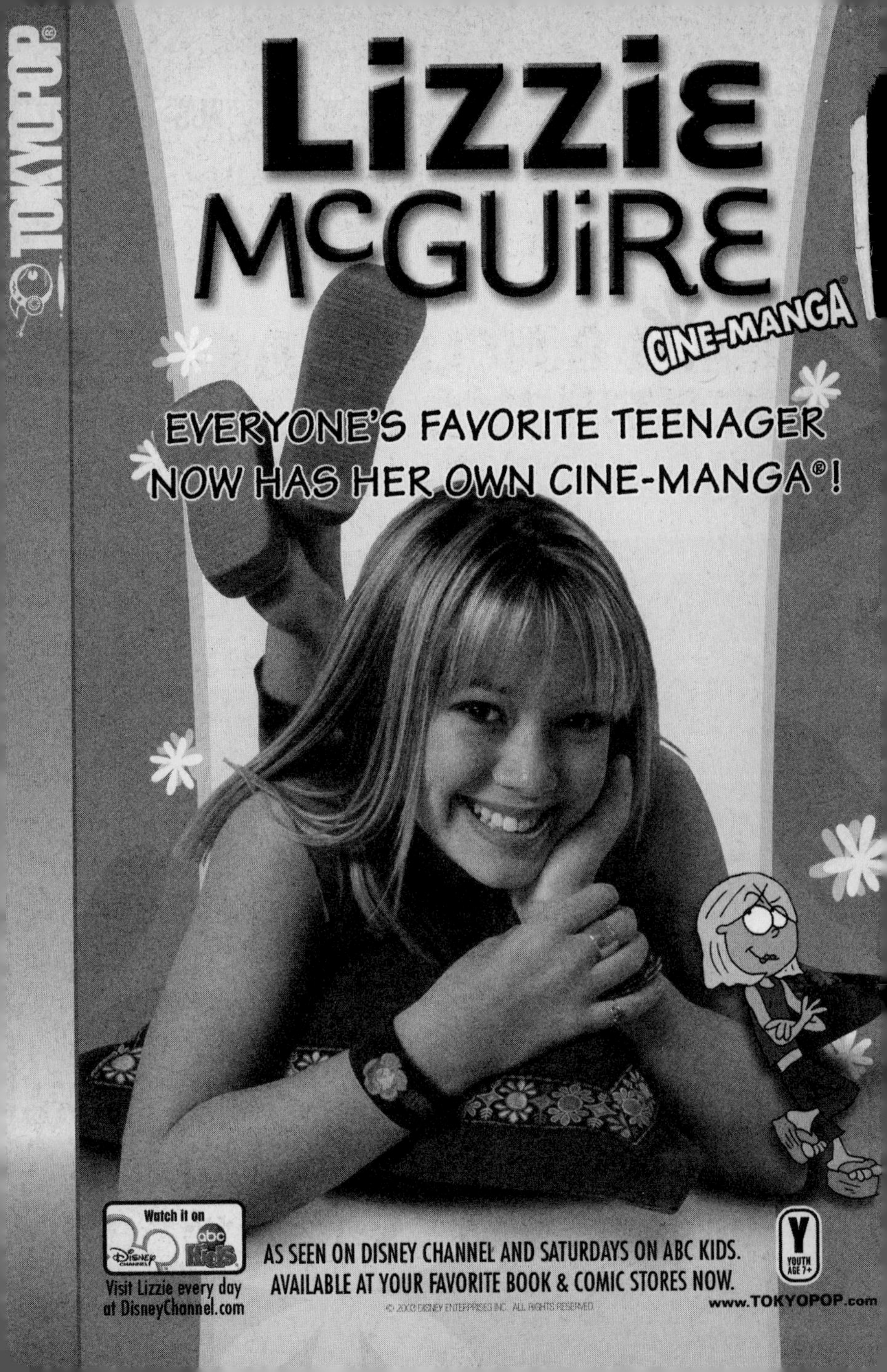
TOKYOPOP
Lizzie McGUiRE
CINE-MANGA®
EVERYONE'S FAVORITE TEENAGER
NOW HAS HER OWN CINE-MANGA®!
Watch it on
Disney Channel
abc Kids
Visit Lizzie every day
at DisneyChannel.com
AS SEEN ON DISNEY CHANNEL AND SATURDAYS ON ABC KIDS.
AVAILABLE AT YOUR FAVORITE BOOK & COMIC STORES NOW.
© 2003 DISNEY ENTERPRISES INC. ALL RIGHTS RESERVED.
Y
YOUTH
AGE 7+
www.TOKYOPOP.com

STOP!

This is the back of the book.
You wouldn't want to spoil a great ending!

This book is printed "manga-style," in the authentic Japanese right-to-left format. Since none of the artwork has been flipped or altered, readers get to experience the story just as the creator intended. You've been asking for it, so TOKYOPOP® delivered: authentic, hot-off-the-press, and far more fun!

DIRECTIONS

If this is your first time reading manga-style, here's a quick guide to help you understand how it works.

It's easy... just start in the top right panel and follow the numbers. Have fun, and look for more 100% authentic manga from TOKYOPOP®!